Expert .NET 2.0 IL Assembler

Serge Lidin

Apress®

Expert .NET 2.0 IL Assembler

Copyright © 2006 by Serge Lidin

Softcover reprint of the hardcover 1st edition 2006

ISBN 978-1-4842-2024-5   ISBN 978-1-4302-0223-3   (eBook)

DOI 10.1007/978-1-4302-0223-3

Lead Editor: Ewan Buckingham

Technical Reviewers: Jim Hogg, Vance Morrison

Editorial Board: Steve Anglin, Ewan Buckingham, Gary Cornell, Jason Gilmore, Jonathan Gennick, Jonathan Hassell, James Huddleston, Chris Mills, Matthew Moodie, Dominic Shakeshaft, Jim Sumser, Keir Thomas, Matt Wade

Project Manager: Sofia Marchant

Copy Edit Manager: Nicole LeClerc

Copy Editor: Kim Wimpsett

Assistant Production Director: Kari Brooks-Copony

Senior Production Editor: Laura Cheu

Compositor: Diana Van Winkle, Van Winkle Design

Proofreader: Linda Seifert

Indexer: Broccoli Information Management

Artist: Diana Van Winkle, Van Winkle Design

Cover Designer: Kurt Krames

Manufacturing Director: Tom Debolski

Distributed to the book trade worldwide by Springer-Verlag New York, Inc., 233 Spring Street, 6th Floor, New York, NY 10013. Phone 1-800-SPRINGER, fax 201-348-4505, e-mail orders-ny@springer-sbm.com, or visit http://www.springeronline.com.

For information on translations, please contact Apress directly at 2560 Ninth Street, Suite 219, Berkeley, CA 94710. Phone 510-549-5930, fax 510-549-5939, e-mail info@apress.com, or visit http://www.apress.com.

The source code for this book is available to readers at http://www.apress.com in the Source Code section. You will need to answer questions pertaining to this book in order to successfully download the code.

To Alenushka, with all my love.

Contents at a Glance

PART 1 ▪ ▪ ▪ Quick Start

PART 2 ▪ ▪ ▪ Underlying Structures

PART 3 ▪ ▪ ▪ Fundamental Components

PART 4 ▪ ▪ ▪ Inside the Execution Engine

PART 5 ■ ■ ■ Special Components

PART 6 ■ ■ ■ Appendixes

Contents

PART 1 ▪▪▪ Quick Start

PART 2 ▪▪▪ Underlying Structures

PART 3 ▨▧▨ Fundamental Components

PART 4 ▪ ▪ ▪ Inside the Execution Engine

PART 5 ▪ ▪ ▪ **Special Components**

PART 6 ▪▪▪ Appendixes

About the Author

 **SERGE LIDIN**, a Russian-born Canadian with more than 20 years in the computer industry, has programmed in more languages and for more platforms than he can recall, in areas varying from astrophysics models to industrial process simulations to transaction processing in financial systems. From 1999 to mid-2005, he worked on the Microsoft .NET common language runtime team, where he designed and developed the IL assembler, IL disassembler, Metadata validator, and run-time metadata validation in the execution engine. Currently, Serge works on the Microsoft Phoenix team, developing future frameworks for code generation and transformation. When not writing software or sleeping, he plays tennis, skis, and reads books (his literary taste is below any criticism). Serge shares his time between Vancouver, British Columbia, where his heart is, and Redmond, Washington, where his brain is.

About the Technical Reviewers

JIM HOGG joined Microsoft seven years ago as a program manager—first on the .NET runtime team, working on metadata, and now with the compiler team, working on optimizations. His previous experience includes stints in computational physics, seismic processing, and operating systems.

VANCE MORRISON has been working at Microsoft for the past seven years and has been involved in the design of the .NET runtime since its inception. He drove the design for the .NET intermediate language (IL) and was the lead for the just-in-time (JIT) compiler team for much of that time. He is currently the compiler architect for Microsoft's .NET runtime.

Acknowledgments

First I would like to thank the editing team from Apress who worked with me on this book: Ewan Buckingham, Sofia Marchant, Kim Wimpsett (ah, those unforgettable discussions about subjunctive tense vs. indicative tense!), and Laura Cheu. It was a pleasure and an honor to work with such a highly professional team.

I would also like to thank my colleagues Jim Hogg and Vance Morrison, who were the principal technical reviewers of this book. Jim worked on the common language runtime team for quite a while and was the driving force of the ECMA/ISO standardization effort concerning the .NET common language infrastructure. Vance has worked on the CLR team since the team's inception in 1998, he led the just-in-time compiler team for a long time, and he helped me a lot with the IL assembler. Jim and Vance provided invaluable feedback on the draft of the book, leaving no stone unturned.

And of course I would like to extend my thanks to my colleagues who helped me write this book and the first IL assembler book by answering my questions and digging into the specifications and source code with me: Larry Sullivan, Jim Miller, Bill Evans, Chris Brumme, Mei-Chin Tsai, Erik Meijer, Thorsten Brunklaus, Ronald Laeremans, Kevin Ransom, Suzanne Cook, Shajan Dasan, Craig Sinclair, and many others.

Introduction

Why was this book written? To tell the truth, I don't think I had much choice in this matter. This book is a revision and extension of my earlier book, *Inside Microsoft .NET IL Assembler*, which hit the shelves in early 2002, about a month after the release of version 1.0 of the .NET common language infrastructure (CLI). So, it is fairly obvious why I had to write this new book now, more than four years later, when the more powerful version 2.0 of the .NET CLI has just been released. And I don't think I had much choice in the matter of writing the first book either, because somebody had to start writing about the .NET CLI inner workings.

The .NET universe, like other information technology universes, resembles a great pyramid turned upside down and standing on its tip. The tip on which the .NET pyramid stands is the common language runtime. The runtime converts the intermediate language (IL) binary code into platform-specific (native) machine code and executes it. Resting on top of the runtime are the .NET Framework class library, the compilers, and environments such as Microsoft Visual Studio. And above them begin the layers of application development, from instrumental to end user oriented. The pyramid quickly grows higher and wider.

This book is not exactly about the common language runtime—even though it's only the tip of the .NET pyramid, the runtime is too vast a topic to be described in detail in any book of reasonable (say, luggable) size. Rather, this book focuses on the next best thing: the .NET IL assembler. IL assembly language (ILAsm) is a low-level language, specifically designed to describe every functional feature of the common language runtime. If the runtime can do it, ILAsm must be able to express it.

Unlike high-level languages, and like other assembly languages, ILAsm is platform-driven rather than concept-driven. An assembly language usually is an exact linguistic mapping of the underlying platform, which in this case is the common language runtime. It is, in fact, so exact a mapping that this language is used for describing aspects of the runtime in the ECMA/ISO standardization documents regarding the .NET common language infrastructure. (ILAsm itself, as part of the common language infrastructure, is a subject of this standardization effort as well.) As a result of the close mapping, it is impossible to describe an assembly language without going into significant detail about the underlying platform. So, to a great extent, this book *is* about the common language runtime after all.

The IL assembly language is very popular among .NET developers. No, I am not claiming that all .NET developers prefer to program in ILAsm rather than in Visual C++/CLI, C#, or Visual Basic. But all .NET developers use the IL disassembler now and then, and many use it on a regular basis. A cyan thunderbolt—the IL disassembler icon (a silent praise for David Drake and his "Hammer's Slammers")—glows on the computer screens of .NET developers regardless of their language preferences and problem areas. And the text output of the IL disassembler is ILAsm source code.

Virtually all books about .NET-based programming that are devoted to high-level programming languages such as C# or Visual Basic or to techniques such as ADO.NET at some moment mention the IL disassembler as a tool of choice to analyze the innards of a .NET managed executable. But these volumes stop short of explaining what the disassembly text means and how to interpret it. This is an understandable choice, given the topics of these books; the detailed description of metadata structuring and IL assembly language represents a separate issue.

Now perhaps you see what I mean when I say I had no choice but to write this book. *Someone* had to, and because I had been given the responsibility of designing and developing the IL assembler and disassembler, it was my obligation to see it through all the way.

History of ILAsm, Part I

The first versions of the IL assembler and IL disassembler were developed in early 1998 by Jonathan Forbes. The current language is very different from this original one, the only distinct common feature being the leading dots in the directive keywords. The assembler and disassembler were built as purely internal tools facilitating the ongoing development of the common language runtime and were used rather extensively inside the runtime development team.

When Jonathan left the common language runtime team in the beginning of 1999, the assembler and disassembler fell in the lap of Larry Sullivan, head of a development group with the colorful name Common Runtime Odds and Ends Development Team (CROEDT). In April of that year, I joined the team, and Larry passed the assembler and disassembler to me. When an alpha version of the common language runtime was presented at a Technical Preview in May 1999, the assembler and disassembler attracted significant attention, and I was told to rework the tools and bring them up to production level. So I did, with great help from Larry, Vance Morrison, and Jim Miller. The tools were still considered internal, so we (Larry, Vance, Jim, and I) could afford to redesign the language—not to mention the implementation of the tools—radically.

A major breakthrough occurred in the second half of 1999, when the IL assembler input and IL disassembler output were synchronized enough to achieve limited round-tripping. *Round-tripping* means you can take a managed (IL) executable compiled from a particular language, disassemble it, add or change some ILAsm code, and reassemble it back into a modified executable. The round-tripping technique opened new avenues, and shortly thereafter it began to be used in certain production processes both inside Microsoft and by its partners.

At about the same time, third-party .NET-oriented compilers that used ILAsm as a base language started to appear. The best known is probably Fujitsu's NetCOBOL, which made quite a splash at the Professional Developers Conference in July 2000, where the first pre-beta version of the common language runtime, along with the .NET Framework class library, compilers, and tools, was released to the developer community.

Since the release of the beta 1 version in late 2000, the IL assembler and IL disassembler have been fully functional in the sense that they reflect all the features of metadata and IL, support complete round-tripping, and maintain synchronization of their changes with the changes in the runtime itself.

ILAsm Marching On

These days the IL assembler is used more and more in the compiler and tool implementation, in education, and in academic research. The following compilers (for example), ranging from purely academic projects to industrial-strength systems, produce ILAsm code as their output and let the IL assembler take care of emitting the managed executables:

- Ada# (USAF Academy, Colorado)

- Alice.NET (Saarland University, Saarbrücken)

- Boo (codehaus.org)

- NetCOBOL (Fujitsu)

- COBOL2002 for .NET Framework (NEC/Hitachi)

- NetExpress COBOL (Microfocus)

- CommonLarceny.NET (Northeastern University, Boston)

- CULE.NET (CULEPlace.com)

- Component Pascal (Queensland University of Technology, Australia)

- Fortran (Lahey/Fujitsu)

- Hotdog Scheme (Northwestern University, Chicago)

- Lagoona.NET (University of California, Irvine)

- LCC (ANSI C) (Microsoft Research, Redmond)

- Mercury (University of Melbourne, Australia)

- Modula-2 (Queensland University of Technology, Australia)

- Moscow ML.NET (Royal Veterinary and Agricultural University, Denmark)

- Oberon.NET (Swiss Federal Institute of Technology, Zürich)

- S# (Smallscript.com)

- SML.NET (Microsoft Research, Cambridge, United Kingdom)

The ability of the IL disassembler and IL assembler to work in tandem gave birth to a slew of interesting tools and techniques based on "creative round-tripping" of managed executables (disassembling—text manipulation—reassembling). For example, Preemptive Software (a company known for its Java and .NET-oriented obfuscators and code optimizers) built its DotFuscator system on this base. The DotFuscator is a commercial, industrial-strength obfuscation and optimization system, well known on the market. I discuss some other interesting examples of application of "creative round-tripping" in Chapter 19.

Practically all academic courses on .NET programming use ILAsm to some extent (how else could the authors of these courses show the innards of .NET managed executables?). Some courses are completely ILAsm based, such as the course developed by Dr. Regeti Govindarajulu at International Institute of Informational Technologies (Hyderabad, India) and the course developed by Drs. Andrey Makarov, Sergey Skorobogatov, and Andrey Chepovskiy at Lomonosov University and Bauman Technical University (Moscow, Russia).

Who Should Read This Book

This book targets all the .NET-oriented developers who, working at a sufficiently advanced level, care about what their programs compile into or who are willing to analyze the end results of their programming. Here these readers will find the information necessary to interpret disassembly texts and metadata structure summaries, allowing them to develop more efficient programming techniques.

This analysis of disassemblies and metadata structuring is crucial in assessing the correctness and efficiency of any .NET-oriented compiler, so this book should also prove especially useful for compiler developers who are targeting .NET. A narrower but growing group of readers who will find the book extremely helpful includes developers who use the IL assembly language directly, such as compiler developers targeting ILAsm as an intermediate step, developers contemplating multilanguage projects, and developers willing to exploit the capabilities of the common language runtime that are inaccessible through the high-level languages.

Finally, this book can be valuable in all phases of software development, from conceptual design to implementation and maintenance.

Organization of This Book

I begin in Part 1, "Quick Start," with a quick overview of ILAsm and common language runtime features, based on a simple sample program. This overview is in no way complete; rather, it is intended to convey a general impression about the runtime and ILAsm as a language.

The following parts discuss features of the runtime and corresponding ILAsm constructs in a detailed, bottom-up manner. Part 2, "Underlying Structures," describes the structure of a managed executable file and general metadata organization. Part 3, "Fundamental Components," is dedicated to the components that constitute a necessary base of any application: assemblies, modules, classes, methods, fields, and related topics. Part 4, "Inside the Execution Engine," brings you, yes, inside the execution engine, describing the execution of IL instructions and managed exception handling. Part 5, "Special Components," discusses metadata representation and the usage of the additional components: events, properties, and custom and security attributes. And Part 6, "Interoperation," describes the interoperation between managed and unmanaged code and discusses practical applications of the IL assembler and IL disassembler to multilanguage projects.

The book's five appendixes contain references concerning ILAsm grammar, metadata organization, and IL instruction set and tool features, including the IL assembler, the IL disassembler, and the offline metadata validation tool.

PART 1

Quick Start

CHAPTER 1

■ ■ ■

Simple Sample

This chapter offers a general overview of ILAsm, the MSIL assembly language. (MSIL stands for *Microsoft intermediate language*, which will soon be discussed in this chapter.) The chapter reviews a relatively simple program written in ILAsm, and then I suggest some modifications that illustrate how you can express the concepts and elements of Microsoft .NET programming in this language.

This chapter does not teach you how to write programs in ILAsm. But it should help you understand what the IL assembler (ILASM) and the IL disassembler (ILDASM) do and how to use that understanding to analyze the internal structure of a .NET-based program with the help of these ubiquitous tools. You'll also learn some intriguing facts about the mysterious affairs that take place behind the scenes within the common language runtime—intriguing enough, I hope, to prompt you to read the rest of the book.

■**Note** For your sake and mine, I'll abbreviate *IL assembly language* as ILAsm throughout this book. Don't confuse it with ILASM, which is the abbreviation for the IL assembler (in other words, the ILAsm compiler) in the .NET documentation.

Basics of the Common Language Runtime

The .NET common language runtime is but one of many aspects of .NET, but it's the core of .NET. (Note that, for variety's sake, I'll sometimes refer to the common language runtime as *the runtime*.) Rather than focusing on an overall description of the .NET platform, I'll concentrate on the part of .NET where the action really happens: the common language runtime.

■**Note** For excellent discussions of the general structure of .NET and its components, see *Introducing Microsoft .NET*, Third Edition (Microsoft Press, 2003), by David S. Platt, and *Inside C#*, Second Edition (Microsoft Press, 2002), by Tom Archer and Andrew Whitechapel.

Simply put, the common language runtime is a run-time environment in which .NET applications run. It provides an operating layer between the .NET applications and the underlying operating system. In principle, the common language runtime is similar to the runtimes of interpreted languages such as GBasic. But this similarity is only in principle: the common language runtime is not an interpreter.

The .NET applications generated by .NET-oriented compilers (such as Microsoft Visual C#, Microsoft Visual Basic .NET, ILAsm, and many others) are represented in an abstract, intermediate form, independent of the original programming language and of the target machine and its operating system. Because they are represented in this abstract form, .NET applications written in different languages can interoperate closely, not only on the level of calling each other's functions but also on the level of class inheritance.

Of course, given the differences in programming languages, a set of rules must be established for the applications to allow them to get along with their neighbors nicely. For example, if you write an application in Visual C# and name three items MYITEM, MyItem, and myitem, Visual Basic .NET, which is case insensitive, will have a hard time differentiating them. Likewise, if you write an application in ILAsm and define a global method, Visual C# will be unable to call the method because it has no concept of global (out-of-class) items.

The set of rules guaranteeing the interoperability of .NET applications is known as the Common Language Specification (CLS), outlined in Partition I of the Common Language Infrastructure standard of Ecma International and the International Organization for Standardization (ISO). It limits the naming conventions, the data types, the function types, and certain other elements, forming a common denominator for different languages. It is important to remember, however, that the CLS is merely a recommendation and has no bearing whatsoever on common language runtime functionality. If your application is not CLS compliant, it might be valid in terms of the common language runtime, but you have no guarantee that it will be able to interoperate with other applications on all levels.

The abstract intermediate representation of the .NET applications, intended for the common language runtime environment, includes two main components: metadata and managed code. *Metadata* is a system of descriptors of all structural items of the application—classes, their members and attributes, global items, and so on—and their relationships. This chapter provides some examples of metadata, and later chapters describe all the metadata structures.

The *managed code* represents the functionality of the application's methods (functions) encoded in an abstract binary form known as *Microsoft intermediate language* (MSIL) or *common intermediate language* (CIL). To simplify things, I'll refer to this encoding simply as *intermediate language* (IL). Of course, other intermediate languages exist in the world, but as far as our endeavors are concerned, let's agree that IL means MSIL, unless specified otherwise.

The runtime "manages" the IL code. Common language runtime management includes, but is not limited to, three major activities: type control, structured exception handling, and garbage collection. *Type control* involves the verification and conversion of item types during execution. *Managed exception handling* is functionally similar to "unmanaged" structured exception handling, but it is performed by the runtime rather than by the operating system. *Garbage collection* involves the automatic identification and disposal of objects no longer in use.

A .NET application, intended for the common language runtime environment, consists of one or more *managed executables*, each of which carries metadata and (optionally) managed code. Managed code is optional because it is always possible to build a managed executable containing no methods. (Obviously, such an executable can be used only as an auxiliary part of an application.) Managed .NET applications are called *assemblies*. (This statement is somewhat simplified; for more details about assemblies, application domains, and applications, see Chapter 6.) The managed executables are referred to as *modules*. You can create single-module assemblies and multimodule assemblies. As illustrated in Figure 1-1, each assembly contains one prime module, which carries the assembly identity information in its metadata.

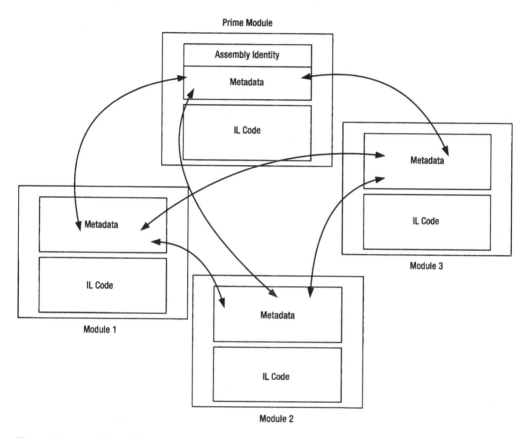

Figure 1-1. *A multimodule .NET assembly*

Figure 1-1 also shows that the two principal components of a managed executable are the metadata and the IL code. The two major common language runtime subsystems dealing with each component are, respectively, the loader and the just-in-time (JIT) compiler.

In brief, the *loader* reads the metadata and creates in memory an internal representation and layout of the classes and their members. It performs this task on demand, meaning a class is loaded and laid out only when it is referenced. Classes that are never referenced are never loaded. When loading a class, the loader runs a series of consistency checks of the related metadata.

The *JIT compiler*, relying on the results of the loader's activity, compiles the methods encoded in IL into the native code of the underlying platform. Because the runtime is not an interpreter, it does not execute the IL code. Instead, the IL code is compiled in memory into the native code, and the native code is executed. The JIT compilation is also done on demand, meaning a method is compiled only when it is called. The compiled methods stay cached in memory. If memory is limited, however, as in the case of a small computing device such as a handheld PDA or a smart phone, the methods can be discarded if not used. If a method is called again after being discarded, it is recompiled.

Figure 1-2 illustrates the sequence of creating and executing a managed .NET application. Arrows with hollow circles at the base indicate data transfer; the arrow with the black circle represents requests and control messages.

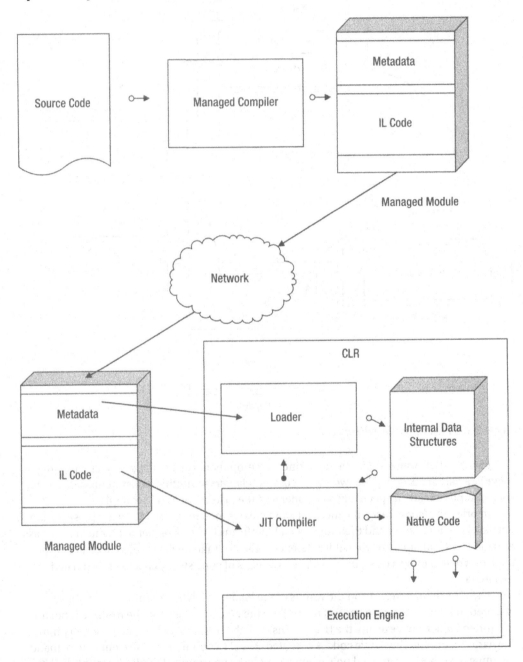

Figure 1-2. *The creation and execution of a managed .NET application*

You can precompile a managed executable from IL to the native code using the NGEN utility. You can do this when the executable is expected to run repeatedly from a local disk in order to save time on JIT compilation. This is standard procedure, for example, for managed components of the .NET Framework, which are precompiled during installation. (Tom Archer refers to this as *install-time code generation*.) In this case, the precompiled code is saved to the local disk or other storage, and every time the executable is invoked, the precompiled native-code version is used instead of the original IL version. The original file, however, must also be present because the precompiled version must be authenticated against the original file before it is allowed to execute.

With the roles of the metadata and the IL code established, I'll now cover the ways you can use ILAsm to describe them.

Simple Sample: The Code

No, the sample will not be "Hello, world!" This sample is a simple managed console application that prompts the user to enter an integer and then identifies the integer as odd or even. When the user enters something other than a decimal number, the application responds with "How rude!" and terminates. (See the source file Simple.il on the Apress Web site at http://www.apress.com.)

The sample, shown in Listing 1-1, uses managed console APIs from the .NET Framework class library for console input and output, and it uses the unmanaged function sscanf from the C run-time library for input string conversion to an integer.

Note To increase code readability throughout this book, all ILAsm keywords within the code listings appear in bold.

Listing 1-1. *OddOrEven Sample Application*

```
//----------- Program header
.assembly extern mscorlib { auto }
.assembly OddOrEven  { }
.module OddOrEven.exe
//----------- Class declaration
.namespace Odd.or {
    .class public auto ansi Even extends [mscorlib]System.Object {
//----------- Field declaration
        .field public static int32 val
//----------- Method declaration
        .method public static void check( ) cil managed {
            .entrypoint
            .locals init (int32 Retval)
        AskForNumber:
            ldstr "Enter a number"
            call void [mscorlib]System.Console::WriteLine(string)
```

```
        call string [mscorlib]System.Console::ReadLine ()
        ldsflda valuetype CharArray8 Format
        ldsflda int32 Odd.or.Even::val
        call vararg int32 sscanf(string,int8*,...,int32*)
        stloc Retval
        ldloc Retval
        brfalse Error
        ldsfld int32 Odd.or.Even::val
        ldc.i4 1
        and
        brfalse ItsEven
        ldstr "odd!"
        br PrintAndReturn
    ItsEven:
        ldstr "even!"
        br PrintAndReturn
    Error:
        ldstr "How rude!"
    PrintAndReturn:
        call void [mscorlib]System.Console::WriteLine(string)
        ldloc Retval
        brtrue AskForNumber
        ret
    } // End of method
  } // End of class
} // End of namespace
//----------- Global items
.field public static valuetype CharArray8 Format at FormatData
//----------- Data declaration
.data FormatData = bytearray(25 64 00 00 00 00 00 00) // % d . . . . . .
//----------- Value type as placeholder
.class public explicit CharArray8
            extends [mscorlib]System.ValueType { .size 8  }
//----------- Calling unmanaged code
.method public static pinvokeimpl("msvcrt.dll" cdecl)
    vararg int32 sscanf(string,int8*) cil managed { }
```

In the following sections, I'll walk you through this source code line by line.

Program Header

This is the program header of the OddOrEven application:

```
.assembly extern mscorlib { auto }
.assembly OddOrEven  { }
.module OddOrEven.exe
```

`.assembly extern mscorlib { auto }` defines a metadata item named `Assembly Reference` (or `AssemblyRef`), identifying the external managed application (assembly) used in this program. In this case, the external application is Mscorlib.dll, the main assembly of the .NET Framework classes. (The topic of the .NET Framework class library itself is beyond the scope of this book; for further information, consult the detailed specification of the .NET Framework class library published as Partition IV of the Ecma International/ISO standard.)

The Mscorlib.dll assembly contains declarations of all the base classes from which all other classes are derived. Although theoretically you could write an application that never uses anything from Mscorlib.dll, I doubt that such an application would be of any use. (One obvious exception is Mscorlib.dll itself.) Thus, it's a good habit to begin a program in ILAsm with a declaration of `AssemblyRef` to Mscorlib.dll, followed by declarations of other `AssemblyRef`s (if any).

The scope of an `AssemblyRef` declaration (between the curly braces) can contain additional information identifying the referenced assembly, such as the version or culture (previously known as `locale`). Because this information is not relevant to understanding this sample, I have omitted it here. (Chapter 5 describes this additional information in detail.) Instead, I used the keyword `auto`, which prompts ILASM to automatically discover the latest version of the referenced assembly.

Note that the assembly autodetection feature is specific to ILASM 2.0 and newer. Versions 1.0 and 1.1 have no autodetection, but they allow referencing Mscorlib.dll (and only it) without additional identifying information. So when using older versions of ILASM, just leave the `AssemblyRef` scope empty.

Note also that although the code references the assembly Mscorlib.dll, `AssemblyRef` is declared by filename only, without the extension. Including the extension causes the loader to look for Mscorlib.dll.dll or Mscorlib.dll.exe, resulting in a run-time error.

`.assembly OddOrEven { }` defines a metadata item named `Assembly`, which, to no one's surprise, identifies the current application (assembly). Again, you could include additional information identifying the assembly in the assembly declaration—see Chapter 6 for details—but it is not necessary here. Like `AssemblyRef`, the assembly is identified by its filename, without the extension.

Why do you need to identify the application as an assembly? If you don't, it will not be an application at all; rather, it will be a nonprime module—part of some other application (assembly)—and as such will not be able to execute on its own. Giving the module an .exe extension changes nothing; only assemblies can be executed.

`.module OddOrEven.exe` defines a metadata item named `Module`, identifying the current module. Each module, prime or otherwise, carries this identification in its metadata. Note that the module is identified by its full filename, including the extension. The path, however, must not be included.

Class Declaration

This is the class declaration of the OddOrEven application:

```
.namespace Odd.or {
    .class public auto ansi Even extends [mscorlib]System.Object {
        ...
    }
    ...
}
```

`.namespace Odd.or { … }` declares a namespace. A namespace does not represent a separate metadata item. Rather, a namespace is a common prefix of the full names of all the classes declared within the scope of the namespace declaration.

`.class public auto ansi Even extends [mscorlib]System.Object { ... }` defines a metadata item named Type Definition (`TypeDef`). Each class, structure, or enumeration defined in the current module is described by a respective `TypeDef` record in the metadata. The name of the class is `Even`. Because it is declared within the scope of the namespace `Odd.or`, its full name (by which it can be referenced elsewhere and by which the loader identifies it) is `Odd.or.Even`. You could forgo the namespace declaration and just declare the class by its full name; it would not make any difference.

The keywords `public`, `auto`, and `ansi` define the flags of the `TypeDef` item. The keyword `public`, which defines the visibility of the class, means the class is visible outside the current assembly. (Another keyword for class visibility is `private`, the default, which means the class is for internal use only and cannot be referenced from outside.)

The keyword `auto` in this context defines the class layout style (automatic, the default), directing the loader to lay out this class however it sees fit. Alternatives are `sequential` (which preserves the specified sequence of the fields) and `explicit` (which explicitly specifies the offset for each field, giving the loader exact instructions for laying out the class).

The keyword `ansi` defines the mode of string conversion within the class when interoperating with the unmanaged code. This keyword, the default, specifies that the strings will be converted to and from "normal" C-style strings of bytes. Alternative keywords are `unicode` (strings are converted to and from UTF-16 Unicode) and `autochar` (the underlying platform determines the mode of string conversion).

The clause `extends [mscorlib]System.Object` defines the parent, or base class, of the class `Odd.or.Even`. The code `[mscorlib]System.Object` represents a metadata item named Type Reference (`TypeRef`). This particular `TypeRef` has `System` as its namespace, `Object` as its name, and `AssemblyRef mscorlib` as the resolution scope. Each class defined outside the current module is addressed by `TypeRef`. You can also address the classes defined in the current module by `TypeRefs` instead of `TypeDefs`, which is considered harmless enough but not nice.

By default, all classes are derived from the class `System.Object` defined in the assembly Mscorlib.dll. Only `System.Object` itself and the interfaces have no base class, as explained in Chapter 7.

The structures—referred to as *value types* in .NET lingo—are derived from the `[mscorlib]System.ValueType` class. The enumerations are derived from the `[mscorlib]System.Enum` class. Because these two distinct kinds of `TypeDefs` are recognized solely by the classes they extend, you must use the `extends` clause every time you declare a value type or an enumeration.

You have probably noticed that the declaration of `TypeDef` in the sample contains three default items: the flags `auto` and `ansi` and the `extends` clause. Yes, in fact, I could have declared the same `TypeDef` as `.class public Even { ... }`, but then I would not be able to discuss the `TypeDef` flags and the `extends` clause.

Finally, I must emphasize one important fact about the class declaration in ILAsm. (Please pay attention, and don't say I haven't told you!) Some languages require that all of a class's attributes and members be defined within the lexical scope of the class, defining the class as a whole in one place. In ILAsm the class needn't be defined all in one place.

In ILAsm, you can declare a `TypeDef` with some of its attributes and members, close the `TypeDef`'s scope, and then reopen the same `TypeDef` later in the source code to declare more of its attributes and members. This technique is referred to as *class amendment*.

When you amend a TypeDef, the flags, the extends clause, and the implements clause (not discussed here in the interests of keeping the sample simple) are ignored. You should define these characteristics of a TypeDef the first time you declare it.

There is no limitation on the number of TypeDef amendments or on how many source files a TypeDef declaration might span. You are required, however, to completely define a TypeDef within one module. Thus, it is impossible to amend the TypeDefs defined in other assemblies or other modules of the same assembly.

Chapter 7 provides detailed information about ILAsm class declarations.

USING PSEUDOFLAGS TO DECLARE A VALUE TYPE AND AN ENUMERATION

You might want to know about a little cheat that will allow you to circumvent the necessity of repeating the extends clause. ILAsm has two keywords, value and enum, that can be placed among the class flags to identify, respectively, value types and enumerations if you omit the extends clause. (If you include the extends clause, these keywords are ignored.) This is, of course, not a proper way to represent the meta-data, because it can give the incorrect impression that value types and enumerations are identified by certain TypeDef flags. I am ashamed that ILAsm contains such lowly tricks, but I am too lazy to type extends [mscorlib]System.ValueType again and again. ILDASM never resorts to these cheats and always truthfully prints the extends clause, but ILDASM has the advantage of being a software utility.

Field Declaration

This is the field declaration of the OddOrEven application:

```
.field public static int32 val
```

`.field public static int32 val` defines a metadata item named Field Definition (FieldDef). Because the declaration occurs within the scope of class Odd.or.Even, the declared field belongs to this class.

The keywords public and static define the flags of the FieldDef. The keyword public identifies the accessibility of this field and means the field can be accessed by any member for whom this class is visible. Alternative accessibility flags are as follows:

- The assembly flag specifies that the field can be accessed from anywhere within this assembly but not from outside.

- The family flag specifies that the field can be accessed from any of the classes descending from Odd.or.Even.

- The famandassem flag specifies that the field can be accessed from any of those descendants of Odd.or.Even that are defined in this assembly.

- The famorassem flag specifies that the field can be accessed from anywhere within this assembly as well as from any descendant of Odd.or.Even, even if the descendant is declared outside this assembly.

- The private flag specifies that the field can be accessed from Odd.or.Even only.

- The privatescope flag specifies that the field can be accessed from anywhere within current module. This flag is the default. The privatescope flag is a special case, and I strongly recommend you do not use it. Private scope items are exempt from the requirement of having a unique parent/name/signature triad, which means you can define two or more private scope items within the same class that have the same name and the same type. Some compilers emit private scope items for their internal purposes. It is the compiler's problem to distinguish one private scope item from another; if you decide to use private scope items, you should at least give them unique names. Because the default accessibility is privatescope, which can be a problem, it's important to remember to specify the accessibility flags.

The keyword static means the field is static—that is, it is shared by all instances of class Odd.or.Even. If you did not designate the field as static, it would be an instance field, individual to a specific instance of the class.

The keyword int32 defines the type of the field, a 32-bit signed integer. (Chapter 8 describes types and signatures.) And, of course, val is the name of the field.

You can find a detailed explanation of field declarations in Chapter 9.

Method Declaration

This is the method declaration of the OddOrEven application:

```
.method public static void check( ) cil managed {
    .entrypoint
    .locals init (int32 Retval)
...
}
```

.method public static void check( ) cil managed { ... } defines a metadata item named Method Definition (MethodDef). Because it is declared within the scope of Odd.or.Even, this method is a member of this class.

The keywords public and static define the flags of MethodDef and mean the same as the similarly named flags of FieldDef discussed in the preceding section. Not all the flags of FieldDefs and MethodDefs are identical—see Chapter 9 as well as Chapter 10 for details—but the accessibility flags are, and the keyword static means the same for fields and methods.

The keyword void defines the return type of the method. If the method had a calling convention that differed from the default, you would place the respective keyword after the flags but before the return type. Calling convention, return type, and types of method parameters define the signature of the MethodDef. Note that a lack of parameters is expressed as ( ), never as (void). The notation (void) would mean that the method has one parameter of type void, which is an illegal signature.

The keywords cil and managed define so-called implementation flags of the MethodDef and indicate that the method body is represented in IL. A method represented in native code rather than in IL would carry the implementation flags native unmanaged.

Now, let's proceed to the method body. In ILAsm, the method body (or method scope) generally contains three categories of items: instructions (compiled into IL code), labels marking the instructions, and directives (compiled into metadata, header settings, managed exception handling clauses, and so on—in short, anything but IL code). Outside the method body, only directives exist. Every declaration discussed so far has been a directive.

.entrypoint identifies the current method as the entry point of the application (the assembly). Each managed EXE file must have a single entry point. The ILAsm compiler will refuse to compile a module without a specified entry point, unless you use the /DLL command-line option.

.locals init (int32 Retval) defines the single local variable of the current method. The type of the variable is int32, and its name is Retval. The keyword init means the local variables will be initialized at run time before the method executes. If the local variables are not designated with this keyword in even one of the assembly's methods, the assembly will fail verification (in a security check performed by the common language runtime) and will be able to run only in full-trust mode, when verification is disabled. For that reason, you should never forget to use the keyword init with the local variable declaration. If you need more than one local variable, you can list them, separated by commas, within the parentheses—for example, .locals init (int32 Retval, string TempStr).

```
AskForNumber:
    ldstr "Enter a number"
    call void [mscorlib]System.Console::WriteLine(string)
```

AskForNumber: is a label. It needn't occupy a separate line; the IL disassembler marks every instruction with a label on the same line as the instruction. Labels are not compiled into metadata or IL; rather, they are used solely for the identification of certain offsets within IL code at compile time.

A label marks the first instruction that follows it. Labels don't mark directives. In other words, if you moved the AskForNumber label two lines up so that the directives .entrypoint and .locals separated the label and the first instruction, the label would still mark the first instruction.

An important note before I go on to the instructions: IL is strictly a stack-based language. Every instruction takes something (or nothing) from the top of the stack and puts something (or nothing) onto the stack. Some instructions have parameters in addition to arguments and some don't, but the general rule does not change: instructions take all required arguments (if any) from the stack and put the results (if any) onto the stack. No IL instruction can address a local variable or a method parameter directly, except the instructions of load and store groups, which, respectively, put the value or the address of a variable or a parameter onto the stack or take the value from the stack and put it into a variable or a parameter.

Elements of the IL stack are not bytes or words, but slots. When I talk about IL stack depth, I am talking in terms of items put onto the stack, with no regard for the size of each item. Each slot of the IL stack carries information about the type of its current "occupant." And if you put an int32 item on the stack and then try to execute an instruction, which expects, for instance, a string, the JIT compiler becomes very unhappy and very outspoken, throwing an Unexpected Type exception and aborting the compilation.

ldstr "Enter a number" is an instruction that creates a string object from the specified string constant and loads a reference to this object onto the stack. The string constant in this case is stored in the metadata. You can refer to such strings as *common language runtime string constants* or *metadata string constants*. You can store and handle the string constants in another way, as explained in a few moments, but ldstr deals exclusively with common language runtime string constants, which are always stored in Unicode (UTF-16) format.

`call void [mscorlib]System.Console::WriteLine(string)` is an instruction that calls a console output method from the .NET Framework class library. The string is taken from the stack as the method argument, and nothing is put back, because the method returns void.

The parameter of this instruction is a metadata item named Member Reference (`MemberRef`). It refers to the static method named `WriteLine`, which has the signature `void(string)`; the method is a member of class `System.Console`, declared in the external assembly `mscorlib`. The `MemberRefs` are members of `TypeRefs`—discussed earlier in this chapter in the section "Class Declaration"—just as `FieldDefs` and `MethodDefs` are `TypeDef` members. However, there are no separate `FieldRefs` and `MethodRefs`; the `MemberRefs` cover references to both fields and methods.

You can distinguish field references from method references by their signatures. `MemberRefs` for fields and for methods have different calling conventions and different signature structures. Chapter 8 discusses signatures, including those of `MemberRefs`, in detail.

How does the IL assembler know what type of signature should be generated for a `MemberRef`? Mostly from the context. For example, if a `MemberRef` is the parameter of a `call` instruction, it must be a `MemberRef` for a method. In certain cases in which the context is not clear, the compiler requires explicit specifications, such as `method void Odd.or.Even::check( )` or `field int32 Odd.or.Even::val`.

```
call string [mscorlib]System.Console::ReadLine()
ldsflda valuetype CharArray8 Format
ldsflda int32 Odd.or.Even::val
call vararg int32 sscanf(string,int8*,...,int32*)
```

`call string [mscorlib]System.Console::ReadLine()` is an instruction that calls a console input method from the .NET Framework class library. Nothing is taken from the stack, and a string is put onto the stack as a result of this call.

`ldsflda valuetype CharArray8 Format` is an instruction that loads the address of the static field `Format` of type `valuetype CharArray8`. (Both the field and the value type are declared later in the source code and are discussed in later sections.) IL has separate instructions for loading instance and static fields (`ldfld` and `ldsfld`) or their addresses (`ldflda` and `ldsflda`). Also note that the "address" loaded onto the stack is not exactly an address (or a C/C++ pointer) but rather a reference to the item (a field in this sample).

As you probably guessed, `valuetype CharArray8 Format` is another `MemberRef`, this time to the field `Format` of type `valuetype CharArray8`. Because this `MemberRef` is not attributed to any `TypeRef`, it must be a global item. (The following section discusses declaring global items.) In addition, this `MemberRef` is not attributed to any external resolution scope, such as `[mscorlib]`. Hence, it must be a global item defined somewhere in the current module.

`ldsflda int32 Odd.or.Even::val` is an instruction that loads the address of the static field `val`, which is a member of the class `Odd.or.Even`, of type `int32`. But because the method being discussed is also a member of `Odd.or.Even`, why do you need to specify the full class name when referring to a member of the same class? Such are the rules of ILAsm: all references must be fully qualified. It might look a bit cumbersome, compared to most high-level languages, but it has its advantages. You don't need to keep track of the context, and all references to the same item look the same throughout the source code. And the IL assembler doesn't need to load and inspect the referenced assemblies to resolve the ambiguous references, which means the IL assembler can compile a module in the absence of the referenced assemblies and modules (if you are not using the autodetection of the referenced assemblies, which, of course, doesn't work without the assemblies to detect).

Because both class Odd.or.Even and its field val are declared in the same module, the ILAsm compiler will not generate a MemberRef item but instead will use a FieldDef item. This way there will be no need to resolve the reference at run time.

call vararg int32 sscanf(string,int8*,...,int32*) is an instruction that calls the global static method sscanf. This method takes three items currently on the stack (the string returned from System.Console::ReadLine, the reference to the global field Format, and the reference to the field Odd.or.Even::val) and puts the result of type int32 onto the stack.

This method call has two major peculiarities. First, it is a call to an unmanaged method from the C run-time library. I'll defer the explanation of this issue until I discuss the declaration of this method. (I have a formal excuse for that because, after all, at the call site managed and unmanaged methods look the same.)

The second peculiarity of this method is its calling convention, vararg, which means this method has a variable argument list. The vararg methods have some (or no) mandatory parameters, followed by an unspecified number of optional parameters of unspecified types— unspecified, that is, at the moment of the method declaration. When the method is invoked, all the mandatory parameters (if any) plus all the optional parameters used in this invocation (if any) should be explicitly specified.

Let's take a closer look at the list of arguments in this call. The ellipsis refers to a pseudoargument of a special kind, known as a *sentinel*. A sentinel's role can be formulated as "separating the mandatory arguments from the optional ones," but I think it would be less ambiguous to say that a sentinel immediately precedes the optional arguments and it is a prefix of the optional part of a vararg signature.

What is the difference? An ironclad common language runtime rule concerning the vararg method signatures dictates that a sentinel cannot be used when no optional arguments are specified. Thus, a sentinel can never appear in MethodDef signatures—only mandatory parameters are specified when a method is declared—and it should not appear in call site signatures when only mandatory arguments are supplied. Signatures containing a trailing sentinel are illegal. That's why I think it is important to look at a sentinel as the beginning of optional arguments and not as a separator between mandatory and optional arguments or (heaven forbid!) as the end of mandatory arguments.

For those less familiar with the C runtime, I should note that the function sscanf parses and converts the buffer string (the first argument) according to the format string (the second argument), puts the results in the rest of the pointer arguments, and returns the number of successfully converted items. In this sample, only one item will be converted, so sscanf will return 1 on success or 0 on failure.

```
stloc Retval
ldloc Retval
brfalse Error
```

stloc Retval is an instruction that takes the result of the call to sscanf from the stack and stores it in the local variable Retval. You need to save this value in a local variable because you will need it later.

ldloc Retval copies the value of Retval back onto the stack. You need to check this value, which was taken off the stack by the stloc instruction.

`brfalse` Error takes an item from the stack, and if it is 0, it branches (switches the computation flow) to the label Error.

```
ldsfld int32 Odd.or.Even::val
ldc.i4 1
and
brfalse ItsEven
ldstr "odd!"
br PrintAndReturn
```

`ldsfld int32 Odd.or.Even::val` is an instruction that loads the value of the static field Odd.or.Even::val onto the stack. If the code has proceeded this far, the string-to-integer conversion must have been successful, and the value that resulted from this conversion must be sitting in the field val. The last time you addressed this field, you used the instruction ldsflda to load the field address onto the stack. This time you need the value, so you use ldsfld.

`ldc.i4 1` is an instruction that loads the constant 1 of type int32 onto the stack.

Instruction and takes two items from the stack—the value of the field val and the integer constant 1—performs a bitwise AND operation and puts the result onto the stack. Performing the bitwise AND operation with 1 zeroes all the bits of the value of val except the least-significant bit.

`brfalse ItsEven` takes an item from the stack (the result of the bitwise AND operation), and if it is 0, it branches to the label ItsEven. The result of the previous instruction is 0 if the value of val is even, and it is 1 if the value is odd.

`ldstr "odd!"` is an instruction that loads the string odd! onto the stack.

`br PrintAndReturn` is an instruction that does not touch the stack and branches unconditionally to the label PrintAndReturn.

The rest of the code in the Odd.or.Even::check method should be clear. This section has covered all the instructions used in this method except ret, which is fairly obvious: it returns whatever is on the stack. If the method's return type does not match the type of the item on the stack, the JIT compiler will disapprove, throw an exception, and abort the compilation. It will do the same if the stack contains more than one item by the time ret is reached or if the method is supposed to return void (that is, not return anything) and the stack still contains an item—or, conversely, if the method is supposed to return something and the stack is empty.

Global Items

These are the global items of the OddOrEven application:

```
{
...
} // End of namespace
.field public static valuetype CharArray8 Format at FormatData
```

`.field public static valuetype CharArray8 Format at FormatData` declares a static field named Format of type valuetype CharArray8. As you might remember, you used a reference to this field in the method Odd.or.Even::check.

This field differs from, for example, the field Odd.or.Even::val because it is declared outside any class scope and hence does not belong to any class. It is thus a global item. Global items belong to the module containing their declarations. As you've learned, a module is a managed executable file (EXE or DLL); one or more modules constitute an assembly, which is the primary building block of a managed .NET application; and each assembly has one prime module, which carries the assembly identification information in its metadata.

Actually, a little trick is connected with the concept of global items not belonging to any class. In fact, the metadata of every module contains one special TypeDef named <Module>, which represents...any guesses? Yes, you are absolutely right.

This TypeDef is always present in the metadata, and it always holds the honorable first position in the TypeDef table. However, <Module> is not a proper TypeDef, because its attributes are limited compared to "normal" TypeDefs (classes, value types, and so on). This sounds almost like real life—the more honorable the position you hold, the more limited your options are.

<Module> cannot be public, that is, visible outside its assembly. <Module> can have only static members, which means all global fields and methods must be static. In addition, <Module> cannot have events or properties because events and properties cannot be static. (Consult Chapter 15 for details.) The reason for this limitation is obvious: given that an assembly always contains exactly one instance of every module, the concept of instantiation becomes meaningless.

The accessibility of global fields and methods differs from the accessibility of member fields and methods belonging to a "normal" class. Even public global items cannot be accessed from outside the assembly. <Module> does not extend anything—that is, it has no base class—and no class can inherit from <Module>. However, all the classes declared within a module have full access to the global items of this module, including the private ones.

This last feature is similar to class nesting and is quite different from class inheritance. (Derived classes don't have access to the private items of their base classes.) A *nested class* is a class declared within the scope of another class. That other class is usually referred to as an *enclosing class* or an *encloser*. A nested class is not a member class or an inner class in the sense that it has no implicit access to the encloser's instance reference (*this*). A nested class is connected to its encloser by three facts only: it is declared within the encloser's lexical scope; its visibility is "filtered" by the encloser's visibility (that is, if the encloser is private, the nested class will not be visible outside the assembly, regardless of its own visibility); and it has access to all of the encloser's members.

Because all the classes declared within a module are by definition declared within the lexical scope of the module, it is only logical that the relationship between the module and the classes declared in it is that of an encloser and nested classes.

As a result, global item accessibilities public, assembly, and famorassem all amount to assembly; private, family, and famandassem amount to private; and privatescope is, well, privatescope. The metadata validity rules explicitly state that only three accessibilities are permitted for the global fields and methods: public (which is actually assembly), private, and privatescope. The loader, however, is more serene about the accessibility flags of the global items: it allows any accessibility flags to be set, interpreting them as just described (as assembly, private, or privatescope).

Mapped Fields

This is the mapped field of the OddOrEven application:

```
.field public static valuetype CharArray8 Format at FormatData
```

The declaration of the field Format contains one more new item, the clause at FormatData. This clause indicates the Format field is located in the data section of the module and its location is identified by the data label FormatData. (The following section discusses data declaration and labeling.)

Compilers widely use this technique of mapping fields to data for field initialization. This technique does have some limitations, however. First, mapped fields must be static. This is logical. After all, the mapping itself is static, because it takes place at compile time. And even if you manage to map an instance field, all the different instances of this field will be physically mapped to the same memory, which means you'll wind up with a static field anyway. Because the loader, encountering a mapped instance field, decides in favor of "instanceness" and completely ignores the field mapping, the mapped instance fields are laid out just like all other instance fields.

Second, the mapped fields belong in the data section and hence are unreachable for the garbage collection subsystem of the common language runtime, which automatically disposes of unused objects. For this reason, mapped fields cannot be of a type that is subject to garbage collection (such as class or array). Value types are permitted as types of the mapped fields, as long as these value types have no members of types that are subject to garbage collection. If this rule is violated, the loader throws a Type Load exception and aborts loading the module.

Third, mapping a field to a predefined memory location leaves this field wide open to access and manipulation. This is perfectly fine from the point of view of security as long as the field does not have an internal structure whose parts are not intended for public access. That's why the type of a mapped field cannot be any value type that has nonpublic member fields. The loader enforces this rule strictly and checks for nonpublic fields all the way down. For example, if the type of a mapped field is value type A, the loader will check whether its fields are all public. If among these fields is one field of value type B, the loader will check whether value type B's fields are also all public. If among these fields are two fields of value types C and D—well, you get the picture. If the loader finds a nonpublic field at any level in the type of a mapped field, it throws a Type Load exception and aborts the loading.

Data Declaration

This is the data declaration of the OddOrEven application:

```
.field public static valuetype CharArray8 Format at FormatData
.data FormatData = bytearray(25 64 00 00 00 00 00 00)
```

.data FormatData = bytearray(25 64 00 00 00 00 00 00) defines a data segment labeled FormatData. This segment is 8 bytes long and has ASCII codes of the characters % (0x25) and d (0x64) in the first 2 bytes and zeros in the remaining 6 bytes.

The segment is described as bytearray, which is the most ubiquitous way to describe data in ILAsm. The numbers within the parentheses represent the hexadecimal values of the bytes, without the 0x prefix. The byte values should be separated by spaces, and I recommend you always use the two-digit form, even if one digit would suffice (as in the case of 0, for example).

It is fairly obvious you can represent literally any data as a bytearray. For example, instead of using the quoted string in the instruction ldstr "odd!", you could use a bytearray presentation of the string:

```
ldstr bytearray(6F 00 64 00 64 00 21 00 00 00)
```

The numbers in parentheses represent the Unicode characters *o, d, d,* and *!* and the zero terminator. When you use ILDASM, you can see bytearrays everywhere. A bytearray is a universal, type-neutral form of data representation, and ILDASM uses it whenever it cannot identify the type associated with the data as one of the elementary types, such as int32.

On the other hand, you could define the data FormatData as follows:

```
.data FormatData = int64(0x0000000000006425)
```

This would result in the same data segment size and contents. When you specify a type declaring a data segment (for instance, int64), no record concerning this type is entered into metadata or anywhere else. The ILAsm compiler uses the specified type for two purposes only: to identify the size of the data segment being allocated and to identify the byte layout within this segment.

Value Type As Placeholder

This is the value type used as a placeholder:

```
.field public static valuetype CharArray8 Format at FormatData
.data FormatData = bytearray(25 64 00 00 00 00 00 00)
.class public explicit CharArray8
              extends [mscorlib]System.ValueType { .size 8  }
```

.class public explicit CharArray8 extends [mscorlib]System.ValueType { .size 8 } declares a value type that has no members but has an explicitly specified size, 8 bytes. Declaring such a value type is a common way to declare "just a piece of memory." In this case, you don't need to declare any members of this value type because you aren't interested in the internal structure of this piece of memory; you simply want to use it as a type of your global field Format to specify the field's size. In a sense, this value type is nothing but a placeholder.

Could you use an array of 8 bytes instead and save yourself the declaration of another value type? You could if you did not intend to map the field to the data. Because arrays are subject to garbage collection, they are not allowed as types of mapped fields.

Using value types as placeholders is popular with managed C/C++ compilers because of the need to store and address numerous ANSI string constants. The Visual C# and Visual Basic .NET compilers, which deal mostly with Unicode strings, are less enthusiastic about this technique because they can directly use the common language runtime string constants, which are stored in metadata in Unicode format.

Calling Unmanaged Code

This is how the OddOrEven application declares the unmanaged method, which is called from the managed method check:

```
.method public static pinvokeimpl("msvcrt.dll" cdecl)
    vararg int32 sscanf(string,int8*) cil managed { }
```

The line .method public static pinvokeimpl("msvcrt.dll" cdecl) vararg int32 sscanf(string, int8*) cil managed { } declares an unmanaged method, to be called from managed code. The attribute pinvokeimpl("msvcrt.dll" cdecl) indicates that this is an unmanaged method, called using the mechanism known as *platform invocation* or P/Invoke.

This attribute also indicates that this method resides in the unmanaged DLL Msvcrt.dll and has the calling convention cdecl. This calling convention means the unmanaged method handles the arguments the same way an ANSI C function does.

The method takes two mandatory parameters of types string and int8* (the equivalent of C/C++ char*) and returns int32. Being a vararg method, sscanf can take any number of optional parameters of any type, but as you know already, neither the optional parameters nor a sentinel is specified when a vararg method is declared.

Platform invocation is the mechanism the common language runtime provides to facilitate the calls from the managed code to unmanaged functions. Behind the scenes, the runtime constructs the so-called stub, or *thunk*, which allows the addressing of the unmanaged function and conversion of managed argument types to the appropriate unmanaged types and back. This conversion is known as *parameter marshaling*.

What is being declared here is not an actual unmanaged method to be called but a stub generated by the runtime, as it is seen from the managed code, which explains the implementation flags cil managed. Specifying the method signature as int32(string, int8*), you specify the "managed side" of parameter marshaling. The unmanaged side of the parameter marshaling is defined by the actual signature of the unmanaged method being invoked.

The actual signature of the unmanaged function sscanf in C is int sscanf(const char*, const char*, ...). So, the first parameter is marshaled from managed type string to unmanaged type char*. Recall that when I declared the class Odd.or.Even, I specified the ansi flag, which means the managed strings by default are marshaled as ANSI C strings, that is, char*. And because the call to sscanf is made from a member method of class Odd.or.Even, you don't need to provide special information about marshaling the managed strings.

The second parameter of the sscanf declaration is int8*, which is a direct equivalent of char*; as a result, little marshaling is required. (ILAsm has type char as well, but it indicates a Unicode character rather than ANSI, equivalent to "unsigned short" in C, so you cannot use this type here.)

The optional parameters of the original (unmanaged) sscanf are supposed to be the pointers to items (variables) you want to fill while parsing the buffer string. The number and base types of these pointers are defined according to the format specification string (the second argument of sscanf). In this case, given the format specification string "%d", sscanf will expect a single optional argument of type int*. When I call the managed thunk of sscanf, I provide the optional argument of type int32*, which might require marshaling to a native integer pointer only if you are dealing with a platform other than a 32-bit Intel platform (for example, an AMD or Intel 64-bit platform).

The P/Invoke mechanism is very useful because it gives you full access to rich and numerous native libraries and platform APIs. But don't overestimate the ubiquity of P/Invoke. Different platforms tend to have different APIs, so overtaxing P/Invoke can easily limit the portability of your applications. It's better to stick with the .NET Framework class library and take some consolation in the thought that by now you can make a fair guess about what lies at the bottom of this library.

Now that I've finished showing you the source code, find the sample file Simple.il on the Apress Web site, copy it into your working directory, compile it using the console command ilasm simple (assuming you have installed the .NET Framework and the Platform software development kit [SDK]), and try running the resulting Simple.exe.

Forward Declaration of Classes

This section is relevant only to earlier versions (1.0 and 1.1) of ILASM, but I still think it is useful information. Considering the size of the install base of the .NET Framework of these versions, chances are you will encounter older ILASM more than once.

If you have an older version of the .NET Framework installed, you can carry out a little experiment with the sample code. Open the source file Simple.il in any text editor, and modify it by moving the declaration of the value type CharArray8 in front of the declaration of the field Format:

```
{
    ...
} // End of namespace
.class public explicit CharArray8
            extends [mscorlib]System.ValueType { .size 8  }
.field public static valuetype CharArray8 Format at FormatData
```

Everything seems to be in order. But when you try to recompile the file, ILAsm compilation fails with the error message Unresolved MemberRef 'Format'.

Now modify the source file again, this time moving the declaration of value type CharArray8 before the declaration of the namespace Odd.or:

```
.class public explicit CharArray8
            extends [mscorlib]System.ValueType { .size 8  }
.namespace Odd.or {
    .class public auto ansi Even extends [mscorlib]System.Object {
        .field public static int32 val
        .method public static void check( ) cil managed {
            ...
            ldsflda valuetype CharArray8 Format
            ...
        } // End of method
    } // End of class
} // End of namespace
.field public static valuetype CharArray8 Format at FormatData
```

Now when you save the source code and try to recompile it, everything is back to normal. What's going on here?

After the first change, when the field Format was being referenced in the ldsflda instruction in the method check, the value type CharArray8 had not been declared yet, so the respective TypeRef was emitted for it, and the signature of the field reference received the TypeRef as its type.

Then the value type CharArray8 was declared, and a new TypeDef was created. After that, when the field Format was actually declared, its type was recognized as a locally declared value type, and the signature of the field definition received the TypeDef as its type. But, no field named Format with a TypeRef as its type was declared anywhere in this module. Hence, you get the reference-to-definition resolution failure.

(This is an inviting moment to criticize the ILAsm compiler's lack of ability to match the signatures on a pragmatic level, with type analysis and matching the TypeRefs to TypeDefs by full name and resolution scope. Have patience, however.)

After the second change in the source code, the value type CharArray8 was declared first so that all references to it, no matter where they happen, refer to it as TypeDef. This is a rather obvious solution.

The solution becomes not so obvious when you consider two classes, members of which use each other's class as the type. Which class to declare first? Actually, both of them.

In the "Class Declaration" section I mentioned the class amendment technique, based on that ILAsm allows you to reopen a class scope to declare more class attributes and members. The general solution to the declaration/reference problem is to specify the empty-scope class definitions for all classes first. Following that, you can specify all the classes in full, with their attributes and members, as amendments. The "first wave" of class declarations should carry all class flags, extends clauses, and implements clauses and should include all nested classes (also with empty scopes). You should leave all the member declarations for later.

This technique of the forward declaration of classes guards against declaration/reference errors and, as a side effect, reduces the metadata size because it is unnecessary to emit redundant TypeRefs for locally defined classes.

(And the answer to the aforementioned criticism of the ILAsm compiler is that the compiler does signature matching in the fastest possible way, without needing more sophisticated and slower methods, as long as you use the class forward declaration.)

The need for the class forward declaration has been eliminated in version 2.0 of the ILAsm compiler.

Summary

This chapter touched briefly on the most important features of the common language runtime and ILAsm. You now know (in general terms) how the runtime functions, how a program in ILAsm is written, and how to define the basic components (classes, fields, and methods). You learned that the managed code can interoperate with the unmanaged (native) code and what the common language runtime is doing to facilitate this interoperation.

In the next chapter, you will continue working with the simple OddOrEven sample to learn some sophisticated features of the runtime and ILAsm.

CHAPTER 2

■ ■ ■

Enhancing the Code

In this chapter, I'll continue tweaking the simple sample; maybe I can make it better. There are two aspects of "better" I will discuss in this chapter: first, reducing code size and, second, protecting the code from unpleasant surprises. I'll start with the code size.

Compacting the Code

The sample code presented in the previous chapter is compact. If you don't believe me, carry out a simple experiment: write a similar application in your favorite high-level Microsoft .NET language, compile it to an executable (and make sure it runs!), disassemble the executable, and compare the result to the sample offered in Chapter 1. Now let's try to make the code even more compact.

First, given what you know about field mapping and value types as placeholders, I don't need to continue employing this technique. If sscanf accepts string as the first argument, it can just as well accept string as the second argument too. Second, I can use certain "short-cuts" (which I'll discuss later in this section) in the IL instruction set.

Let's have a look at the simple sample with slight modifications (source file Simple1.il) shown in Listing 2-1. I've marked the portions of interest with the CHANGE! comment.

Listing 2-1. *OddOrEven Sample Application with Changes*

```
//----------- Program header
.assembly extern mscorlib { auto }
.assembly OddOrEven { }
.module OddOrEven.exe
//----------- Class declaration
.namespace Odd.or {
  .class public auto ansi Even
         extends [mscorlib]System.Object {
//----------- Field declaration
    .field public static int32 val
//----------- Method declaration
    .method public static void check( ) cil managed {
      .entrypoint
      .locals init (int32 Retval)
    AskForNumber:
      ldstr "Enter a number"
```

```
  call void [mscorlib]System.Console::WriteLine(string)
  call string [mscorlib]System.Console::ReadLine()
  ldstr "%d" // CHANGE!
  ldsflda int32 Odd.or.Even::val
  call vararg int32 sscanf(string,string,...,int32*) // CHANGE!
  stloc.0 // CHANGE!
  ldloc.0 // CHANGE!
  brfalse.s Error // CHANGE!
  ldsfld int32 Odd.or.Even::val
  ldc.i4.1 // CHANGE!
  and
  brfalse.s ItsEven // CHANGE!
  ldstr "odd!"
  br.s PrintAndReturn // CHANGE!
ItsEven:
  ldstr "even!"
  br.s PrintAndReturn // CHANGE!
Error:
  ldstr "How rude!"
PrintAndReturn:
  call void [mscorlib]System.Console::WriteLine(string)
  ldloc.0 // CHANGE!
  brtrue.s AskForNumber // CHANGE!
  ret
    } // End of method
  } // End of class
} // End of namespace
//---------- Calling unmanaged code
.method public static pinvokeimpl("msvcrt.dll" cdecl)
    vararg int32 sscanf(string,string) cil managed { }
```

The program header, class declaration, field declaration, and method header look the same. The first change comes within the method body, where the loading of the address of the global field Format is replaced with the loading of a metadata string constant, ldstr "%d". As noted earlier, you can abandon defining and using an ANSI string constant as the second argument of the call to sscanf in favor of using a metadata string constant (internally represented in Unicode), relying on the marshaling mechanism provided by P/Invoke to do the necessary conversion work.

Because I am no longer using an ANSI string constant, the declarations of the global field Format, the placeholder value type used as the type of this field, and the data to which the field was mapped are omitted. As you've undoubtedly noticed, I don't need to explicitly declare a metadata string constant in ILAsm—the mere mention of such a constant in the source code is enough for the ILAsm compiler to automatically emit this metadata item.

Having thus changed the nature of the second argument of the call to sscanf, I need to modify the signature of the sscanf P/Invoke thunk so that necessary marshaling can be provided. Hence, you'll see changes in the signature of sscanf, both in the method declaration and at the call site.

Another set of changes results from replacing the local variable loading/storing instructions ldloc Retval and stloc Retval with the instructions ldloc.0 and stloc.0, respectively. IL defines special operation codes for loading/storing the first four local variables on the list, numbered 0 to 3. This is advantageous because the canonic form of the instruction (ldloc Retval) compiles into the operation code (ldloc) followed by an unsigned integer indexing the local variable (in this case 0), and the instructions ldloc.*n* compile into single-byte operation codes without parameters.

You might also notice that all branching instructions (br, brfalse, and brtrue) in the method check are replaced with the short forms of these instructions (br.s, brfalse.s, and brtrue.s). A standard (long) form of an instruction compiles into an operation code followed by a 4-byte parameter (in the case of branching instructions, offset from the current position), whereas a short form compiles into an operation code followed by a 1-byte parameter. This limits the range of branching to a maxima of 128 bytes backward and 127 bytes forward from the current point in the IL stream, but in this case you can safely afford to switch to short forms because the method is rather small.

Short forms that take an integer or unsigned integer parameter are defined for all types of IL instructions. So even if you declare more than four local variables, you still could save a few bytes by using the instructions ldloc.s and stloc.s instead of ldloc and stloc, as long as the index of a local variable does not exceed 255.

The high-level language compilers, emitting the IL code, automatically estimate the ranges and choose whether a long form or a short form of the instruction should be used in each particular case. The ILAsm compiler, of course, does nothing of the sort. If you specify a long or short instruction, the compiler takes it at face value—you are the boss, and you are supposed to know better. But if you specify a short branching instruction and place the target label out of range, the ILAsm compiler will diagnose an error.

Once, a colleague of mine came to me complaining that the IL assembler obviously could not compile the code the ILDASM produced. The disassembler and the assembler are supposed to work in absolute concert, so I was quite startled by this discovery. A short investigation uncovered the grim truth. In an effort to work out a special method for automatic test program generation, my colleague was compiling the initial programs written in Visual C# and Visual Basic .NET, disassembling the resulting executables, inserting test-specific ILAsm segments, and reassembling the modified code into new executables. The methods in the initial executables, produced by Visual C# and Visual Basic .NET compilers, were rather small, so the compilers were emitting the short branching instructions, which, of course, were shown in the disassembly as is. And every time my colleague's automatic utility inserted enough additional ILAsm code between a short branching instruction and its destination, the branching instruction, figuratively speaking, kissed its target label good-bye.

One more change to note in the sample: the instruction ldc.i4 1 was replaced with ldc.i4.1. The logic here is the same as in the case of replacing ldloc Retval with ldloc.0—in other words, a shortcut operation code to get rid of a 4-byte integer parameter. The shortcuts ldc.i4.*n* exist for *n* from 0 to 8, and (–1) can be loaded using the operation code ldc.i4.m1. The short form of the ldc.i4 instruction—ldc.i4.s—works for the integers in the byte range (from –128 to 127).

Now copy the source file Simple1.il from the Apress Web site, compile it with the console command ilasm simple1 into an executable (Simple1.exe), and ensure that it runs exactly as Simple.exe does. Then disassemble both executables side by side using the console commands ildasm simple.exe /bytes and ildasm simple1.exe /bytes. (The *bytes* option makes the disassembler show the actual byte values constituting the IL flow.) Find the check methods in the tree views of both instances of ILDASM, and double-click them to open disassembly windows, in which you can compare the two implementations of the same method to see whether the code compaction worked.

Protecting the Code

Thus far, I could have been quite confident that nothing bad would happen when I called the unmanaged function sscanf from the managed code, so I simply called it. But who knows what terrible dangers lurk in the deep shadows of unmanaged code? I don't. So I'd better take steps to make sure the application behaves in an orderly manner. For this purpose, I can employ the mechanism of exception handling, which is well known to C++ and Visual C# .NET programmers.

Examine the light modifications of the sample (source file Simple2.il) shown in Listing 2-2. As before, I've marked the modifications with the CHANGE! comment.

Listing 2-2. *Simple2.il, Modified Again*

```
//----------- Program header
.assembly extern mscorlib { auto }
.assembly OddOrEven { }
.module OddOrEven.exe
//----------- Class Declaration
.namespace Odd.or {
  .class public auto ansi Even
           extends [mscorlib]System.Object {
//------------ Field declaration
    .field public static int32 val
//------------ Method declaration
    .method public static void check( ) cil managed {
      .entrypoint
      .locals init (int32 Retval)
    AskForNumber:
      ldstr "Enter a number"
      call void [mscorlib]System.Console::WriteLine(string)
      .try { // CHANGE!
        // Guarded block begins
        call string [mscorlib]System.Console::ReadLine()
        // pop // CHANGE!
        // ldnull // CHANGE!
        ldstr "%d"
        ldsflda int32 Odd.or.Even::val
        call vararg int32 sscanf(string,string,...,int32*)
        stloc.0
        leave.s DidntBlowUp // CHANGE!
        // Guarded block ends
      } // CHANGE!
```

```
    // CHANGE block begins! --->
    catch [mscorlib]System.Exception
    { // Exception handler begins
      pop
      ldstr "KABOOM!"
      call void [mscorlib]System.Console::WriteLine(string)
      leave.s Return
    } // Exception handler ends
  DidntBlowUp:
    // <--- CHANGE block ends!
    ldloc.0
    brfalse.s Error
    ldsfld int32 Odd.or.Even::val
    ldc.i4.1
    and
    brfalse.s ItsEven
    ldstr "odd!"
    br.s PrintAndReturn
  ItsEven:
    ldstr "even!"
    br.s PrintAndReturn
  Error:
    ldstr "How rude!"
  PrintAndReturn:
    call void [mscorlib]System.Console::WriteLine(string)
    ldloc.0
    brtrue.s AskForNumber
  Return: // CHANGE!
    ret
  } // End of method
 } // End of class
} // End of namespace
//----------- Calling unmanaged code
.method public static pinvokeimpl("msvcrt.dll" cdecl)
    vararg int32 sscanf(string,string) cil managed { }
```

What are these changes? One involves enclosing the "dangerous" part of the code in the scope of the so-called try block (or guarded block), which prompts the runtime to watch for exceptions thrown while executing this code segment. The exceptions are thrown if anything out of order happens—for example, a memory access violation or a reference to an undefined class or method.

```
.try {
  // Guarded block begins
  call string [mscorlib]System.Console::ReadLine()
  ldstr "%d"
  ldsflda int32 Odd.or.Even::val
  call vararg int32 sscanf(string,string,...,int32*)
```

```
stloc.0
leave.s DidntBlowUp
// Guarded block ends
}
```

Note that the try block ends with the instruction leave.s DidntBlowUp. This instruction—leave.s being a short form of leave—switches the computation flow to the location marked with the label DidntBlowUp. You cannot use a branching instruction here because, according to the rules of the common language runtime exception handling mechanism strictly enforced by the JIT compiler, the only legal way out of a try block is via a leave instruction.

This limitation is caused by an important function performed by the leave instruction: before switching the computation flow, it unwinds the stack (strips off all the items currently on the stack), and if these items are references to object instances, it disposes of them. That is why I need to store the value returned by the sscanf function in the local variable Retval before using the leave instruction; if I tried to do it later, the value would be lost.

catch [mscorlib]System.Exception indicates I plan to intercept any exception thrown within the protected segment and handle this exception:

```
{
    ...
    leave.s DidntBlowUp
    // Guarded block ends
}
catch [mscorlib]System.Exception
{ // Exception handler begins
    pop
    ...
}
```

Because I am intercepting *any* exception, I specified a base managed exception type ([mscorlib]System.Exception), a type from which all managed exception types are derived. Technically, I could call [mscorlib]System.Exception the "mother of all exceptions," but the proper term is somehow less colloquial: the "inheritance root of all exceptions."

Mentioning another, more specific, type of exception in the catch clause—in this case, [mscorlib]System.NullReferenceException—would indicate I am prepared to handle only this particular type of exception and that exceptions of other types should be handled elsewhere. This approach is convenient if you want to have different handlers for different types of exceptions (which is less error prone and is considered a better programming style), and it's the reason this mechanism is referred to as *structured* exception handling.

Immediately following the catch clause is the exception handler scope (the handler block):

```
catch [mscorlib]System.Exception
{ // Exception handler begins
    pop
    ldstr "KABOOM!"
    call void [mscorlib]System.Console::WriteLine(string)
    leave.s Return
} // Exception handler ends
```

When an exception is intercepted and the handler block is entered, the only thing present on the stack is always the reference to the intercepted exception—an instance of the exception type. In implementing this handler, I don't want to take pains analyzing the caught exception, so I can simply get rid of it using the instruction pop. In this simple application, it's enough to know that an exception has occurred, without reviewing the details.

Then I load the string constant "KABOOM!" onto the stack, print this string by using the console output method [mscorlib]System.Console::WriteLine(string), and switch to the label Return by using the instruction leave.s. The rule "leave only by leave" applies to the handler blocks as well as to the try blocks. I could not simply load the string "KABOOM!" onto the stack and leave to PrintAndReturn; the leave.s instruction would remove this string from the stack, leaving nothing with which to call WriteLine.

You might be wondering why, if I am trying to protect the call to the unmanaged function sscanf, I included three preceding instructions in the try block? Why not include only the call to sscanf in the scope of .try?

```
ldstr "Enter a number"
call void [mscorlib]System.Console::WriteLine(string)
.try {
    // Guarded block begins
    call string [mscorlib]System.Console::ReadLine()
    ldstr "%d"
    ldsflda int32 Odd.or.Even::val
    call vararg int32 sscanf(string,string,..., int32*)
    stloc.0
    leave.s DidntBlowUp
    // Guarded block ends
}
```

According to the exception handling rules, a guarded segment (a try block) can begin only when the method stack is empty. The closest such moment before the call to sscanf was immediately after the call to [mscorlib]System.Console::WriteLine(string), which took the string "Enter a number" from the stack and put nothing back. Because the three instructions immediately preceding the call to sscanf are loading the call arguments onto the stack, you must open the guarded segment before any of these instructions are executed.

Perhaps you're puzzled by what seems to be a rather strict limitation. Why can't you begin and end a try block anywhere you want, as you can in C++? Well, the truth is that you can do it the same way you do it in C++, but no better.

The high-level language compilers work in such a way that every completed statement in a high-level language is compiled into a sequence of instructions that begins and ends with the stack empty. In C++, the try block would look like this:

```
try {
    Retval = sscanf(System.Console::ReadLine(),
                    "%d", &val);
}
```

This feature of high-level language compilers is so universal that all high-level language decompilers use these empty-stack points within the instruction sequence to identify the beginnings and ends of completed statements.

The last task remaining is to test the protection. Copy the source file Simple2.il from the Apress Web site into your working directory, and compile it with the console command ilasm simple2 into the executable Simple2.exe. Test it to ensure it runs exactly as the previous samples do.

Now I'll simulate A Horrible Disaster Within Unmanaged Code. Load the source file Simple2.il into any text editor, and uncomment the instructions pop and ldnull within the try block:

```
.try {
    // Guarded block begins
    call string [mscorlib]System.Console::ReadLine()
    pop
    ldnull
    ldstr "%d"
    ldsflda int32 Odd.or.Even::val
    call vararg int32 sscanf(string,string,..., int32*)
    stloc.0
    leave.s DidntBlowUp
    // Guarded block ends
}
```

The instruction pop removes from the stack the string returned by ReadLine, and ldnull loads a null reference instead. The null reference is marshaled to the unmanaged sscanf as a null pointer. Sscanf is not prepared to take it and will try to dereference the null pointer. The platform operating system will throw the unmanaged exception Memory Access Violation, which is intercepted by the common language runtime and converted to a managed exception of type System.NullReferenceException, which in turn is intercepted by the .try-catch protection. The application will then terminate gracefully.

Recompile Simple2.il, and try to run the resulting executable. You will get nothing worse than "KABOOM!" displayed on the console.

You can then modify the source code in Simple.il or Simple1.il, adding the same two instructions, pop and ldnull, after the call to System.Console::ReadLine. Recompile the source file to see how it runs without structured exception handling protection.

Summary

Now you know how to write more compact IL code and how to use managed exception handling to protect it from crashes.

Managed exception handling is important in .NET programming because the managed methods of the .NET Framework class library (and even separate IL instructions) routinely throw exceptions instead of returning error codes.

In the next chapter, I will show you how to make IL programming a little less boring.

CHAPTER 3

Making the Coding Easier

I don't know about you, but for me this endless typing and retyping of the same code again and again is fun way below the average. Let's see how ILAsm 2.0 can make this work less tedious. There are three useful additions to the assembler syntax that can be exploited: aliasing, compilation control directives, and special keywords for the current class and its parent.

Aliasing

In the sample Simple2.il presented in the previous chapter, the methods of console input/output were called four times (one time for input and three times for output). And every time I had to type [mscorlib]System.Console::WriteLine or [mscorlib]System.Console::ReadLine. In ILAsm 1.0 and 1.1 I had no choice, but in ILAsm 2.0 I can use *aliasing*, assigning new short names to methods, classes, and so on.

Listing 3-1 shows the simple sample from the previous chapters with aliasing (source file Simple3.il). And, by the way, while at it, let's get rid of unnecessary default declarations.

Listing 3-1. *Simple3.il with Aliasing*

```
//----------- Program header
.assembly extern mscorlib { auto }
.assembly OddOrEven { }
.module OddOrEven.exe
//---------- Aliasing
.typedef [mscorlib]System.Console as TTY
.typedef method void TTY::WriteLine(string) as PrintLine
//---------- Class Declaration
.class public Odd.Or.Even {
//----------- Field declaration
  .field public static int32 val
//----------- Method declaration
  .method public static void check( ) {
    .entrypoint
    .locals init (int32 Retval)
  AskForNumber:
    ldstr "Enter a number"
    call PrintLine
    .try {
```

```
    // Guarded block begins
    call string TTY::ReadLine()
    // pop
    // ldnull
    ldstr "%d"
    ldsflda int32 Odd.or.Even::val
    call vararg int32 sscanf(string,string,...,int32*)
    stloc.0
    leave.s DidntBlowUp
    // Guarded block ends
  }
  catch [mscorlib]System.Exception
  { // Exception handler begins
    pop
    ldstr "KABOOM!"
    call PrintLine
    leave.s Return
  } // Exception handler ends
DidntBlowUp:
  ldloc.0
  brfalse.s Error
  ldsfld int32 Odd.or.Even::val
  ldc.i4.1
  and
  brfalse.s ItsEven
  ldstr "odd!"
  br.s PrintAndReturn
ItsEven:
  ldstr "even!"
  br.s PrintAndReturn
Error:
  ldstr "How rude!"
PrintAndReturn:
  call PrintLine
  ldloc.0
  brtrue.s AskForNumber
Return:
  ret
} // End of method
} // End of class
//------------ Calling unmanaged code
.method public static pinvokeimpl("msvcrt.dll" cdecl)
    vararg int32 sscanf(string,string) { }
```

Right after the program header, I have defined the aliases of class [mscorlib]System.Console and of its method WriteLine(string):

```
//----------- Aliasing
.typedef [mscorlib]System.Console as TTY
.typedef method void TTY::WriteLine(string) as PrintLine
```

Aliases in ILAsm are introduced by the .typedef keyword—this is similar to the typedef keyword in C. (Note that this is not related to the TypeDef mentioned in Chapter 1—an entry in a metadata table that describes a class or value type.) Aliases can be defined for a class, a method, a field, or a custom attribute. (Custom attributes are described in Chapter 16.) Once an alias is introduced, it can be used anywhere instead of the aliased item. You have probably noticed that the second aliasing directive uses the alias defined by the first aliasing directive.

When a method is being aliased, its definition starts with the keyword method and includes the full name and signature of the aliased method. The same approach is used when aliasing a field, but in this case, of course, the leading keyword is field. Aliasing the custom attributes should not concern you at the moment (because I have not explained yet what a custom attribute is), so I suggest waiting until Chapter 16.

The aliases are defined modulewide, which means once you define an alias, you can use it anywhere in this module. It also means once you define an alias, you cannot redefine it within this module. This is different from the C++ aliasing provided by the typedef directive, which can be scoped to a class or a method.

The aliases must be defined lexically before they are used.

The alias names must be unique within the module; you cannot alias two different things and name both of them, say, Foo. On the other hand, you can alias the same item (class, method, field, or custom attribute) more than once. The following is perfectly legal:

```
.typedef [mscorlib]System.Console as TTY
.typedef [mscorlib]System.Console as CON
...
    call void TTY::WriteLine(string)
...
    call void CON::WriteLine(string)
```

An interesting feature of aliases is that they survive round-tripping (assembling and disassembling). If you compile Simple3.il and then disassemble the resulting file Simple3.exe, you will see the aliases TTY and PrintLine all present and accounted for. This is because the ILAsm compiler stores all aliases in the metadata of the emitted module, and the disassembler looks for the aliases and uses them.

You might also notice that I got rid of the .namespace directive and declared the class Odd.Or.Even by its full name. This is another feature of ILAsm 2.0 that, in my opinion, makes the programmer's life easier, because this way the classes are defined and referenced uniformly. Besides, using the .namespace directive led to interesting questions such as, "If I define a global method Z within namespace X.Y, should I refer to this method as X.Y::Z?" (The answer is no, you refer to it as Z; namespaces are for the classes only.)

This does not mean, of course, that ILAsm 2.0 does not understand the .namespace directive. ILAsm 2.0 is fully backward compatible, which means it can compile the sources the previous versions could compile.

Compilation Control Directives

Those of you who have programmed in C/C++ (and I suspect it is the majority of the readers of this book) are probably holding nostalgic memories of useful preprocessor directives such as #include, #define, #ifdef, and so on. Rejoice, my friends, for ILAsm 2.0 supports some of those directives. No, it does not support all of them; there are way too many.

Listing 3-2 shows some light modifications of the sample (source file Simple4.il).

Listing 3-2. *Simple4.il*

```
// #define USE_MAPPED_FIELD
// #define BLOW_UP
//----------- Program header
.assembly extern mscorlib { auto }
.assembly OddOrEven { }
.module OddOrEven.exe
//----------- Aliasing
.typedef [mscorlib]System.Console as TTY
.typedef method void TTY::WriteLine(string) as PrintLine
//----------- Class Declaration
.class public Odd.Or.Even {
  //------------ Field declaration
  .field public static int32 val
  //------------ Method declaration
  .method public static void check( ) {
    .entrypoint
    .locals init (int32 Retval)
AskForNumber:
    ldstr "Enter a number"
    call PrintLine
    .try {
      // Guarded block begins
      call string TTY::ReadLine()
#ifdef BLOW_UP
      pop
      ldnull
#endif

#ifdef USE_MAPPED_FIELD
      ldsflda valuetype CharArray8 Format
      ldsflda int32 Odd.or.Even::val
      call vararg int32 sscanf(string,int8*,...,int32*)
#else
      ldstr "%d"
      ldsflda int32 Odd.or.Even::val
      call vararg int32 sscanf(string,string,...,int32*)
#endif
      stloc.0
```

```
      leave.s DidntBlowUp
       // Guarded block ends
    }
   catch [mscorlib]System.Exception
   { // Exception handler begins
      pop
      ldstr "KABOOM!"
      call PrintLine
      leave.s Return
   } // Exception handler ends
 DidntBlowUp:
   ldloc.0
   brfalse.s Error
   ldsfld int32 Odd.or.Even::val
   ldc.i4.1
   and
   brfalse.s ItsEven
   ldstr "odd!"
   br.s PrintAndReturn
 ItsEven:
   ldstr "even!"
   br.s PrintAndReturn
 Error:
   ldstr "How rude!"
 PrintAndReturn:
   call PrintLine
   ldloc.0
   brtrue.s AskForNumber
 Return:
   ret
 } // End of method
} // End of class
#ifdef USE_MAPPED_FIELD
//----------- Global items
.field public static valuetype CharArray8 Format at FormatData
//----------- Data declaration
.data FormatData = bytearray(25 64 00 00 00 00 00 00)
//----------- Value type as placeholder
.class public explicit value CharArray8 { .size 8  }
//----------- Calling unmanaged code
.method public static pinvokeimpl("msvcrt.dll" cdecl)
    vararg int32 sscanf(string,int8*) { }
#else
//------------ Calling unmanaged code
.method public static pinvokeimpl("msvcrt.dll" cdecl)
     vararg int32 sscanf(string,string) { }
#endif
```

This sample shows how to use the conditional compilation directives #ifdef, #else, and #endif. You need only to uncomment the directive #define USE_MAPPED_FIELD to switch back to passing the format string to sscanf as a byte array (as in sample Simple.il from Chapter 1). And if you uncomment the directive #define BLOW_UP, you will be able to simulate A Horrible Disaster Within Unmanaged Code (as in the sample Simple2.il from Chapter 2).

The compilation control directives supported by the ILAsm 2.0 compiler include the following:

#include "MyHeaderFile.il": Effectively inserts the contents of the file MyHeaderFile.il at the present location. I say "effectively" because the compilation control directives of ILAsm 2.0 are not in fact the preprocessor directives, so no intermediate preprocessed file is created like during C/C++ compilation. Instead, the ILAsm compiler, having encountered an #include directive, suspends the parsing of the current source file and switches to the included file. Once done with the included file, the compiler resumes the parsing of the current file. Note that the name of the included file must be in quotes. The form #include <MyHeaderFile.il> is not supported. The compiler looks for the included file in the current directory and on the include path, which may be specified in the command-line option /INC=<include_path> or in the environment variable ILASM_INCLUDE. Alternatively, you can specify the path to the included file in the #include directive itself. In this case, the compiler does not search the include path even if it is specified. If the included file is not found, the compiler aborts the compilation.

#define SYM1: Defines a compilation control symbol named SYM1. You can define the compilation control symbols only once in the source code; there is no command-line option to set these symbols (yes, I realize it's an omission).

#define SYM2 "SomeText": Defines a substitution symbol named SYM2 with the content "SomeText". The content must be in quotes always. The compiler will replace every occurrence of SYM2 in the source code with SomeText. The content of a substitution symbol can be whatever you like, but it cannot be part of a syntactic unit (such as a number, a name, or a keyword), only a full syntactic unit or a combination of those. For example, you could write the following:

```
#define MyFld="int32 Odd.Or.Even::val"
...
    ldflda MyFld
```

#undef SYM1: Undefines the compilation control symbol or substitution symbol named SYM1. You cannot use SYM1 in the code lexically following this directive. But you can redefine SYM1 by another #define directive and use it again after that.

#ifdef SYM: Compiles the following code if symbol SYM is defined.

#ifndef SYM: Compiles the following code if symbol SYM is not defined.

#else: I don't think I need to explain this one.

#endif: Ends the #ifdef/#ifndef or #ifdef/#ifndef-#else block. You can nest the conditional compilation blocks, just like in C/C++.

Referencing the Current Class and Its Relatives

Does it not look silly that in a member method check, of class Odd.Or.Even, we have to address this very class's member field as Odd.Or.Even::val?

ILAsm 2.0 offers three special keywords to refer to current class, the parent of the current class, and the encloser of the current class if the current class is nested (see Chapter 7 for details).

The keyword .this means the current class (not the current instance of the class, like the this keyword in C++ or C#). When used outside class scope, this keyword causes a compilation error. In the sample's code, instead of the following:

```
ldsflda int32 Odd.or.Even::val
```

you could use this:

```
ldsflda int32 .this::val
```

The keyword .base means the parent of the current class. This keyword must also be used only within a class scope, and the class must have a parent (an explicit or implicit extends clause). I haven't used a reference to the parent of the Odd.Or.Even class in the samples, but such references usually are numerous in code. For example, class Odd.Or.Even has no constructor, because it has only static members, so you don't need to instantiate it. But most classes have constructors, and the first step the class's constructor must take is to call the parent's constructor. Even if you don't need to do something special during the class construction, you still need a default constructor if you plan to instantiate the class. The following example defines a default constructor and is very useful in IL programming:

```
#define DEFLT_CTOR
   ".method public specialname void .ctor()
     { ldarg.0; call instance void .base::.ctor(); ret;}"
```

(Did you notice the semicolons? ILAsm 2.0 allows the semicolons to be used for source readability, such as when you want to put several instructions on the same line. Semicolons are not required and have no role except a cosmetic one.)

And after DEFLT_CTOR symbol has been defined, you can use it every time you need to declare a default constructor of some class:

```
.class public A.B.C extends X.Y.Z
{
  DEFLT_CTOR
  ...
}
.class public D.E extends [mscorlib]System.Object
{
  DEFLT_CTOR
  ...
}
```

Could you use aliasing (the .typedef directive) to define DEFLT_CTOR? No, because the definition of DEFLT_CTOR contains .base, which is defined only in a class scope and means different classes in different class scopes. This is the principal difference between .typedef and #define directives: the first provides an alternative name for a certain metadata item (class, method, field, custom attribute), and the second provides just "a named piece of text" to be inserted into the source code and interpreted according to the context.

The keyword .nester denotes the enclosing class of a nested class. A *nested class* is a class defined within the scope of another class (see Chapter 7 for details). This keyword can be used only within the scope of a nested class.

Summary

Please don't forget that the features discussed in this chapter are supported only in ILAsm 2.0.

These first three chapters *did* make for a quick start, didn't they? Well, I promised you a light cavalry raid into hostile territories, and you got just that. By now you should be able to understand in general the text output the IL disassembler produces. I hope too you are interested in a more detailed and systematic discussion of what is going on inside the common language runtime and how you can use ILAsm to describe it.

From now on, the operative words are detailed and systematic. No more cavalry charges!

PART 2

Underlying Structures

CHAPTER 4

■■■

The Structure of a
Managed Executable File

Chapter 1 introduced the managed executable file, known as a *managed module* and executed in the environment of the common language runtime. In this chapter, I'll show you the general structure of such a file. The file format of a managed module is an extension of the standard Microsoft Windows Portable Executable and Common Object File Format (PE/COFF). Thus, formally, any managed module is a proper PE/COFF file, with additional features that identify it as a managed executable file.

The file format of a managed module conforms to the Windows PE/COFF standard, and the operating system treats the managed module as an executable. And the extended, common language runtime–specific information allows the runtime to immediately seize control over the module execution as soon as the operating system invokes the module. Figure 4-1 shows the structure of a managed PE/COFF file.

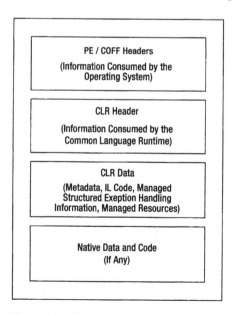

Figure 4-1. *The general structure of a managed executable file*

Since ILAsm produces only PE files, this chapter concentrates on managed PE files—executables, also known as *image files* because they can be thought of as "memory images"—rather than pure COFF object files. (Actually, only one of the current managed compilers, Microsoft Visual C++, produces object files as an intermediate step to PE files.)

This analysis of the managed PE file structure employs the following common definitions:

File pointer: The location of an item within the file itself, before it is processed by the loader. This location is a position (an offset) within the file as it is stored on disk.

Relative virtual address (RVA): The address of an item once it has been loaded into memory, with the base address of the image file subtracted from it—in other words, the offset of an item within the image file loaded into memory. The RVA of an item almost always differs from its position within the file on disk (the file pointer).

Virtual address (VA): The same as the RVA except that the base address of the image file is not subtracted. The address is referred to as *virtual* because the operating system creates a distinct virtual address space for each process, independent of physical memory. For almost all purposes, a virtual address should be considered simply as an address. A virtual address is not as predictable as an RVA because the loader might not load the image at its preferred location if a conflict exists with any image file already loaded—a *base address conflict*.

Section: The basic unit of code or data within a PE/COFF file. In addition to code and data sections, an image file can contain a number of sections, such as *.tls* (thread local storage) or *.reloc* (relocations), that have special purposes. All the raw data in a section must be loaded contiguously.

Throughout this chapter (and indeed throughout the book), I use the term *managed compiler* to mean a compiler that targets the common language runtime and produces managed PE files. The term does not necessarily imply that the compiler itself is a managed application.

PE/COFF Headers

Figure 4-2 illustrates the structure of operating system–specific headers of a PE file. The headers include an MS-DOS header and stub, the PE signature, the COFF header, the PE header, and section headers. The following sections discuss all these components and the data directory table in the PE header.

MS-DOS Header/Stub and PE Signature

The MS-DOS header and stub are present in image files only. Placed at the beginning of an image file, they represent a valid application that runs under MS-DOS. (Isn't that exciting?) The default stub prints the message "This program cannot be run in DOS mode" when the image file is run in MS-DOS. This is probably the least interesting part of operating system–specific headers; the only relevant fact is that the MS-DOS header, at offset 0x3C, contains the file pointer to the PE signature, which allows the operating system to properly execute the image file.

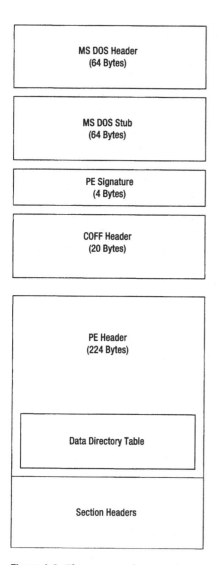

Figure 4-2. *The memory layout of operating system–specific headers*

The PE signature that usually (but not necessarily) immediately follows the MS-DOS stub is a 4-byte item, identifying the file as a PE format image file. The signature contains the characters *P* and *E*, followed by 2 null bytes.

COFF Header

A standard COFF header is located immediately after the PE signature. The COFF header provides the most general characteristics of a PE/COFF file, applicable to both object and executable files. Table 4-1 describes the structure of the COFF header and the meaning of its fields.

Table 4-1. *The Format of a COFF Header*

Offset	Size	Field Name	Description
0	2	Machine	Number identifying the type of target machine. (See Table 4-2.) If the managed PE file is intended for various machine types, this field should be set to IMAGE_FILE_MACHINE_I386 (0x014C). The IL assembler has the command options */ITANIUM* and */X64* to specify IMAGE_FILE_MACHINE_IA64 and IMAGE_FILE_MACHINE_AMD64 values, respectively.
2	2	NumberOfSections	Number of entries in the section table, which immediately follows the headers.
4	4	TimeDateStamp	Time and date of file creation.
8	4	PointerToSymbolTable	File pointer of the COFF symbol table. As this table is never used in managed PE files, this field must be set to 0.
12	4	NumberOfSymbols	Number of entries in the COFF symbol table. This field must be set to 0 in managed PE files.
16	2	SizeOfOptionalHeader	Size of the PE header. This field is specific to PE files; it is set to 0 in COFF files.
18	2	Characteristics	Flags indicating the attributes of the file. (See Table 4-3.)

The structure of the standard COFF header is defined in Winnt.h as follows:

```
typedef struct _IMAGE_FILE_HEADER {
    WORD    Machine;
    WORD    NumberOfSections;
    DWORD   TimeDateStamp;
    DWORD   PointerToSymbolTable;
    DWORD   NumberOfSymbols;
    WORD    SizeOfOptionalHeader;
    WORD    Characteristics;
} IMAGE_FILE_HEADER, *PIMAGE_FILE_HEADER;
```

The Machine types are also defined in Winnt.h, as listed in Table 4-2. Each type is named IMAGE_FILE_MACHINE_XXX, which I will abbreviate to _XXX to avoid repetition.

Table 4-2. *The Machine Field Values*

Constant (IMAGE_FILE_MACHINE...)	Value	Description
_UNKNOWN	0	Contents assumed to be applicable to any machine type—for unmanaged PE files only.
_I386	0x014c	Intel 386 or later. For pure managed PE files, contents are applicable to any machine type.
_R3000	0x0162	MIPS little endian—the least significant byte precedes the most significant byte. 0x0160 big endian—the most significant byte precedes the least significant byte.
_R4000	0x0166	MIPS little endian.

Continued

Table 4-2. *Continued*

Constant (IMAGE_FILE_MACHINE...)	Value	Description
_R10000	0x0168	MIPS little endian.
_WCEMIPSV2	0x0169	MIPS little endian running Microsoft Windows CE 2.
_ALPHA	0x0184	Alpha AXP.
_SH3	0x01a2	SH3 little endian.
_SH3DSP	0x01a3	SH3DSP little endian.
_SH3E	0x01a4	SH3E little endian.
_SH4	0x01a6	SH4 little endian.
_ARM	0x01c0	ARM little endian.
_THUMB	0x01c2	ARM processor with Thumb decompressor.
_AM33	0x01d3	AM33 processor.
_POWERPC	0x01F0	IBM PowerPC little endian.
_POWERPCFP	0x01F1	IBM PowerPC little endian with floating-point unit (FPU).
_IA 64	0x0200	Intel IA64 (Itanium).
_MIPS16	0x0266	MIPS.
_ALPHA64	0x0284	ALPHA AXP64.
_AXP64	0x0284	ALPHA AXP64.
_MIPSFPU	0x0366	MIPS with FPU.
_MIPSFPU16	0x0466	MIPS16 with FPU.
_TRICORE	0x0520	Infineon.
_AMD64	0x8664	AMD X64 and Intel E64T architecture.
_M32R	0x9041	M32R little endian.

The Characteristics field of a COFF header contains flags that indicate attributes of the PE/COFF file. These flags are defined in Winnt.h, as shown in Table 4-3. Notice that the table refers to pure-IL managed PE files; *pure IL* indicates that the image file contains no embedded native code.

The names of the flags all begin with IMAGE_FILE, which I will omit for clarity.

Table 4-3. *The Characteristics Field Values*

Flag (IMAGE_FILE...)	Value	Description
_RELOCS_STRIPPED	0x0001	Image file only. This flag indicates that the file contains no base relocations and must be loaded at its preferred base address. In the case of base address conflict, the OS loader reports an error. This flag should not be set for managed PE files.
_EXECUTABLE_IMAGE	0x0002	Flag indicates that the file is an image file (EXE or DLL). This flag should be set for managed PE files. If it is not set, this generally indicates a linker error.

Continued

Table 4-3. *Continued*

Flag (IMAGE_FILE...)	Value	Description
_LINE_NUMS_STRIPPED	0x0004	COFF line numbers have been removed. This flag should be set for managed PE files because they do not use the debug information embedded in the PE file itself. Instead, the debug information is saved in accompanying program database (PDB) files.
_LOCAL_SYMS_STRIPPED	0x0008	COFF symbol table entries for local symbols have been removed. This flag should be set for managed PE files, for the reason given in the preceding entry.
_AGGRESIVE_WS_TRIM	0x0010	Aggressively trim the working set. This flag should not be set for pure-IL managed PE files.
_LARGE_ADDRESS_AWARE	0x0020	Application can handle addresses beyond the 2GB range. This flag should not be set for pure-IL managed PE files of versions 1.0 and 1.1 but can be set for v2.0 files.
_BYTES_REVERSED_LO	0x0080	Little endian. This flag should not be set for pure-IL managed PE files.
_32BIT_MACHINE	0x0100	Machine is based on 32-bit architecture. This flag is usually set by the current versions of code generators producing managed PE files. Version 2.0 and newer, however, can produce 64-bit specific images, which don't have this flag set.
_DEBUG_STRIPPED	0x0200	Debug information has been removed from the image file.
_REMOVABLE_RUN_FROM_SWAP	0x0400	If the image file is on removable media, copy and run it from the swap file. This flag should not be set for pure-IL managed PE files.
_NET_RUN_FROM_SWAP	0x0800	If the image file is on a network, copy and run it from the swap file. This flag should not be set for pure-IL managed PE files.
_SYSTEM	0x1000	The image file is a system file (for example, a device driver). This flag should not be set for pure-IL managed PE files.
_DLL	0x2000	The image file is a DLL rather than an EXE. It cannot be directly run.
_UP_SYSTEM_ONLY	0x4000	The image file should be run on a uniprocessor machine only. This flag should not be set for pure-IL managed PE files.
_BYTES_REVERSED_HI	0x8000	Big endian. This flag should not be set for pure-IL managed PE files.

The typical Characteristics value produced by existing PE file generators—the one employed by the VC++ linker as well as the one used by all the rest of the Microsoft managed compilers, including ILAsm—for an EXE image file is 0x010E (IMAGE_FILE_EXECUTABLE_ IMAGE | IMAGE_FILE_LINE_NUMS_STRIPPED | IMAGE_FILE_LOCAL_SYMS_STRIPPED | IMAGE_FILE_32BIT_MACHINE).

For a DLL image file, this value is 0x210E (IMAGE_FILE_EXECUTABLE_IMAGE | IMAGE_ FILE_LINE_NUMS_STRIPPED | IMAGE_FILE_LOCAL_SYMS_STRIPPED | IMAGE_FILE_ 32BIT_MACHINE | IMAGE_FILE_DLL).

In version 2.0 of the common language runtime (CLR), the Characteristics value may have no IMAGE_FILE_32BIT_MACHINE flag if the image is generated for a 64-bit target platform.

PE Header

The PE header, which immediately follows the COFF header, provides information for the OS loader. Although this header is referred to as the *optional header*, it is optional only in the sense that object files usually don't contain it. For PE files, this header is mandatory.

The size of the PE header is not fixed. It depends on the number of data directories defined in the header and is specified in the SizeOfOptionalHeader field of the COFF header. The structure of the PE header is defined in Winnt.h as follows:

```
typedef struct _IMAGE_OPTIONAL_HEADER {
    // Standard fields
    WORD    Magic;
    BYTE    MajorLinkerVersion;
    BYTE    MinorLinkerVersion;
    DWORD   SizeOfCode;
    DWORD   SizeOfInitializedData;
    DWORD   SizeOfUninitializedData;
    DWORD   AddressOfEntryPoint;
    DWORD   BaseOfCode;
    DWORD   BaseOfData;
    // NT additional fields
    DWORD   ImageBase;
    DWORD   SectionAlignment;
    DWORD   FileAlignment;
    WORD    MajorOperatingSystemVersion;
    WORD    MinorOperatingSystemVersion;
    WORD    MajorImageVersion;
    WORD    MinorImageVersion;
    WORD    MajorSubsystemVersion;
    WORD    MinorSubsystemVersion;
    DWORD   Win32VersionValue;
    DWORD   SizeOfImage;
    DWORD   SizeOfHeaders;
    DWORD   CheckSum;
    WORD    Subsystem;
    WORD    DllCharacteristics;
    DWORD   SizeOfStackReserve;
    DWORD   SizeOfStackCommit;
    DWORD   SizeOfHeapReserve;
    DWORD   SizeOfHeapCommit;
    DWORD   LoaderFlags;
    DWORD   NumberOfRvaAndSizes;
    IMAGE_DATA_DIRECTORY
        DataDirectory[IMAGE_NUMBEROF_DIRECTORY_ENTRIES] ;
} IMAGE_OPTIONAL_HEADER32, *PIMAGE_OPTIONAL_HEADER32;
```

Table 4-4 describes the fields of the PE header.

Table 4-4. *PE Header Fields*

Offset 32/64	Size 32/64	Field	Description
0	2	Magic	"Magic number" identifying the state of the image file. Acceptable values are 0x010B for a 32-bit PE file, 0x020B for a 64-bit PE file, and 0x107 for a ROM image file. Managed PE files must have this field set to 0x010B or 0x020B (version 2.0 and later only, for 64-bit images).
2	1	MajorLinkerVersion	Linker major version number. The VC++ linker sets this field to 8; the pure-IL file generator employed by other compilers does the same. In earlier versions, this field was set to 7 and 6, respectively.
3	1	MinorLinkerVersion	Linker minor version number.
4	4	SizeOfCode	Size of the code section (.*text*) or the sum of all code sections if multiple code sections exist. The IL assembler always emits a single code section.
8	4	SizeOfInitializedData	Size of the initialized data section (held in the field SizeOfRawData of the respective section header) or the sum of all such sections. The initialized data is defined as specific values, stored in the disk image file.
12	4	SizeOfUninitializedData	Size of the uninitialized data section (.*bss*) or the sum of all such sections. This data is not part of the disk file and does not have specific values, but the OS loader commits memory space for this data when the file is loaded.
16	4	AddressOfEntryPoint	RVA of the entry point function. For unmanaged DLLs, this can be 0. For managed PE files, this value always points to the common language runtime invocation stub.
20	4	BaseOfCode	RVA of the beginning of the file's code section(s).
24/–	4/–	BaseOfData	RVA of the beginning of the file's data section(s). This entry doesn't exist in the 64-bit Optional header.

Continued

Table 4-4. *Continued*

Offset 32/64	Size 32/64	Field	Description
28/24	4/8	ImageBase	Image's preferred starting virtual address; must be aligned on the 64KB boundary (0x10000). In ILAsm, this field can be specified explicitly by the directive .imagebase <integer value> and/or the command-line option /BASE=<integer value>. The command-line option takes precedence over the directive.
32	4	SectionAlignment	Alignment of sections when loaded in memory. This setting must be greater than or equal to the value of the FileAlignment field. The default is the memory page size.
36	4	FileAlignment	Alignment of sections in the disk image file. The value should be a power of 2, from 512 to 64,000 0x200 (to 0x10000). If SectionAlignment is set to less than the memory page size, FileAlignment must match SectionAlignment. In ILAsm, this field can be specified explicitly by the directive .file alignment <integer value> and/or the command-line option /ALIGNMENT=<integer value>. The command-line option takes precedence over the directive.
40	2	MajorOperatingSystemVersion	Major version number of the required operating system.
42	2	MinorOperatingSystemVersion	Minor version number of the required operating system.
44	2	MajorImageVersion	Major version number of the application.
46	2	MinorImageVersion	Minor version number of the application.
48	2	MajorSubsystemVersion	Major version number of the subsystem.
50	2	MinorSubsystemVersion	Minor version number of the subsystem.
52	4	Win32VersionValue	Reserved.
56	4	SizeOfImage	Size of the image file (in bytes), including all headers. This field must be set to a multiple of the SectionAlignment value.

Continued

Table 4-4. *Continued*

Offset 32/64	Size 32/64	Field	Description
60	4	SizeOfHeaders	Sum of the sizes of the MS-DOS header and stub, the COFF header, the PE header, and the section headers, rounded up to a multiple of the FileAlignment value.
64	4	CheckSum	Checksum of the disk image file.
68	2	Subsystem	User interface subsystem required to run this image file. The values are defined in Winnt.h and are as follows: NATIVE (1): No subsystem required (for example, a device driver). WINDOWS_GUI (2): Runs in the Windows GUI subsystem. WINDOWS_CUI (3): Runs in Windows console mode. OS2_CUI (5): Runs in OS/2 1.x console mode. POSIX_CUI (7): Runs in POSIX console mode. NATIVE_WINDOWS (8): The image file is a native Win9x driver. WINDOWS_CE_GUI (9): Runs in the Windows CE GUI subsystem. In ILAsm, this field can be specified explicitly by the directive .subsystem <integer value> and/or the command-line option /SUBSYSTEM=<integer value>. The command-line option takes precedence over the directive.
70	2	DllCharacteristics	In managed files of v1.0, always set to 0. In managed files of v1.1 and later, always set to 0x400: no unmanaged Windows structural exception handling.
72	4/8	SizeOfStackReserve	Size of virtual memory to reserve for the initial thread's stack. Only the SizeOfStackCommit field is committed; the rest is available in one-page increments. The default is 1MB for 32-bit images and 4MB for 64-bit images. In ILAsm, this field can be specified explicitly by the directive .stackreserve <integer value> and/or the command-line option /STACK=<integer value>. The command-line option takes precedence over the directive.
76/80	4/8	SizeOfStackCommit	Size of virtual memory initially committed for the initial thread's stack. The default is one page (4KB) for 32-bit images and 16KB for 64-bit images.
80/88	4/8	SizeOfHeapReserve	Size of virtual memory to reserve for the initial process heap. Only the SizeOfHeapCommit field is committed; the rest is available in one-page increments. The default is 1MB for both 32-bit and 64bit images.

Continued

Table 4-4. *Continued*

Offset 32/64	Size 32/64	Field	Description
84/96	4/8	SizeOfHeapCommit	Size of virtual memory initially committed for the process heap. The default is 4KB (one operating system memory page) for 32-bit images and 2KB for 64-bit images.
88/ 104	4	LoaderFlags	Obsolete, set to 0.
92/ 108	4	NumberOfRvaAndSizes	Number of entries in the DataDirectory array; at least 16. Although it is theoretically possible to emit more than 16 data directories, all existing managed compilers emit exactly 16 data directories, with the 16th (last) data directory never used (reserved).

Data Directory Table

The data directory table starts at offset 96 in a 32-bit PE header and at offset 112 in a 64-bit PE header. Each entry in the data directory table contains the RVA and size of a table or a string that this particular directory entry describes; this information is used by the operating system. The data directory table entry is an 8-byte structure defined in Winnt.h as follows:

```
typedef struct _IMAGE_DATA_DIRECTORY {
    DWORD   VirtualAddress;
    DWORD   Size;
} IMAGE_DATA_DIRECTORY, *PIMAGE_DATA_DIRECTORY;
```

The first field, named VirtualAddress, is, however, not a virtual address but rather an RVA. The RVAs given in this table do not necessarily point to the beginning of a section, and the sections containing specific tables do not necessarily have specific names. The second field is the size in bytes.

Sixteen standard data directories are defined in the data directory table:

[0] Export Directory table address and size: The Export Directory table contains information about four other tables, which hold data describing unmanaged exports of the PE file. Among managed compilers, only the VC++ linker and ILAsm are capable of exposing the managed methods exported by a managed PE file as unmanaged exports, to be consumed by an unmanaged caller. See Chapter 18 for details.

[1] Import table address and size: This table contains data on unmanaged imports consumed by the PE file. Among managed compilers, only the VC++ linker make nontrivial use of this table, importing the unmanaged external functions used in the unmanaged native code that is embedded within the current, managed PE file. Other compilers, including the IL assembler, do not embed the unmanaged native code in the managed PE files, so Import tables of the files produced by these compilers contain a single entry, that of the CLR entry function.

[2] Resource table address and size: This table contains unmanaged resources embedded in the PE file; managed resources aren't part of this data.

[3] Exception table address and size: This table contains information on unmanaged exceptions only.

[4] Certificate table address and size: The address entry points to a table of attribute certificates (used for the file authentication), which are not loaded into memory as part of the image file. As such, the first field of this entry is a file pointer rather than an RVA. Each entry of the table contains a 4-byte file pointer to the respective attribute certificate and the 4-byte size of it.

[5] Base Relocation table address and size: The base relocations are discussed in detail later in this chapter; see "Relocation Section."

[6] Debug data address and size: A managed PE file does not carry embedded debug data; the debug data is emitted into a PDB file, so this data directory either is all zero or points to single 30-byte debug directory entry of type 2 (IMAGE_DEBUG_TYPE_CODEVIEW), which in turn points to a CodeView-style header, containing path to the PDB file. IL assembler and C# and VB .NET compilers emit this data into the *.text* section.

[7] Architecture data address and size: Architecture-specific data. This data directory is not used (set to all zeros) for I386, IA64, or AMD64 architecture.

[8] Global pointer: RVA of the value to be stored in the global pointer register. The size must be set to 0. This data directory is set to all zeros if the target architecture (for example, I386 or AMD64) does not use the concept of a global pointer.

[9] TLS table address and size: Among managed compilers, only the VC++ linker and the IL assembler are able to produce the code that would use the thread local storage data.

[10] Load Configuration table address and size: Data specific to Windows NT family of operating system (for example, the GlobalFlag value).

[11] Bound Import table address and size: This table is an array of bound import descriptors, each of which describes a DLL this image was bound up with at the time of the image creation. The descriptors also carry the time stamps of the bindings, and if the bindings are up-to-date, the OS loader uses these bindings as a "shortcut" for API import. Otherwise, the loader ignores the bindings and resolves the imported APIs through the Import tables.

[12] Import Address table address and size: The Import Address table (IAT) is referenced from the Import Directory table (data directory 1).

[13] Delay import descriptor address and size: Contains an array of 32-byte ImgDelayDescr structures, each structure describing a delay-load import. Delay-load imports are DLLs described as implicit imports but loaded as explicit imports (via calls to the LoadLibrary API). The load of delay-load DLLs is executed on demand—on the first call into such a DLL. This differs from the implicit imports, which are loaded eagerly when the importing executable is initialized.

[14] Common language runtime header address and size: The CLR header structure is described in detail later in this chapter (see "Common Language Runtime Header").

[15] Reserved: Set to all zeros.

Section Headers

The table of section headers must immediately follow the PE header. Since none of the file headers has a direct pointer to the section table, the location of this table is calculated as the total size of the file headers plus 1.

The NumberOfSections field of the COFF header defines the number of entries in the section header table. The section header indexing in the table is one-based, with the order of the sections defined by the linker. The sections follow one another contiguously in the order defined by the section header table, with (as you already know) starting RVAs aligned by the value of the SectionAlignment field of the PE header.

A section header is a 40-byte structure defined in Winnt.h as follows:

```
typedef struct _IMAGE_SECTION_HEADER {
    BYTE    Name[8];
    union {
            DWORD   PhysicalAddress;
            DWORD   VirtualSize;
    } Misc;
    DWORD   VirtualAddress;
    DWORD   SizeOfRawData;
    DWORD   PointerToRawData;
    DWORD   PointerToRelocations;
    DWORD   PointerToLinenumbers;
    WORD    NumberOfRelocations;
    WORD    NumberOfLinenumbers;
    DWORD   Characteristics;
} IMAGE_SECTION_HEADER, *PIMAGE_SECTION_HEADER;
```

The fields contained in the IMAGE_SECTION_HEADER structure are as follows:

Name (8-byte ASCII string): Represents the name of the section. Section names start with a dot (for instance, *.reloc*). If the section name contains exactly eight characters, the null terminator is omitted. If the section name has fewer than eight characters, the array Name is padded with null characters. Image files cannot have section names with more than eight characters. In object files, however, section names can be longer. (Imagine a long-winded file generator emitting a section named *.myownsectionnobodyelsecouldevergrok*.) In this case, the name is placed in the string table, and the field contains the slash (/) character in the first byte, followed by an ASCII string containing a decimal representation of the respective offset in the string table.

PhysicalAddress/VirtualSize (4-byte unsigned integer): In image files, this field holds the actual (unaligned) size in bytes of the code or data in this section.

VirtualAddress (4-byte unsigned integer): Despite its name, this field holds the RVA of the beginning of the section.

SizeOfRawData (4-byte unsigned integer): In an image file, this field holds the size in bytes of the initialized data on disk, rounded up to a multiple of the FileAlignment value specified in the PE header. If SizeOfRawData is less than VirtualSize, the rest of the section is padded with null bytes when laid out in memory.

PointerToRawData (4-byte unsigned integer): This field holds a file pointer to the section's first page. In image files, this value should be a multiple of the FileAlignment value specified in the PE header.

PointerToRelocations (4-byte unsigned integer): This is a file pointer to the beginning of relocation entries for the section. In image files, this field is not used and should be set to 0.

PointerToLinenumbers (4-byte unsigned integer): This field holds a file pointer to the beginning of line-number entries for the section. In managed PE files, the COFF line numbers are stripped, and this field must be set to 0.

NumberOfRelocations (2-byte unsigned integer): In managed image files, this field should be set to 0.

NumberOfLinenumbers (2-byte unsigned integer): In managed image files, this field should be set to 0.

Characteristics (4-byte unsigned integer): This field specifies the characteristics of an image file and holds a combination of binary flags, described in Table 4-5.

The section Characteristics flags are defined in Winnt.h. Some of these flags are reserved, and some are relevant to object files only. Table 4-5 lists the flags that are valid for PE files. Names of all flags begin with IMAGE_SCN, which I will omit as usual; in other words, IMAGE_SCN_SCALE_INDEX will become _SCALE_INDEX.

Table 4-5. *The Section Characteristics Flags in PE Files*

Flag (IMAGE_SCN...)	Value	Description
_SCALE_INDEX	0x00000001	TLS descriptor table index is scaled.
_CNT_CODE	0x00000020	Section contains executable code. In IL assembler–generated PE files, only the *.text* section carries this flag.
_CNT_INITIALIZED_DATA	0x00000040	Section contains initialized data.
_CNT_UNINITIALIZED_DATA	0x00000080	Section contains uninitialized data.
_LNK_INFO	0x00000200	Section contains comments or some other type of auxiliary information.
_NO_DEFER_SPEC_EXC	0x00004000	Reset speculative exception handling bits in the translation lookaside buffer (TLB) entries for this section.
_LNK_NRELOC_OVFL	0x01000000	Section contains extended relocations.
_MEM_DISCARDABLE	0x02000000	Section can be discarded as needed.
_MEM_NOT_CACHED	0x04000000	Section cannot be cached.
_MEM_NOT_PAGED	0x08000000	Section cannot be paged.
_MEM_SHARED	0x10000000	Section can be shared in memory.
_MEM_EXECUTE	0x20000000	Section can be executed as code. In IL assembler–generated PE files, only the *.text* section carries this flag.
_MEM_READ	0x40000000	Section can be read.
_MEM_WRITE	0x80000000	Section can be written to. In PE files generated by IL assembler, only the *.sdata* and *.tls* sections carry this flag.

The following flags are not allowed in the sections of managed files: IMAGE_SCN_SCALE_INDEX, IMAGE_SCN_NO_DEFER_SPEC_EXC, IMAGE_SCN_LNK_NRELOC_OVFL, and IMAGE_SCN_MEM_SHARED.

The IL assembler generates the following sections in a PE file:

.text: A read-only section containing the common language runtime header, the metadata, the IL code, managed exception handling information, and managed resources

.sdata: A read/write section containing data

.reloc: A read-only section containing relocations

.rsrc: A read-only section containing unmanaged resources

.tls: A read/write section containing thread local storage data

Common Language Runtime Header

The 15th directory entry of the PE header contains the RVA and size of the runtime header in the image file. The runtime header, which contains all of the runtime-specific data entries and other information, should reside in a read-only section of the image file. The IL assembler puts the common language runtime header in the *.text* section.

Header Structure

The common language runtime header is defined in CorHdr.h—a header file distributed as part of the Microsoft .NET Framework SDK—as follows:

```
typedef struct IMAGE_COR20_HEADER
{
    ULONG                   cb;
    USHORT                  MajorRuntimeVersion;
    USHORT                  MinorRuntimeVersion;
    // Symbol table and startup information
    IMAGE_DATA_DIRECTORY    MetaData;
    ULONG                   Flags;
    union {
        DWORD               EntryPointToken;
        DWORD               EntryPointRVA;
    };

    // Binding information
    IMAGE_DATA_DIRECTORY    Resources;
    IMAGE_DATA_DIRECTORY    StrongNameSignature;

    // Regular fixup and binding information
    IMAGE_DATA_DIRECTORY    CodeManagerTable;
    IMAGE_DATA_DIRECTORY    VTableFixups;
    IMAGE_DATA_DIRECTORY    ExportAddressTableJumps;

    IMAGE_DATA_DIRECTORY    ManagedNativeHeader;
} IMAGE_COR20_HEADER;
```

Table 4-6 provides a closer look at the fields of the header.

Table 4-6. *Common Language Runtime Header Fields*

Offset	Size	Field	Description
0	4	Cb	Size of the header in bytes.
4	2	MajorRuntimeVersion	Major number of the minimum version of the runtime required to run the program.
6	2	MinorRuntimeVersion	Minor number of the version of the runtime required to run the program.
8	8	MetaData	RVA and size of the metadata.
16	4	Flags	Binary flags, discussed in the following section. In ILAsm, you can specify this value explicitly by the directive .corflags <integer value> and/or the command-line option /FLAGS=<integer value>. The command-line option takes precedence over the directive.
20	4	EntryPointToken/EntryPointRVA	Metadata identifier (token) of the entry point for the image file; can be 0 for DLL images. This field identifies a method belonging to this module or a module containing the entry point method. In images of version 2.0 and newer, this field may contain RVA of the embedded native entry point method.
24	8	Resources	RVA and size of managed resources.
32	8	StrongNameSignature	RVA and size of the hash data for this PE file, used by the loader for binding and versioning.
40	8	CodeManagerTable	RVA and size of the Code Manager table. In the existing releases of the runtime, this field is reserved and must be set to 0.
48	8	VTableFixups	RVA and size in bytes of an array of virtual table (v-table) fixups. Among current managed compilers, only the VC++ linker and the IL assembler can produce this array.
56	8	ExportAddressTableJumps	RVA and size of an array of addresses of jump thunks. Among managed compilers, only the VC++ of versions pre-8.0 could produce this table, which allows the export of unmanaged native methods embedded in the managed PE file. In v2.0 of CLR this entry is obsolete and must be set to 0.
64	8	ManagedNativeHeader	Reserved for precompiled images; set to 0.

Flags Field

The Flags field of the common language runtime header holds a combination of the following bit flags:

COMIMAGE_FLAGS_ILONLY (0x00000001): The image file contains IL code only, with no embedded native unmanaged code except the start-up stub (which simply executes an indirect jump to the CLR entry point). Common language runtime–aware operating systems (such as Windows XP and newer) ignore the start-up stub and invoke the CLR automatically, so for all practical purposes the file can be considered pure IL. However, setting this flag can cause certain problems when running under Windows XP and newer. If this flag is set, the OS loader of Windows XP and newer ignores not only the start-up stub but also the *.reloc* section, which in this case contains single relocation (or single pair of relocations in IA64-specific images) for the CLR entry point. However, the *.reloc* section can contain relocations for the beginning and end of the *.tls* section as well as relocations for what is referred to as *data on data* (that is, data constants that are pointers to other data constants). Among existing managed compilers, only the VC++ and the IL assembler can produce these items. The VC++ of v7.0 and v7.1 (corresponding to CLR versions 1.0 and 1.1) never set this flag because the image file it generated was never pure IL. In v2.0 this situation has changed, and currently, the VC++ and IL assembler are the only two capable of producing pure-IL image files that might require additional relocations in the *.reloc* section. To resolve this problem, the IL assembler, if TLS-based data or data on data is emitted, clears this flag and, if the target platform is 32-bit, sets the COMIMAGE_FLAGS_32BITREQUIRED flag instead.

COMIMAGE_FLAGS_32BITREQUIRED (0x00000002): The image file can be loaded only into a 32-bit process. This flag is set alone when native unmanaged code is embedded in the PE file or when the *.reloc* section contains additional relocations or is set in combination with _ILONLY when the executable does not contain additional relocations but is in some way 32-bit specific (for example, invokes an unmanaged 32-bit specific API or uses 4-byte integers to store pointers).

COMIMAGE_FLAGS_IL_LIBRARY (0x00000004): This flag is obsolete and should not be set. Setting it—as the IL assembler allows, using the .corflags directive—will render your module unloadable.

COMIMAGE_FLAGS_STRONGNAMESIGNED (0x00000008): The image file is protected with a strong name signature. The *strong name signature* includes the public key and the signature hash and is a part of an assembly's identity, along with the assembly name, version number, and culture information. This flag is set when the strong name signing procedure is applied to the image file. No compiler, including ILAsm, can set this flag explicitly.

COMIMAGE_FLAGS_NATIVE_ENTRYPOINT (0x00000010): The executable's entry point is an unmanaged method. The EntryPointToken/EntryPointRVA field of the CLR header contains the RVA of this native method. This flag was introduced in version 2.0 of the CLR.

COMIMAGE_FLAGS_TRACKDEBUGDATA (0x00010000): The CLR loader and the JIT compiler are required to track debug information about the methods. This flag is not used.

EntryPointToken Field

The EntryPointToken field of the common language runtime header contains a token (metadata identifier) of either a method definition (MethodDef) or a file reference (File). A MethodDef token identifies a method defined in the module (a managed PE file) as the entry point method. A File token is used in one case only: in the runtime header of the prime module of a multimodule assembly, when the entry point method is defined in another module (identified by the file reference) of this assembly. In this case, the module identified by the file reference must contain the respective MethodDef token in the EntryPointToken field of its runtime header.

EntryPointToken must be specified in runnable executables (EXE files). The IL assembler, for example, does not even try to generate an EXE file if the source code does not define the entry point. The CLR loader imposes limitations on the signature of the entry point method: the method must return a signed or unsigned 4-byte integer or void, and it must have at most one parameter of type string or string[] (vector of strings).

With nonrunnable executables (DLL files), it's a different story. Pure-IL DLLs don't need the entry point method defined, and the EntryPointToken field in their runtime headers should be set to 0.

Mixed-code DLLs—DLLs containing IL and embedded unmanaged code—generated by the VC++ compiler and linker must run the unmanaged native function DllMain immediately at the DLL invocation in order to perform the initialization necessary for the unmanaged native components of the DLL. The signature of this unmanaged function must be as follows:

```
int DllMain(HINSTANCE, DWORD, void *);
```

To be visible from the managed code and the runtime, the function DllMain must be declared as a platform invocation of an embedded native method (local P/Invoke, also known in enlightened circles as IJW—It Just Works). See Chapter 18 for details about the interoperation of managed and unmanaged code.

Starting with version 2.0, you can specify the unmanaged entry point method without local platform invocation. In this case, indicated by setting flag COMIMAGE_FLAGS_NATIVE_ENTRYPOINT, the field EntryPointRVA (alias of EntryPointToken) contains the RVA of the native entry point method.

The method referred to by the EntryPointToken/EntryPointRVA field of the common language runtime header has nothing to do with the function to which the AddressOfEntryPoint field of the PE header points. AddressOfEntryPoint always points to the runtime invocation stub, which is invisible to the runtime, is not reflected in metadata and hence cannot have a token.

VTableFixups Field

The VTableFixups field of the CLR header is a data directory containing the RVA and the size of the image file's v-table fixup table. Managed and unmanaged methods use different data formats, so when a managed method must be called from unmanaged code, the common language runtime creates a marshaling thunk for it, which performs the data conversions, and the address of this thunk is placed in the respective address table. If the managed method is called from the unmanaged code embedded in the current managed PE file, the thunk address goes to the file's v-table. If the managed method is exported as unmanaged and is consumed somewhere outside the managed PE file, the address of the respective v-table entry must also go to the Export Address table. At loading time (and in the disk image file), the entries of this v-table contain the respective method tokens.

These v-table fixups represent the initializing information necessary for the runtime to create the thunks. v-table fixup is defined in CorHdr.h as follows:

```
typedef struct _IMAGE_COR_VTABLEFIXUP {
    ULONG       RVA;
    USHORT      Count;
    USHORT      Type;
} IMAGE_COR_VTABLEFIXUP;
```

In this definition, RVA points to the location of the v-table slot containing the method token(s). Count specifies the number of entries in the slot, 1 or greater if, for example, multiple implementations of the same method exist, overriding one another. Type is a combination of the following flags, providing the runtime with information about the slot and what to do with it:

COR_VTABLE_32BIT (0x01): Each entry is 32 bits wide.

COR_VTABLE_64BIT (0x02): Each entry is 64 bits wide.

COR_VTABLE_FROM_UNMANAGED (0x04): The thunk created by the common language runtime must provide data marshaling between managed and unmanaged code.

COR_VTABLE_CALL_MOST_DERIVED (0x10): This flag is not currently used.

Obviously, the first two flags are mutually exclusive. The slots of the v-table must follow each other immediately—that is, the v-table must be contiguous.

The v-table is located in a read/write section because it should be fixed up after the image has been loaded into memory. In contrast, the v-table in an unmanaged image is located in a read-only section.

Among existing managed compilers, only the VC++ and the IL assembler can define the v-table and its fixups.

StrongNameSignature Field

The StrongNameSignature field of the common language runtime header contains the RVA and size of the strong name hash, which is used by the runtime to establish the authenticity of the image file. After the image file has been created, it is hashed using the private encryption keys provided by the producer of the image file, and the resulting hash blob is written into the space allocated inside the image file.

If even a single byte in the image file is subsequently modified, the authenticity check fails, and the image file cannot be loaded. The strong name signature does not survive a round-tripping procedure; if you disassemble a strong-named module using the IL disassembler and then reassemble it, the module must be strong name signed again.

The IL assembler puts the strong name signature in the *.text* section of the image file.

Relocation Section

The *.reloc* section of the image file contains the Fixup table, which holds entries for all fixups in the image file. The RVA and size of the *.reloc* section are defined by the Base Relocation table directory of the PE header. The Fixup table consists of blocks of fixups, each block holding the fixups for a 4KB page. Blocks are 4-byte aligned.

Each fixup describes the location of a specific address within the image file as well as how the OS loader should modify the address at this location when loading the image file into memory.

Each fixup block starts with two 4-byte unsigned integers: the RVA of the page containing the addresses to be fixed up and the size of the block. The fixup entries for this page immediately follow. Each entry is 16 bits wide, of which four most significant bits contain the type of relocation required. The remaining 12 bits contain the relocated address's offset within the page.

To relocate an address, the OS loader calculates the difference (delta) between the preferred base address (the ImageBase field of the PE header) and the actual base address where the image file has been loaded. This delta is then applied to the address according to the type of relocation. If the image file is loaded at its preferred address, no fixups need be applied.

The following relocation types are defined in Winnt.h:

IMAGE_REL_BASED_ABSOLUTE (0): This type has no meaning in an image file, and the fixup is skipped.

IMAGE_REL_BASED_HIGH (1): The high 16 bits of the delta are added to the 16-bit field at the offset. The 16-bit field in this case is the high half of the 32-bit address being relocated.

IMAGE_REL_BASED_LOW (2): The low 16 bits of the delta are added to the 16-bit field at the offset. The 16-bit field in this case is the low half of the 32-bit address being relocated.

IMAGE_REL_BASED_HIGHLOW (3): The delta is added to the 32-bit address at the offset. Relocation of this type is equivalent to a combination of IMAGE_REL_BASED_LOW and IMAGE_REL_BASED_HIGH relocations and is a preferred type of 32-bit address relocation.

IMAGE_REL_BASED_HIGHADJ (4): The high 16 bits of the delta are added to the 16-bit field at the offset. The 16-bit field in this case is the high part of the 32-bit address being relocated. The low 16 bits of the address are stored in the 16-bit word that follows this relocation. A fixup of this type occupies two slots.

IMAGE_REL_BASED_MIPS_JMPADDR (5): The fixup applies to a MIPS jump instruction.

IMAGE_REL_BASED_SECTION (6): Reserved.

IMAGE_REL_BASED_REL32 (7): Reserved.

IMAGE_REL_BASED_MIPS_JMPADDR16 (9): The fixup applies to a MIPS16 jump function.

IMAGE_REL_BASED_IA64_IMM64 (9): This is the same type as IMAGE_REL_BASED_MIPS_JMPADDR16.

IMAGE_REL_BASED_DIR64 (10): The delta is added to the 64-bit field at the offset.

IMAGE_REL_BASED_HIGH3ADJ (11): The fixup adds the high 16 bits of the delta to the 16-bit field at the offset. The 16-bit field is the high one-third of a 48-bit address. The low 32 bits of the address are stored in the 32-bit double word that follows this relocation. A fixup of this type occupies three slots.

The only fixup type emitted by the existing managed compilers in 32-bit executables is IMAGE_REL_BASED_HIGHLOW. In 64-bit executables, it is IMAGE_REL_BASED_DIR64.

A 32-bit pure-IL PE file, as a rule, contains only one fixup in the *.reloc* section. This is for the benefit of the common language runtime start-up stub, the only segment of native code in a pure-IL image file. This fixup is for the image file's IAT, containing a single entry: the CLR entry point.

A 64-bit pure-IL PE file contains one fixup on X64 architecture and two fixups on Itanium architecture (additional fixup needed for the global pointer).

Windows XP or newer, as a common language runtime–aware operating system, needs neither the runtime start-up stub nor the IAT to invoke the runtime. Thus, if the common language runtime header flags indicate that the image file is IL only (COMIMAGE_FLAGS_ILONLY), the operating system ignores the *.reloc* section altogether.

This optimization plays a bad joke with some image files generated by the IL assembler, which produces pure-IL image files but needs relocations executed if any data is located in thread local storage or if data on data is defined. To have these relocations executed when the image file is loaded under Windows XP, the IL assembler is forced to cheat and set the common language runtime header flags as if the image file contained embedded native code (COMIMAGE_FLAGS_32BITREQUIRED for 32-bit target platform, or none for 64-bit target platforms).

Other compilers don't have these problems. Compilers generating pure-IL image files (such as Visual C# and Visual Basic .NET) don't define TLS-based data or data on data.

As the VC++ compiler and linker can produce mixed-code image files, the *.reloc* sections of these image files can contain any number of relocations. But mixed-code image files never carry IL-only common language runtime header flags, so their relocations are always executed.

Text Section

The *.text* section of a PE file is a read-only section. In a managed PE file, it contains metadata tables, IL code, the Import tables, the common language runtime header, and an unmanaged start-up stub for the CLR. In the image files generated by the IL assembler, this section also contains managed resources, the strong name signature hash, the debug data, and unmanaged export stubs.

Figure 4-3 summarizes the general structure of the *.text* section of an image file generated by the IL assembler.

The IL assembler emits data to the *.text* section in a particular order. When the PE file generator is initialized during the IL assembler start-up, space is allocated in the *.text* section for the Import Address table (which carries one lonely entry, for the entry point of the CLR) and for the CLR header described earlier in this chapter.

While IL assembler is parsing the source code and forming metadata and IL structures in memory, the *.text* section gets a temporary break; nothing is emitted to it until the parsing is done and the IL assembler is ready to emit the PE file.

Then the IL assembler, if so ordered (by specifying the public key in the .assembly directive; see Chapter 6 for details), allocates sufficient space in the *.text* section for the strong name signature. The strong name signature is a hash of the prime module encrypted with the assembly publisher's private key. The signature itself is emitted into allocated space later, as the last step of the prime module generation.

Then comes the turn of method bodies, which include method headers, IL code, and managed exception handling tables (see Chapter 10 for details).

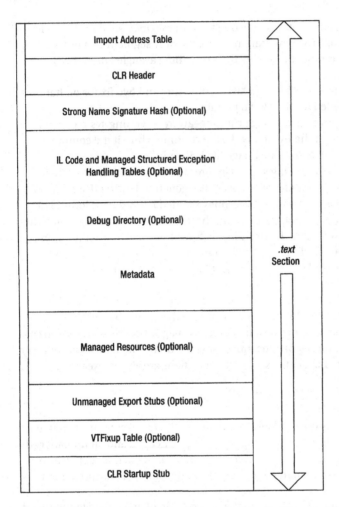

Figure 4-3. *Structure of a* .text *section emitted by the IL assembler*

After the method bodies have been emitted, and if you ordered the generation of the PDB file, which contains the debug data, the IL assembler emits the debug directory entry and CodeView-style header containing the path to the PDB file.

Then the metadata, which is fully defined by then, is emitted to the *.text* section, followed by managed resources (if any). Metadata format is described in detail in the next chapter, and the managed resources are discussed in the "Resources" section later in this chapter.

After the metadata and managed resources, the unmanaged export stubs are emitted for those managed methods that are exposed as unmanaged exports. Chapter 18 describes exporting of managed methods to unmanaged clients.

The next item emitted (if present) to the *.text* section is the v-table fixup table (VTFixup table) described earlier in this chapter.

And the last item emitted to the *.text* section is the unmanaged start-up stub of the CLR, whose RVA is assigned to the AddressOfEntryPoint field of the PE header.

Data Sections

The data section (*.sdata*) of an image file generated by the IL assembler is a read/write section. It contains data constants, the v-table described in the "V-Table" section, the unmanaged export table, and the thread local storage directory structure. The data declared as thread-specific is located in a different section, the *.tls* section.

Data Constants

The term *data constants* might be a little misleading. Located in a read/write section, data constants can certainly be overwritten, so technically they can hardly be called *constants*. The term, however, refers to the usage of the data rather than to the nature of the data. Data constants represent the mappings of the static fields and usually contain data initializing the mapped fields. (Chapter 1 described the peculiarities of this field mapping.)

Field mapping is a convenient way to initialize any static field with ANSI strings, blobs, or structures. An alternative way to initialize static fields—and a more orthodox way in terms of the common language runtime—is to do it explicitly by executing code in class constructors, as discussed in Chapter 9. But this alternative is much more tedious, so no one can really blame the managed compilers for resorting to field mapping for initialization. The VC++ compiler maps all the global fields, whether they will be initialized or not.

Mapping static fields to data has its caveats. Fields mapped to the data section are, on the one hand, out of reach of runtime controlling mechanisms such as type control and garbage collection and, on the other hand, wide open to unrestricted access and modification. This causes the loader to prevent certain field types from being mapped; types of mapped fields might contain no references to objects, vectors, arrays, or any nonpublic substructures. No such problems arise if a class constructor is used for static field initialization. Philosophically speaking, this is only natural: throughout the history of humanity, deviations from orthodoxy, however tempting, have always brought some unpleasant complications.

V-Table

The v-table in a pure-managed module is used for exposing the managed methods for consumption from the unmanaged code and consists of entries, each entry consisting of one or more slots. The entries and slots of the v-table are defined in the v-table fixups discussed earlier in the section "VTableFixups Field." Each fixup specifies the number and width (4 or 8 bytes) of slots in each entry. Each slot of the v-table contains a metadata token of the respective method, which at execution time is replaced with the address of the method itself or the address of a marshaling thunk providing unmanaged entry to the method. As these fixups are performed at execution time, the v-table of a managed PE file must be located in a read/write section. The IL assembler puts the v-table in the *.sdata* section, unlike the VTFixup table, which resides in the *.text* section.

V-tables of unmanaged image files are completely defined at link time and need base relocation fixups only, performed by the OS loader. Since no changes are made to v-tables at execution time (such as replacing method tokens with addresses in managed images), unmanaged image files carry their v-tables in read-only sections.

Unmanaged Export Table

The unmanaged export table in an unmanaged image file occupies a separate section named *.edata*. In image files generated by the IL assembler, the unmanaged export table resides in the *.sdata* section, together with the v-table it references.

The unmanaged export table contains information about methods that unmanaged image files can access through dynamic linking. The unmanaged export table is not a single table but rather a contiguous set of five tables: the Export Directory table, the Export Address table, the Name Pointer table, the Ordinal table, and the Export Name table. Figure 4-4 shows the relationship between the export tables of a module YDD.DLL exporting the functions Yabba, Dabba, and Doo.

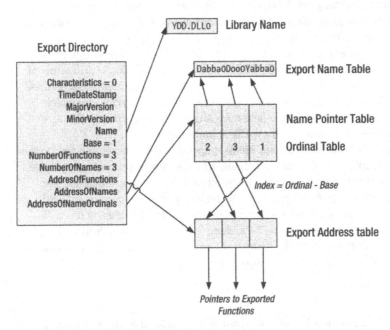

Figure 4-4. *Structure of unmanaged export tables*

The unmanaged export information starts with the Export Directory table, which describes the rest of the export information. It is a table with only one element, containing the locations and sizes of other export tables. The structure of the sole row of the Export Directory table is defined in Winnt.h as follows:

```
typedef struct _IMAGE_EXPORT_DIRECTORY {
    DWORD   Characteristics;
    DWORD   TimeDateStamp;
    WORD    MajorVersion;
    WORD    MinorVersion;
    DWORD   Name;
    DWORD   Base;
    DWORD   NumberOfFunctions;
    DWORD   NumberOfNames;
    DWORD   AddressOfFunctions;
```

```
    DWORD    AddressOfNames;
    DWORD    AddressOfNameOrdinals;
} IMAGE_EXPORT_DIRECTORY,
  *PIMAGE_EXPORT_DIRECTORY;
```

Briefly, the fields of IMAGE_EXPORT_DIRECTORY are the following:

Characteristics: Reserved. This field should be set to 0.

TimeDateStamp: The time and date the export data was generated.

MajorVersion: The major version number. This field and the MinorVersion field are for information only; the IL assembler does not set them.

MinorVersion: The minor version number.

Name: The RVA of the ASCII string containing the name of the exporting module.

Base: The ordinal base (usually 1). This is the starting ordinal number for exports in the image file.

NumberOfFunctions: The number of entries in the Export Address table.

NumberOfNames: The number of entries in the Export Name table.

AddressOfFunctions: The RVA of the Export Address table.

AddressOfNames: The RVA of the Export Name table.

AddressOfNameOrdinals: The RVA of the Name Pointer table.

The Export Address table contains the RVAs of exported entry points. The export ordinal of an entry point is defined as its zero-based index within the Export Address table plus the ordinal base (the value of the Base field of IMAGE_EXPORT_DIRECTORY structure).

In a managed file, the Export Address table contains the RVAs not of the exported entry points (methods) themselves but rather of unmanaged export stubs giving access to these entry points. (See "Text Section" earlier in this chapter.) Export stubs, in turn, contain references to respective v-table slots.

An RVA in an Export Address table can be a *forwarder RVA*, identifying a reexported entry point—that is, an entry point this module imports from another module and exports as its own. In such a case, the RVA points to an ASCII string containing the import name. The import name might be a DLL name and the name of the imported entry (SomeDLL.someFunc) or a DLL name and the imported entry's ordinal in this DLL (SomeDLL.#12).

The IL assembler does not allow reexport, so the entries in an Export Address table of an image file generated by this compiler always represent the RVAs of unmanaged export stubs.

The Export Name table contains zero-terminated ASCII strings representing the export names of the methods exported by the module. Strictly speaking, the Export Name table is not a table but a sequence of zero-terminated strings. The export names in the Export Name table are sorted alphabetically to facilitate binary searches of the entry points by name. The export names might differ from the names under which the methods were declared in the module. An exported method might have no exported name at all if it is being exported by ordinal only. In this case, its ordinal is not included in the Ordinal table. The IL assembler does not allow unnamed exports.

The Name Pointer table contains RVAs of the export names from the Export Name table.

The Ordinal table contains 2-byte indexes to the Export Address table. The Name Pointer table and the Ordinal table form two parallel arrays and operate as one intermediate lookup table, rearranging the entries so that they are lexically ordered by name. When an entry is to be identified by name, the binary search is conducted in the Name Pointer table, and if it's found that the sought entry matches the name at address number N in the Name Pointer table, the ordinal of this entry is taken from element number N of the Ordinal table. By this ordinal, the address of the entry is retrieved from the Export Address table.

Chapter 18 examines unmanaged export information and the details of exposing managed methods as unmanaged exports.

Thread Local Storage

ILAsm and VC++ allow you to define data constants belonging to thread local storage and to map static fields to these data constants. TLS is a special storage class in which a data object is not a stack variable but is nevertheless local to each separate thread. Consequently, each thread can maintain a different value for such a variable.

The TLS data is described in the TLS directory, which the IL assembler puts in the *.sdata* section. The structure of the TLS directory for 32-bit image files is defined in Winnt.h as follows:

```
typedef struct _IMAGE_TLS_DIRECTORY32 {
    ULONG   StartAddressOfRawData;
    ULONG   EndAddressOfRawData;
    ULONG   AddressOfIndex;
    ULONG   AddressOfCallBacks;
    ULONG   SizeOfZeroFill;
    ULONG   Characteristics;
} IMAGE_TLS_DIRECTORY32;
```

The structure of the TLS directory for a 64-bit image (IMAGE_TLS_DIRECTORY64) is similar, except the first four fields are 8-byte unsigned integers (ULONGLONG) instead of 4-byte unsigned integers (ULONG). The fields of this structure are as follows:

StartAddressOfRawData: The starting virtual address (not an RVA) of the TLS data constants. The TLS data constants plus uninitialized TLS data together form the *TLS template*. The operating system makes a copy of the TLS template every time a thread is created, thus providing each thread with its "personal" data constants and field mapping.

EndAddressOfRawData: The ending VA of the TLS data constants. The rest of the TLS data (if any) is filled with zeros. The IL assembler allows no uninitialized TLS data, presuming that TLS data constants represent the whole TLS template, so nothing is left for the zero fill.

AddressOfIndex: The VA of the 4-byte TLS index, located in the ordinary data section. The IL assembler puts the TLS index in the *.sdata* section, immediately after the TLS directory structure and the callback function pointer array terminator.

AddressOfCallBacks: The VA of a null-terminated array of TLS callback function pointers. The array is null terminated, and as a result this field is never null and points to an all-zero pointer if no callback functions are specified. The IL assembler does not support

TLS callback functions, so the entire array of TLS callback function pointers consists of a null terminator. This null terminator immediately follows the TLS directory structure in the *.sdata* section.

SizeOfZeroFill: The size of the uninitialized part of the TLS template, filled with zeros when a copy of the TLS template is being made. The IL assembler sets this field to 0.

Characteristics: Reserved. This field should be set to 0.

The StartAddressOfRawData, EndAddressOfRawData, AddressOfIndex, and AddressOfCallBacks fields hold VAs rather than RVAs, so you need to define the base relocations for them in the *.reloc* section.

The RVA and size of the TLS directory structure are stored in the 10th data directory (TLS) of the PE header. TLS data constants, which form the TLS template, reside in the *.tls* section of the image file.

Resources

You can embed two distinct kinds of resources in a managed PE file: unmanaged platform-specific resources and managed resources specific to CLR. These two kinds of resources, which have nothing in common, reside in different sections of a managed image file and are accessed by different sets of APIs.

Unmanaged Resources

Unmanaged resources reside in the *.rsrc* section of the image file. The starting RVA and size of embedded unmanaged resources are represented in the Resource data directory of the PE header.

Unmanaged resources are indexed by type, name, and language and are binary sorted by these three characteristics in that order. A set of Resource directory tables represents this indexing as follows: each directory table is followed by an array of directory entries, which contain the integer reference number (ID) or name of the respective level (the type, name, or language level) and the address of the next-level directory table or of a data description (a leaf node of the tree). Thanks to the use of three indexing characteristics, any data description can be reached by analyzing at most three directory tables.

By the time the data description is reached, its type, name, and language are known from the path the search algorithm traversed to arrive at the data description.

The *.rsrc* section has the following structure:

Resource directory tables and entries: As described previously.

Resource directory strings: Unicode (UTF-16) strings representing the string data addressed by the directory entries. These strings are 2-byte aligned. Each string is preceded by a 2-byte unsigned integer representing the string's length in 2-byte characters.

Resource data description: A set of records addressed by directory entries, containing the size and location of actual resource data.

Resource data: Raw undelimited resource data, consisting of individual resource data whose address and size are defined by data description records.

A Resource directory table structure is defined in Winnt.h as follows:

```
typedef struct _IMAGE_RESOURCE_DIRECTORY {
    DWORD    Characteristics;
    DWORD    TimeDateStamp;
    WORD     MajorVersion;
    WORD     MinorVersion;
    WORD     NumberOfNamedEntries;
    WORD     NumberOfIdEntries;
} IMAGE_RESOURCE_DIRECTORY, *PIMAGE_RESOURCE_DIRECTORY;
```

The roles of these fields should be evident, in light of the preceding discussion about structuring unmanaged resources and the Resource directory tables. One exception might be the Characteristics field, which is reserved and should be set to 0.

Name entries, which use strings to identify the type, name, or language, immediately follow the Resource directory table. After them, ID entries are stored.

A Resource directory entry (either a name entry or an ID entry) is an 8-byte structure consisting of two 4-byte unsigned integers, defined in Winnt.h as follows:

```
typedef struct _IMAGE_RESOURCE_DIRECTORY_ENTRY {
    union {
        struct {
            DWORD NameOffset:31;
            DWORD NameIsString:1;
        };
        DWORD    Name;
        WORD     Id;
    };
    union {
        DWORD    OffsetToData;
        struct {
            DWORD    OffsetToDirectory:31;
            DWORD    DataIsDirectory:1;
        };
    };
} IMAGE_RESOURCE_DIRECTORY_ENTRY,
    *PIMAGE_RESOURCE_DIRECTORY_ENTRY;
```

If the top bit of the first 4-byte component is set, the entry is a name entry, and the remaining 31 bits represent the name string offset; otherwise, the entry is an ID entry, and 16 less significant bits of it hold the ID value.

If the top bit of the second 4-byte component is set, the item, whose offset is represented by the remaining 31 bits, is a next-level Resource directory table; otherwise, it is a Resource data description.

A Resource data description is a 16-byte structure defined in Winnt.h as follows:

```
typedef struct _IMAGE_RESOURCE_DATA_ENTRY {
    DWORD    OffsetToData;
    DWORD    Size;
    DWORD    CodePage;
    DWORD    Reserved;
} IMAGE_RESOURCE_DATA_ENTRY,
    *PIMAGE_RESOURCE_DATA_ENTRY;
```

The fields OffsetToData and Size characterize the respective chunks of resource data that constitute an individual resource. OffsetToData is specified relatively to the beginning of the resource directory. CodePage is the ID of the code page used to decode the code point values in the resource data. Usually this is the Unicode code page. Finally—no surprise here—the Reserved field is reserved and must be set to 0.

The IL assembler creates the *.rsrc* section and embeds the unmanaged resources from the respective .res file if this file is specified in command-line options. The assembler can embed only one unmanaged resource file per module.

When the IL disassembler analyzes a managed PE file and finds the *.rsrc* section, it reads the data and its structure from the section and emits the .res file containing all the unmanaged resources embedded in the PE file.

Managed Resources

The Resources field of the CLR header contains the RVA and size of the managed resources embedded in the PE file. It has nothing to do with the Resource directory of the PE header, which specifies the RVA and size of unmanaged platform-specific resources.

In PE files created by the IL assembler, unmanaged resources reside in the *.rsrc* section of the image file, whereas managed resources are located in the *.text* section, along with the metadata, the IL code, and so on. Managed resources are stored in the *.text* section contiguously. Metadata carries ManifestResource records, one for each managed resource, containing the name of the managed resource and the offset of the beginning of the resource from the starting RVA specified in the Resources field of the CLR header. At this offset, a 4-byte unsigned integer indicates the length in bytes of the resource. The resource itself immediately follows.

When the IL disassembler processes a managed image file and finds embedded managed resources, it writes each resource to a separate file, named according to the resource name.

When the IL assembler creates a PE file, it reads all managed resources defined in the source code as embedded from the file according to the resource names and writes them to the *.text* section, each preceded by its specified length.

As an exercise, I offer you to open any managed executable (say, one of the simple samples) in the IL disassembler and select the View/Headers menu entry. You will see all headers and their fields "live."

Summary

Having discussed the structure of the managed image files and the ways the IL assembler goes about generating these files, I'll summarize the steps the IL assembler takes to create a managed PE file. The PE file creation is performed in four phases.

Phase 1: Initialization

1. Internal buffers are initialized.

2. The empty template of a PE file is created in memory, including an MS-DOS header and stub, a PE signature, a COFF header, and a PE header.

3. The Import Address table, and the CLR header are allocated in the *.text* section.

Phase 2: Source Code Parsing

1. Metadata is collected in internal buffers.

2. The method bodies (IL code and managed exception handling tables) are collected in internal buffers.

3. Data constants are emitted to the *.sdata* and *.tls* sections.

Phase 3: Image Generation

1. Space for the strong name signature is allocated in the *.text* section.

2. Metadata is analyzed and rearranged.

3. Internal (to the module) references are resolved in the IL code.

4. Method bodies are emitted to the *.text* section.

5. The TLS directory table is emitted to the *.sdata* section.

6. The debug directory is emitted to the *.text* section.

7. Space for metadata is allocated in the *.text* section.

8. Space for embedded managed resources is allocated in the *.text* section.

9. Unmanaged export stubs are emitted to the *.text* section.

10. The VTFixup table is emitted to the *.text* section.

11. The v-table is emitted to the *.sdata* section.

12. Unmanaged export tables are emitted to the *.sdata* section.

13. Last changes in the metadata—the RVAs of mapped fields are fixed up.

14. Metadata is emitted into the preallocated space in the *.text* section.

15. Managed resources are emitted into the preallocated space in the *.text* section.

16. The runtime start-up stub is emitted to the .*text* section.

17. Unmanaged resources are read from the .res file and emitted to the .*rsrc* section.

18. Necessary base relocations are emitted to the .*reloc* section.

Phase 4: Completion

1. The image file is written as a disk file.

2. The strong name signing procedure is applied to the file by invoking the strong name utility (sn.exe).

The IL assembler allows you to explicitly set certain values in the image file headers, by means of both source code directives and the compiler's command-line options, as shown in Table 4-7. In all the cases discussed in this chapter, the command-line options take precedence over the respective source code directives.

Table 4-7. *Directives and Command-Line Options for Setting Header Fields*

Header	Field	Directive	Command-Line Option
COFF	Machine		/*ITANIUM*, /*X64* (default is I386)
PE	Header type		/*PE64* (default is PE32)
PE	ImageBase	`.imagebase <integer value>`	/*BASE=<integer value>*
PE	SizeOfStackReserve	`.stackreserve <integer_value>`	/*STACK=<integer value>*
PE	FileAlignment	`.file alignment <integer value>`	/*ALIGNMENT=<integer value>*
PE	Subsystem	`.subsystem <integer value>`	/*SUBSYSTEM=<integer value>*
CLR	Flags	`.corflags <integer value>`	/*FLAGS=<integer value>*

CHAPTER 5

■■■

Metadata Tables Organization

This chapter provides an overview of metadata and how it is structured. It also describes metadata validation. Later chapters will analyze individual metadata items based on the foundation presented here. I understand your possible impatience—"When will this guy quit stalling and get to the real stuff?"—but nevertheless I urge you not to skip this chapter. Far from stalling, I'm simply approaching the subject systematically. It might look the same, but the motivation is quite different, and that's what matters.

What Is Metadata?

Metadata is, by definition, data that describes data. Like any general definition, however, this one is hardly informative. In the context of the common language runtime, *metadata* means a system of descriptors of all items that are declared or referenced in a module. The common language runtime programming model is inherently object oriented, so the items represented in metadata are classes and their members, with their accompanying attributes, properties, and relationships.

From a pragmatic point of view, the role played by metadata is similar to that played by type libraries in the COM world. At this general level, however, the similarities end, and the differences begin. Metadata, which describes the structural aspect of a module or an assembly in minute detail, is vastly richer than the data provided by type libraries, which carry only information regarding the COM interfaces exposed by the module. The important difference is that metadata is an integral part of a managed module, which means each managed module always carries a complete, high-level, formal description of its logical structure.

Structurally, metadata is a normalized relational database. This means that metadata is organized as a set of cross-referencing rectangular tables—as opposed to, for example, a hierarchical database that has a tree structure. Each column of a metadata table contains either data or a reference to a row of another table. Metadata does not contain any duplicate data fields; each category of data resides in only one table of the metadata database. If another table needs to employ the same data, it references the table that holds the data.

For example, as Chapter 1 explained, a class definition carries certain binary attributes (flags). The behavior and features of methods of this class are affected by the class's flags, so it would be tempting to duplicate some of the class attributes, including flags, in a metadata record describing one of the methods. But data duplication leads not only to increased database size but also to the problem of keeping all the duplications consistent.

Instead, method descriptors are stored in such a way that the parent class can always be found from a given method descriptor. Such referencing does require a certain amount of searching, which is more expensive, but for typical .NET–based applications, processor speed is not the problem—communication bandwidth and data integrity are.

If this arrangement seems less than efficient to you, think of how you would usually access the metadata if you were the runtime's class loader. Being a class loader, you would want to load a whole class with all its methods, fields, and other members. And, as I mentioned, the class descriptor (record) carries a reference to the record of the method table that represents the first method of this class. The end of the method records belonging to this class is defined by the beginning of the next class's method records or (for the last class) by the end of the method table. It's the same story with the field records.

Obviously, this technique requires that the records in the method table be sorted by their parent class. The same applies to other table-to-table relationships (class-to-field, method-to-parameter, and so on). If this requirement is met, the metadata is referred to as *optimized* or *compressed*. Figure 5-1 shows an example of such metadata. The ILAsm compiler always emits optimized metadata.

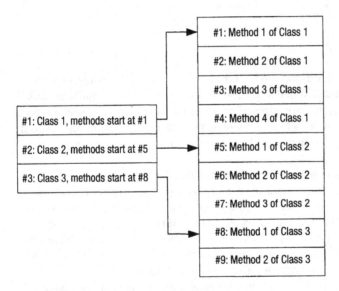

Figure 5-1. *An example of optimized metadata*

It is possible, however—perhaps as a result of sloppy metadata emission or of incremental compilation—to have the child tables interleaved with regard to their owner classes. For example, class record A might be emitted first, followed by class record B, the method records of class B, and then the method records of class A; or the sequence might be class record A, then some of the method records of class A, followed by class record B, the method records of class B, and then the rest of the method records of class A.

In such a case, additional intermediate metadata tables are engaged, providing noninterleaved lookup tables sorted by the owner class. Instead of referencing the method records, class records reference the records of an intermediate table (a *pointer* table), and those records in turn reference the method records, as diagrammed in Figure 5-2. Metadata that uses such intermediate lookup tables is referred to as *unoptimized* or *uncompressed*.

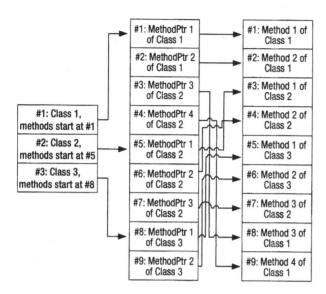

Figure 5-2. *An example of unoptimized metadata*

Two scenarios usually result in the emission of an uncompressed metadata structure: an "edit-and-continue" scenario, in which metadata and the IL code of a module are modified while the module is loaded in memory, and an incremental compilation scenario, in which metadata and IL code are modified in "installments."

Heaps and Tables

Logically, metadata is represented as a set of named streams, with each stream representing a category of metadata. These streams are divided into two types: metadata heaps and metadata tables.

Heaps

A *metadata heap* is a storage of trivial structure, holding a contiguous sequence of items. Heaps are used in metadata to store strings and binary objects. There are three kinds of metadata heaps:

String heap: This kind of heap contains zero-terminated character strings, encoded in UTF-8. The strings follow each other immediately. The first byte of the heap is always 0, and as a result the first string in the heap is always an empty string. The last byte of the heap must be 0 as well (in other words, the last string in the heap must be zero-terminated just like the others).

GUID heap: This kind of heap contains 16-byte binary objects, immediately following each other. The size of the binary objects is fixed, so length parameters or terminators are not needed.

Blob heap: This kind of heap contains binary objects of arbitrary size. Each binary object is preceded by its length (in compressed form). Binary objects are aligned on 4-byte boundaries.

The length compression formula is fairly simple. If the length (which is an unsigned integer) is 0x7F or less, it is represented as 1 byte; if the length is greater than 0x7F but no larger than 0x3FFF, it is represented as a 2-byte unsigned integer with the most significant bit set. Otherwise, it is represented as a 4-byte unsigned integer with two most significant bits set. Table 5-1 summarizes this formula.

Table 5-1. *The Length Compression Formula for the Blob*

Value Range	Compressed Size	Compressed Value (Big Endian)
0–0x7F	1 byte	<value>
0x80–0x3FFF	2 bytes	0x8000	<value>
0x4000–0x1FFFFFFF	4 bytes	0xC0000000	<value>

This compression formula is widely used in metadata. Of course, the compression works only for numbers not exceeding 0x1FFFFFFF (536,870,911), but this limitation isn't a problem because the compression is usually applied to such values as lengths and counts.

General Metadata Header

The general metadata header consists of a storage signature and a storage header. The storage signature, which must be 4-byte aligned, has the structure described in Table 5-2.

Table 5-2. *Structure of the Metadata Storage Signature*

Type	Field	Description
DWORD	lSignature	"Magic" signature for physical metadata, currently 0x424A5342, or, read as characters, BSJB—the initials of four "founding fathers" Brian Harry, Susan Radke-Sproull, Jason Zander, and Bill Evans (I'd better make it "founders"; Susan might object to be called a father), who started the runtime development in 1998
WORD	iMajorVer	Major version (1)
WORD	iMinorVer	Minor version (1)
DWORD	iExtraData	Reserved; set to 0
DWORD	iVersionString	Length of the version string
BYTE[]	pVersion	Version string

The storage header follows the storage signature, aligned on a 4-byte boundary. Its structure is simple, as described in Table 5-3.

Table 5-3. *Metadata Storage Header Structure*

Type	Field	Description
BYTE	fFlags	Reserved; set to 0
BYTE		[padding]
WORD	iStreams	Number of streams

The storage header is followed by an array of stream headers. Table 5-4 describes the structure of a stream header.

Table 5-4. *Metadata Stream Header Structure*

Type	Field	Description
DWORD	iOffset	Offset in the file for this stream.
DWORD	iSize	Size of the stream in bytes.
char[32]	rcName	Name of the stream; a zero-terminated ASCII string no longer than 31 characters (plus zero terminator). The name might be shorter, in which case the size of the stream header is correspondingly reduced, padded to the 4-byte boundary.

Six named streams can be present in the metadata:

#Strings: A string heap containing the names of metadata items (class names, method names, field names, and so on). The stream does *not* contain literal constants defined or referenced in the methods of the module.

#Blob: A blob heap containing internal metadata binary objects, such as default values, signatures, and so on.

#GUID: A GUID heap containing all sorts of globally unique identifiers.

#US: A blob heap containing user-defined strings. This stream contains string constants defined in the user code. The strings are kept in Unicode (UTF-16) encoding, with an additional trailing byte set to 1 or 0, indicating whether there are any characters with codes greater than 0x007F in the string. This trailing byte was added to streamline the encoding conversion operations on string objects produced from user-defined string constants. This stream's most interesting characteristic is that the user strings are never referenced from any metadata table but can be explicitly addressed by the IL code (with the ldstr instruction). In addition, being actually a blob heap, the #US heap can store not only Unicode strings but any binary object, which opens some intriguing possibilities.

#~: A compressed (optimized) metadata stream. This stream contains an optimized system of metadata tables.

#-: An uncompressed (unoptimized) metadata stream. This stream contains an unoptimized system of metadata tables, which includes at least one intermediate lookup table (pointer table).

The streams #~ and #- are mutually exclusive—that is, the metadata structure of the module is either optimized or unoptimized; it cannot be both at the same time or be something in between. If no items are stored in a stream, the stream is absent, and the iStreams field of the storage header is correspondingly reduced. At least three streams are guaranteed to be present: a metadata stream (#~ or #-), a string stream (#Strings), and a GUID stream (#GUID). Metadata items must be present in at least a minimal configuration in even the most trivial module, and these metadata items must have names and GUIDs.

Figure 5-3 illustrates the general structure of metadata. In Figure 5-4, you can see the way streams are referenced by other streams as well as by external "consumers" such as metadata APIs and the IL code.

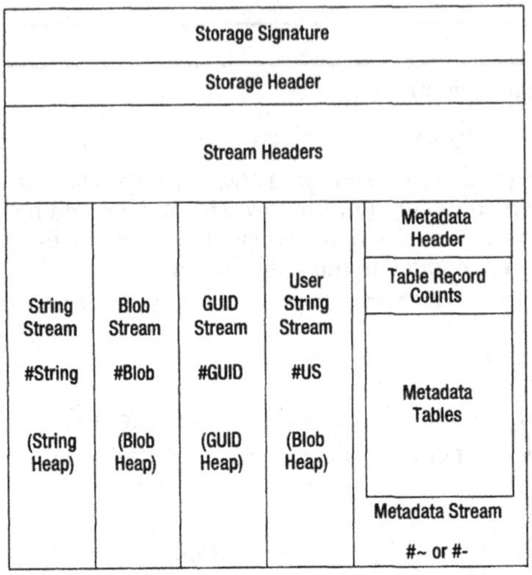

Storage Signature
Storage Header
Stream Headers
String Stream
#String
(String Heap)
Blob Stream
#Blob
(Blob Heap)
GUID Stream
#GUID
(GUID Heap)
User String Stream
#US
(Blob Heap)
Metadata Header
Table Record Counts
Metadata Tables
Metadata Stream
#~ or #-

Figure 5-3. *The general structure of metadata*

Tools, Compilers
IL Code
Metadata API
Metadata Tables Stream
#~ or #-
User String Stream
#US
GUID Stream
#GUID
Blob Stream
#Blob
String Stream
#String
METADATA

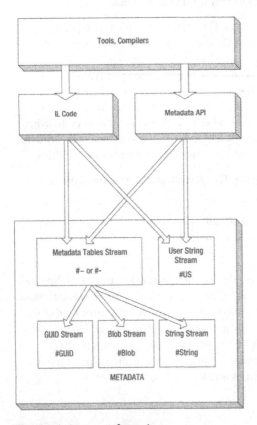

Figure 5-4. *Stream referencing*

Metadata Table Streams

The metadata streams #~ and #- begin with the header described in Table 5-5.

Table 5-5. *Metadata Table Stream Header Structure*

Size	Field	Description
4 bytes	Reserved	Reserved; set to 0.
1 byte	Major	Major version of the table schema (1 for v1.0 and v1.1; 2 for v2.0).
1 byte	Minor	Minor version of the table schema (0 for all versions).
1 byte	Heaps	Binary flags indicate the offset sizes to be used within the heaps. A 4-byte unsigned integer offset is indicated by 0x01 for a string heap, 0x02 for a GUID heap, and 0x04 for a blob heap. If a flag is not set, the respective heap offset is a 2-byte unsigned integer. A #- stream can also have special flags set: flag 0x20, indicating that the stream contains only changes made during an edit-and-continue session, and flag 0x80, indicating that the metadata might contain items marked as deleted.
1 byte	Rid	Bit width of the maximal record index to all tables of the metadata; calculated at run time (during the metadata stream initialization).
8 bytes	MaskValid	Bit vector of present tables, each bit representing one table (1 if present).
8 bytes	Sorted	Bit vector of sorted tables, each bit representing a respective table (1 if sorted).

This header is followed by a sequence of 4-byte unsigned integers indicating the number of records in each table marked 1 in the MaskValid bit vector.

Like any database, metadata has a schema. The *schema* is a system of descriptors of metadata tables and columns—in this sense, it is "meta-metadata." A schema is not a part of metadata, and it is not an attribute of a managed PE file. Rather, a metadata schema is an attribute of the common language runtime and is hard-coded. It does not change unless there's a major overhaul of the runtime, and even then it changes incrementally (as it changed between versions 1.0 and 2.0 of the runtime), by adding new tables and leaving the old tables unchanged.

Each metadata table has a descriptor of the structure described in Table 5-6.

Table 5-6. *Metadata Table Descriptor Structure*

Type	Field	Description
pointer	pColDefs	Pointer to an array of column descriptors
BYTE	cCols	Number of columns in the table
BYTE	iKey	Index of the key column
WORD	cbRec	Size of a record in the table

Column descriptors, to which the pColDefs fields of table descriptors point, have the structure described in Table 5-7.

Table 5-7. *Metadata Table Column Descriptor Structure*

Type	Field	Description
BYTE	Type	Code of the column's type
BYTE	oColumn	Offset of the column
BYTE	cbColumn	Size of the column in bytes

Type, the first field of a column descriptor, is especially interesting. The metadata schema of the existing releases of the common language runtime identifies the codes for column types described in Table 5-8.

Table 5-8. *Metadata Table Column Type Codes*

Code	Description
0–63	Column holds the record index (RID) in another table; the specific code value indicates which table. RID is used as column type when the column can reference records of only one table. The width of the column is defined by the Rid field of the metadata stream header.
64–95	Column holds a coded token referencing another table; the specific code value indicates the type of coded token. Tokens are references carrying the indexes of both the table and the record being referenced. Token is used as a column type when the column can reference records of more than one table. The table being addressed and the index of the record are defined by the coded token value.
96	Column holds a 2-byte signed integer.
97	Column holds a 2-byte unsigned integer.
98	Column holds a 4-byte signed integer.
99	Column holds a 4-byte unsigned integer.
100	Column holds a 1-byte unsigned integer.
101	Column holds an offset in the string heap (the #Strings stream).
102	Column holds an offset in the GUID heap (the #GUID stream).
103	Column holds an offset in the blob heap (the #Blob stream).

The metadata schema defines 45 tables. Given the range of RID type codes, the common language runtime definitely has room for growth. At the moment, the following tables are defined:

[0] Module: The current module descriptor.

[1] TypeRef: Class reference descriptors.

[2] TypeDef: Class or interface definition descriptors.

[3] FieldPtr: A class-to-fields lookup table, which does not exist in optimized metadata (#~ stream).

[4] Field: Field definition descriptors.

[5] MethodPtr: A class-to-methods lookup table, which does not exist in optimized metadata (#~ stream).

[6] Method: Method definition descriptors.

[7] ParamPtr: A method-to-parameters lookup table, which does not exist in optimized metadata (#~ stream).

[8] Param: Parameter definition descriptors.

[9] InterfaceImpl: Interface implementation descriptors.

[10] MemberRef: Member (field or method) reference descriptors.

[11] Constant: Constant value descriptors that map the default values stored in the #Blob stream to respective fields, parameters, and properties.

[12] CustomAttribute: Custom attribute descriptors.

[13] FieldMarshal: Field or parameter marshaling descriptors for managed/unmanaged interoperations.

[14] DeclSecurity: Security descriptors.

[15] ClassLayout: Class layout descriptors that hold information about how the loader should lay out respective classes.

[16] FieldLayout: Field layout descriptors that specify the offset or ordinal of individual fields.

[17] StandAloneSig: Stand-alone signature descriptors. Signatures per se are used in two capacities: as composite signatures of local variables of methods and as parameters of the call indirect (calli) IL instruction.

[18] EventMap: A class-to-events mapping table. This is not an intermediate lookup table, and it does exist in optimized metadata.

[19] EventPtr: An event map–to–events lookup table, which does not exist in optimized metadata (#~ stream).

[20] Event: Event descriptors.

[21] PropertyMap: A class-to-properties mapping table. This is not an intermediate lookup table, and it does exist in optimized metadata.

[22] PropertyPtr: A property map–to–properties lookup table, which does not exist in optimized metadata (#~ stream).

[23] Property: Property descriptors.

[24] MethodSemantics: Method semantics descriptors that hold information about which method is associated with a specific property or event and in what capacity.

[25] MethodImpl: Method implementation descriptors.

[26] ModuleRef: Module reference descriptors.

[27] TypeSpec: Type specification descriptors.

[28] ImplMap: Implementation map descriptors used for the platform invocation (P/Invoke) type of managed/unmanaged code interoperation.

[29] FieldRVA: Field-to-data mapping descriptors.

[30] ENCLog: Edit-and-continue log descriptors that hold information about what changes have been made to specific metadata items during in-memory editing. This table does not exist in optimized metadata (#~ stream).

[31] ENCMap: Edit-and-continue mapping descriptors. This table does not exist in optimized metadata (#~ stream).

[32] Assembly: The current assembly descriptor, which should appear only in the prime module metadata.

[33] AssemblyProcessor: This table is unused.

[34] AssemblyOS: This table is unused.

[35] AssemblyRef: Assembly reference descriptors.

[36] AssemblyRefProcessor: This table is unused.

[37] AssemblyRefOS: This table is unused.

[38] File: File descriptors that contain information about other files in the current assembly.

[39] ExportedType: Exported type descriptors that contain information about public classes exported by the current assembly, which are declared in other modules of the assembly. Only the prime module of the assembly should carry this table.

[40] ManifestResource: Managed resource descriptors.

[41] NestedClass: Nested class descriptors that provide mapping of nested classes to their respective enclosing classes.

[42] GenericParam: Type parameter descriptors for generic (parameterized) classes and methods.

[43] MethodSpec: Generic method instantiation descriptors.

[44] GenericParamConstraint: Descriptors of constraints specified for type parameters of generic classes and methods.

The last three tables were added in version 2.0 of the common language runtime. They did not exist in versions 1.0 and 1.1.

I'll discuss the structural aspects of the various tables and their validity rules in later chapters, along with the corresponding ILAsm constructs.

RIDs and Tokens

Record indexes and tokens are the unsigned integer values used for indexing the records in metadata tables. RIDs are simple indexes, applicable only to an explicitly specified table, and tokens carry the information identifying metadata tables they reference.

RIDs

A RID is a record identifier, which is simply a one-based row number in the table containing the record. The range of valid RIDs stretches from 1 to the record count of the addressed table, inclusive. RIDs are used in metadata internally only; metadata emission and retrieval APIs do not use RIDs as parameters.

The RID column type codes (0–63) serve as zero-based table indexes. Thus, the type of the column identifies the referenced table, while the value of the table cell identifies the referenced record. This works fine as long as we know that a particular column always references one particular table and no other. Now if we only could combine RID with table identification.

Tokens

Actually, we can. The combined identification entity, referred to as a *token*, is used in all metadata APIs and in all IL instructions. A token is a 4-byte unsigned integer whose most significant byte carries a zero-based table index (the same as the internal metadata RID type). The remaining 3 bytes are left for the RID.

There is a significant difference between token types and internal metadata RID types, however: whereas internal RID types cover all metadata tables, the token types are defined for only a limited subset of the tables, as noted in Table 5-9.

Table 5-9. *Token Types and Their Referenced Tables*

Token Type	Value (RID	(Type << 24))	Referenced Table
mdtModule	0x00000000	Module
mdtTypeRef	0x01000000	TypeRef
mdtTypeDef	0x02000000	TypeDef
mdtFieldDef	0x04000000	Field
mdtMethodDef	0x06000000	Method
mdtParamDef	0x08000000	Param
mdtInterfaceImpl	0x09000000	InterfaceImpl
mdtMemberRef	0x0A000000	MemberRef
mdtCustomAttribute	0x0C000000	CustomAttribute
mdtPermission	0x0E000000	DeclSecurity
mdtSignature	0x11000000	StandAloneSig
mdtEvent	0x14000000	Event
mdtProperty	0x17000000	Property
mdtModuleRef	0x1A000000	ModuleRef

Continued

Table 5-9. *Continued*

Token Type	Value (RID	(Type << 24))	Referenced Table
mdtTypeSpec	0x1B000000	TypeSpec
mdtAssembly	0x20000000	Assembly
mdtAssemblyRef	0x23000000	AssemblyRef
mdtFile	0x26000000	File
mdtExportedType	0x27000000	ExportedType
mdtManifestResource	0x28000000	ManifestResource
mdtGenericParam	0x2A000000	GenericParam
mdtMethodSpec	0x2B000000	MethodSpec
mdtGenericParamConstraint	0x2C000000	GenericParamConstraint

The 22 tables that do not have associated token types are not intended to be accessed from "outside," through metadata APIs or from IL code. These tables are of an auxiliary or intermediate nature and should be accessed indirectly only, through the references contained in the "exposed" tables, which have associated token types.

The validity of these tokens can be defined simply: a valid token has a type from Table 5-9, and it has a valid RID—that is, a RID in the range from 1 to the record count of the table of a specified type.

An additional token type, quite different from the types listed in Table 5-9, is mdtString (0x70000000). Tokens of this type are used to refer to the user-defined Unicode strings stored in the #US stream.

Both the type component and the RID component of user-defined string tokens differ from those of metadata table tokens. The type component of a user-defined string token (0x70) has nothing to do with column types (the maximal column type is 103 = 0x67), which is not surprising, considering that no column type corresponds to an offset in the #US stream. As metadata tables never reference the user-defined strings, it's not necessary to define a column type for the strings. In addition, the RID component of a user-defined string token does not represent a RID because no table is being referenced. Instead, the 3 lower bytes of a user-defined string token hold an offset in the #US stream. A side effect of this arrangement is that you cannot have the #US stream much larger than 16MB, or more exactly, all your user-defined strings except the last one must fit into 16MB short of 1B. You can make the last string as long as you like, but it must start at offset below 2^{24}, or in other words, below the 16MB boundary.

The definition of the validity of a user-defined string token is more complex. The RID (or offset) component is valid if it is greater than 0 and if the string it defines starts at a 4-byte boundary and is fully contained within the #US stream. The last condition is checked in the following way: the bytes at the offset specified by the RID component of the token are interpreted as the compressed length of the string. (Don't forget that the #US stream is a blob heap.) If the sum of the offset and the size of compressed length brings us to a 4-byte boundary and if this sum plus the calculated length are within the #US stream size, everything is fine and the token is valid.

Coded Tokens

The discussion thus far has focused on the "external" form of tokens. You have every right to suspect that the "internal" form of tokens, used inside the metadata, is different—and it is.

Why can't the external form also be used as internal? Because the external tokens are huge. Imagine 4 bytes for each token when we fight for each measly byte, trying to squeeze the metadata into as small a footprint as possible. (Bandwidth! Don't forget about the bandwidth!) Compression? Alas, having the type component occupying the most significant byte, external tokens represent very large unsigned integers and thus cannot be efficiently compressed, even though their middle bytes are full of zeros. We need a fresh approach.

The internal encoding of tokens is based on a simple idea: a column must be given a token type only if it might reference several tables. (Columns referencing only one table have a respective RID type.) But any such column certainly does not need to reference *all* the tables.

So our first task is to identify which group of tables each such column might reference and form a set of such groups. Let's assign each group a number, which will be a coded token type of the column. The coded token types occupy a range from 64 to 95, so we can define up to 32 groups.

Now, every group contains two or more table types. Let's enumerate them within the group and see how many bits we will need for this enumeration. This bit count will be a characteristic of the group and hence of the respective coded token type. The number assigned to a table within the group is called a *tag*.

This tag plays a role roughly equivalent to that of the type component of an external token. But, unwilling to once again create large tokens full of zeros, we will this time put the tag not in the most significant bits of the token but rather in the least significant bits. Then let's left-shift the RID n bits and add the left-shifted RID to the tag, where n is the bit width of the tag. Now we've got a coded token. For example, an uncoded TypeSpec token 0x1B000123 will be converted into coded TypeDefOrRef token 0x0000048E.

What about the coded token size? We know which metadata tables form each group and we know the record count of each table, so we know the maximal possible RID within the group. Say, for example, that we would need m bits to encode the maximal RID. If we can fit the maximal RID (m bits) and the tag (n bits) into a 2-byte unsigned integer (16 bits), we win, and the coded token size for this group will be 2 bytes. If we can't, we are out of luck and will have to use 4-byte coded tokens for this group. No, we won't even consider 3 bytes—it's unbecoming.

To summarize, a coded token type has the following attributes:

- Number of referenced tables (part of the schema)

- Array of referenced table IDs (part of the schema)

- Tag bit width (part of the schema, derived from the number of referenced tables)

- Coded token size, either 2 or 4 bytes (computed at the metadata opening time from the tag width and the maximal record count among the referenced tables)

Table 5-10 lists the 13 coded token types defined in the metadata schema of the existing releases of the common language runtime.

Table 5-10. *Coded Token Types*

Coded Token Type	Tag
TypeDefOrRef (64): 3 referenced tables, tag size 2	
TypeDef	0
TypeRef	1
TypeSpec	2
HasConstant (65): 3 referenced tables, tag size 2	
Field	0
Param	1
Property	2
HasCustomAttribute (66): 22 referenced tables, tag size 5	
Method	0
Field	1
TypeRef	2
TypeDef	3
Param	4
InterfaceImpl	5
MemberRef	6
Module	7
DeclSecurity	8
Property	9
Event	10
StandAloneSig	11
ModuleRef	12
TypeSpec	13
Assembly	14
AssemblyRef	15
File	16
ExportedType	17
ManifestResource	18
GenericParam (v2.0 only)	19
GenericParamConstraint (v2.0 only)	20
MethodSpec (v2.0 only)	21
HasFieldMarshal (67): 2 referenced tables, tag size 1	
Field	0
Param	1

Continued

Table 5-10. *Continued*

Coded Token Type	Tag
HasDeclSecurity (68): 3 referenced tables, tag size 2	
TypeDef	0
Method	1
Assembly	2
MemberRefParent (69): 5 referenced tables, tag size 3	
TypeDef	0
TypeRef	1
ModuleRef	2
Method	3
TypeSpec	4
HasSemantics (70): 2 referenced tables, tag size 1	
Event	0
Property	1
MethodDefOrRef (71): 2 referenced tables, tag size 1	
Method	0
MemberRef	1
MemberForwarded (72): 2 referenced tables, tag size 1	
Field	0
Method	1
Implementation (73): 3 referenced tables, tag size 2	
File	0
AssemblyRef	1
ExportedType	2
CustomAttributeType (74): 5 referenced tables, tag size 3	
TypeRef (obsolete, must not be used)	0
TypeDef (obsolete, must not be used)	1
Method	2
MemberRef	3
String (obsolete, must not be used)	4
ResolutionScope (75): 4 referenced tables, tag size 2	
Module	0
ModuleRef	1
AssemblyRef	2
TypeRef	3
TypeOrMethodDef (76) (v2.0 only): 2 referenced tables, tag size 1	
TypeDef	0
Method	1

The coded token type range (64–95) provides room to add another 19 types in the future, should it ever become necessary.

Coded tokens are part of metadata's internal affairs. The IL assembler, like all other compilers, never deals with coded tokens. Compilers and other tools read and emit metadata through the metadata import and emission APIs, either directly or through managed wrappers provided in the .NET Framework class library—System.Reflection for metadata import and System.Reflection.Emit for metadata emission. The metadata APIs automatically convert standard 4-byte tokens to and from coded tokens. IL code also uses only standard 4-byte tokens.

Nonetheless, the preceding definitions are useful to us for two reasons. First, we will need them when we discuss individual metadata tables in later chapters. Second, these definitions provide a good hint about the nature of relationships between the metadata tables.

Metadata Validation

This "good hint," however, is merely a hint. The definitions in the preceding section provide information about which tables you *can* reference from a column of a certain type. It does not mean you *should* reference all the tables you can. Some of the groups of token types listed in Table 5-10 are wider than is actually acceptable in the existing releases of the common language runtime. For example, the MemberRefParent group, which describes the tables that can contain the parents of a MemberRef record, includes the TypeDef table. But the metadata emission APIs will not accept a TypeDef token as the parent token of a MemberRef; and even if such metadata were somehow emitted, the loader would reject it.

Metadata emission APIs provide very few safeguards (most of them fairly trivial) as far as metadata validity is concerned. Metadata is an extremely complex system, and literally hundreds of validity rules need to be enforced.

High-level language compilers, such as VB .NET or C# compilers, provide a significant level of protection against invalid metadata emission because they shield the actual metadata specification and emission from programmers. The high-level languages are concept driven and concept based, and it is the compiler's duty to translate the language concepts to the metadata structures and IL code constructs, so a compiler can be built to emit valid structures and constructs. (Well, more or less.) On the other hand, ILAsm, like other assemblers, is a platform-oriented language and allows a programmer to generate an enormously wide range of metadata structures and IL constructs, only a fraction of which represent a valid subset.

In view of this bleak situation, we need to rely on external validation and verification tools. (Speaking of "validation and verification" is not an exercise in tautology—in the CLR lingo, the term *validation* is usually applied to metadata and *verification* to IL code.) One such tool is the common language runtime itself. The loader tests metadata against many of the validity rules, especially those whose violation could break the system. The runtime subsystem responsible for JIT compilation performs IL code verification. These processes are referred to as *run-time validation and verification.*

PEVerify, a stand-alone tool included in the .NET Framework SDK, offers more exhaustive validation and verification. PEVerify employs two independent subsystems, MDValidator and ILVerifier. MDValidator can also be invoked through the IL disassembler.

You can find information about PEVerify and the IL disassembler in the appendixes. Later chapters discuss various validity rules along with the related metadata structures and IL constructs.

Summary

Now that you know how the metadata is organized in principle, you are ready to examine the particular metadata items and the tables representing them. All further considerations shall concentrate on four metadata streams—#Strings, #Blob, #US, and #~—because the #GUID stream is referenced in one metadata table only (the Module table) and the #- stream (unoptimized metadata) is never emitted by the ILAsm compiler.

Here's some advice for those of you who wonder whether it would be a good idea to spoof the metadata header to get access to the data beyond the metadata under the pretense of manipulating the metadata: forget it. The CLR loader has safeguards analyzing the consistency of the metadata headers and the metadata itself. If an inconsistency is detected, the loader refuses to open the metadata streams. Tinkering with the metadata headers does not lead to erroneous or unpredictable behavior of the module; instead, it renders the module unloadable, period.

And on this cheerful note, let's proceed to discussion of the "real" metadata items.

PART 3

■ ■ ■

Fundamental Components

CHAPTER 6

■ ■ ■

Modules and Assemblies

This chapter discusses the organization, deployment, and execution of assemblies and modules. It also provides a detailed examination of the metadata segment responsible for assembly and module identity and interaction: the manifest. As you might recall from Chapter 1, an assembly can include several modules (managed PE files). Any module of a multimodule assembly can—and does, as a rule—carry its own manifest, but only one module per assembly carries the manifest that contains the assembly's identity. This module is referred to as the *prime* module. Thus, each assembly, whether multimodule or single-module, contains only one prime module.

What Is an Assembly?

An *assembly* is a deployment unit, a building block of a managed application. Assemblies are reusable, allowing different applications to use the same assembly. Assemblies carry a full self-description in their metadata, including version information that allows the common language runtime to use a specific version of an assembly for a particular application.

This arrangement eliminates what's known as DLL Hell, the situation created when upgrading one application renders another application inoperative because both happen to use identically named DLL(s) of different versions.

Private and Shared Assemblies

Assemblies are classified as either private or shared. Structurally and functionally, these two kinds of assemblies are the same, but they differ in how they are named and deployed and in the level of version checks performed by the loader.

A *private assembly* is considered part of a particular application, not intended for use by other applications. A private assembly is deployed in the same directory as the application or in a subdirectory of this directory. This kind of deployment shields the private assembly from other applications, which should not have access to it.

Being part of a particular application, a private assembly is usually created by the same author (person, group, or organization) as other components specific to this application and is thus considered to be primarily the author's responsibility. Consequently, naming and versioning requirements are relaxed for private assemblies, and the common language runtime does not enforce these requirements. The name of a private assembly must be unique within the application.

A *shared assembly* is not part of a particular application and is designed to be used widely by various applications. Shared assemblies are usually authored by groups or organizations other than those responsible for the applications that use these assemblies. A prominent example of shared assemblies is the set of assemblies constituting the .NET Framework class library.

As a result of such positioning, the naming and versioning requirements for shared assemblies are much stricter than those for private assemblies. Names of shared assemblies must be globally unique. Additional assembly identification is provided by *strong names*, which use cryptographic public/private key pairs to ensure the strong name's uniqueness and to prevent name spoofing. The central part of the strong name is the *strong name signature* (mentioned in Chapter 5)—a hash of the assembly's prime module encrypted with the publisher's private key. Assembly metadata carries the publisher's public key, which is used to verify the strong name signature. A strong name also provides the consumer of the shared assembly with information about the identity of the assembly publisher. If the common language runtime cryptographic checks pass, the consumer can be sure that the assembly comes from the expected publisher, assuming that the publisher's private encryption key was not compromised.

Shared assemblies are deployed into the machine-wide repository called global assembly cache (GAC). The GAC stores multiple versions of shared assemblies side by side. The loader looks for the shared assemblies in the GAC.

Under some circumstances, an application might need to deploy a shared assembly in its directory to ensure that the appropriate version is loaded. In such a case, the shared assembly is being used as a private assembly, so it is not in fact shared, whether it is strong named or not.

Application Domains As Logical Units of Execution

Operating systems and runtimes typically provide some form of isolation between applications running on the system. This isolation is necessary to ensure that code running in one application cannot adversely affect other, unrelated applications. In modern operating systems, this isolation is achieved by using hardware-enforced process boundaries, where a process, occupying a unique virtual address space, runs exactly one application and scopes the resources that are available for that process to use.

Managed code execution has similar needs for isolation. Such isolation can be provided at a lower cost in a managed application, however, considering that managed applications run under the control of the common language runtime and are verified to be type-safe.

The runtime allows multiple applications to be run in a single operating system process, using a construct called an *application domain* to isolate the applications from one another. Since all memory allocation requested by an application is done by the CLR, it is easy for the CLR to give an application access to only those objects that were allocated by the application and to block the application's attempts to access objects allocated in another application domain. In many respects, application domains are the CLR equivalent of an operating system process.

Specifically, isolation in managed applications means the following:

- Different security levels can be assigned to each application domain, giving the host a chance to run the applications with varying security requirements in one process.

- Code running in one application cannot directly access code or resources from another application. (Doing so could introduce a security hole.) An exception to this rule is the base class library assembly of .NET Framework—Mscorlib—which is shared by all application domains within the process. Mscorlib is not shared between the processes.

- Faults in one application cannot affect other applications by bringing down the entire process.

- Each application has control over where the code loaded on its behalf comes from and what version the code being loaded is. In addition, configuration information is scoped by the application.

The following examples describe scenarios in which it is useful to run multiple applications in the same process:

- ASP.NET runs multiple Web applications in the same process. In ASP and Internet Information Services (IIS), application isolation was achieved by process boundaries, which proved too expensive to scale appropriately—it's cheaper to run 20 application domains in one process than to spawn 20 separate processes.

- Microsoft Internet Explorer runs code from multiple sites in the same process as the browser code itself. Obviously, code from one site should not be able to affect code from another site.

- Database engines need to run code from multiple user applications in the same process.

- Application server products might need to run code from multiple applications in a single process.

Hosting environments such as ASP.NET or Internet Explorer need to run managed code on behalf of the user and take advantage of the application isolation features provided by application domains. In fact, it is the host that determines where the application domain boundaries lie and in what domain user code is run, as these examples show:

- ASP.NET creates application domains to run user code. Domains are created per application as defined by the Web server.

- Internet Explorer by default creates one application domain per site (although developers can customize this behavior).

- In Shell EXE, each application launched from the command line runs in a separate application domain occupying one process.

- Microsoft Visual Basic for Applications (VBA) uses the default application domain of the process to run the script code contained in a Microsoft Office document.

- The Windows Foundation Classes (WFC) Forms Designer creates a separate application domain for each form being built. When a form is edited and rebuilt, the old application domain is shut down, the code is recompiled, and a new application domain is created.

Since isolation demands that the code or resources of one application must not be directly accessible from code running in another application, no direct calls are allowed between objects in different application domains. Cross-domain communications are limited to either copying objects or creating special proxy objects, which are the object's "representatives" in other domains, giving the code in other domains access to instance fields and methods of the object. In regard to cross-domain communications, the objects fall into one of the following three categories:

- *Unbound objects* are marshaled by value across domains. This means that the receiving domain gets a copy of the object to play with instead of the original object.

- *AppDomain-bound objects* are marshaled by reference across domains, which means that cross-domain access is always accomplished through proxies.

- *Context-bound objects* are also marshaled by reference across domains as well as between contexts within the same domain. A context is a set of usage rules defining an environment where the objects reside. The rules are enforced when an object is entering or leaving the context.

The CLR relies on the verifiable type safety of the code (discussed in Chapter 13) to provide fault isolation between domains at a much lower cost than that incurred by the process isolation used in operating systems. The isolation is based on static type verification, and as a result, the hardware ring transitions or process switches are not necessary.

Manifest

The metadata that describes an assembly and its modules is referred to as a *manifest*. The manifest carries the following information:

- Identity, including a simple textual name, an assembly version number, an optional culture (if the assembly contains localized managed resources), and an optional public key if the assembly is strong named. This information is defined in two metadata tables: Module and Assembly (in the prime module only).

- Contents, including types and managed resources exposed by this assembly for external use and the location of these types and resources. The metadata tables that contain this information are ExportedType (in the prime module only) and ManifestResource.

- Dependencies, including other (external) assemblies this assembly references and, in the case of a multimodule assembly, other modules of the same assembly. You can find the dependency information in these metadata tables: AssemblyRef, ModuleRef, and File.

- Requested permissions, specific to the assembly as a whole. More specific requested permissions might also be defined for certain types (classes) and methods. This information is defined in the DeclSecurity metadata table. (Chapter 17 describes requested permissions and the ways to declare them.)

- Custom attributes, specific to the manifest components. Custom attributes provide additional information used mostly by compilers and other tools. The CLR recognizes a limited number of custom attributes. Custom attributes are defined in the CustomAttribute metadata table. (Refer to Chapter 16 for more information on this topic.)

Figure 6-1 shows the mutual references that take place between the metadata tables constituting the manifest.

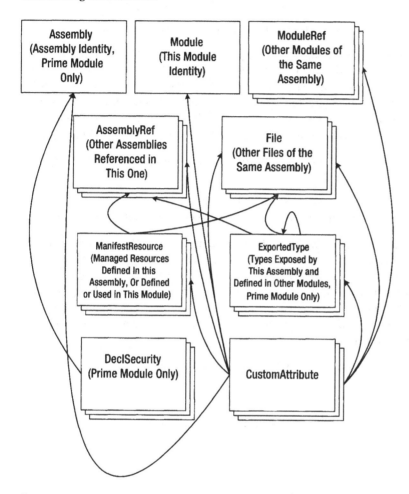

Figure 6-1. *Mutual references between the manifest's metadata tables*

Assembly Metadata Table and Declaration

The Assembly metadata table contains at most one record, which appears in the prime module's metadata. The table has the following column structure:

HashAlgId (4-byte unsigned integer): The ID of the hash algorithm used in this assembly to hash the files. The value must be one of the CALG_* values defined in the header file Wincrypt.h. The default hash algorithm is CALG_SHA (a.k.a. CALG_SHA1) (0x8004). Ecma International/ISO specifications consider this algorithm to be standard, offering the best widely available technology for file hashing.

MajorVersion (2-byte unsigned integer): The major version of the assembly.

MinorVersion (2-byte unsigned integer): The minor version of the assembly.

BuildNumber (2-byte unsigned integer): The build number of the assembly.

RevisionNumber (2-byte unsigned integer): The revision number of the assembly.

Flags (4-byte unsigned integer): Assembly flags indicating whether the assembly is strong named (set automatically by the metadata emission API if PublicKey is present), whether the JIT tracking and/or optimization is enabled (set automatically on assembly load), and whether the assembly can be retargeted at run time to an assembly of a different version. JIT tracking is the mapping of IL instruction offsets to addresses of native code produced by the JIT compiler; this mapping is used during the debugging of the managed code.

PublicKey (offset in the #Blob stream): A binary object representing a public encryption key for a strong-named assembly.

Name (offset in the #Strings stream): The assembly name, which must be nonempty and must not contain a path or a filename extension (for example, mscorlib, System.Data).

Locale (offset in the #Strings stream): The culture (formerly known as locale) name, such as en-US (American English) or fr-CA (Canadian French), identifying the culture of localized managed resources of this assembly. The culture name must match one of hundreds of culture names "known" to the runtime through the .NET Framework class library, but this validity rule is rather meaningless: to use a culture, the specific language support must be installed on the target machine. If the language support is not installed, it doesn't matter whether the culture is "known" to the runtime.

In ILAsm, the Assembly is declared in the following way (for example):

```
.assembly mscorlib
{
  .publickey = (00 00 00 00 00 00 00 00 04 00 00 00 00 00 00 00 )
  .hash algorithm 0x00008004
  .ver 2:0:0:0
}
```

The ILAsm syntax of the Assembly declaration is as follows:

```
.assembly <flags> <name> { <assemblyDecl>* }
```

where <flags> ::=

```
<none> // Assembly cannot be retargeted
| retargetable  // Assembly can be retargeted
```

and <assemblyDecl> ::=

```
.hash algorithm <int32>  // Set hash algorithm ID
| .ver <int32>:<int32>:<int32>:<int32> //  Set version numbers
| .publickey = ( <bytes> ) // Set public encryption key
| .locale <quotedString> // Set assembly culture
| <securityDecl> // Set requested permissions
| <customAttrDecl> // Define custom attribute(s)
```

In this declaration, `<int32>` denotes an integer number, at most 4 bytes in size. The notation `<bytes>` represents a sequence of two-digit hexadecimal numbers, each representing 1 byte; this form, `bytearray`, is often used in ILAsm to represent binary objects of arbitrary size. Finally, `<quotedString>` denotes, in general, a composite quoted string—that is, a construct such as `"ABC"+"DEF"+"GHI"`. The concatenation with the plus sign is useful for defining very long strings, although in this case we don't need concatenation for strings such as `en-US` or `nl-BE`.

AssemblyRef Metadata Table and Declaration

The AssemblyRef (assembly reference) metadata table defines the external dependencies of an assembly or a module. Both prime and nonprime modules can—and do, as a rule—contain this table. The only assembly that does not depend on any other assembly, and hence has an empty AssemblyRef table, is Mscorlib.dll, the root assembly of the .NET Framework class library.

The column structure of the AssemblyRef table is as follows:

MajorVersion (2-byte unsigned integer): The major version of the assembly.

MinorVersion (2-byte unsigned integer): The minor version of the assembly.

BuildNumber (2-byte unsigned integer): The build number of the assembly.

RevisionNumber (2-byte unsigned integer): The revision number of the assembly.

Flags (4-byte unsigned integer): Assembly reference flags, which indicate whether the assembly reference holds a full unhashed public key or a "surrogate" (public key token).

PublicKeyOrToken (offset in the #Blob stream): A binary object representing the public encryption key for a strong-named assembly or a token of this key. A key token is an 8-byte representation of a hashed public key, and it has nothing to do with metadata tokens.

Name (offset in the #Strings stream): The name of the referenced assembly, which must be nonempty and must not contain a path or a filename extension.

Locale (offset in the #Strings stream): The culture name.

HashValue (offset in the #Blob stream): A binary object representing a hash of the metadata of the referenced assembly's prime module. This value is ignored by the loader, so it can safely be omitted.

In ILAsm, an AssemblyRef is declared in the following way (for example):

```
.assembly extern mscorlib
{
  .publickeytoken = (B7 7A 5C 56 19 34 E0 89 )
  .ver 2:0:0:0
}
```

The ILAsm syntax for an AssemblyRef declaration is as follows:

```
.assembly extern <name> { <assemblyRefDecl>* }
```

where <assemblyRefDecl> ::=

```
| .ver <int32>:<int32>:<int32>:<int32> // Set version numbers
| .publickey = ( <bytes> ) // Set public encryption key
| .publickeytoken = ( <bytes> ) // Set public encryption key token
| .locale <quotedString> // Set assembly locale (culture)
| .hash = ( <bytes> ) // Set hash value
| <customAttrDecl> // Define custom attribute(s)
```

As you might have noticed, ILAsm does not provide a way to set the flags in the AssemblyRef declaration. The explanation is simple: the only flag relevant to an AssemblyRef is the flag indicating whether the AssemblyRef carries a full unhashed public encryption key, and this flag is set only when the .publickey directive is used.

When referencing a strong-named assembly, you are required to specify .publickeytoken (or .publickey, which is rarely used in AssemblyRefs) and .ver. The only exception to this rule among the strong-named assemblies is Mscorlib.dll.

If .locale is not specified, the referenced assembly is presumed to be "culture neutral."

An interesting situation arises when you need to use two or more versions of the same assembly side by side. An assembly is identified by its name, version, public key (or public key token), and culture. It would be extremely cumbersome to list all these identifications every time you reference an assembly: "I want to call method Bar of class Foo from assembly SomeOtherAssembly, and I want the version number such-and-such, the culture nl-BE, and...." Of course, if you didn't need to use different versions side by side, you could simply refer to an assembly by name.

ILAsm provides an AssemblyRef aliasing mechanism to deal with such situations. The AssemblyRef declaration can be extended as shown here:

```
.assembly extern <name> as <alias> { <assemblyRefDecl>*  }
```

and whenever you need to reference this assembly, you can use its <alias>, as shown in this example:

```
.assembly extern SomeOtherAssembly as OldSomeOther
{ .ver 1:1:1:1 }
.assembly extern SomeOtherAssembly as NewSomeOther
{ .ver 1:3:2:1 }
...
call int32 [OldSomeOther]Foo::Bar(string)
...
call int32 [NewSomeOther]Foo::Bar(string)
...
```

The alias is not part of metadata. Rather, it is simply a language tool, needed to identify a particular AssemblyRef among several identically named AssemblyRefs. The IL disassembler generates aliases for AssemblyRefs whenever it finds identically named AssemblyRefs in the module metadata.

Autodetection of Referenced Assemblies

Version 2.0 of the IL assembler offers you a way to reference the assemblies without specifying their version, public key token, and other attributes:

```
.assembly extern <name> as <alias> { auto }
```

When the keyword auto is specified, the ILAsm compiler queries the GAC and tries to find an assembly with the specified name. If it succeeds, it reads the assembly attributes (version, public key, culture) and puts these attributes into the generated AssemblyRef metadata record.

Note that the autodetection feature works only for referenced assemblies installed in the GAC.

The referenced assembly attributes may be partially specified and combined with autodetection, thus narrowing the search; for example:

```
.assembly extern OtherAssembly { .ver 1:3:*:* auto }
```

The previous directive will prompt the IL assembler to query the GAC looking for an assembly named OtherAssembly with the major version number equal to 1 and the minor version number equal to 3 and with any build and revision numbers. If such an assembly is found in the GAC, then its missing atrributes are retrieved and put into the respective entries of the AssemblyRef record.

If more than one assembly matching the search criteria is found, the one with the highest version is taken.

In this regard, the IL assembler differs from other managed compilers (VB, C#, VC++), as those compilers require the specification of referenced assemblies via the file path instead of querying the GAC. This might play a bad trick on a programmer, because the CLR loader always tries to load the assemblies from the GAC first (as is described in the next section), and in the unlikely event of a mismatch between referenced assemblies installed in the GAC and those specified by the file path, the application will be executed against assemblies different from those it was built against.

The autodetection feature was introduced in version 2.0 of the IL assembler.

The Loader in Search of Assemblies

When you define an AssemblyRef in the metadata, you expect the loader to find exactly this assembly and load it into the application domain. Let's have a look at the process of finding an external assembly and binding it to the referencing application.

Given an AssemblyRef, the process of binding to that assembly is influenced by these factors:

- The application base (AppBase), which is a URL to the referencing application location (that is, to the directory in which your application is located). For executables, this is the directory containing the EXE file. For Web applications, the AppBase is the root directory of the application as defined by the Web server.

- Version policies specified by the application, by the publisher of the shared assembly being referenced, or by the administrator.

- Any additional search path information given in the application configuration file.
- Any code base (CodeBase) locations provided in the configuration files by the application, the publisher, or the administrator. The CodeBase is a URL to the location of the referenced external assembly. There may be as many code bases as there are referenced assemblies.
- Whether the reference is to a shared assembly with a strong name or to a private assembly. Strong-named assemblies are first sought in the GAC.

As illustrated in Figure 6-2, the loader performs the following steps to locate a referenced assembly:

1. Initiate the binding. Basically, this means taking the relevant AssemblyRef record from the metadata and seeing what it holds—its external assembly name, whether it is strong named, whether culture is specified, and so on.

2. Apply the version policies, which are statements made by the application, by the publisher of the shared assembly being referenced, or by the administrator. These statements are contained in XML configuration files and simply redirect references to a particular version (or set of versions) of an assembly to a different version.

3. The .NET Framework retrieves its configuration from a set of configuration files. Each file represents settings that have different scopes. For example, the configuration file supplied with the installation of the common language runtime has settings that can affect all applications that use that version of the CLR. The configuration file supplied with an application (application configuration file) has settings that affect only that one application; this configuration file resides in the application directory. A publisher policy file is supplied by the publisher of a shared assembly, and it contains information about the assembly compatibility and redirects an assembly reference to a new version of the shared component. A publisher policy file is usually issued when the shared component is updated by its publisher. The publisher policy settings take precedence over the settings of the application configuration file. The administrator policy file, Machine.config, resides in the Configuration subdirectory of the CLR installation directory. This file contains settings defined by the administrator for this machine and takes precedence over any other configuration file. Overrides specified in the Machine.config file affect all applications running on this machine and cannot be in turn overridden.

4. If the referenced assembly is strong named (in other words, the AssemblyRef contains non-null public key or public key token), then look up the assembly in the GAC. Otherwise, since weak-named assemblies cannot be installed in GAC, this step is skipped. If the assembly is found, which is the most common case, the search process is completed.

5. Check the CodeBase. Now that the common language runtime knows which version of the assembly it is looking for, it begins the process of locating it. If the CodeBase has been supplied (in the same XML configuration file), it points the CLR directly at the executable to load; otherwise, the runtime needs to look in the AppBase (see the next step). If the executable specified by the CodeBase matches the assembly reference, the process of finding the assembly is complete, and the external assembly can be loaded. In fact, even if the executable specified by the CodeBase does not match the reference, the CLR stops searching. In this case, of course, the search is considered a failure, and no assembly load follows.

6. Probe the AppBase. The probing involves consecutive searching in the directories defined by the AppBase, the private binary path (binpath) from the same XML configuration file, the culture of the referenced assembly, and its name. The AppBase plus directories specified in the binpath form a set of root directories: {<root$_k$>, k=1…N}. If the AssemblyRef specifies the culture, the search is performed in directories <root$_k$>/<culture> and then in <root$_k$>/<culture>/<name>; otherwise, the directories <root$_k$> and then <root$_k$>/<name> are searched. When searching for a private assembly, the process ignores the version numbers. If the assembly is not found by probing, the binding fails.

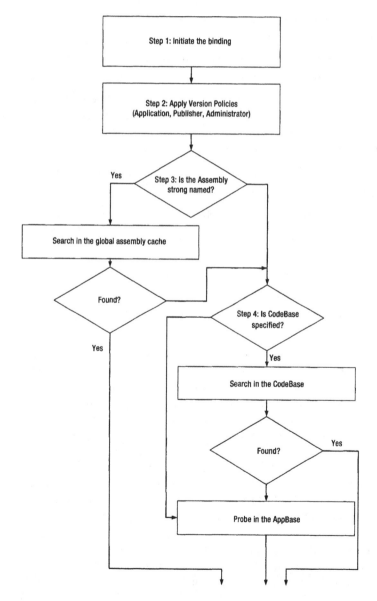

Figure 6-2. *Searching for a referenced assembly*

In version 2.0 of the CLR running under a 64-bit operating system, the problems with assembly binding are exacerbated by the possible presence of both 32-bit and 64-bit versions of assemblies. To deal with the problem, the binding mechanism of the v2.0 assembly loader uses the following classification of the assemblies:

- *Platform-agnostic* assemblies can be executed in native unemulated mode on a 32-bit or 64-bit platform; they don't contain any platform-specific details.

- *32-bit specific* assemblies can be executed natively on 32-bit platforms; on 64-bit platforms such assemblies require 32-bit emulation.

- *Itanium-specific* assemblies can be executed natively on Intel Itanium platform and cannot be executed on any other platform.

- *X64-specific* assemblies can be executed natively on an AMD/Intel X64 platform and cannot be executed on any other platform.

This classification is called Processor Architecture and is an additional part of full assembly identity in version 2.0. The Processor Architecture is derived from the Machine entry of the COFF header, the type of the Optional NT header, and the two least significant bits (flags ILONLY and 32BITREQUIRED) of the CLR header flags (see Chapter 4 for details):

- *Platform-agnostic* assemblies have Machine = I386, 32-bit Optional header, and the two least significant bits of CLR header flags set to ILONLY (0x1).

- *32-bit specific* assemblies have the same Machine and Optional header and the two least significant bits of CLR header flags set to 32BITREQUIRED|ILONLY (0x3), 32BITREQUIRED (0x2), or 0.

- *Itanium-specific* assemblies have Machine = IA64 and 64-bit Optional header; CLR header flags play no role.

- *X64-specific* assemblies have Machine = AMD64 and 64-bit Optional header; CLR header flags play no role.

You should be careful declaring your assembly platform agnostic. To be truly platform agnostic, the assembly has to have no presumptions of pointer size, no unmanaged exports or imports, no embedded native code, and no thread-local storage (*.tls* section), and it has to reference no platform-specific assemblies or platform-specific unmanaged DLLs. The last condition is the worst of them all, because it is transitive. Many times developers have written an application (EXE) and declared it platform agnostic, only to discover that it crashed on 64-bit platforms: the application, being platform agnostic, created a 64-bit process and then tried to load a 32-bit specific referenced assembly into the 64-bit process. Kaboom! Or it tried to load a platform-agnostic assembly A, which in turn referenced assembly B, and B just happened to P/Invoke a 32-bit unmanaged DLL (see Chapter 18). Kaboom! The bright side of it is that such problems are usually discovered right away, not after the application has been shipped.

Version 2.0 of the runtime considers all assemblies produced for versions 1.0 and 1.1 as 32-bit specific assemblies. It is only fair: versions 1.0 and 1.1 of the runtime did not support 64-bit platforms. The assemblies produced for versions 1.0 and 1.1 are identified by the metadata stream header (see Chapter 5); the version specified in this header is 1.0 for v1.0 and v1.1 assemblies and is 2.0 for v2.0 assemblies.

Module Metadata Table and Declaration

The Module metadata table contains a single record that provides the identification of the current module. The column structure of the table is as follows:

Generation (2-byte unsigned integer): Used only at run time, in edit-and-continue mode.

Name (offset in the #Strings stream): The module name, which is the same as the name of the executable file with its extension but without a path. The length should not exceed 512 bytes in UTF-8 encoding, counting the zero terminator.

Mvid (offset in the #GUID stream): A globally unique identifier, assigned to the module as it is generated.

EncId (offset in the #GUID stream): Used only at run time, in edit-and-continue mode.

EncBaseId (offset in the #GUID stream): Used only at run time, in edit-and-continue mode.

Since only one entry of the Module record can be set explicitly (the Name entry), the module declaration in ILAsm is quite simple:

```
.module <name>
```

ModuleRef Metadata Table and Declaration

The ModuleRef metadata table contains descriptors of other modules referenced in the current module. The set of "other modules" includes both managed and unmanaged modules.

The relevant managed modules are the other modules of the current assembly. In ILAsm, they should be declared explicitly, and their declarations should be paired with File declarations (discussed in the following section). IL assembler does not verify whether the referenced modules are present at compile time.

The unmanaged modules described in the ModuleRef table are simply unmanaged DLLs containing methods called from the current module using the platform invocation mechanism—P/Invoke, discussed in Chapter 18. These ModuleRef records usually are not paired with File records. They need not be explicitly declared in ILAsm because in ILAsm the DLL name is part of the P/Invoke specification, so the IL assembler emits respective ModuleRef records automatically.

There is one reason, however, to pair a ModuleRef record referring to an unmanaged module with a File record: you should do that if you want this unmanaged DLL to be part of your deployment. In this case the unmanaged DLL will reside together with managed modules constituting your assembly, and it does not have to be on the path to be discovered.

A ModuleRef record contains only one entry, the Name entry, which is an offset in the #Strings stream. The ModuleRef declaration in ILAsm is not much more sophisticated than the declaration of Module:

```
.module extern <name>
```

As in the case of Module, <name> in ModuleRef is the name of the executable file with its extension but without a path, not exceeding 512 bytes in UTF-8 encoding.

File Metadata Table and Declaration

The File metadata table describes other files of the same assembly that are referenced in the current module. In single-module assemblies, this table is empty (unless you want to specify unmanaged DLLs as part of your deployment, as was described earlier). The table has the following column structure:

Flags (4-byte wide bitfield): Binary flags characterizing the file. This entry is mostly reserved for future use; the only flag currently defined is ContainsNoMetaData (0x00000001). This flag indicates that the file in question is not a managed PE file but rather a pure resource file.

Name (offset in the #Strings stream): The filename, subject to the same rules as the names in Module and ModuleRef. This is the only occurrence of data duplication in the metadata model: the File name matches the name used in the ModuleRef with which this File record is paired. However, since the names in both records are not physical strings but rather offsets in the string heap, the string data might not actually be duplicated; instead, both records might reference the same string in the heap. This doesn't mean there is no data duplication: the offsets are definitely duplicated.

HashValue (offset in the #Blob stream): The blob representing the hash of the file, used to authenticate the files in a multifile assembly. Even in a strong-named assembly, the strong name signature resides only in the prime module and covers only the prime module. Nonprime modules in an assembly are authenticated by their hash values.

The File declaration in ILAsm looks like the following:

```
.file <flag> <name>  .hash = ( <bytes> )
```

where <flag> ::=

```
<none>          // The file is a managed PE file
| nometadata    // The file is a pure resource file
```

If the hash value is not explicitly specified, the IL assembler finds the named file and computes the hash value using the hash algorithm specified in the Assembly declaration. If the file is not available at compile time, the HashValue entry of the respective File record is set to 0.

The File declaration can also carry the .entrypoint directive, as shown in this example:

```
.file MainClass.dll
  .hash = (01 02 03 04 05 06  … )
  .entrypoint
```

This sort of File declaration can occur only in the prime module of a multimodule assembly and only when the entry point method is defined in a nonprime module of the assembly. This clause of the File declaration does not affect the metadata, but it puts the appropriate file token in the EntryPointToken entry of the common language runtime header. See Chapter 4 for details about EntryPointToken and the CLR header.

The prime module of an assembly, especially a runnable application (EXE), must have a valid token in the EntryPointToken field of the CLR header; and this token must be either a Method token, if the entry point method is defined in the prime module, or a File token. In the latter case, the loader loads the relevant module and inspects its common language runtime header, which must contain a valid Method token in the EntryPointToken field.

Managed Resource Metadata and Declaration

A *resource* is nonexecutable data that is logically deployed as part of an application. The data can take any number of forms such as strings, images, persisted objects, and so on. As Chapter 4 described, resources can be either managed or unmanaged (platform specific). These two kinds of resources have different formats and are accessed using managed and unmanaged APIs, respectively.

An application often must be customized for different cultures. A *culture* is a set of preferences based on a user's language, sublanguage, and cultural conventions. In the .NET Framework, the culture is described by the CultureInfo class from the .NET Framework class library. A culture is used to customize operations such as formatting dates and numbers, sorting strings, and so on.

You might also need to customize an application for different countries or regions. A *region* defines a set of standards for a particular country or region of the world. In the .NET Framework, the class library describes a region using the RegionInfo class. A region is used to customize operations such as formatting currency symbols.

Localization of an application is the process of connecting the application's executable code with the application's resources that have been customized for specific cultures. Although a culture and a region together constitute a *locale*, localization is not concerned with customizing an application to a specific region. The .NET Framework and the common language runtime do not support the localization of component metadata, instead relying solely on the managed resources for this task.

The .NET Framework uses a hub-and-spoke model for packaging and deploying resources. The hub is the *main* assembly, which contains the executable code and the resources for a single culture (referred to as the *neutral culture*). The neutral culture is the fallback culture for the application. Each spoke connects to a *satellite* assembly that contains the resources for a single culture. Satellite assemblies do not contain code.

The advantages of this model are obvious. First, resources for new cultures can be added incrementally after an application is deployed. Second, an application needs to load only those satellite assemblies that contain the resources needed for a particular run.

The resources used in or exposed by an assembly can reside in one of the following locations:

- In separate resource file(s) in the same assembly. Each resource file can contain one or more resources. The metadata descriptors of such files carry the `nometadata` flag.

- Embedded in managed modules of the same assembly.

- In another (external) assembly.

The resource data is not directly used or validated by the deployment subsystem or the loader, so it can be of any kind.

All resource data embedded in a managed PE file resides in a contiguous block inside the *.text* section. The Resources data directory in the CLR header provides the RVA and size of embedded managed resources. Each individual resource is preceded by a 4-byte unsigned integer holding the resource's length in bytes. Figure 6-3 shows the layout of embedded managed resources.

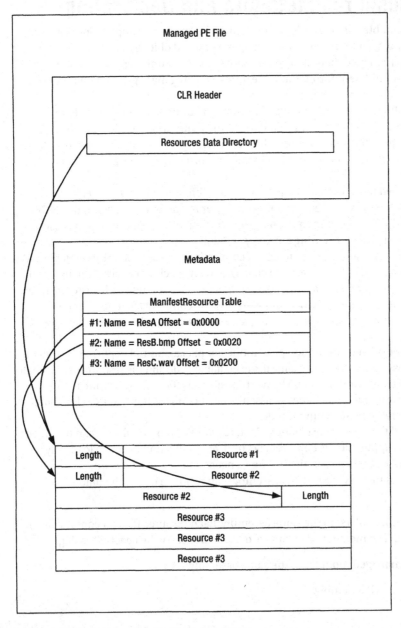

Figure 6-3. *The layout of embedded managed resources*

The ManifestResource metadata table, describing the managed resources, has the following column structure:

Offset (4-byte unsigned integer): Location of the resource within the managed resource segment to which the Resources data directory of the CLR header points. This is *not* an RVA; rather, it is an offset within the managed resource segment.

Flags (4-byte wide bitfield): Binary flags indicating whether the managed resource is public (accessible from outside the assembly) or private (accessible from within the current assembly only).

Name (offset in the #Strings stream): Nonempty name of the resource, unique within the assembly.

Implementation (coded token of type Implementation): Token of the respective AssemblyRef record if the resource resides in another assembly or of the respective File record if the resource resides in another file of the current assembly. If the resource is embedded in the current module, this entry is set to 0. If the resource is imported from another assembly, the offset need not be specified; the loader will ignore it.

ILAsm syntax for the declaration of a managed resource is as follows:

.mresource <flag> <name> { <mResourceDecl>* }

where <flag> ::= **public** | **private** and <mResourceDecl> ::=

```
.assembly extern <alias>        //  Resource is imported from another
                                //  assembly
| .file <name> at <int32>       //  Resource resides in another
                                //  file of this assembly;
                                //  <int32> is the offset
| <customAttrDecl> //  Define custom attribute for this resource
```

The default flag value is private.

The directives .assembly extern and .file in the context of a managed resource declaration refer to the resource's Implementation entry and are mutually exclusive. If Implementation references the AssemblyRef or File before it has been declared, the ILAsm compiler will diagnose an error.

If the Implementation entry is empty, the resource is presumed embedded in the current module. In this case, the IL assembler creates the PE file, loads the resource from the file according to the resource's name, and writes it into the *.text* section of the PE file, automatically setting the Offset entry of the ManifestResource record. When the IL disassembler disassembles a PE file into a text file, the embedded managed resources are saved into binary files named after these resources, which allows the IL assembler to easily pick them up if the PE file needs to be reassembled.

There is a little catch there: names of managed resources may contain characters inappropriate for filenames. In such cases, the managed resources cannot be saved under their true names; on the other hand, you cannot change the resource names, because the resources are addressed by these names in the application. To deal with this situation, version 2.0 of ILAsm offers aliasing of the managed resources similar to aliasing of referenced assemblies:

.mresource <flag> <name> **as** <filename> { <mResourceDecl>* }

The previous directive prompts the IL assembler to load the resource from file <filename> and create the respective ManifestResource metadata record with name <name>. The IL disassembler v2.0, when saving the managed resources to files, analyzes the names of the resources and if it finds colon, semicolon, comma, or backslash characters, it creates an alias for the resource, replacing these characters with exclamation mark, commercial "at" (@), ampersand (&), and currency sign ($), respectively. Then the resource is saved in the alias-named file.

ILAsm does not offer any language constructs to address the managed resources because IL lacks the means to do so. Managed APIs provided by the .NET Framework class library—specifically, the System.Resources.ResourceManager class—are used to load and manipulate managed resources.

ExportedType Metadata Table and Declaration

The ExportedType metadata table contains information about the public classes (visible outside the assembly) that are declared in nonprime modules of the assembly. Only the prime module's manifest can carry this table.

This table is needed because the loader expects the prime module of an assembly to hold information about *all* classes exported by the assembly. The union of the classes defined in the prime module and those in the ExportedType table gives the loader the full picture.

On the other hand, the intersection of the classes defined in the prime module and those in the ExportedType table must be nil. As a result, the ExportedType table can be nonempty only in the prime module of a multimodule assembly: if there are no nonprime modules, then all classes defined by this assembly reside in the prime module itself.

In version 2.0, the ExportedType table serves an additional function: it contains so-called class forwarders, which are close conceptually to reexports in the unmanaged world or a postal address forwarding in everyday life. A forwarder indicates to which assembly class such-and-such (which used to reside in this assembly) has been moved. The forwarding mechanism, obviously, allows you to refactor your multiassembly product without the need for all your customers to rebuild their applications.

The ExportedType table has the following column structure:

Flags (4-byte wide bitfield): Binary flags indicating whether the exported type is a forwarder (forwarder) and the accessibility of the exported type. The accessibility flags we are interested in are public and nested public; other accessibility flags—identical to the class accessibility flags discussed in Chapter 7—are syntactically admissible but are not used to define true exported types. Other flags can be present in pseudo-ExportedTypes only, which the loader can use to resolve unscoped type references in multimodule assemblies.

Some explanation is in order. Any time a type (class) is referenced in a module, the resolution scope should be provided to indicate where the referenced class is defined (in the current module, in another module of this assembly, or in another assembly). If the resolution scope is not provided, the referenced type should be declared in the current module. However, if this type cannot be found in the module referencing it *and* if the manifest of the prime module carries a identically named pseudo-ExportedType record indicating where the type is actually defined, the loader is nevertheless able to resolve the type reference.

None of the current Microsoft managed compilers, excluding the IL assembler, uses this rather bizarre technique. The IL assembler has to, for obvious reasons.

TypeDefId (4-byte unsigned integer): An uncoded token referring to a record of the TypeDef table of the module where the exported class is defined. This is the *only* occasion in the entire metadata model in which a module's metadata contains an explicit value of a metadata token from another module. This token is used as something of a hint for the loader and can be omitted without any ill effects. If the token is supplied, the loader retrieves the specific TypeDef record from the respective module's metadata and checks the full name of ExportedType against the full name of TypeDef. If the names match, the loader has found the class it was looking for; if the names do not match or if the token was not supplied in the first place, the loader finds the needed TypeDef by its full name. My advice: never specify a TypeDefId token explicitly when programming in ILAsm. This shortcut works only for automatic tools such as the Assembly Linker (AL) and only under certain circumstances.

TypeName (offset in the #Strings stream): Exported type's name; must be nonempty.

TypeNamespace (offset in the #Strings stream): Exported type's namespace; can be empty. Class names and namespaces are discussed in Chapter 7.

Implementation (coded token of type Implementation): Token of the File record indicating the file of the assembly where the exported class is defined or the token of another ExportedType, if the current one is nested in another one. The forwarders have AssemblyRef tokens as Implementation, which, in my humble opinion, makes the forwarder flag redundant: the forwarding nature of an exported type can be deduced from its Implementation being an AssemblyRef.

The exported types are declared in ILAsm as follows:

```
.class extern <flag> <namespace>.<name> { <expTypeDecl> * }
```

where <flag> ::= **public** | **nested public** | **forwarder** and where <expTypeDecl> ::=

```
.file <name>       // File where exported class is defined
| .class extern <namespace>.<name> // Enclosing exported type
| .class <int32> // Set TypeDefId explicitly (don't do that!)
| .assembly extern <name> // Forwarder
| <customAttrDecl> // Define custom attribute for this ExportedType
```

The directives .assembly extern, .file, and .class extern define the Implementation entry and are mutually exclusive. As in the case of the .mresource declaration, respective AssemblyRef, File, or ExportedType must be declared before being referenced by the Implementation entry.

It is fairly obvious that if Implementation is specified as .class extern, we are dealing with a nested exported type, and Flags must be set to nested public. Inversely, if Implementation is specified as .file, we are dealing with a top-level unnested class, and Flags must be set to public.

Order of Manifest Declarations in ILAsm

The general rule in ILAsm (and not only in ILAsm) is "declare, then reference." In other words, it's always safer, and in some cases outright required, to declare a metadata item before referencing it. There are times when you can reference a yet-undeclared item—for example, calling a method that is defined later in the source code. But you cannot do this in the manifest declarations.

If we reexamine Figure 6-1, which illustrates the mutual references between the manifest metadata tables, we can discern the following list of dependencies:

- Exported types reference external assemblies, files, and enclosing exported types.

- Manifest resources reference files and external assemblies.

- Every manifest item can have associated custom attributes, and custom attributes reference external assemblies and (rarely) external modules. (See Chapter 16 for details.)

To comply with the "declare, then reference" rule, the following sequence of declarations is recommended for ILAsm programs, with the manifest declarations preceding all other declarations in the source code:

1. AssemblyRef declarations (.assembly extern), because of the custom attributes. The reference to the assembly Mscorlib should lead the pack because most custom attributes reference this assembly.

2. ModuleRef declarations (.module extern), again because of the custom attributes.

3. Assembly declaration (.assembly). The ILAsm compiler takes different paths in compiling Mscorlib.dll and compiling other assemblies, so it is better to let it know which path to take as soon as possible. In version 2.0 you can also use special keyword .mscorlib, indicating that you are compiling Mscorlib.dll. This keyword is best placed at the beginning of the program. However, this is less important if you are *not* compiling Mscorlib.dll; by default the compiler assumes that it is compiling a "conventional" module.

4. File declarations (.file) because ExportedType and ManifestResource declarations might reference them.

5. ExportedType declarations (.class extern), with enclosing ExportedType declarations preceding the nested ExportedType declarations.

6. ManifestResource declarations (.mresource).

Remember that only the manifests of prime modules carry Assembly and ExportedType declarations.

Single-Module and Multimodule Assemblies

A single-module assembly consists of a sole prime module. Manifests of single-module assemblies as a rule carry neither File nor ExportedType tables: there are no other files to declare, and all types are defined in the prime module. However, you might want to declare a File record for an unmanaged DLL you want to be part of the deployment, or your single-module assembly might use type forwarding via the ExportedType table.

The advantages of single-module assemblies include lower overhead, easier deployment, and slightly greater security. Overhead is lower because only one set of headers and metadata tables must be read, transmitted, and analyzed. Assembly deployment is simpler because only one PE file must be deployed. And the level of security can be slightly higher because the prime module of the assembly can be protected with a strong name signature, which is extremely difficult to counterfeit and virtually guarantees the authenticity of the prime module. Nonprime modules are authenticated only by their hash values (referenced in File records of the prime module) and are theoretically easier to spoof.

Manifests of the modules of a multimodule assembly carry File tables, and the manifest of the prime module of such an assembly might or might not carry ExportedType tables, depending on whether any public types are defined in nonprime modules.

The advantages of multimodule assemblies include easier development and…lower overhead. (No, I am not pulling your leg.) Both advantages stem from the obvious modularity of the multimodule assemblies.

Multimodule assemblies are easier to develop because if you distribute the functionality among the modules well, you can develop the modules independently and then incrementally add to the assembly. (I didn't say that a multimodule assembly was easier to *design*.)

Lower overhead at run time results from the way the loader operates: it loads the modules only when they are referenced. So if only part of your assembly's functionality is engaged in a certain execution session, only part of the modules constituting your assembly might be loaded. Of course, you cannot count on any such effect if the functionality is spread all over the modules and if classes defined in different modules cross-reference each other.

A well-known technique for building a multimodule assembly from a set of modules is based on a "spokesperson" approach: the modules are analyzed, and an additional prime module is created, carrying nothing but the manifest and (maybe) a strong name signature. Such a prime module carries no functionality or positive definitions of its own whatsoever—it is only a front for functional modules, a "spokesperson" dealing with the loader on behalf of the functional modules. The Assembly Linker tool, distributed with the .NET Framework, uses this technique to build multimodule assemblies from sets of nonprime modules.

Summary of Metadata Validity Rules

In this section, I'll summarize the validity rules for metadata contained in a manifest. Since some of these rules have a direct bearing on how the loader functions, the respective checks are performed at run time. Other rules describe "well-formed" metadata; violating one of these rules might result in rather peculiar effects during the program execution, but it does not represent a crash or security breach hazard, so the loader does not perform these checks. You can find the complete set of metadata validity rules in Partition II of the ECMA/ISO standard; the sections that follow here review the most important of them.

ILAsm *does* allow you to generate invalid metadata. Thus, it's extremely important to carefully check your modules after compilation.

To find out whether any of the metadata in a module is invalid, you can run the PEVerify utility, included in the .NET Framework SDK, using the option /MD (metadata validation). Alternatively, you can invoke the IL disassembler. Choose View, MetaInfo, and Validate, and then press Ctrl+M. Both utilities use the Metadata Validator (MDValidator), which is built into the common language runtime.

Assembly Table Validity Rules

- The record count of the table must be no more than 1. This is not checked at run time because the loader ignores all Assembly records except the first one. (I will mark all metadata validity rules checked by the loader with a "[run time]" label.)

- The Flags entry must have bits set only as defined in the CorAssemblyFlags enumeration in CorHdr.h. For the version 2.0 of the common language runtime, the valid mask is 0xC101, and only one bit (0x0100, retargetable) can be specified explicitly.

- The Locale entry must be set to 0 or must refer to a nonempty string in the string heap that matches a known culture name. You can obtain a list of known culture names by using a call to the CultureInfo.GetCultures method, from the .NET Framework class library.

- [run time] If Locale is not set to 0, the referenced string must be no longer than 1,023 characters plus the zero terminator.

- [run time] The Name entry must refer to a nonempty string in the string heap. The name must be the module filename excluding the extension, the path, and the drive letter.

- [run time] The PublicKey entry must be set to 0 or must contain a valid offset in the #Blob stream.

AssemblyRef Table Validity Rules

- The Flags entry can have only the least significant bit set (corresponding to the afPublicKey value; see the CorAssemblyFlags enumeration in CorHdr.h).

- [run time] The PublicKeyOrToken entry must be set to 0 or must contain a valid offset in the #Blob stream.

- The Locale entry must comply with the same rules as the Locale entry of the Assembly table (discussed in the preceding section).

- The table must not have duplicate records with simultaneously matching Name, Locale, PublicKeyOrToken, and all Version entries.

- [run time] The Name entry must refer to a nonempty string in the string heap. The name must be the prime module filename excluding the extension, the path, and the drive letter.

Module Table Validity Rules

- [run time] The record count of the table must be at least 1.

- The record count of the table must be exactly 1. This is not checked at run time because the loader uses the first Module record and ignores the others.

- [run time] The Name entry must refer to a nonempty string in the string heap, no longer than 511 characters plus the zero terminator. The name must be the module filename including the extension and excluding the path and the drive letter.

- The Mvid entry must refer to a nonzero GUID in the #GUID stream. The value of the Mvid entry is generated automatically and cannot be specified explicitly in ILAsm.

ModuleRef Table Validity Rules

- [run time] The Name entry must refer to a nonempty string in the string heap, no longer than 511 characters plus the zero terminator. The name must be a filename including the extension and excluding the path and the drive letter.

File Table Validity Rules

- The Flags entry can have only the least significant bit set (corresponding to the ffContainsNoMetaData value; see the CorFileFlags enumeration in CorHdr.h).

- [run time] The Name entry must refer to a nonempty string in the string heap, no longer than 511 characters plus the zero terminator. The name must be a filename including the extension and excluding the path and the drive letter.

- [run time] The string referenced by the Name entry must not match S[N][[C]*], where

```
S ::= con | aux | lpt | prn | nul | com
N ::= 0..9
C ::= $ | :
```

- [run time] The HashValue entry must hold a valid offset in the #Blob stream.

- The table must not contain duplicate records whose Name entries refer to matching strings.

- The table must not contain duplicate records whose Name entries refer to strings matching this module's name.

ManifestResource Table Validity Rules

- [run time] The Implementation entry must be set to 0 or must hold a valid AssemblyRef or File token.

- [run time] If the Implementation entry does not hold an AssemblyRef token, the Offset entry must hold a valid offset within limits specified by the Resources data directory of the common language runtime header of the target file (if the target file is not a pure-resource file with no metadata).

- [run time] The Flags entry must hold either 1 or 2—mrPublic or mrPrivate, respectively.

- [run time] The Name entry must refer to a nonempty string in the string heap.

- The table must not contain duplicate records whose Name entries refer to matching strings.

ExportedType Table Validity Rules

- There must be no rows with TypeName and TypeNamespace matching Name and Namespace, respectively, of any row of the TypeDef table.

- The Flags entry must hold either one of the visibility flags (0x0–0x7) of the enumeration CorTypeAttr (see CorHdr.h) or a forwarder flag (0x00200000).

- [run time] The Implementation entry must hold a valid ExportedType or File or AssemblyRef token. In the last case, the forwarder flag must be set.

- [run time] The Implementation entry must not hold an ExportedType token pointing to this record.

- If the Implementation entry holds an ExportedType token, the Flags entry must hold a nested visibility value in the range 2–7.

- If the Implementation entry holds a File token, the Flags entry must hold the tdNonPublic or tdPublic visibility value (0 or 1).

- [run time] The TypeName entry must refer to a nonempty string in the string heap.

- [run time] The TypeNamespace entry must be set to 0 or must refer to a nonempty string in the string heap.

- [run time] The combined length of the strings referenced by TypeName and TypeNamespace must not exceed 1022 bytes in UTF-8 encoding.

- The table must not contain duplicate records whose Implementation entry holds a File or AssemblyRef token and whose TypeName and TypeNamespace entries refer to matching strings.

- The table must not contain duplicate records whose Implementation entries hold the same ExportedType token and whose TypeName entries refer to matching strings.

CHAPTER 7

■ ■ ■

Namespaces and Classes

As earlier chapters have discussed, the common language runtime computational model is inherently object oriented. The concept of class—or, to use more precise runtime terminology, the concept of a *type*—is the central principle around which the entire computational model is organized. The type of an item—a variable, a constant, a parameter, and so on—defines both data representation and the behavioral features of the item. Hence, one type can be substituted for another only if both these aspects are equivalent for both types—for instance, a derived type can be interpreted as the type from which it is derived.

The Ecma International/ISO standard specification of the common language infrastructure divides types into value types and reference types, depending on whether an item type represents a data item itself or a reference (an address or a location indicator) to a data item.

Reference types include object types, interface types, and pointer types. Object types—classes—are types of self-describing values, either complete or partial. Types with partial self-describing values are called *abstract classes*. Interface types are always types of partial self-describing values. Interfaces usually represent subsets of behavioral features exposed by classes; a class is said to implement the respective interface. Pointer types are simply references to items, indicating item locations.

This is what the Ecma International/ISO specification says, and I am not going to argue the fine points of the theory, such as why classes and interfaces are self-describing and value types are not or why the way of passing the items between functional units—by value or by reference—all of a sudden becomes the inherent attribute of the items themselves.

The common language runtime object model supports only single type inheritance, and multiple inheritance is simulated through the implementation of one or more interfaces. As a result, the runtime object model is absolutely hierarchical, with the System.Object class at the root of the tree (see Figure 7-1). Interface types, however, are not part of the type hierarchy because they are inherently incomplete and have no implementation of their own.

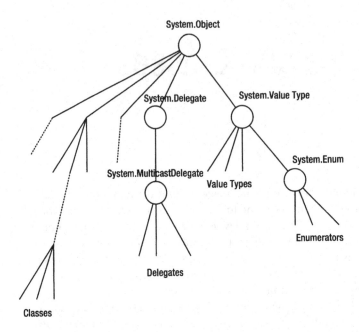

Figure 7-1. *The common language runtime type hierarchy*

The interfaces play an interesting role: they serve as promissory notes of a class. When class X is derived from class Y, X inherits all members of Y, so inheritance directly affects the structure of the derived class. But when you say that class X implements interface IY, you promise only that class X will expose all the methods described in IY, which might be viewed as a *constraint* imposed on class X. Class X does not inherit anything from the interface IY it implements, except a "debt" of implementing the methods of IY.

All types (except interfaces) are derived eventually from System.Object. This chapter examines types and their declarations, dividing the types into five categories: classes, interfaces, value types, enumerations, and delegates. These categories are not mutually exclusive—for example, delegates are classes, and enumerations are value types—but the types of each category have distinct features.

Class Metadata

From a structural point of view, all five categories of types have identical metadata representations. Thus, we can talk about class metadata, or type metadata, in a general sense.

Class metadata is grouped around two distinct concepts: type definition (TypeDef) and type reference (TypeRef). TypeDefs and related metadata describe the types declared in the current module, whereas TypeRefs describe references to types that are declared somewhere else. Since it obviously takes more information to adequately define a type than to refer to one already defined, TypeDefs and related metadata are far more complex than TypeRefs.

When defining a type, you should supply the following information:

- The full name of the type being defined

- Flags indicating special features the type should have

- The type from which this type is derived

- The interfaces this type implements

- How the loader should lay out this type in memory

- Whether this type is nested in another type—and if so, in which one

- Where fields and methods of this type (if any) can be found

When referencing a type, only its name and resolution scope need be specified. The resolution scope indicates where the definition of the referenced type can be found: in this module, in another module of this assembly, or in another assembly. In the case of referencing the nested types, the resolution scope is another TypeRef.

Figure 7-2 shows the metadata tables that engage in type definition and referencing but not the tables related to the identification of type members—fields and methods, for example, and their attributes. The arrows denote cross-table referencing by means of metadata tokens. In the following sections, you'll have a look at all the metadata tables involved.

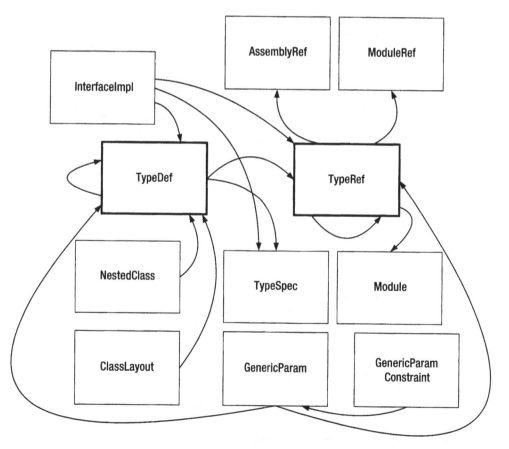

Figure 7-2. *Metadata tables that engage in type definition and referencing*

I must point out that three tables in the lower part of Figure 7-2 (TypeSpec, GenericParam, and GenericParamConstraint) and their associated links have entered the picture (no pun intended) in version 2.0 only. They are related to generic types and will be discussed in Chapter 11.

TypeDef Metadata Table

The TypeDef table is the main table containing type definition information. Each record in this table has six entries:

- Flags (4-byte unsigned integer). Binary flags indicating special features of the type. The TypeDef flags are numerous and important, so this chapter discusses them separately; see "Class Attributes."

- Name (offset in the #Strings stream). The name of the type. This entry must not be empty. Remember class Odd.or.Even from Chapter 1? Odd.or.Even was its full name. The Name of that class was Even—part of the full name to the right of the rightmost dot.

- Namespace (offset in the #Strings stream). The namespace of the type, part of the full name to the left of the rightmost dot. Class Odd.or.Even from Chapter 1 had Namespace Odd.or. The Namespace entry can be empty, if the full name of the class does not contain dots. The namespace and the name constitute the full name of the type.

- Extends (coded token of type TypeDefOrRef). A token of the type's parent—that is, of the type from which this type is derived. This entry must be set to 0 for all interfaces and for one class, the type hierarchy root class System.Object. For all other types, this entry should carry a valid reference to the TypeDef, TypeRef, or TypeSpec table. The TypeSpec table can be referenced only if the parent type is an instantiation of a generic type (see Chapter 11).

- FieldList (record index [RID] in the Field table). An index to the Field table, marking the start of the field records belonging to this type.

- MethodList (RID in the Method table). An index to the Method table, marking the start of the method records belonging to this type.

TypeRef Metadata Table

The TypeRef metadata table has a much simpler structure than the TypeDef table, because it needs to carry only data necessary to identify the referenced type unambiguously, so the CLR loader could resolve the reference at run time. Each record in this table has three entries:

- ResolutionScope (coded token of type ResolutionScope). An indicator of the location of the type definition. This entry is set to 0 if the referenced type is defined somewhere in the current assembly or to 4 (compressed token 1—the Module token) if the referenced type is defined in the same module. Besides these two rather special cases, in general ResolutionScope can be a token referencing the ModuleRef table if the type is defined in another module of the same assembly, a token referencing the AssemblyRef table if the type is defined in another assembly, or a token referencing the TypeRef table if the type is nested in another type. Having TypeRefs for the types defined in the same module does not constitute a metadata error, but it is redundant and should be avoided if possible.

- Name (offset in the #Strings stream). The name of the referenced type. This entry must not be empty.

- Namespace (offset in the #Strings stream). The namespace of the referenced type. This entry can be empty. The namespace and the name constitute the full name of the type.

InterfaceImpl Metadata Table

If the defined type implements one or several interfaces, the corresponding TypeDef record is referenced by one or several records of the InterfaceImpl metadata table. This table serves as a lookup table (describing not some metadata entities but rather relations between entities described in other tables), providing information about "what is implementing what," and it is ordered by implementing type. The InterfaceImpl table has only two entries in each record:

- Class (RID in the TypeDef table). An index in the TypeDef table, indicating the implementing type.

- Interface (coded token of type TypeDefOrRef). A token of the implemented type, which can reside in the TypeDef, TypeRef, or TypeSpec table. The TypeSpec table can be referenced only if the implemented interface is an instantiation of a generic interface (see Chapter 11). The implemented type must be marked as an interface.

NestedClass Metadata Table

If the defined type is nested in another type, its TypeDef record is referenced in another lookup table: the NestedClass metadata table. (For more information about nesting, see "Nested Types" later in this chapter.) Like the InterfaceImpl table, the NestedClass table is a lookup table, and records of which describe some "links" between other tables. Being a lookup table, the NestedClass table has only two entries per record:

- NestedClass (RID in the TypeDef table). An index of the nested type (the *nestee*).

- EnclosingClass (RID in the TypeDef table). An index of the type in which the current type is nested (the encloser, or *nester*).

Since types of both entries are RIDs in the TypeDef table, the nested type and its encloser cannot be defined in different modules or assemblies.

ClassLayout Metadata Table

Usually, the loader has its own ideas about how to lay out the type being loaded: it may add fillers between the fields of the class for alignment, or even shuffle the fields. Certain types, however, must be laid out in a specific manner (for example, suppose you want to introduce a value type describing a COFF header, which has a very definite structure and layout, or you want to create such a simple thing as a union), and they carry metadata information regarding these specifics.

The ClassLayout metadata table provides additional information about the packing order and total size of the type. In Chapter 1, for example, when I declared a "placeholder" type without any internal structure, I used such additional information—the total size of the type.

A record in the ClassLayout metadata table has three entries:

- PackingSize (2-byte unsigned integer). The alignment factor in bytes. This entry must be set to 0 or to a power of 2, from 1 to 128. If this entry is not zero, its value will be used as the alignment factor for fields instead of a "natural" alignment characteristic of the field types ("natural" alignment usually coincides with the size of the type or nearest greater power of 2). For example, if PackingSize is set to 2, and you have two fields—a byte and a pointer—then your layout will include a byte (first field), another byte (filler), and a pointer; the pointer in this case will be 2-byte aligned, which is a bad thing on almost all processor architectures. If, however, the PackingSize value is greater than the "natural" alignment of a field, the "natural" alignment is used; if, for example, PackingSize is set to 2, and you have two 1-byte fields, then your layout will include just 2 bytes (first field, second field) without any filler between them.

- ClassSize (4-byte unsigned integer). The total requested layout size of the type. If the type has instance fields and the summary size of these fields, aligned by PackingSize, is different from ClassSize, the loader allocates the larger of the two sizes for the type.

- Parent (RID in the TypeDef table). An index of the type definition record to which this layout belongs. The ClassLayout table should not contain any duplicate records with the same Parent entry value.

Namespace and Full Class Name

It is time to talk seriously about names in the common language runtime and ILAsm. So far, in Chapter 6, you've encountered only names that were in fact filenames and hence had to conform to well-known filename conventions. From now on, however, you'll need to deal with names in general, so it is important to know the rules.

ILAsm Naming Conventions

Names in ILAsm are either simple or composite. Composite names are composed of simple names and special connection symbols such as a dot. For example, System and Object are simple names, and System.Object is a composite name. The length of either kind of name in ILAsm is not limited syntactically, but metadata rules impose certain limitations on the name length.

The simplest form of a simple name is an identifier, which in ILAsm must begin with an alphabetic character or one of the following characters:

#, $, @, _

and continue with alphanumeric characters or one of the following:

?, $, @, _, `

(The last symbol is not an apostrophe; it is a backtick.)

These are examples of valid ILAsm identifiers:

- `Object`

- `_Never_Say_Never_Again_`

- `men@work`

- `` GType`1 ``

Caution One obvious limitation on ILAsm identifiers is that an ILAsm identifier must not match any of the (rather numerous) ILAsm keywords.

The common language runtime accepts a wide variety of names with very few limitations. Certain names—for example, `.ctor` (an instance constructor), `.cctor` (a class constructor, a.k.a. type initializer), and `_Deleted*` (a metadata item marked for deletion during an edit-and-continue session)—are reserved for internal use by the runtime. Generally, however, the runtime is liberal about names. As long as a name serves its purpose—identifying a metadata item unambiguously—and cannot be misinterpreted, it is perfectly fine. This liberalism, of course, includes names beginning with wrong (from the ILAsm point of view) symbols and names continuing with wrong symbols, not to mention the names that happen to match ILAsm keywords.

To cover this variety, ILAsm offers an alternative way to present a simple name: as a single-quoted literal. For example, these are valid ILAsm simple names:

- `'123'`

- `'Space Between'`

- `'&%!'`

One of the most frequently encountered kinds of composite names is the dotted name, a name composed of simple names separated by a dot:

`<dotted_name> ::= <simple_name>[.<simple_name>*]`

Examples of dotted names include the following:

- `System.Object`

- `'123'.'456'.'789'`

- `Foo.Bar.'&%!'`

Namespaces

Simply put, namespaces are the common prefixes of the full names of classes. The full name of a class is a dotted name; the last simple name it contains is the class name, and the rest is the namespace of the class.

It takes longer, perhaps, to explain what namespaces are *not*. Namespaces are not metadata items—they do not have an associated metadata table, and they cannot be referenced by tokens. Namespaces also have no direct bearing on assemblies. The name of an assembly might or might not match in full or in part the namespace(s) used in the assembly. One assembly might use several namespaces, and the same namespace can be used in different assemblies (an assembly using a namespace means an assembly defining classes with names belonging to this namespace).

So why does the metadata model even bother with namespaces and class names instead of simply using the full class names? The answer is simple: economy of space. Let's suppose you define two classes with the full names Foo.Bar and Foo.Baz. Since the names are different, in the full-name model you would have to store two full names in the string heap: Foo.Bar\0Foo.Baz\0. But if you split the full names into namespaces and names, you need to store only Foo\0Bar\0Baz\0. This is quite a difference when you consider the number of possible classes.

Namespaces in ILAsm are declared in the following way:

```
.namespace MyNamespace
{
    ...
    // Classes declared here
    // Have full name "MyNamespace.<simple_name>"
}
```

Namespaces can be nested, as shown here:

```
.namespace MyNamespace
{
    ...
    // Classes declared here
    // Have full name "MyNamespace.<simple_name>"
    .namespace X
    {
        ...
        // Classes declared here
        // Have full name "MyNamespace.X.<simple_name>"
    }
}
```

or they can be unnested. This is how the IL disassembler versions 1.0 and 1.1 used to represent namespaces in the disassembly text:

```
.namespace MyNamespace
{
    ...
```

```
    // Classes declared here
    // Have full name "MyNamespace.<simple_name>"
}
.namespace MyNamespace.X
{
    ...
    // Classes declared here
    // Have full name "MyNamespace.X.<simple_name>"
}
```

In version 2.0, it is recommended that you use full class names instead of the specifica-tion of namespaces, and the IL disassembler version 2.0 follows this pattern. The .namespace directive is still recognized by the IL assembler for backward-compatibility reasons.

Full Class Names

As the preceding section explained, a full class name in general case is a dotted name, com-posed of the class's namespace and the name of the class. The loader resolves class references by their full names and resolution scopes, so the general rule is that no classes with identical full names must be defined in the same module. For multimodule assemblies, an additional (less strict) rule prohibits defining public classes—classes visible outside the assembly—with identical full names in the same assembly.

In ILAsm, a class is always referenced by its full name, even if it is referenced from within the same namespace. This makes class referencing context independent.

ILAsm v1.0 and v1.1 did not allow dotted names as class names, but you could bypass this restriction by quoting the dotted name, thus turning it into a simple name and avoiding a syn-tax error:

```
.namespace X
{
    .class public 'Y.Z'
    {
        ...
    }
}
```

And a class is always referenced by its full name, so a class with a dotted name will not pose any resolution problems (it will be referenced as X.Y.Z anyway), and the module will compile and work. But if you disassemble the module, you'll find that the left part of the dot-ted name of the class has migrated to the namespace, courtesy of the metadata emission API:

```
.namespace X.Y
{
    .class public Z
    {
        ...
    }
}
```

Although this is not what you intended, it has no dire consequences—just a case of mild confusion. If you know and expect this effect and don't get confused that easily, you can even forgo the namespace declarations altogether and declare classes by their full names, to match the way they are referenced:

```
.class public 'X.Y.Z'{
...
}
```

That's exactly how it is done in ILAsm v2.0, only without single quotes around the full class name, because ILAsm v2.0 allows dotted names as class or method names.

The reason for switching from the namespace/name model of class declaration to the full-name model in ILAsm v2.0 is twofold. First, this way, the classes are declared and referenced uniformly by their full names. Second, this resolves the problem of naming the nested classes: if namespace A contains declaration of class B, which contains declaration of nested class C, what is the full name of the nested class? A.C? A.B.C? (Actually, it's C, because the encloser's namespace has nothing to do with the nested class's namespace.)

The common language runtime imposes a limitation on the full class name length, specifying that it should not exceed 1,023 bytes in UTF-8 encoding. The ILAsm compiler, however, does *not* enforce this limitation. Single quotes, should they be used for simple names in ILAsm, are a purely lexical tool and don't make it to the metadata; thus, they don't contribute to the total length of the full class name.

Class Attributes

An earlier section ("Class Metadata") listed the various pieces of information included in a type definition. In the simplest case, when only the TypeDef metadata table is involved, the ILAsm syntax for a type definition is as follows:

```
.class <flags> <dotted_name> extends <class_ref> {
    ...
}
```

The <dotted_name> value specified in the .class directive defines the TypeDef's Namespace and Name entries, <class_ref> specified in the extends clause defines the Extends entry, and <flags> defines the Flags entry.

Flags

The numerous TypeDef flags can be divided into several groups, as described here.

- Visibility flags (binary mask 0x00000007):

  - private (0x00000000). The type is not visible outside the assembly. This is the default.

  - public (0x00000001). The type is visible outside the assembly.

- nested public (0x00000002). The nested type has public visibility.

- nested private (0x00000003). The nested type has private visibility; it is not visible outside the enclosing class.

- nested family (0x00000004). The nested type has family visibility—that is, it is visible to descendants of the enclosing class only.

- nested assembly (0x00000005). The nested type is visible within the assembly only.

- nested famandassem (0x00000006). The nested type is visible to the descendants of the enclosing class residing in the same assembly.

- nested famorassem (0x00000007). The nested type is visible to the descendants of the enclosing class either within or outside the assembly and to every type within the assembly with no regard to "lineage."

- Layout flags (binary mask 0x00000018):

  - auto (0x00000000). The type fields are laid out automatically, at the loader's discretion. This is the default.

  - sequential (0x00000008). The loader shall preserve the order of the instance fields.

  - explicit (0x00000010). The type layout is specified explicitly, and the loader shall follow it. (See Chapter 9 for information about field declaration.)

- Type semantics flags (binary mask 0x000005A0):

  - interface (0x00000020). The type is an interface. If this flag is not specified, the type is presumed to be a class or a value type; if this flag is specified, the default parent (the class that is assumed to be the parent if the extends clause is not specified, usually [mscorlib]System.Object) is set to nil.

  - abstract (0x00000080). The class is abstract—for example, it has abstract member methods. As such, this class cannot be instantiated and can be used only as a parent of another type or types. This flag is invalid for value types.

  - sealed (0x00000100). No types can be derived from this type. All value types and enumerations must carry this flag.

  - specialname (0x00000400). The type has a special name. How special it is depends on the name itself. This flag indicates to the metadata API and the loader that the name has a meaning in which they might be interested—for instance, _Deleted*.

- Type implementation flags (binary mask 0x00103000):

  - import (0x00001000). The type (a class or an interface) is imported from a COM type library.

  - serializable (0x00002000). The type can be serialized into sequential data by the serializer provided in the Microsoft .NET Framework class library.

- `beforefieldinit` (0x00100000). The type can be initialized (its `.cctor` run) any time before the first access to a static field. If this flag is not set, the type is initialized before the first access to one of its static fields or methods or before the first instantiation of the type. I discuss this flag and its effect on type initialization in more detail in Chapter 10.

- String formatting flags (binary mask 0x00030000):

  - `ansi` (0x00000000). When interoperating with native methods, the managed strings are by default marshaled to and from ANSI strings. Managed strings are instances of the `System.String` class defined in the .NET Framework class library. Marshaling is a general term for data conversion on the managed and unmanaged code boundaries. (See Chapter 18 for detailed information.) String formatting flags specify only default marshaling and are irrelevant when marshaling is explicitly specified. This flag, `ansi`, is the default flag for a class and hence represents a "default default" string marshaling.

  - `unicode` (0x00010000). By default, managed strings are marshaled to and from Unicode (UTF-16).

  - `autochar` (0x00020000). The default string marshaling is defined by the underlying platform.

- Reserved flags (binary mask 0x0004080):

  - `rtspecialname` (0x00000800). The name is reserved by the common language runtime and has a special meaning. This flag is legal only in combination with the `specialname` flag. The keyword `rtspecialname` has no effect in ILAsm and is provided for informational purposes only. The IL disassembler uses this keyword to show the presence of this reserved flag. Reserved flags cannot be set at will—this flag, for example, is set automatically by the metadata emission API when it emits an item with the `specialname` flag set and the name recognized as specific to the common language runtime, for example `.ctor` or `.cctor`.

  - <no keyword> (0x00040000). The type has declarative security metadata associated with it. This flag is set by the metadata emission API when respective declarative security metadata is emitted.

- Semantics pseudoflags (no binary mask). These are not true binary flags that define the `Flags` entry of a `TypeDef` record but rather are lexical pseudoflags modifying the default parent of the class:

  - `value`. The type is a value type. The default parent is `System.ValueType`.

  - `enum`. The type is an enumeration. The default parent is `System.Enum`.

Class Visibility and Friend Assemblies

Flag `public` means that the class is visible and can be referenced outside the assembly where it is declared. Flag `private` means the opposite, so probably a more proper name for this flag would be `assembly`. In version 2.0 of the common language runtime, it is possible to declare certain assemblies "friends" of the current assembly by using custom attribute

System.Runtime.CompilerServices.InternalsVisibleToAttribute. If assembly A declares assembly B as its "friend," then all classes and members inside A that have assemblywide visibility and accessibility become visible and accessible to assembly B. At the same time, these classes and members remain invisible and inaccessible to other assemblies.

There are significant differences between "friend" assemblies of the managed world and friend classes and functions of unmanaged C++. First, in the managed world the granularity of friendship does not go below the assembly level, while in unmanaged C++ the friendship is defined at the class or function level. Second, in unmanaged C++ a friend class or method has full access to all members of this class, including private members, while in the managed world a friend assembly has access only to internal (assemblywide) classes and members but not to private or protected ones.

Class References

The nonterminal symbol <class_ref> in the extends clause represents a reference to a type and translates into a TypeDef, a TypeRef, or a TypeSpec (if the parent is an instantiation of a generic type). The general syntax of a class reference is as follows:

```
<class_ref> ::= [<resolution_scope>]<full_type_name>
```

where

```
<resolution_scope> ::= [<assembly_ref_alias>]
    | [.module <module_ref_name>]
```

Note that the square brackets in the definition of <resolution_scope> are syntactic elements; they do not indicate that any portion of the definition is optional.

The previous syntax does not describe instantiations of generic types, which are presented in Chapter 11.

Here are a few examples of class references:

```
[mscorlib]System.ValueType // Type is defined in another assembly
[.module Second.dll]Foo.Bar // Type is defined in another module
Foo.Baz  // Type is defined in this module
```

If the resolution scope of a class reference points to an external assembly or module, the class reference is translated into a TypeRef metadata token, with the full type name providing values for the Name and Namespace entries and the resolution scope providing an AssemblyRef or a ModuleRef token for the ResolutionScope entry.

If the resolution scope is not defined—that is, if the referenced type is defined somewhere in the current module—the class reference is translated into the respective TypeDef token.

Parent of the Type

Having resolved the class reference to a TypeRef or TypeDef token, I thus provided the value for the Extends entry of the TypeDef record under construction. This token references the type's parent—that is, the type from which the current type is derived.

The type referenced in the extends clause must not be sealed and must not be an interface; otherwise, the loader will fail to load the type. When a type is sealed, no types can be derived from it.

If the extends clause is omitted, the ILAsm compiler assigns a default parent depending on the flags specified for the type:

- interface. No parent. The interfaces are not derived from other types.

- value. The parent is [mscorlib]System.ValueType.

- enum. The parent is [mscorlib]System.Enum.

- None of the above. The parent is [mscorlib]System.Object.

If the extends clause is present, the value and enum flags are ignored, and the interface flag causes a compilation error. This difference in ILAsm's reaction to erroneous flags can be easily explained: the value and enum are pseudoflags, like hints for the IL assembler, while the interface flag is a true metadata flag, and in combination with extends clause it represents invalid metadata.

If the type layout is specified as sequential or explicit, the type's parent must also have the corresponding layout, unless the parent is [mscorlib]System.Object, [mscorlib]System.ValueType, or [mscorlib]System.Enum. The rationale is that the type might inherit fields from its parent, and the type cannot have a mixed layout—that is, it cannot have some fields laid out automatically and some laid out explicitly or sequentially. However, an autolayout type can be derived from a type having any layout; in this case, information about the parent's field layout plays no role in laying out the instance fields of the derived type.

Interface Implementations

If the type being defined implements one or more interfaces, the type declaration has an additional clause, the implements clause, as shown here:

```
.class <flags> <dotted_name>
   extends <class_ref>
   implements <class_refs> {
      ...
}
```

The nonterminal symbol <class_refs> simply means a comma-separated list of class references:

```
<class_refs> ::= <class_ref>[,<class_ref>*]
```

For example:

```
.class public MyNamespace.MyClass
   extends MyNamespace.MyClassBase
   implements MyNamespace.IOne,
              MyNamespace.ITwo,
              MyNamespace.IThree {
      ...
}
```

The types referenced in the `implements` clause must be interfaces. A type implementing an interface must provide the implementation for all of the interface's instance methods. The only exception to this rule is an abstract class.

The `implements` clause of a type declaration creates as many records in the InterfaceImpl metadata table as there are class references listed in this clause. In the preceding example, three `InterfaceImpl` records would be created.

And, while an interface cannot extend any type, including another interface, it certainly can implement one or more other interfaces. I discussed the difference between one type extending (inheriting from) another type and a type implementing an interface earlier in this chapter.

Class Layout Information

To provide additional information regarding type layout (field alignment, total type size, or both), you need to use the `.pack` and `.size` directives, as shown in this example:

```
.class public value explicit MyNamespace.MyStruct {
    .pack 4
    .size 1024
    ...
}
```

These directives, obviously enough, set the entries `PackingSize` and `ClassSize`, respectively, of the `ClassLayout` record associated with a given class.

The `.pack` and `.size` directives appear within the scope of the type declaration, in any order. If `.pack` is not specified, the field alignment defaults to 1. If `.pack` or `.size` is specified, a `ClassLayout` record is created for this `TypeDef`.

Integer values specified in a `.pack` directive must be 0 or a power of 2, in the range 2^0 to 2^7 (1 to 128). Breaking this rule results in a compilation error. When the value is 0, the field alignment defaults to the "natural" value defined by the type of the field—the size of the type or the nearest greater power of 2.

Class layout information should not be specified for the autolayout types. Formally, defining the class layout information for an autolayout type represents invalid metadata. In reality, however, it is simply a waste of metadata space; when the loader encounters an autolayout type, it never checks to see whether this type has a corresponding `ClassLayout` record.

Interfaces

An interface is a special kind of type, defined in Partition I of the Ecma International/ISO standard as "a named group of methods, locations, and other contracts that shall be implemented by any object type that supports the interface contract of the same name." In other words, an interface is not a "real" type but merely a named descriptor of methods and properties exposed by other types—an IOU note of a type. Conceptually, an interface in the common language runtime is similar to a COM interface—or at least the general idea is the same.

Not being a real type, an interface is not derived from any other type, and other types cannot be derived from an interface. But an interface can "implement" other interfaces. This is not a true implementation, of course. When I say that "interface IA implements interfaces IB and IC," I mean only that the contracts defined by IB and IC are subcontracts of the contract defined by IA.

As a descriptor of items (methods, properties, events) exposed by other types, an interface cannot offer its own implementation of these items and thus is, by definition, an abstract type. When you define an interface in ILAsm, you can omit the keyword abstract because the compiler adds this flag automatically when it encounters the keyword interface.

For the same reason, an interface cannot have instance fields, because a declaration of a field is the field's implementation. However, an interface must offer the implementation of its static members—the items shared by all instances of a type—if it has any. Bear in mind, of course, that the definition of static as "shared by all instances" is general for all types and does not imply that interfaces can be instantiated. They cannot be. Interfaces are inherently abstract and cannot even have instance constructors.

Static members (fields, methods) of an interface are not part of the contract defined by the interface and have no bearing on the types that implement the interface. A type implementing an interface must implement all instance members of the interface, but it has nothing to do with the static members of the interface. Static members of an interface can be accessed directly like static members of any type, and you don't need an "instance" of an interface (meaning an instance of a class implementing this interface) for that.

The nature of an interface as a descriptor of items exposed by other types requires that the interface itself and all its instance members must be public, which makes reasonable sense—I am, after all, talking about *exposed* items.

Interfaces have several limitations. One is obvious: since an interface is not a real type, it does not have layout. It simply doesn't make sense to talk about the packing size or total size of a contract descriptor.

Another limitation stems from the fact that the instance methods declared by an interface must be virtual, because they are implemented elsewhere, namely, by the class implementing the interface. Chapter 10 discusses the virtual methods and their implementation in details.

Yet another limitation is not so obvious: interfaces should not be sealed. This might sound contradictory because, as just noted, no types can be derived from interfaces—which is precisely the definition of *sealed*. The logic behind this limitation is as follows: since a sealed type cannot extend any other type, its virtual methods cannot be overridden and become simple instance methods; and, as you may recall, an interface may provide implementation only of its static methods, so these instance (formerly known as *virtual*) methods are left unimplemented.

From this logic stems a more general rule, applicable to all types, that dictates an abstract type should not be sealed unless it has only static members. At least that is what the Ecma International/ISO specification says. I personally think that the correct formulation of a general rule would be that an abstract type cannot be sealed *unless it has no abstract (unimplemented) virtual methods*. And a type may be declared abstract even if it contains no abstract methods. You may just not want this particular type to ever be instantiated. There is quite a difference between "no instance members" and "no abstract virtual methods," don't you agree?

On the other hand, what is the use of the instance members of a type if you cannot instantiate this type (it's abstract) or derive something "instantiatable" from it (it's sealed)? So maybe the Ecma International/ISO spec is right—the abstract types with only nonabstract instance members *could* be declared sealed, but they *should not* be declared sealed.

Instance methods of an interface, however, are all abstract virtual by definition, so there is no "should"/"could" dilemma.

Value Types

Value types are the closest thing in the common language runtime model to C++ structures. These types are values with either a trivial structure (for example, a 4-byte integer) or a complex structure. When you declare a variable of a class type, you don't automatically create a class instance. You create only a reference to the class, initially pointing at nothing. But when you declare a variable of value type, the instance of this value type is allocated immediately, by the variable declaration itself, because a value type is primarily a data structure. As such, a value type must have instance fields or size defined. A zero-size value type (with no instance fields and no total size specified) represents invalid metadata; however, as in many other cases, the loader is more forgiving than the official metadata validity rules: when it encounters a zero-size value type, the loader assigns it a 1-byte size by default.

Value types are the types passed by value, as opposed to the reference types passed by reference. It means that the code a = b;, when a and b are value types, is translated into copying the contents of b into a, and when a and b are reference types, it is translated into copying the reference to some class instance from b to a. So in the end we wind up with two identical instances in the case of a and b being of a value type and with two identical references to the same instance in the case of a and b being of a reference type.

Although an instance of a value type is created at the moment a variable having this value type is declared, the default instance constructor method (should it be defined for the value type in question) is not called at this moment. (See Chapter 10 for information about the instance constructor method.) Declaring a variable creates a "blank" instance of the value type, and if this value type has a default instance constructor, it should be called explicitly.

Please don't ask me why the runtime does not execute the instance constructor of a value type (if available) automatically when it allocates the instance of this type—this question is of the same rhetorical nature as "why does runtime ignore the default values specified for fields and parameters?" (See Chapters 9 and 10 for details.) The correct answer is "because the runtime is built this way."

Boxed and Unboxed Values

As a data structure, a value type must sometimes be represented as an object to satisfy the requirements of certain generic APIs, which expect object references as input parameters. The common language runtime provides the means to produce a class representation of a value type and to extract a value type (data structure) from its class representation. These operations, called *boxing* and *unboxing*, respectively, are defined for every value type.

Recall from the beginning of this chapter that types can be classified as either value types or reference types. Simply put, boxing transforms a value type into a reference type (an object reference), and unboxing does just the opposite. You can box any value type and get an object reference, but this does not mean, however, that you can unbox any object and get a value type: in the .NET type system, every value type has its reference-type "hat," but not vice versa. Why that is so, when it is obviously possible to extract the data part from any reference type that has it, is another of those rhetoric questions.

When we declare a value type variable, we create a data structure. When we box this variable, an object (a class instance) is created whose data part is an exact bit copy of the data structure. Then we can deal with this instance the same way we would deal with an ordinary object—for example, we could use it in a call to a method, which takes an object reference as a parameter. It is important to understand that the "original" instance of a value type does not go anywhere after it has been boxed. Its copy does. And what happens to this copy is not reflected back to the original instance of the value type. This effect is known as a problem of mutability of the boxed value types. It is up to the author of the code to propagate possible changes inflicted upon the boxed instance of the value type back to the original instance.

When a boxed value type is being unboxed, no instance copying is involved. The unboxing operation simply produces a managed pointer to the data part of the object to which it is applied.

Instance Members of Value Types

Value types, like other types, can have static and instance members, including methods and fields. To access an instance member of a class, you need to provide the instance pointer (known in C++ as this). In the case of a value type, you simply use a managed reference as an instance pointer.

Let's suppose, for example, that you have a variable of type 4-byte integer. (What can be more trivial than that, except maybe type fewer-byte integer?) This value type is defined as [mscorlib]System.Int32 in the .NET Framework class library. Instead of boxing this variable and getting a reference to an instance of System.Int32 as the class, you can simply take the reference to this variable and call the instance methods of this value type, say, ToString(), which returns a string representation of the integer in question:

```
...
.locals init (int32 J)  // Declare variable J as value type
...
ldc.i4 12345
stloc J   // J = 12345
...
ldloca J // Get managed reference to J as instance pointer
// Call method of this instance
call instance string [mscorlib]System.Int32::ToString()
...
```

Can value types have virtual methods? Yes, they can. However, to call the virtual methods of a value type, you have to box this value type first. I must clarify, though, that you need to box the value type only if you are calling its virtual method as a virtual method, through the virtual table dispatch, using the callvirt instruction (methods and method call instructions are discussed in Chapters 10, 12, and 13). If you are calling a virtual method of a value type as simply an instance method, using the call instruction, you don't need to box the value type. That's why I didn't need to box the variable J in the previous code snippet before calling the ToString() method despite that ToString() is a virtual method.

Derivation of Value Types

All value types are derived from the [mscorlib]System.ValueType class. More than that, anything derived from [mscorlib]System.ValueType is a value type by definition, with one important exception: the [mscorlib]System.Enum class, which is a parent of all enumerations (discussed in the next section).

Unlike C++, in which derivation of a structure from another structure is commonplace, the common language runtime object model does not allow any derivations from value types. All value types must be sealed. (And you probably thought I was too lazy to draw further derivation branches from value types in Figure 7-1!) As to why all value types must be sealed, I am afraid it's another one of those rhetorical questions.

Enumerations

Enumerations (a.k.a. enumeration types, a.k.a. enums) make up a special subset of value types. All enumerations are derived from the [mscorlib]System.Enum class, which is the only reference type derived from [mscorlib]System.ValueType. Enums are possibly the most primitive of all types that have some structure, and the rules regarding them are the most restrictive.

Unlike other value types in their boxed form, enumerators don't show any of the characteristics of a "true class." Enums can have only fields as members—no methods, properties, or events. Enums cannot implement interfaces; since enums cannot have methods, the question of implementing interfaces is moot.

Here is an example of a simple enumeration:

```
.class public enum Color
{
    .field public specialname int32 __value
    .field public static literal valuetype Color Red = int32(1)
    .field public static literal valuetype Color Green = int32(2)
    .field public static literal valuetype Color Blue = int32(3)
}
```

Even with the fields the enums have no leeway: an enum must have exactly one instance field and at least one static field. The instance field of an enum represents the value of the current instance of the enum and must be of integer, Boolean, or character type. The type of the instance field is the underlying type of the enum. The enum itself as a value type is completely interchangeable with its underlying type in all operations except boxing. If an operation, other than boxing, expects a Boolean variable as its argument, a variable of a Boolean-based enumeration type can be used instead, and vice versa. A boxing operation, however, always results in a boxed enum and not in a boxed underlying type.

The static fields represent the values of the enum itself and have the type of the enum. As values of the enum, these fields must be not only static (shared by all instances of the type) but also literal—they represent constants defined in the metadata. The literal fields are not true fields because they do not occupy memory allocated by the loader when the enum is loaded and laid out. (Chapter 9 discusses this and other aspects of fields.)

Generally speaking, you can think of an enumeration as a restriction of its underlying type to a predefined, finite set of values (however, the CLR does not enforce this restriction). As such, an enumeration obviously cannot have any specific layout requirements and must have the auto layout flag set.

Delegates

Delegates are a special kind of reference type, designed with the specific purpose of representing function pointers. All delegates are derived from the [mscorlib]System.MulticastDelegate type, which in turn is derived from the [mscorlib]System.Delegate type. The delegates themselves are sealed (just like the value types), so no types can be derived from them.

Limitations imposed on the structure of a delegate are as strict as those imposed on the enumerator structure. Delegates have no fields, events, or properties. They can have only instance methods, either two or four of them, and the names and signatures of these methods are predefined.

Two mandatory methods of a delegate are the instance constructor (.ctor) and Invoke. The instance constructor returns void (as all instance constructors do) and takes two parameters: the object reference to the type defining the method being delegated and the function pointer to the managed method being delegated. (See Chapter 10 for details about instance constructors.)

This leads to a question: if you can get a function pointer per se, why do you need delegates at all? Why not use the function pointers directly? You could, but then you would need to introduce fields or variables of function pointer types to hold these pointers—and function pointer types are considered a security risk (because the pointer value can be modified after it was acquired from a particular function) and deemed unverifiable. If a module is unverifiable, it can be executed only from a local drive in full trust mode, when all security checks are disabled. Another drawback is that managed function pointers cannot be marshaled to unmanaged function pointers when calling unmanaged methods, whereas delegates can be. (See Chapter 18 for information on managed and unmanaged code interoperation.)

Delegates are secure, verifiable, and type-safe representations of function pointers first of all because the function pointers in delegate representation cannot be tampered with and as such are preferable over function pointer types. Besides, delegates can offer additional useful features, as I'll describe in a moment.

The second mandatory method (Invoke) must have the same signature as the delegated method. Two mandatory methods (.ctor and Invoke) are sufficient to allow the delegate to be used for synchronous calls, which are the usual method calls when the calling thread is blocked until the called method returns. The first method (.ctor) creates the delegate instance and binds it to the delegated method. The Invoke method is used to make a synchronous call of the delegated method.

Delegates also can be used for asynchronous calls, when the called method is executed on a separate thread created by the common language runtime for this purpose and does not block the calling thread. So that it can be called asynchronously, a delegate must define two additional methods, BeginInvoke and EndInvoke.

BeginInvoke is a thread starter. It takes all the parameters of the delegated method plus two more: a delegate of type [mscorlib]System.AsyncCallback representing a callback method that is invoked when the call completes, and an object you choose to indicate the final status of the call thread. BeginInvoke returns an instance of the interface [mscorlib]System.IAsyncResult, carrying the object you passed as the last parameter. Remember that since interfaces, delegates, and objects are reference types, when I say "takes a delegate" or "returns an interface," I actually mean a reference.

If you want to be notified immediately when the call is completed, you must specify the AsyncCallback delegate. The respective callback method is called upon the completion of the asynchronous call. This event-driven technique is the most widely used way to react to the completion of the asynchronous calls.

You might choose another way to monitor the status of the asynchronous call thread: polling from the main thread. The returned interface has the method bool get_IsCompleted(), which returns true when the asynchronous call is completed. You can call this method from time to time from the main thread to find out whether the call is finished.

You can also call another method of the returned interface, get_AsyncWaitHandle, which returns a wait handle, an instance of the [mscorlib]System.Threading.WaitHandle class. After you get the wait handle, you can monitor it any way you please (similar to the use of the Win32 APIs WaitForSingleObject and WaitForMultipleObjects). If you are curious, disassemble Mscorlib.dll and take a look at this class.

If you have chosen to employ a polling technique, you can forgo the callback function and specify null instead of the System.AsyncCallback delegate instance.

The EndInvoke method takes the [mscorlib]System.IAsyncResult interface, returned by BeginInvoke, as its single argument and returns void. This method waits for the asynchronous call to complete, blocking the calling thread, so calling it immediately after BeginInvoke is equivalent to a synchronous call using Invoke. EndInvoke must be called eventually in order to clear the corresponding runtime threading table entry, but it should be done when you know that the asynchronous call has been completed.

All four methods of a delegate are virtual, and their implementation is provided by the CLR itself—the user does not need to write the body of these methods. When defining a delegate, we can simply declare the methods without providing implementation for them, as shown here:

```
.class public sealed MyDelegate
    extends [mscorlib]System.MulticastDelegate
{
    .method public hidebysig instance
        void .ctor(object MethodsClass,
                    native unsigned int MethodPtr)
            runtime managed { }

    .method public hidebysig virtual instance
        int32 Invoke(void* Arg1, void* Arg2)
            runtime managed { }

    .method public hidebysig newslot virtual instance
        class [mscorlib]System.IAsyncResult
            BeginInvoke(void* Arg1, void* Arg2,
                        class [mscorlib]System.AsyncCallback callBkPtr,
                        object) runtime managed { }
```

```
.method public hidebysig newslot virtual instance
    void EndInvoke(class [mscorlib]System.IAsyncResult res )
        runtime managed { }
}
```

Nested Types

Nested types are types (classes, interfaces, value types) that are defined within other types. However, being defined within another type does not make the nested type anything like the member classes or Java inner classes. The instance pointers (this) of a nested type and its enclosing type are in no way related. A nested class does not automatically get access to the this pointer of its enclosing class when the instance of the enclosing class is created.

In addition, instantiating the enclosing class does not involve instantiating the class(es) nested in it. The nested classes must be instantiated separately. Instantiating a nested class does not require the enclosing class to be instantiated.

Type nesting is not about membership and joint instantiation; rather, it's all about visibility. As explained earlier in "Class Attributes," nested types at any level of nesting have their own specific visibility flags. When one type is nested in another type, the visibility of the nested type is "filtered" by the visibility of the enclosing type. If, for example, a class whose visibility is set to nested public is nested in a private class, this nested class will not be visible outside the assembly despite its own specified visibility.

This visibility filtering works throughout all levels of nesting. The final visibility of a nested class is defined by its own declared visibility and then is limited in sequence by the visibilities of all classes enclosing it, directly or indirectly.

Nested classes are defined in ILAsm the same way they are defined in other languages—that is, the nested classes are declared within the lexical scope of their encloser declaration:

```
.class public MyNameSpace.Encl {
    ...
    .class nested public Nestd1 {
        ...
        .class nested family Nestd2 {
            ...
        }
    }
}
```

According to this declaration, the Nestd2 class is nested in the Nestd1 class, which in turn is nested in MyNameSpace.Encl, which is not a nested class.

Full names of the nested classes are not in any way affected by the names of their enclosers: neither the namespace nor the name of the encloser automatically becomes (or is required to be) part of the nested class's full name. The full name of a nested class must be unique within the encloser scope, meaning that a class cannot have two identically named classes nested in it.

Since the nested classes are identified by their full name and their encloser (which is in turn identified by its scope and full name), the nested classes are referenced in ILAsm as a concatenation of the encloser reference, nesting symbol / (forward slash), and full name of the nested class:

```
<nested_class_ref> ::= <encloser_ref> / <full_type_name>
```

where

```
<encloser_ref> ::= <nested_class_ref> | <class_ref>
```

and `<class_ref>` has already been defined earlier as follows:

```
<class_ref> ::= [<resolution_scope>]<full_type_name>
```

According to these definitions, classes Nestd1 and Nestd2 will be referenced respectively as MyNameSpace.Encl/Nestd1 and MyNameSpace.Encl/Nestd1/Nestd2. Names of nested classes must be unique within their nester, as opposed to the full names of top-level classes, which must be unique within the module or (for public classes) within the assembly.

Unlike C#, which uses a dot delimiter for all hierarchical relationships without discrimination—so that One.Two.Three might mean "class Three of namespace One.Two" or "class Three nested in class Two of namespace One" or even "field Three of class Two nested in class One"—ILAsm uses different delimiters for different hierarchies. A dot is used for the full class name hierarchy; a forward slash (/) indicates the nesting hierarchy; and a double colon (::), as in "classic" C++, denotes the class-member relationship. I used the qualifier "classic" because the *managed* version of Visual C++ uses a double colon instead of a dot delimiter in dotted names, so it has the same ambiguity problem as C#, only instead of the ambiguous One.Two.Three, it uses the equally ambiguous One::Two::Three. That's a huge difference indeed.

Thus far, the discussion has focused mainly on what nested classes are not. One more important negative to note is that nested classes have no effect on the layout of their enclosers. If you want to declare a substructure of a structure, you must declare a nested value type (substructure) within the enclosing value type (structure) and then define a field of the substructure type:

```
.class public value Struct {
    ...
    .class nested public value Substruct {
        ...
    }
    .field public valuetype Struct/Substruct Substr
}
```

Now I need to say something positive about nested classes. Members of a nested class have access to all members of the enclosing class without exception, including access to private members. In this regard, the nesting relationship is even stronger than inheritance and stronger than the member class relationship in C++, where member classes don't have access to private members of their owner. Of course, to get access to the encloser's instance members, the nested type members should first obtain the instance pointer to the encloser. This "full disclosure" policy works one-way only; the encloser has no access to private members of the nested class.

Nested types can be used as base classes for other types that don't need to be nested:

```
.class public X {
   ...
   .class nested public Y {
     ...
   }
}
.class public Z extends X/Y {
   ...
}
```

Of course, class Z, derived from a nested class (Y), does not have any access rights to private members of the encloser (X). The "full disclosure" privilege is not inheritable.

A nested class can be derived from its encloser. In this case, it retains access to the encloser's private members, and it also acquires an ability to override the encloser's virtual methods. The enclosing class cannot be derived from any of its nested classes.

Note A metadata validity rule states that a nested class must be defined in the same module as its encloser. In ILAsm, however, the only way to define a nested class is to declare it within the encloser's lexical scope, which means you could not violate this validity rule in ILAsm even if you tried.

Class Augmentation

In ILAsm, as in Visual Basic and C#, all members, attributes, and nested classes of a class are declared within the lexical scope of that class. However, ILAsm allows you to reopen a once-closed class scope and define additional items:

```
.class public X extends Y implements IX,IY {
   ...
}
...
// Later in the source, possibly in another source file...
.class X {
   ... // More items defined
}
```

This reopening of the class scope is known as *class augmentation*. A class can be augmented any number of times throughout the source code, and the augmenting segments can reside in different source files. The following simple safety rules govern class augmentation:

- The class must be fully defined within the module—in other words, you cannot augment a class that is defined somewhere else. (Wouldn't that be nice? Good-bye, security—fare thee well!)

- Class flags, the extends clause, and the implements clause must be fully defined at the lexically first opening of class scope, because these attributes are ignored in augmenting segments.

- None of the augmenting segments can contain duplicate item declarations. If you declare field int32 X in one segment and then declare it in another segment, the ILAsm compiler will not appreciate that you probably have the same field in mind and will read it as an attempt to define two identical fields in the same class, which is not allowed.

- The augmenting segments are not explicitly numbered, and the class is augmented according to the sequence of augmenting segments in the source code. This means the sequence of class item declarations will change if you swap augmenting segments, which in turn might affect the class layout.

A good strategy for writing an ILAsm program in versions 1.0 and 1.1 was to use forward class declaration, explained in the Chapter 1. This strategy allows you to declare *all* classes of the current module, including nested ones, without any members and attributes, and to define the members and attributes in augmenting segments. This way, the IL assembler gets the full picture of the module's type declaration structure before any type is referenced. By the time locally declared types are referenced, they all are already defined and have corresponding TypeDef metadata records.

There is no need for forward class declaration in version 2.0 of ILAsm, though. In v2.0, the IL assembler implicitly declares a class whenever this class is mentioned, as a declaration or as a reference. Of course, the class implicitly declared on a reference is just a dummy—a placeholder. It turns from a dummy to "real" class declaration when the declaration of the class (.class ... { ... }) is encountered in the source code. If all compilands are parsed, and there still are "dummies" remaining, the compilation fails.

This method of class "bookkeeping" messes up royally the order of class declaration on round-tripping (disassembling and reassembling of a module), because the classes in the round-tripped module are emitted not in the order they were emitted in the original module, but rather in the order they were mentioned in the disassembly. This is a minor issue, because the order of class definitions (TypeDef records) does not really matter, except in the case of nested classes (enclosing class must be declared before the nested class), and this case is handled properly by the IL assembler.

If, however, you want to preserve the order of class declarations or you have some considerations to emit the class declarations in some particular order, you can use directive .typelist:

.typelist { FirstClass SecondClass ThirdClass ...}

The .typelist directive is best placed right on top of the first source file, even before the manifest declarations but after the .mscorlib directive, if present. The reason for such placing is obvious: the IL assembler needs to know right away if you are compiling Mscorlib.dll or something else, and the manifest declarations might have custom attributes, or other class references, that could mix up the intended order of class declaration.

Manifest declarations, described in Chapter 6, plus forward class declarations (v1.0, v1.1) or the .typelist directive (v2.0), look a lot like a program header, so I would not blame you if you put them in a separate source file. Just don't forget that this file must be first on the list of source files when you assemble your module.

Summary of the Metadata Validity Rules

Recall that the type-related metadata tables (except those related to generic types, which will be discussed in Chapter 11) include TypeDef, TypeRef, InterfaceImpl, NestedClass, and ClassLayout. The records of these tables contain the following entries:

- The TypeDef table contains the Flags, Name, Namespace, Extends, FieldList, and MethodList entries.

- The TypeRef table contains the ResolutionScope, Name, and Namespace entries.

- The InterfaceImpl table contains the Class and Interface entries.

- The NestedClass table contains the NestedClass and EnclosingClass entries.

- The ClassLayout table contains the PackingSize, ClassSize, and Parent entries.

TypeDef Table Validity Rules

- The Flags entry can have only those bits set that are defined in the enumeration CorTypeAttr in CorHdr.h except the tdForwarder flag, reserved for exported types (validity mask: 0x00173DBF).

- [run time] The Flags entry cannot have the sequential and explicit bits set simultaneously.

- [run time] The Flags entry cannot have the unicode and autochar bits set simultaneously.

- If the rtspecialname flag is set in the Flags entry, the Name field must be set to _Deleted*, and vice versa.

- [run time] If the bit 0x00040000 is set in the Flags entry, either a DeclSecurity record or a custom attribute named SuppressUnmanagedCodeSecurityAttribute must be associated with the TypeDef, and vice versa.

- [run time] If the interface flag is set in the Flags entry, abstract must be also set.

- [run time] If the interface flag is set in the Flags entry, sealed must not be set.

- [run time] If the interface flag is set in the Flags entry, the TypeDef must have no instance fields.

- [run time] If the interface flag is set in the Flags entry, all the TypeDef's instance methods must be abstract.

- [run time] The visibility flag of a non-nested TypeDef must be set to private or public.

- [run time] If the visibility flag of a TypeDef is set to nested public, nested private, nested family, nested assembly, nested famorassem, or nested famandassem, the TypeDef must be referenced in the NestedClass entry of one of the records in the NestedClass metadata table, and vice versa.

- The Name field must reference a nonempty string in the #Strings stream.

- The combined length of the strings referenced by the Name and Namespace entries must not exceed 1,023 bytes.

- The TypeDef table must contain no duplicate records with the same full name (the namespace plus the name) unless the TypeDef is nested or deleted.

- [run time] The Extends entry must be nil for TypeDefs with the interface flag set and for the TypeDef System.Object of the Mscorlib assembly.

- [run time] The Extends entry of all other TypeDefs must hold a valid reference to the TypeDef, TypeRef, or TypeSpec table, and this reference must point at a nonsealed class (not an interface or a value type).

- [run time] The Extends entry must not point to the type itself or to any of the type descendants (inheritance loop).

- [run time] The FieldList entry can be nil or hold a valid reference to the Field table.

- [run time] The MethodList entry can be nil or hold a valid reference to the Method table.

Enumeration-Specific Validity Rules

If the TypeDef is an enum—that is, if the Extends entry holds the reference to the class [mscorlib]System.Enum—the following additional rules apply:

- [run time] The interface, abstract, sequential, and explicit flags must not be set in the Flags entry.

- The sealed flag must be set in the Flags entry.

- The TypeDef must have no methods, events, or properties.

- The TypeDef must implement no interfaces—that is, it must not be referenced in the Class entry of any record in the InterfaceImpl table.

- [run time] The TypeDef must have at least one instance field of integer type or of type bool or char.

- [run time] All static fields of the TypeDef must be literal.

- The type of the static fields of the TypeDef must be the current TypeDef itself.

TypeRef Table Validity Rules

- [run time] The ResolutionScope entry must hold either 0 or a valid reference to the AssemblyRef, ModuleRef, Module, or TypeRef table. In the last case, TypeRef refers to a type nested in another type (a nested TypeRef).

- If the ResolutionScope entry is nil, the ExportedType table of the prime module of the assembly must contain a record whose TypeName and TypeNamespace entries match the Name and Namespace entries of the TypeRef record, respectively.

- [run time] The Name entry must reference a nonempty string in the #Strings stream.

- [run time] The combined length of the strings referenced by the Name and Namespace entries must not exceed 1,023 bytes.

- The table must contain no duplicate records with the same full name (the namespace plus the name) and ResolutionScope value.

InterfaceImpl Table Validity Rules

A Class entry set to nil means a deleted InterfaceImpl record. If the Class entry is non-nil, however, the following rules apply:

- [run time] The Class entry must hold a valid reference to the TypeDef table.

- [run time] The Interface entry must hold a valid reference to the TypeDef or TypeRef table.

- If the Interface field references the TypeDef table, the corresponding TypeDef record must have the interface flag set in the Flags entry.

- The table must contain no duplicate records with the same Class and Interface entries.

NestedClass Table Validity Rules

- The NestedClass entry must hold a valid reference to the TypeDef table.

- [run time] The EnclosingClass entry must hold a valid reference to the TypeDef table, one that differs from the reference held by the NestedClass entry.

- The table must contain no duplicate records with the same NestedClass entries.

- The table must contain no records with the same EnclosingClass entries and NestedClass entries referencing TypeDef records with matching names—in other words, a nested class must have a unique name within its encloser.

- The table must contain no sets of records forming a circular nesting pattern—for example, A nested in B, B nested in C, C nested in A.

ClassLayout Table Validity Rules

A Parent entry set to nil means a deleted ClassLayout record. However, if the Parent entry is non-nil, the following rules apply:

- The Parent entry must hold a valid reference to the TypeDef table, and the referenced TypeDef record must have the Flags bit explicit or sequential set and must have the interface bit not set.

- [run time] The PackingSize entry must be set to 0 or to a power of 2 in the range 1 to 128.

- The table must contain no duplicate records with the same Parent entries.

CHAPTER 8

■■■

Primitive Types and Signatures

Having looked at how types are defined in the common language runtime and ILAsm, let's proceed to the question of how these types and their derivatives are assigned to program items—fields, variables, methods, and so on. The constructs defining the types of program items are known as the *signatures* of these items. Signatures are built from encoded references to various classes and value types; I'll discuss signatures in detail in this chapter.

But before we start analyzing the signatures of program items, let's consider the building blocks of these signatures.

Primitive Types in the Common Language Runtime

All types have to be defined somewhere. The Microsoft .NET Framework class library defines hundreds of types, and other assemblies build their own types based on the types defined in the class library. Some of the types defined in the class library are recognized by the common language runtime as primitive types and are given special encoding in the signatures. This is done only for the sake of performance—theoretically, the signatures could have been built from type tokens only, given that every type is defined somewhere and hence has a token. But resolving all these tokens simply to find that they reference trivial items such as a 4-byte integer or a Boolean value can hardly be considered a sensible way to work at the run time.

Primitive Data Types

The term *primitive data types* refers to the types defined in the .NET Framework class library that are given specific individual type codes to be used in signatures. Because all these types are defined in the assembly Mscorlib and all belong to the namespace System, I have omitted the prefix [mscorlib]System when supplying the class library type name for a type.

The individual type codes are defined in the enumeration CorElementType in the header file CorHdr.h. The names of all these codes begin with ELEMENT_TYPE_, which I have either omitted in this chapter or abbreviated as E_T_.

Table 8-1 describes primitive data types and their respective ILAsm notation.

Table 8-1. *Primitive Data Types Defined in the Runtime*

Code	Constant Name	.NET Framework Type Name	ILAsm Notation	Comments
0x01	VOID	Void	void	
0x02	BOOLEAN	Boolean	bool	Single-byte value, true = 1, false = 0
0x03	CHAR	Char	char	2-byte unsigned integer, representing a Unicode character
0x04	I1	SByte	int8	Signed 1-byte integer, the same as char in C/C++
0x05	U1	Byte	unsigned int8	Unsigned 1-byte integer
0x06	I2	Int16	int16	Signed 2-byte integer
0x07	U2	UInt16	unsigned int16	Unsigned 2-byte integer
0x08	I4	Int32	int32	Signed 4-byte integer
0x09	U4	UInt32	unsigned int32	Unsigned 4-byte integer
0x0 A	I8	Int64	int64	Signed 8-byte integer
0x0 B	U8	UInt64	unsigned int64	Unsigned 8-byte integer
0x0 C	R4	Single	float32	4-byte floating point
0x0 D	R8	Double	float64	8-byte floating point
0x16	TYPEDBYREF	TypedReference	typedref	Typed reference, carrying both a reference to a type and information identifying the referenced type
0x18	I	IntPtr	native int	Pointer-size integer; size dependent on the target platform, which explains the use of the keyword native
0x19	U	UIntPtr	native unsigned int	Pointer-size unsigned integer

Data Pointer Types

The common language runtime distinguishes between pointers that must point at the beginning of an object allocated on the garbage-collected heap (called *object references*; see "Representing Classes") and other pointers.

Two data pointer types are defined in the common language runtime: the managed pointer and the unmanaged pointer. The difference is that a managed pointer is managed by the runtime's garbage collection subsystem and stays valid even if the referenced item is moved in memory during the process of garbage collection, whereas an unmanaged pointer can be safely used only in association with "unmovable" items.

Both pointer types must be followed by the referent types to which the pointers point. As types constructed from referent types, the pointers have no corresponding types defined in the .NET Framework class library and cannot be boxed. Table 8-2 describes the two pointer types and their ILAsm notations. Neither of them has an associated .NET Framework type.

Table 8-2. *Pointer Types Defined in the Runtime*

Code	Constant Name	ILAsm Notation	Comments
0x0F	PTR	<type>*	Unmanaged pointer to <type>
0x10	BYREF	<type>&	Managed pointer to <type>

Note Although ILAsm notation places the pointer character after the pointed type, in signatures E_T_PTR and E_T_BYREF always precede the referent type.

Pointers of both types are subject to standard pointer arithmetic: an integer can be added to or subtracted from a pointer, resulting in a pointer; and one pointer can be subtracted from another, resulting in an integer value. The difference between pointer arithmetic in, say, C/C++ (see Listing 8-1) and in IL is that in IL—and hence in ILAsm (see Listing 8-2)—the increments and decrements of pointers are always specified in bytes, regardless of the size of the item the pointer represents.

Listing 8-1. *C/C++*

```
long L, *pL=&L;
...
pL += 4; //  pL is incremented by 4*sizeof(long) = 16 bytes
```

Listing 8-2. *ILAsm*

```
.locals init(int32 L, int32& pL)
ldloca L    // Load pointer to L on stack
stloc pL    // pL = &L
...
ldloc pL    // Load pL on stack
ldc.i4 4    // Load 4 on stack
add
stloc pL    // pL += 4, pL is incremented by 4 bytes
```

By the same token...now, this is just a common expression. I'm not referring to metadata tokens. (I think I'd better be extra careful with phrases like "by the same token" or "token of appreciation" in this book.) In the same way, the delta of two pointers in IL is always expressed in bytes, not in the items pointed at.

Using unmanaged pointers in IL is never considered safe (verifiable). Because of the unlimited access that C-style pointer arithmetic gives to anybody for anything, IL code, which has unmanaged pointers dereferenced, is deemed unverifiable and can be run when the code comes from a trusted source (such as a local drive).

Managed pointers are tamed, domesticated pointers, fully owned by the common language runtime type control and the garbage collection subsystem. These pointers dwell in a safe but not too spacious corral, fenced along the following lines:

- Managed pointers are always references to an item in existence—a field, an array element, a local variable, or a method argument.

- Array elements and fields *cannot* have managed pointer types.

- Managed pointer types can be used only for method attributes—local variables, parameters, or a return type, and it is not a simple coincidence that all these items are stack allocated.

- Managed pointers that point to "managed memory" (the garbage collector heap, which contains object instances and arrays) cannot be converted to unmanaged pointers.

- Managed pointers that don't point to the garbage collector heap can be converted to unmanaged pointers, but such conversion renders the IL code unverifiable.

- The underlying type of a managed pointer cannot be another pointer, but it can be an object reference.

Managed pointers are different from object references. In Chapter 7, which described boxing and unboxing of the value types, you saw that it takes boxing to create an object reference to a value type. Using a simple reference—that is, a managed pointer—is not enough.

The difference is that an object reference points to the start (method table) of an object, whereas a managed pointer points to the object's interior—the value (data) part of the item. When you take a managed pointer to an instance of a value type, you address the data part. You can have only this much because instances of value types, not being objects, have no method tables.

When you box a value type instance, you create an object, a class instance with its own method table and data part copied from the value type instance. This object is represented by an object reference.

Function Pointer Types

Chapter 7 briefly described the use of managed function pointers and compared them with delegate types. Managed function pointers are represented by type E_T_FNPTR, which is indicated by the value 0x1B and doesn't have a .NET Framework type associated.

Just like a data pointer type, a function pointer type is a constructed type that does not exist by itself and must be followed by the full signature of the method to which it points. (Method signatures are discussed later in this chapter; see "Signatures.")

The ILAsm notation for a function pointer is as follows:

```
method <call_conv> <return_type> * (<type>[,<type>*])
```

where <call_conv> is a calling convention, <return_type> is the return type, and the <type> sequence in the parentheses is the argument list. You'll find more details in the "Signatures" section.

Vectors and Arrays

The common language runtime recognizes two types of arrays: vectors and multidimensional arrays, as described in Table 8-3. Vectors are single-dimensional arrays with a zero lower bound. Multidimensional arrays, which I'll refer to as *arrays,* can have more than one dimension and nonzero lower bounds. Both array types are constructed types, so neither of them has an associated .NET Framework type.

Table 8-3. *Arrays Supported in the Runtime*

Code	Constant Name	ILAsm Notation	Comments
0x1D	SZARRAY	\<type\>[ ]	Vector of \<type\>
0x14	ARRAY	\<type\>[\<bounds\> [,\<bounds\>*]]	Array of \<type\>

All vectors and arrays are objects (class instances) derived from the abstract class [mscorlib]System.Array.

Vector encoding is simple: E_T_SZARRAY followed by the encoding of the underlying type, which can be anything except void. The size of the vector is not part of the encoding. Since arrays and vectors are object references, it is not enough to simply declare an array—you must create an instance of it, using the instruction newarr for a vector or calling an array constructor. It is at that point that the size of the vector or array instance is specified. Thus, the size of an array is an attribute of an instance of an array, not the type of the array.

Array encoding is more sophisticated:

E_T_ARRAY\<underlying_type\>\<rank\>\<num_sizes\>\<size1\>...\<sizeN\>
       \<num_lower_bounds\>\<lower_bound1\>...\<lower_boundM\>

where the following is true:

\<underlying_type\> cannot be void
\<rank\> is the number of array dimensions (K>0)
\<num_sizes\> is the number of specified sizes for dimensions (N <= K)
\<sizen\> is an unsigned integer specifying the size (n = 1,...,N)
\<num_lower_bounds\> is the number of specified lower bounds (M <= K)
\<lower_boundm\> is a signed integer specifying the lower bound (m = 1,...,M)

All the unsigned integer values among the previous are compressed according to the length compression formula discussed in Chapter 5. To save you a trip three chapters back, I will repeat this formula in Table 8-4.

Table 8-4. *The Length Compression Formula for Unsigned Integers*

Value Range	Compressed Size	Compressed Value (Big Endian)
0–0x7F	1 byte	\<value\>
0x80–0x3FFF	2 bytes	0x8000 | \<value\>
0x4000–0x1FFFFFFF	4 bytes	0xC0000000 | \<value\>

Signed integer values (lower bound values) are compressed according to a different compression procedure. First the signed integer is encoded as an unsigned integer by taking the absolute value of the original integer, shifting it left by 1 bit, and setting the least significant bit according to the most significant (sign) bit of the original value. Then compression is applied according to the formula shown in Table 8-4.

If size and/or the lower bound for a dimension are not specified, they are not presumed to be 0; rather, they are marked as not specified. The specification of size and lower bound cannot have "holes"—that is, if you have an array of rank 5 and want to specify size (or lower bound) for its third dimension, you must specify size (or lower bound) for the first and second dimensions as well.

An array specification in ILAsm looks like this:

```
<type> [ <bounds>[, <bounds>*] ]
```

where

```
<bounds> ::= [<lower_bound>] ... [<upper_bound>]
```

The following is an example:

```
int32[..., ...] // Two-dimensional array with undefined lower bounds
                // And sizes
int32[2...5]  // One-dimensional array with lower bound 2 and size 4
int32[0..., 0...] // Two-dimensional array with zero lower bounds
                  // And undefined sizes
```

If neither lower bound nor upper bound is specified for a dimension in a multidimensional array declaration, the ellipsis can be omitted. Thus, int32[...,...] and int32[,] mean the same: a two-dimensional array with no lower bounds or sizes specified.

This omission does not work in the case of single-dimensional arrays, however. The notation int32[] indicates a vector (<E_T_SZARRAY><E_T_I4>), and int32[...] indicates an array of rank 1 whose lower bound and size are undefined (<E_T_ARRAY><E_T_I4><1><0><0>).

The common language runtime treats multidimensional arrays and vectors of vectors (of vectors, and so on) completely differently. The specifications int32[,] and int32[ ][ ] result in different type encoding, are created differently, and are laid out differently when created:

int32[,]: This specification has the encoding <E_T_ARRAY><E_T_I4><2><0><0>, is created by a single call to an array constructor, and is laid out as a contiguous two-dimensional array of int32.

int32[ ][ ]: This specification has the encoding <E_T_SZARRAY><E_T_SZARRAY><E_T_I4>, is created by a series of newarr instructions, and is laid out as a vector of vector references, each pointing to a contiguous vector of int32, with no guarantee regarding the location of each vector. Vectors of vectors are useful for describing jagged arrays, when the size of the second dimension varies depending on the first dimension index.

Modifiers

Four built-in common language runtime type codes, described in Table 8-5, do not denote any specific data or pointer type but rather are used as modifiers of data and pointer types. None of these modifiers has an associated .NET Framework type.

Table 8-5. *Modifiers Defined in the Runtime*

Code	Constant Name	ILAsm Notation	Comments
0x1F	CMOD_REQD	modreq(<class_ref>)	Required custom modifier
0x20	CMOD_OPT	modopt(<class_ref>)	Optional custom modifier
0x41	SENTINEL	...	Start of optional arguments in a vararg method call
0x45	PINNED	pinned	Marks a local variable as unmovable by the garbage collector

The modifiers modreq and modopt indicate that the item to which they are attached—an argument, a return type, or a field, for example—must be treated in some special way. These modifiers are followed by TypeDef or TypeRef tokens, and the classes corresponding to these tokens indicate the special way the item is to be handled.

The tokens following modreq and modopt are compressed according to the following algorithm. As you might remember, an uncoded (external) metadata token is a 4-byte unsigned integer, which has the token type in its senior byte and an RID in its 3 lower bytes. It so happens that the tokens appearing in the signatures and hence requiring compression are of three types only: TypeDef, TypeRef, or TypeSpec. (See "Signatures" later in this chapter for information about TypeSpecs.) Because of that, only 2 bits, rather than a whole byte, are required for the token type: 00 denotes TypeDef, 01 is used for TypeRef, and 10 specifies TypeSpec. The token compression procedure resembles the procedure used to compress the signed integers: the RID part of the token is shifted left by 2 bits, and the 2-bit type encoding is placed in the least significant bits. The result is compressed just as any unsigned integer would be, according to the formula shown earlier in Table 8-4.

The modifiers modreq and modopt are used primarily by tools other than the common language runtime, such as compilers or program analyzers. The modreq modifier indicates that the modifier must be taken into account, whereas modopt indicates that the modifier is optional and can be ignored. The ILAsm compiler does not use these modifiers for its internal purposes.

The only use of the modreq and modopt modifiers recognized by the common language runtime is when these modifiers are applied to return types or parameters of methods subject to managed/unmanaged marshaling. For example, to specify that a managed method must have the cdecl calling convention when it is marshaled as unmanaged, you can use the following modifier attached to the method's return type:

modopt([mscorlib]System.Runtime.CompilerServices.CallConvCdecl)

When used in the context of managed/unmanaged marshaling, the modreq and modopt modifiers are equivalent.

Although the modreq and modopt modifiers have no effect on the managed types of the items to which they are attached, signatures with and without these modifiers are considered different. The same is true for signatures differing only in classes referenced by these modifiers. This allows, for example, the overloading of functions having arguments of type int and long. In C/C++, int and long are two different types, but for CLR they are the same—32-bit signed integers (E_T_I4). So in order to distinguish these two types, C++ compiler emits long as modopt([mscorlib]System.Runtime.CompilerServices.IsLong)int32. Another modifier often used by the C++ compiler is modopt([mscorlib]System.Runtime.CompilerServices.IsConst), to distinguish, for example, the C types int* and const int*. Custom modifiers were introduced to accommodate C++ type system, but they are not specific to C++. Other high-level languages might also require distinguishing certain types, which are indistinguishable from the CLR's point of view.

The sentinel modifier (...) was introduced in Chapter 1, when we analyzed the declaration and calling of methods with a variable-length argument list (vararg methods). A sentinel signifies the beginning of optional arguments supplied for a vararg method call. This modifier can appear in only one context: at the call site, because the optional parameters of a vararg method are not specified when such a method is declared. The runtime treats a sentinel appearing in any other context as an error. The method arguments at the call site can contain only one sentinel, and the sentinel is used only if optional arguments are supplied:

```
// Declaration of vararg method - mandatory parameters only:
.method public static vararg int32 Print(string Format)
{
    ...
}
...
// Calling vararg method with two optional arguments:
call vararg int32 Print(string, ..., int32, int32)
...
// Calling vararg method without optional arguments:
call vararg int32 Print(string)
```

The pinned modifier is applicable to the method's local variables only. Its use means that the object referenced by the local variable cannot be relocated by the garbage collector and must stay put throughout the method execution. If a local variable representing an object reference or a managed pointer is "pinned," it is safe to convert it to an unmanaged pointer and then to dereference this unmanaged pointer, because the unmanaged pointer is guaranteed to still be valid when it is dereferenced (it is safe in the sense of dereferencing, but it is still unverifiable, as is any usage of an unmanaged pointer):

```
.locals init(class Foo A, class Foo pinned B, int32* pA, int32* pB)
ldloc A
ldflda int32 Foo::x
stloc pA        // pA = &A->x
ldloc B
ldflda int32 Foo::x
stloc pB        // pB = &B->x
...
ldloc pA
ldc.i4 123
```

```
stind.i4       // *pA=123 - unsafe, A could have been moved
ldloc pB
ldc.i4 123
stind.i4       // *pB=123 - safe, B is pinned and cannot move
```

Native Types

When managed code calls unmanaged methods or exposes managed fields to unmanaged code, it is sometimes necessary to provide specific information about how the managed types should be marshaled to and from the unmanaged types. The unmanaged types recognizable by the common language runtime, also referred to as *native*, are listed in CorHdr.h in the enumeration CorNativeType. All constants in this enumeration have names that begin with NATIVE_TYPE_* ; for the purposes of this discussion, I have omitted these parts of the names or abbreviated them as N_T_. The same constants are also listed in the .NET Framework class library in the enumerator System.Runtime.InteropServices.UnmanagedType.

Some of the native types are obsolete and are ignored by the runtime interoperability subsystem. But since these native types are not retired altogether, ILAsm must have ways to denote them—and since ILAsm denotes these types, I cannot help but list obsolete types along with others, all of which you'll find in Table 8-6.

Table 8-6. *Native Types Defined in the Runtime*

Code	Constant Name	.NET Framework Type Name	ILAsm Notation	Comments
0x01	VOID		void	Obsolete and thus should not be used; recognized by ILAsm but ignored by the runtime interoperability subsystem
0x02	BOOLEAN	Bool	bool	4-byte Boolean value; true = nonzero, false = 0
0x03	I1	I1	int8	Signed 1-byte integer
0x04	U1	U1	unsigned int8, uint8	Unsigned 1-byte integer
0x05	I2	I2	int16	Signed 2-byte integer
0x06	U2	U2	unsigned int16, uint16	Unsigned 2-byte integer
0x07	I4	I4	int32	Signed 4-byte integer
0x08	U4	U4	unsigned int32, uint32	Unsigned 4-byte integer
0x09	I8	I8	int64	Signed 8-byte integer
0x0A	U8	U8	unsigned int64, uint64	Unsigned 8-byte integer
0x0B	R4	R4	float32	4-byte floating point
0x0C	R8	R8	float64	8-byte floating point
0x0D	SYSCHAR		syschar	Obsolete

Continued

Table 8-6. *Continued*

Code	Constant Name	.NET Framework Type Name	ILAsm Notation	Comments
0x0E	VARIANT		variant	Obsolete
0x0F	CURRENCY	Currency	currency	Currency value
0x10	PTR		*	Obsolete; use native int
0x11	DECIMAL		decimal	Obsolete
0x12	DATE		date	Obsolete
0x13	BSTR	BStr	bstr	Unicode Visual Basic–style string, used in COM interoperations
0x14	LPSTR	LPStr	lpstr	Pointer to a zero-terminated ANSI string
0x15	LPWSTR	LPWStr	lpwstr	Pointer to a zero-terminated Unicode string
0x16	LPTSTR	LPTStr	lptstr	Pointer to a zero-terminated ANSI or Unicode string, depending on platform
0x17	FIXEDSYSSTRING	ByValTStr	fixed sysstring [<size>]	Fixed-size system string of size <size> bytes; applicable to field marshaling only
0x18	OBJECTREF		objectref	Obsolete
0x19	IUNKNOWN	IUnknown	iunknown	IUnknown interface pointer
0x1A	IDISPATCH	IDispatch	idispatch	IDispatch interface pointer
0x1B	STRUCT	Struct	struct	C-style structure, for marshaling the formatted managed types
0x1C	INTF	Interface	interface	Interface pointer
0x1D	SAFEARRAY	SafeArray	safearray <variant_type>	Safe array of type <variant_type>
0x1E	FIXEDARRAY	ByValArray	fixed array [<size>]	Fixed-size array, of size <size> bytes
0x1F	INT	IntPtr	int	Signed pointer-size integer
0x20	UINT	UIntPtr	unsigned int, uint	Unsigned pointer-size integer
0x21	NESTEDSTRUCT		nested struct	Obsolete; use struct
0x22	BYVALSTR	VBByRefStr	byvalstr	Visual Basic–style string in a fixed-length buffer
0x23	ANSIBSTR	AnsiBStr	ansi bstr	ANSI Visual Basic–style string
0x24	TBSTR	TBStr	tbstr	bstr or ansi bstr, depending on the platform
0x25	VARIANTBOOL	VariantBool	variant bool	2-byte Boolean; true = –1, false = 0

Continued

Table 8-6. *Continued*

Code	Constant Name	.NET Framework Type Name	ILAsm Notation	Comments
0x26	FUNC	FunctionPtr	method	Function pointer
0x28	ASANY	AsAny	as any	Object; type defined at run time
0x2A	ARRAY	LPArray	<n_type> [<sizes>]	Fixed-size array of a native type <n_type>
0x2B	LPSTRUCT	LPStruct	lpstruct	Pointer to a C-style structure
0x2C	CUSTOMMARSHALER	CustomMarshaler	custom (<class_str>, <cookie_str>)	Custom marshaler
0x2D	ERROR	Error	error	Maps int32 to VT_HRESULT

The <sizes> parameter in the ILAsm notation for N_T_ARRAY, shown in Table 8-6, can be empty or can be formatted as <size> + <size_param_number>:

```
<sizes> ::= <>
          | <size>
          | + <size_param_number>
          | <size> + <size_param_number>
```

If <sizes> is empty, the size of the native array is derived from the size of the managed array being marshaled.

The <size> parameter specifies the native array size in array items. The zero-based method parameter number <size_param_number> indicates which of the method parameters specifies the size of the native array. The total size of the native array is <size> plus the additional size specified by the method parameter that is indicated by <size_param_number>.

A custom marshaler declaration (shown in Table 8-6) has two parameters, both of which are quoted strings. The <class_str> parameter is the name of the class representing the custom marshaler, using the string conventions of Reflection.Emit. The <cookie_str> parameter is an argument string (cookie) passed to the custom marshaler at run time. This string identifies the form of the marshaling required, and its notation is specific to the custom marshaler.

Variant Types

Variant types (popular in COM) are defined in the enumeration VARENUM in the Wtypes.h file, which is distributed with Microsoft Visual Studio. Not all variant types are applicable as safe array types, according to Wtypes.h, but ILAsm provides notation for all of them nevertheless, as shown in Table 8-7. It might look strange, considering that variant types appear in ILAsm only in the context of safe array specification, but we should not forget that one of ILAsm's principal applications is the generation of test programs, which contain known, preprogrammed errors.

Table 8-7. *Variant Types Defined in the Runtime*

Code	Constant Name	Applicable to Safe Array?	ILAsm Notation
0x00	VT_EMPTY	No	<empty>
0x01	VT_NULL	No	null
0x02	VT_I2	Yes	int16
0x03	VT_I4	Yes	int32
0x04	VT_R4	Yes	float32
0x05	VT_R8	Yes	float64
0x06	VT_CY	Yes	currency
0x07	VT_DATE	Yes	date
0x08	VT_BSTR	Yes	bstr
0x09	VT_DISPATCH	Yes	idispatch
0x0A	VT_ERROR	Yes	error
0x0B	VT_BOOL	Yes	bool
0x0C	VT_VARIANT	Yes	variant
0x0D	VT_UNKNOWN	Yes	iunknown
0x0E	VT_DECIMAL	Yes	decimal
0x10	VT_I1	Yes	int8
0x11	VT_UI1	Yes	unsigned int8, uint8
0x12	VT_UI2	Yes	unsigned int16, uint16
0x13	VT_UI4	Yes	unsigned int32, uint32
0x14	VT_I8	No	int64
0x15	VT_UI8	No	unsigned int64, uint64
0x16	VT_INT	Yes	int
0x17	VT_UINT	Yes	unsigned int, uint
0x18	VT_VOID	No	void
0x19	VT_HRESULT	No	hresult
0x1A	VT_PTR	No	*
0x1B	VT_SAFEARRAY	No	safearray
0x1C	VT_CARRAY	No	carray
0x1D	VT_USERDEFINED	No	userdefined
0x1E	VT_LPSTR	No	lpstr
0x1F	VT_LPWSTR	No	lpwstr
0x24	VT_RECORD	Yes	record
0x40	VT_FILETIME	No	filetime
0x41	VT_BLOB	No	blob
0x42	VT_STREAM	No	stream
0x43	VT_STORAGE	No	storage

Continued

Table 8-7. *Continued*

Code	Constant Name	Applicable to Safe Array?	ILAsm Notation
0x44	VT_STREAMED_OBJECT	No	streamed_object
0x45	VT_STORED_OBJECT	No	stored_object
0x46	VT_BLOB_OBJECT	No	blob_object
0x47	VT_CF	No	cf
0x48	VT_CLSID	No	clsid
0x1000	VT_VECTOR	Yes	<v_type> vector
0x2000	VT_ARRAY	Yes	<v_type> [ ]
0x4000	VT_BYREF	Yes	<v_type> &

Representing Classes in Signatures

Remember the local variables signature from the "Modifiers" code snippet? It contained two references to some class Foo:

`.locals init(class Foo A, class Foo pinned B, int32* pA, int32* pB)`

The classes and value types in general are represented in signatures by their TypeDef or TypeRef tokens, preceded by E_T_CLASS or E_T_VALUETYPE, respectively, as shown in Table 8-8.

Table 8-8. *Representation of* CLASS *and* VALUETYPE

Code	Constant Name	.NET Framework Type Name	ILAsm Notation	Comments
0x11	VALUETYPE		valuetype <class_ref>	Value type
0x12	CLASS		class <class_ref>	Class or interface, except [mscorlib]System.Object and [mscorlib]System.String
0x0E	STRING	String	string	[mscorlib]System.String class
0x1C	OBJECT	Object	object	[mscorlib]System.Object class

As you can see in Table 8-8, two classes, String and Object, are assigned their own codes and hence should have been listed along with the primitive data types in Table 8-1, if it were not for their class nature. This is important: if a type (class or value type) is given its own code, it cannot be referenced in signatures other than by this code. In other words, the class [mscorlib]System.Object must appear in signatures as E_T_OBJECT and never as E_T_CLASS<token_of_Object>, and the value type [mscorlib]System.Int32 must appear in signatures as E_T_I4 and never as E_T_VALUETYPE<token_of_Int32>. This rule was introduced in the early stages of CLR development in an attempt to somehow reduce the anarchy reigning in the signature domain, where semantically identical signatures could be expressed in a dozen different ways. A nice side effect of this rule is that it minimizes the signatures.

The JIT compiler does not accept "long forms" of type encoding for types that have dedicated type codes assigned to them, and run-time signature validation procedures reject such signatures.

■**Caution** If a type (class or value type) is given its own code, it cannot be referenced in signatures other than by this code.

Signatures

Now that you know more about type encoding, let's look at how the types of the various items you find in a program are set in the common language runtime. Program items such as fields, methods, and local variables are not characterized by simply encoded types; rather, they are characterized by signatures. A *signature* is a byte array containing one or more encoded types and residing in the #Blob stream of metadata.

The following metadata tables refer to the signatures:

Field table: Field declaration signature

Method table: Method declaration signature

Property table: Property declaration signature

MemberRef table: Field or method referencing signature

StandAloneSig table: Local variables or indirect call signature

TypeSpec table: Type specification signature

Calling Conventions

The first byte of a signature identifies the type of the signature, which for historical reasons is called the calling convention of the signature, be it a method signature or some other signature. The CorHdr.h file defines the following calling convention constants in the enumeration CorCallingConvention:

- IMAGE_CEE_CS_CALLCONV_DEFAULT (0x0). Default ("normal") method with a fixed-length argument list. ILAsm has no keyword for this calling convention.

- IMAGE_CEE_CS_CALLCONV_VARARG (0x5). Method with a variable-length argument list. The ILAsm keyword is vararg.

- IMAGE_CEE_CS_CALLCONV_FIELD (0x6). Field. ILAsm has no keyword for this calling convention.

- IMAGE_CEE_CS_CALLCONV_LOCAL_SIG (0x7). Local variables. ILAsm has no keyword for this calling convention.

- IMAGE_CEE_CS_CALLCONV_PROPERTY (0x8). Property. ILAsm has no keyword for this calling convention.

- IMAGE_CEE_CS_CALLCONV_UNMGD (0x9). Unmanaged calling convention, not currently used by the common language runtime and not recognized by ILAsm.

- IMAGE_CEE_CS_CALLCONV_HASTHIS (0x20). Instance method that has an instance pointer (this) as an implicit first argument. The ILAsm keyword is instance.

- IMAGE_CEE_CS_CALLCONV_EXPLICITTHIS (0x40). Method call signature. The first explicitly specified parameter is the instance pointer. The ILAsm keyword is explicit.

The calling conventions instance and explicit are the modifiers of the default and vararg method calling conventions. The calling convention explicit can be used only in conjunction with instance and only at the call site, never in the method declaration.

Calling conventions for field, property, and local variables signatures don't need special ILAsm keywords because they are inferred from the context.

Field Signatures

A *field signature* is the simplest kind of signature. It consists of a single encoded type (SET), which of course follows the calling convention byte:

```
<field_sig> ::= <callconv_field> <SET>
```

Although this type encoding (SET) can be quite long, especially in the case of a multidimensional array or a function pointer, it is nevertheless a single type encoding. In a field signature, SET cannot have the &, pinned, and sentinel modifiers, and it cannot be void. The reasons are plain enough: only method parameters and local variables can be managed pointers and have the & modifier, only local variables can be pinned, only method references of vararg methods can have sentinel in signature, and only a method's return type can be void. And a field is none of those.

The field calling convention is always equal to IMAGE_CEE_CS_CALLCONV_FIELD, regardless of whether the field is static or instance. As a result, it is necessary to keep two sets of field manipulation instructions in the IL instruction set (described in Chapter 13)—for instance fields and for static fields. At the same time there is only one set of method call instructions, suitable for both instance and static methods, which are recognized by bit IMAGE_CEE_CS_CALLCONV_HASTHIS in calling conventions of their signatures.

Method and Property Signatures

The structures of method and property signatures (and I am talking about method and property *declarations* here) are similar:

```
<method_sig> ::= <callconv_method> <num_of_args> <return_type>
                 [<arg_type>[,<arg_type>*] ]
<prop_sig> ::= <callconv_prop> <num_of_args> <return_type>
               [<arg_type>[,<arg_type>*] ]
```

The difference is in the calling convention. The calling convention for a method signature is the following:

```
< callconv_method > ::= <default>  // Static method, default
                                   // calling convention
                     | vararg      // Static vararg method
                     | instance    // Instance method, default
                                   // calling convention
                     | instance vararg //  Instance vararg method
```

The calling convention for a property signature is always equal to `IMAGE_CEE_CS_CALLCONV_PROPERTY`.

Having noted this difference, you might as well forget about property signatures and concentrate on method signatures. The truth is that a property signature—excluding the calling convention—is a composite of signatures of the property's access methods, so it is no great wonder that method and property signatures have similar structures.

Remember that in the method calling convention, the combined calling conventions, such as `instance vararg`, are the products of bitwise OR operations performed on the respective calling convention constants. The calling convention is always represented by one (the first) byte of a signature.

The value `<num_of_args>`, a compressed unsigned integer, is the number of parameters, not counting the return type. The values `<return_type>` and `<arg_type>` are SETs. The difference between them and the field's SET is that the modifier & is allowed in both `<return_type>` and `<arg_type>`. The difference between `<return_type>` and `<arg_type>` is that `<return_type>` can be void and `<arg_type>` cannot.

Instance methods have the implicit first argument `this`, which is not reflected in the argument list. This implicit argument is a reference to the instance of the method's parent type. It is a class reference if the parent is a class or an interface and a managed pointer if the parent is a value type.

MemberRef Signatures

Member references, which are kept in the MemberRef metadata table, are the references to fields and methods, usually those defined outside the current module. There are no specific `MethodRefs` and `FieldRefs`, so you must look at the calling convention of a `MemberRef` signature to tell a field reference from a method reference, which is not exactly convenient or fast. On the flip side, this design solution saves 17 bytes per image loaded in memory (8 bytes for table descriptor and 3 * 3 bytes for column descriptors of a separate FieldRef table; see Chapter 5), which is undoubtedly a significant gain.

`MemberRef` signatures for field references are the same as the field declaration signatures discussed earlier; see "Field Signatures." `MemberRef` signatures for method references are structurally similar to method declaration signatures, although in the argument list of a `vararg` method reference, a sentinel can precede the optional arguments. The sentinel itself does not count as an additional argument, so if you call a `vararg` method with one mandatory argument and two optional arguments, the `MemberRef` signature will have an argument count of three and an argument list structure that looks like this:

```
<mandatory_arg><sentinel><opt_arg1><opt_arg2>
```

Indirect Call Signatures

To call methods indirectly, IL has the special instruction `calli`. This instruction takes argument values plus a function pointer from the stack and uses the `StandAloneSig` token as a parameter. The signature indexed by the token is the signature by which the call is made. Effectively, `calli` takes a function pointer and a signature and presumes that the signature is the correct one to use in calling this function:

```
ldc.i4.0     // Load first argument
ldc.i4.1     // Load second argument
ldftn   void Foo::Bar(int32, int32) // Load function pointer
calli   void(int32, int32)   // Call Foo::Bar indirectly
```

Indirect call signatures are similar to the method signatures of `MemberRefs`, but the calling convention can contain the modifier `explicit`, which indicates that the instance pointer of the parent object (`this`) is explicitly specified in the method signature as the first parameter.

Also, the calling convention of indirect call signature might be one of the unmanaged calling conventions, if the method called indirectly is in fact unmanaged.

Unmanaged calling conventions are defined in CorHdr.h in the `CorUnmanagedCallingConvention` enumeration as follows:

- `IMAGE_CEE_UNMANAGED_CALLCONV_C` (0x1). C/C++-style calling convention. The call stack is cleaned up by the caller. The ILAsm notation is `unmanaged cdecl`.

- `IMAGE_CEE_UNMANAGED_CALLCONV_STDCALL` (0x2). Win32 API calling convention. The call stack is cleaned up by the callee. The ILAsm notation is `unmanaged stdcall`.

- `IMAGE_CEE_UNMANAGED_CALLCONV_THISCALL` (0x3). C++ member method (non-vararg) calling convention. The callee cleans the stack, and the `this` pointer is passed through the ECX register. The ILAsm notation is `unmanaged thiscall`.

- `IMAGE_CEE_UNMANAGED_CALLCONV_FASTCALL` (0x4). Arguments are passed in registers when possible. The ILAsm notation is `unmanaged fastcall`. This calling convention is not supported in the first release of the runtime.

Local Variables Signatures

Local variables signatures are the second type of signatures referenced by the StandAloneSig metadata table. Each such signature contains type encodings for all local variables used in a method. The method header can contain the `StandAloneSig` token, which identifies the local variables signature. This signature is retrieved by the loader when it prepares the method for JIT compilation.

Local variables signatures are to some extent similar to method declaration signatures, with three differences:

- The calling convention is `IMAGE_CEE_CS_CALLCONV_LOCAL_SIG`.

- Local variables signatures have no return type. The local variable count is immediately followed by the sequence of encoded local variable types:

```
<locals_sig> ::= <callconv_locals> <num_of_vars>
                    <var_type>[,<var_type>*] ]
```

where <var_type> is the same SET as <arg_type> in method declaration signatures—it can be anything except void.

- The SETs may have the pinned modifier.

Type Specifications

Type specifications are special metadata items residing in the TypeSpec table and representing constructed types (pointers, arrays, function types, and so on)—as opposed to TypeDefs and TypeRefs, which represent types (classes, interfaces, and value types).

A common example of a constructed type is a vector or an array of classes or value types. Consider the following code snippet:

```
.locals init(int32[0...,0...] iArr) // Declare 2-dim array reference
ldc.i4 5      // Load size of first dimension
ldc.i4 10    // Load size of second dimension
// Create array by calling array constructor:
newobj instance void int32[0...,0...]::.ctor(int32,int32)
stloc iArr   // Store reference to new array in iArr
```

In the newobj instruction, we specified a MemberRef of the constructor method, parented not by a type but by a constructed type, int32[0...,0...]. The question is, "Whose .ctor is it, anyway?"

The arrays and vectors are generic types and can be instantiated only in conjunction with some nongeneric type, producing a new class—in this case, a two-dimensional array of 4-byte integers with zero lower bounds. So the constructor we called was the constructor of this class.

And, of course, about the only possible way to represent a constructed type is by a signature. That's why TypeSpec records have only one entry, containing an offset in the #Blob stream, pointing at the signature. Personally, I think it's a pity the TypeSpec record contains only one entry; a Name entry could be of some use. We could go pretty far with named TypeSpecs. Most obvious possibilities include type aliasing and type forwarding.

The TypeSpec signature has no calling convention and consists of one SET, which, however, can be fairly long. Consider, for example, a multidimensional array of function pointers that have function pointers among their arguments.

TypeSpec tokens can be used with all IL instructions that accept TypeDef or TypeRef tokens. In addition, as you've seen, MemberRefs can be scoped to TypeSpecs as well as TypeRefs. The only places where TypeSpecs could not replace TypeDefs or TypeRefs in versions 1.0 and 1.1 were the extends and implements clauses of the class declaration, but in version 2.0 the TypeSpecs can be used there as well, because the generic type instantiations are represented by TypeSpecs (more about generic types and instantiations in Chapter 11).

Two additional kinds of TypeSpecs, other than vectors and arrays, are unmanaged pointers and function pointers, which are not true generics, in that no abstract class exists from which all pointers inherit. Of course, both types of pointers can be cast to the value type int ([mscorlib]System.IntPtr), but this can hardly help—the int value type is oblivious to the type being pointed at, so such casting results only in loss of information. Pointer kinds of TypeSpecs are rarely used, compared to array kinds, and have limited application.

Summary of Signature Validity Rules

Let's wrap up the basic facts discussed in this chapter:

- [run time] Signature entries of records in the Method, Field, Property, MemberRef, StandaloneSig, and TypeSpec metadata tables must hold valid offsets in the #Blob stream. Nil values of these entries are not acceptable.

- Signatures are built from SETs. Each SET describes the type of a field, a parameter, a variable, or other such item.

- [run time] Each SET is a sequence of primitive type codes and optional integer parameters, such as metadata tokens or array dimension sizes. A SET cannot end with codes of the following primitive types: a sentinel, *, &, [ ], or pinned. These primitive types are modifiers for the types whose encodings follow them in the SET.

- [run time] A field signature, which is referenced from the Field or MemberRef table, consists of the calling convention IMAGE_CEE_CS_CALLCONV_FIELD and one valid SET, which cannot be void or <type>& and cannot contain a sentinel or a pinned modifier.

- A method reference signature, which is referenced from the MemberRef table, consists of a calling convention, an argument count, a return SET, and a sequence of argument SETs, corresponding in number to the argument count.

- [run time] The calling convention of a method reference signature is one of the following: the default, vararg, instance, or instance vararg.

- [run time] The return SET of a method reference signature cannot contain a sentinel or a pinned modifier.

- [run time] No more than one argument SET of a method reference signature can contain a sentinel, and it can do so only if the calling convention includes vararg.

- [run time] The argument SETs of a method reference signature cannot be void and cannot contain a pinned modifier.

- A method declaration signature, which is referenced from the Method table, has the same structure as a method reference signature and must comply with the same requirements, plus no argument SET can contain a sentinel.

- A property declaration signature, which is referenced from the Property table, has the same structure as a method declaration signature and must comply with the same requirements except that the calling convention of a property declaration signature must be IMAGE_CEE_CS_CALLCONV_PROPERTY.

- An indirect call signature, which is referenced from the StandAloneSig table, has the same structure as a method reference signature and must comply with the same requirements except that the calling convention of an indirect call can be instance explicit or instance explicit vararg, and the calling convention of an indirect call to an unmanaged method can be unmanaged cdecl, unmanaged stdcall, unmanaged thiscall, or unmanaged fastcall.

- A local variables signature, which is referenced from the StandAloneSig table, consists of the calling convention IMAGE_CEE_CS_CALLCONV_LOCAL_SIG, a local variable count, and a sequence of local variable SETs, corresponding in number to the variable count.

- [run time] No local variable SET can be void or can contain a sentinel.

- A type specification signature, which is referenced from the TypeSpec table, consists of one SET not preceded by the calling convention. The SET may represent an array, a vector, an unmanaged pointer, or a function pointer, and it cannot contain a pinned modifier.

CHAPTER 9

■ ■ ■

Fields and Data Constants

Fields are one of two kinds of typed and named data locations, the second kind being method local variables, which are discussed in Chapter 10. Fields correspond to the data members and global variables of the C++ world. Apart from their own characteristics, fields can have additional information associated with them that defines the way the fields are laid out by the loader, how they are allocated, how they are marshaled to unmanaged code, and whether they have default values. This chapter examines all aspects of member and global fields and the metadata used to describe these aspects.

Field Metadata

To define a field, you must first provide basic information: the field's name and signature and the flags indicating the field's characteristics, stored in the Field metadata table. Then comes optional information, specific to certain kinds of fields: field marshaling information, found in the FieldMarshal table; field layout information in the FieldLayout table; field mapping information in the FieldRVA table; and a default value in the Constant table.

To reference a field, you must know its owner—TypeRef, TypeDef, or ModuleRef—as well as the field's name and signature. The references to the fields are kept in the MemberRef table. Figure 9-1 shows the general structure of the field metadata group.

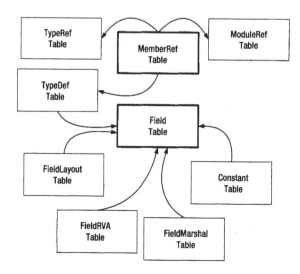

Figure 9-1. *Field metadata group*

Defining a Field

The central metadata table of the group, the Field table, has the associated token type mdtFieldDef (0x04000000). A record in this table has three entries:

- Flags (2-byte unsigned integer). Binary flags indicating the field's characteristics.

- Name (offset in the #Strings stream). The field's name.

- Signature (offset in the #Blob stream). The field's signature.

As you can see, a Field record does not contain one vital piece of information: which class or value type owns the field. The information about field ownership is furnished by the class descriptor itself: records in the TypeDef table have FieldList entries, which hold the RID in the Field table where the first of the type's fields can be found.

In the simplest case, the ILAsm syntax for a field declaration is as follows:

.field <flags> <type> <name>

The owner of a field is the class or value type in the lexical scope of which the field is defined.

A field's binary flags are defined in the CorHdr.h file in the enumeration CorFieldAttr and can be divided into four groups, as described in the following list. I'm using ILAsm keywords instead of the constant names from CorFieldAttr, as I don't think the constant names are relevant.

- Accessibility flags (mask 0x0007):

  - privatescope (0x0000). This is the default accessibility. A private scope field is exempt from the requirement of having a unique triad of owner, name, and signature and hence must always be referenced by a FieldDef token and never by a MemberRef token (0x0A000000), because member references are resolved to the definitions by exactly this triad. The privatescope fields are accessible from anywhere within current module.

  - private (0x0001). The field is accessible from its owner and from classes nested in the field's owner. Global private fields are accessible from anywhere within current module.

  - famandassem (0x0002). The field is accessible from types belonging to the owner's family defined in the current assembly. The term *family* here means the type itself and all its descendants.

  - assembly (0x0003). The field is accessible from types defined in the current assembly.

  - family (0x0004). The field is accessible from the owner's family (defined in this or any other assembly).

  - famorassem (0x0005). The field is accessible from the owner's family (defined in this or any other assembly) and from all types (of the owner's family or not) defined in the current assembly.

  - public (0x0006). The field is accessible from any type.

- Contract flags (mask 0x02F0):

  - static (0x0010). The field is static, shared by all instances of the type. Global fields must be static.

  - initonly (0x0020). The field can be initialized only and cannot be written to later. Initialization takes place in an instance constructor (.ctor) for instance fields and in a class constructor (.cctor) for static fields. This flag is not enforced by the CLR; it exists for the compilers' reference only.

  - literal (0x0040). The field is a compile-time constant. The loader does not lay out this field and does not create an internal handle for it. The field cannot be directly addressed from IL and can be used only as a Reflection reference to retrieve an associated metadata-held constant. If you try to access a literal field directly—for example, through the ldsfld instruction—the JIT compiler throws a MissingField exception and aborts the task.

  - notserialized (0x0080). The field is not serialized when the owner is remoted. This flag has meaning only for instance fields of the serializable types.

  - specialname (0x0200). The field is special in some way, as defined by the name. An example is field value__ of an enumeration type.

- Reserved flags (cannot be set explicitly; mask 0x9500):

  - rtspecialname (0x0400). The field has a special name that is reserved for the internal use of the common language runtime. Two field names are reserved: value_, for instance fields in enumerations, and _Deleted*, for fields marked for deletion but not actually removed from metadata. The keyword rtspecialname is ignored by the IL assembler (the flag is actually set automatically by the metadata emission API) and is displayed by the IL disassembler for informational purposes only. This flag must be accompanied in the metadata by a specialname flag.

  - marshal(<native_type>) (0x1000). The field has an associated FieldMarshal record specifying how the field must be marshaled when consumed by unmanaged code. The ILAsm construct marshal(<native_type>) defines the marshaling information emitted to the FieldMarshal table but does not set the flag directly. Rather, the flag is set behind the scenes by the metadata emission API when the marshaling information is emitted. Chapter 8 discusses native types.

  - [no ILAsm keyword] (0x8000). The field has an associated Constant record. The flag is set by the metadata emission API when the respective Constant record is emitted. See the section "Default Values" later in this chapter.

  - [no ILAsm keyword] (0x0100). The field is mapped to data and has an associated FieldRVA record. The flag is set by the metadata emission API when the respective FieldRVA record is emitted. See the section "Mapped Fields" later in this chapter.

In the field declaration, the type of the field (<type> in the previous syntax formula) is the ILAsm notation of the appropriate single encoded type, which together with the calling convention forms the field's signature. If you forgot what a field signature looks like, see Chapter 8.

The name of the field (<name> in the previous syntax formula), also included in the declaration, can be a simple name or a composite (dotted) name. ILAsm v1.0 and v1.1 did not allow composite field names, although one could always cheat and put a composite name in single quotation marks, turning it into a simple name.

Examples of field declarations include the following:

```
.field public static marshal(int) int32 I
.field family string S
.field private int32& pJ    // ERROR! ByRef in field signature!
```

Referencing a Field

Field references in ILAsm have the following notation:

```
<field_ref> ::= <type>[<class_ref>::]< name>
```

where <class_ref>—as you know from Chapter 7—is defined as follows:

```
<class_ref> ::= [<resolution_scope>]<full_type_name>
```

where

```
<resolution_scope> ::= [<assembly_ref_alias>]
                     | [.module <module_ref_name>]
```

For instance, this example uses the IL instruction ldfld, which loads the field value on the stack:

```
ldfld  int32 [.module Another.dll]Foo.Bar::idx
```

When it is not possible to infer unambiguously from the context whether the referenced member is a field or a method, <field_ref> is preceded by the keyword field. Note that the keyword does not contain a leading dot. The following example uses the IL instruction ldtoken, which loads an item's runtime handle on the stack:

```
ldtoken field int32 [.module Another.dll]Foo.Bar::idx
```

The field references reside in the MemberRef metadata table, which has associated token type 0x0A000000. A record of this table has only three entries:

- Class (coded token of type MemberRefParent). This entry references the TypeRef or ModuleRef table. Method references, residing in the same table, can have their Class entries referencing the Method and TypeSpec tables as well.

- Name (offset in the #Strings stream).

- Signature (offset in the #Blob stream).

Instance and Static Fields

Instance fields are created every time a type instance is created, and they belong to the type instance. Static fields, which are shared by all instances of the type, are created when the type is loaded. Some of the static fields (literal and mapped fields) are never allocated. The loader simply notes where the mapped fields reside and addresses these locations whenever the fields are to be addressed. And all the references to the literal fields are replaced with the constants at compile time by the high-level compilers (the IL assembler does not do that, leaving it to the programmer).

A field signature contains no indication of whether the field is static or instance. But since the loader keeps separate books for instance fields and for two out of three kinds of static fields—not for literal static fields—the kind of referenced field is easily discerned from the field's token. When a field token is found in the IL stream, the JIT compiler does not have to dive into the metadata, retrieve the record, and check the field's flags; by that time, all the fields have been accounted for and duly classified by the loader.

IL has two sets of instructions for field loading and storing. The instructions for instance fields are ldfld, ldflda, and stfld; those for static fields are ldsfld, ldsflda, and stsfld. An attempt to use a static field instruction with an instance field would result in a JIT compilation failure. The inverse combination would work, but it requires loading the instance pointer on the stack, which is, of course, completely redundant for a static field. The good thing about the possibility of using instance field instructions for static fields is that it allows for accessing both static and instance fields in the same way.

Default Values

Default values reside in the Constant metadata table. Three kinds of metadata items can have a default value assigned and therefore can reference the Constant table: fields, method parameters, and properties. A record of the Constant table has three entries:

- Type (unsigned 1-byte integer). The type of the constant—one of the ELEMENT_TYPE_* codes. (See Chapter 8.)

- Parent (coded token of type HasConstant). A reference to the owner of the constant—a record in the Field, Property, or Param table.

- Value (offset in the #Blob stream). A constant value blob.

The current implementation of the common language runtime and ILAsm allows the constant types described in Table 9-1. (As usual, I've dropped the ELEMENT_TYPE_ part of the name.)

Table 9-1. *Constant Types*

Constant Type	ILAsm Notation	Comments
I1	int8	Signed 1-byte integer.
I2	int16	Signed 2-byte integer.
I4	int32	Signed 4-byte integer.
I8	int64	Signed 8-byte integer.
R4	float32	4-byte floating point.
R8	float64	8-byte floating point.
CHAR	char	2-byte Unicode character.
BOOLEAN	bool	1-byte Boolean, true = 1, false = 0.
STRING	<quoted_string>, bytearray	Unicode string.
CLASS	nullref	Null object reference. The value of the constant of this type must be a 4-byte integer containing 0.

The ILAsm syntax for defining the default value of a field is as follows:

```
<field_def_const> ::= .field <flags> <type> <name>
   = <const_type> [( <value> )]
```

The value in parentheses is mandatory for all constant types except `nullref`. For example:

```
.field public int32 i = int32(123)
.field public static literal bool b = bool(true)
.field private float32 f = float32(1.2345)
.field public static int16 ii = int16(0xFFE0)
.field public object o = nullref
```

Defining integer and Boolean constants—not to mention `nullref`—is pretty straightforward, but floating-point constants and strings can present some difficulties.

Floating-point numbers have special cases, such as positive infinity, negative infinity, and not-a-number (NAN), that cannot be presented textually in simple floating-point format. In these special cases, the floating-point constants can alternatively be represented as integer values with a matching byte count. The integer values are not converted to floating-point values; instead, they represent an exact bit image of the floating-point values (in IEEE-754 floating-point format used by the CLR). For example:

```
.field public float32 fPosInf = float32(0x7F800000)
.field public float32 fNegInf = float32(0xFF800000)
.field public float32 fNAN = float32(0xFFC00000)
```

Like all other constants, string constants are stored in the #Blob stream. In this regard, they differ from user-defined strings, which are stored in the #US stream. What both kinds of strings have in common is that they are supposed to be Unicode (UTF-16). I say "supposed to be" because the only Unicode-specific restrictions imposed on these strings are that their sizes are reported in Unicode characters and that their byte counts must be even. Otherwise, these strings are simply binary objects and might or might not contain invalid Unicode characters.

Notice that the type of the constant does not need to match the type of the item to which this constant is assigned—in this case, the type of the field. That is, the match is not required by the CLR, which cares nothing about the constants: the constants are provided for compilers' information only, and the high-level compilers, having encountered a reference to a constant in the source code, emit explicit instructions to assign respective values to fields or parameters.

In ILAsm, a string constant can be defined either as a composite quoted string or as a byte array:

```
.field public static string str1 = "Isn't" + " it " + "marvelous!"
.field public static string str2 = bytearray(00 01 FF FE 1A 00 00 )
```

When a string constant is defined as a simple or composite quoted string, this string is converted to Unicode before being stored in the #Blob stream. In the case of a `bytearray` definition, the specified byte sequence is stored "as is" and padded with one 0 byte if necessary to make the byte count even. In the example shown here, the default value for the `str2` field will be padded to bring the byte count to eight (four Unicode characters). And if the bytes specified in the `bytearray` are invalid Unicode characters, it will surely be discovered when we try to print the string, but not before.

Assigning default values to fields (and parameters) seems to be such a compelling technique that you might wonder why we did not employ it in the simple sample discussed in Chapter 1. Really, defining the default values is a great way to initialize fields—right? Wrong. Here's a tricky question. Suppose that we define a member field as follows:

```
.field public static int32 ii = int32(12345)
```

What will the value of the field be when the class is loaded? Correct answer: 0. Why? Default values specified in the Constant table are not used by the loader to initialize the items to which they are assigned. If you want to initialize a field to its default value, you must explicitly call the respective Reflection method to retrieve the value from metadata and then store this value in the field. This doesn't sound too nice, and I think that the CLR could probably do a better job with field initialization—and with literal fields as well.

Let me remind you once again that literal fields are not true fields. They are not laid out by the loader, and they cannot be directly accessed from IL. From the point of view of metadata, however, literal fields are nevertheless valid fields having valid tokens, which allow the constant values corresponding to these fields to be retrieved by Reflection methods. The common language runtime does not provide an implicit means of accessing the Constant table, which is a pity. It would certainly be much nicer if the JIT compiler would compile the ldsfld instruction into the retrieval of the respective constant value, instead of failing, when this instruction is applied to a literal field. But such are the facts of life, and I am afraid we cannot do anything about it at the moment.

Given this situation, literal fields without associated Constant records are legal from the loader's point of view, but they are utterly meaningless. They serve no purpose except to inflate the Field metadata table.

But how do the compilers handle literal fields? If every time a constant from an enumeration—represented, as we know, by a literal field—was used, the compiler emitted a call to the Reflection API to get this constant value, then one could imagine where it would leave the performance. Most compilers are smarter than that and resolve the literal fields at compile time, replacing references to literal fields with explicit constant values of these fields so that the literal fields never come into play at run time.

ILAsm, following common language runtime functionality to the letter, allows the definition of the Constant metadata but does nothing about the symbol-to-value resolution at compile time. From the point of view of ILAsm and the runtime, the enumeration types are real, as distinctive types, but the symbolic constants listed in the enumerations are not. You can reference an enum, but you can never reference its literal fields.

Mapped Fields

It is possible to provide unconditional initialization for static fields by mapping the fields to data defined in the PE file and setting this data to the initializing values. The syntax for mapping a field to data in ILAsm is as follows:

```
<mapped_field_decl> ::= .field <flags> <type> <name> at <data_label>
```

Here's an example:

```
.field public static int64 ii at data_ii
```

The nonterminal symbol <data_label> is a simple name labeling the data segment to which the field is mapped. The ILAsm compiler allows a field to be mapped either to the "normal" data section (.sdata) or to the thread local storage (.tls), depending on the data declaration to which the field mapping refers. A field can be mapped only to data residing in the same module as the field declaration. (For information about data declaration, see the following section, "Data Constants Declaration.")

Mapping a field results in emitting a record into the FieldRVA table, which contains two entries:

- RVA (4-byte unsigned integer). The relative virtual address of the data to which the field is mapped.

- Field (RID to the Field table). The index of the Field record being mapped.

Two or more fields can be mapped to the same location, but each field can be mapped to one location only. Duplicate FieldRVA records with the same Field values and different RVA values are therefore considered invalid metadata. The loader is not particular about duplicate FieldRVA records, however; it simply uses the first one available for the field and ignores the rest.

The field mapping technique has some catches. The first catch (well, not much of a catch, actually) is that, obviously, only static fields can be mapped. Even if we could map instance fields, each instance would be mapped to the same physical memory, making the fields de facto static—shared by all instances—anyway. Mapping instance fields is considered invalid metadata, but it has no serious consequences for the loader—if a field is not static, the loader does not even check to see whether the field is mapped. The only real effect of mapping instance fields is a bloated FieldRVA table. The IL assembler treats mapping of an instance field as an error and produces an error message.

The second catch is to an extent a derivative from the first catch: the mapped static fields are "the most static of them all." When multiple application domains are sharing the same process (as in the case of ASP.NET, for example) and several application domains are sharing a loaded assembly, the mapped fields of this assembly are shared by all application domains, unlike the "normal" static fields, which are individual per application domain.

The third catch is that a field cannot be mapped if its type contains object references (objects or arrays). The data sections are out of the garbage collector's reach, so the validity of object references placed in the data sections cannot be guaranteed. If the loader finds object references in a mapped field type, it throws a TypeLoad exception and aborts the loading, even if the code is run in full-trust mode from a local drive and all security-related checks are disabled. The loader checks for the presence of object references on all levels of the field type—in other words, it checks the types of all the fields that make up the type, checks the types of fields that make up those types, and so on.

The fourth catch is that in the verifiable code a field cannot be mapped if its type (value type, of course) contains nonpublic instance fields. The reasoning behind this limitation is that if we map a field with a type containing nonpublic members, we can map another field of some all-public type to the same location and, through this second mapping, get unlimited access to nonpublic member fields of the first type. The loader checks for the presence of nonpublic members on all levels of the mapped field type and throws a TypeLoad exception if it finds such members. This check, unlike the check for object references, is performed only when code verification is required; it is disabled when the code is run from the local drive in full-trust mode.

Note, however, that a mapped field itself can be declared nonpublic without ill consequences. This is based on the simple assumption that if developers decide to overlap their own nonpublic field and thus defy the accessibility control mechanism of the common language runtime object model, they probably know what they are doing.

The last catch worth mentioning is that the initialization data is provided "as is," exactly as it is defined in the PE file. And if you run the code on a platform other than the one on which the PE file was created, you can face some unpleasant consequences. As a trivial example, suppose you map an int32 field to data containing bytes 0xAA, 0xBB, 0xCC, and 0xDD. On a little endian platform (for instance, an Intel platform), the field is initialized to 0xDDCCBBAA, while on a big endian platform...well, you get the picture.

All these catches do not preclude the compilers from using field mapping for initialization.

Version 2.0 of the IL assembler provides a means of mapping the fields onto an explicitly specified memory address. In this case, the <data label> name must have the form @<RVA in decimal format>. This technique can hardly be recommended for general use because of the obvious hazards associated with it (you usually don't know the target RVA before the program has been compiled), but in certain limited cases (when you *do* know the RVA beforehand) it can be useful. Consider, for example, the following declaration:

```
.field public static int16 NTHeaderMagic at @152
```

Data Constants Declaration

A data constant declaration in ILAsm has the following syntax:

```
<data_decl> ::= .data [ tls ] [<data_label> = ] <data_items>
```

where <data_label> is a simple name, unique within the module

```
<data_items> ::= { <data_item> [ , <data_item>* ] } | <data_item>
```

and where

```
<data_item> ::= <data_type> [ ( <value> ) ] [ [ <count> ] ]
```

Data constants are emitted to the .sdata section or the .tls section, depending on the presence of the tls keyword, in the same sequence in which they were declared in the source code. The unlabeled data declarations can be used for padding between the labeled data declarations and probably for nothing else, since without a label it's impossible to map a field to this data. Unlabeled—or, more precisely, unreferenced—data might not survive round-tripping (disassembly-reassembly) because the IL disassembler outputs only referenced data.

The nonterminal symbol <data_type> specifies the data type. (See Table 9-2.) The data type is used by the IL assembler exclusively for identifying the size and byte layout of <value> (in order to emit the data correctly) and is not emitted as any part of metadata or the data itself. Having no way to know what the type was intended to be when the data was emitted, the IL disassembler always uses the most generic form, a byte array, for data representation.

Table 9-2. *Types Defined for Data Constants*

Data Type	Size	Value	Comments
float32	4 bytes	Floating point, single precision	If an integer value is used, it is converted to floating point. If the value overflows float32, the ILAsm compiler issues a warning.
float64	8 bytes	Floating point, double precision	If an integer value is used, it is converted to floating point.
int64	8 bytes	8-byte signed integer	
int32	4 bytes	4-byte signed integer	If the value overflows int32, the ILAsm compiler issues a warning.
int16	2 bytes	2-byte signed integer	If the value overflows int16, the ILAsm compiler issues a warning.
int8	1 byte	1-byte signed integer	If the value overflows int8, the ILAsm compiler issues a warning.
bytearray	var	Sequence of two-digit hexadecimal numbers, without the 0x prefix	The value cannot be omitted because it defines the size. The repetition parameter ([<count>]) cannot be used.
char*	var	Composite quoted string	The value cannot be omitted because it defines the size. The repetition parameter ([<count>]) cannot be used. The string is converted to Unicode before being emitted to data.
&	pointer size	Another data label	Data on data; the data containing the value of the unmanaged pointer—the virtual address—of another named data segment. The value cannot be omitted, and the repetition parameter ([<count>]) cannot be used. The referenced data segment must be declared before being referenced in a data-on-data declaration. Using data on data results in the emission of additional relocations, which makes the module unverifiable and platform dependent.

If <value> is not specified, the data is initialized to a value with all bits set to zeros. Thus, it is still "initialized data" in terms of the PE file structure—meaning that this data is part of the PE file disk image.

The optional <count> in square brackets indicates the repetition count of the data item. Here are some examples:

```
.data tls T_01 = int32(1234)
// 4 bytes in .tls section, value 0x000004D2
.data tls int32
// unnamed 4 bytes padding in .tls section, value doesn't matter
.data D_01 = int32(1234)[32] // 32 4-byte integers in .sdata section,
                             // Each equal to 0x000004D2
.data D_02 = char*("Hello world!") // Unicode string in .sdata section
```

Explicit Layouts and Union Declaration

Although instance fields cannot be mapped to data, it is possible to specify the positioning of these fields directly. As you might remember from Chapter 7, a class or a value type can have an explicit flag—a special flag indicating that the metadata contains an exact recipe for the loader regarding the layout of this class. This information is kept in the FieldLayout metadata table, whose records contain these two entries:

- OffSet (4-byte unsigned integer). The relative offset of the field in the class layout (*not* an RVA) or the field's ordinal in case of sequential layout. The offset is relative to the start of the class instance's data.

- Field (RID to the Field table). The index of the field for which the offset is specified.

In ILAsm, the field offset is specified by putting the offset value in square brackets immediately after the .field keyword, as shown here:

```
.class public value sealed explicit MyStruct
{
    .field [0] public int32 ii
    .field [4] public float64 dd
    .field [12] public bool bb
}
```

Only instance fields can have offsets specified. Since static fields are not part of the class instance layout, specifying explicit offsets for them is meaningless and is considered a metadata error. If an offset is specified for a static field, the loader behaves the same way it does with mapped instance fields: if the field is static, the loader does not check to see whether the field has an offset specified. Consequently, FieldLayout records referencing the static fields are nothing more than a waste of memory.

In a class that has an explicit layout, *all* the instance fields must have specified offsets. If one of the instance fields does not have an associated FieldLayout record, the loader throws a TypeLoad exception and aborts the loading. Obviously, a field can have only one offset, so duplicate FieldLayout records that have the same Field entry are illegal. This is not checked at run time because this metadata invalidity is not critical: the loader takes the first available FieldLayout record for the current field and ignores any duplicates. It's worth remembering, though, that while supplying wrong metadata doesn't always lead to aborted program, it almost certainly leads to unexpected (by the programmer) behavior of the application.

The placement of object references (classes, arrays) is subject to a general limitation: the fields of object reference types must be aligned on pointer size—either 4 or 8 bytes, depending on the platform:

```
.class public value sealed explicit MyStruct
{
    .field [0] public int16 ii
    .field [2] public string str //Illegal on 32-bit and 64-bit
    .field [6] public int16 jj
    .field [8] public int32 kk
    .field [12] public object oo //Illegal on 64-bit platform
    .field [16] public int32[] iArr //Legal on both platforms
}
```

This alignment requirement may cause platform dependence, unless you decide to always align the fields of object reference types on 8 bytes, which would suit both 32-bit and 64-bit platforms.

Value types with an explicit layout containing object references must have a total size equal to a multiple of the pointer size. The reason is pretty obvious: imagine what happens if you declare an array of such value types.

Explicit layout is a standard way to implement unions in IL. By explicitly specifying field offsets, you can make fields overlap however you want. Let's suppose, for example, that you want to treat a 4-byte unsigned integer as such, as a pair of 2-byte words, or as 4 bytes. In C++ notation, the respective constructs look like this:

```
union MultiDword {
    DWORD dw;
    union {
        struct {
            WORD w1;
            WORD w2;
        };
        struct {
            BYTE b1;
            BYTE b2;
            BYTE b3;
            BYTE b4;
        };
    };
};
```

In ILAsm, the same union will be written like so:

```
.class public value sealed explicit MultiDword
{
    .field [0] public uint32 dw

    .field [0] public uint16 w1
    .field [2] public uint16 w2

    .field [0] public uint8 b1
    .field [1] public uint8 b2
    .field [2] public uint8 b3
    .field [3] public uint8 b4
}
```

The only limitation imposed on the explicit-layout unions is that if the overlapping fields contain object references, these object references must not overlap with any other field:

```
.class public value sealed explicit StrAndIndex
{
    .field [0] public string Str // Reference, size 4 bytes
                                 // on 32-bit platform
```

```
    .field [4] public uint32 Index
}
.class public value sealed explicit MyUnion
{
    .field [0] public valuetype StrAndIndex str_and_index
    .field [0] public uint64 whole_thing // Illegal!
    .field [0] public string str // Illegal!
    .field [2] public uint32 half_and_half // Illegal!
    .field [4] public uint32 index // Legal, object reference
                                   //  not overlapped
}
```

Such "unionizing" of the object references would provide the means for directly modifying these references, which could thoroughly disrupt the functioning of the garbage collector. The loader checks explicit layouts for object reference overlap; if any is found, it throws a TypeLoad exception and aborts the loading.

This rule has an interesting exception, though: the object references can be overlapped with other object references (only full overlapping is allowed; partial overlapping is forbidden). This looks to me like a gaping hole in the type safety. On the other hand, this overlapping is allowed only in full-trust mode, and in full-trust mode you can do even worse things (run native unmanaged code, for example).

A field can also have an associated FieldLayout record if the type that owns this field has a sequential layout. In this case, the Offset entry of the FieldLayout record holds a field ordinal rather than an offset. The fields belonging to a sequential-layout class needn't have associated FieldLayout records, but if one of the class's fields has such an associated record, all the rest must have one too. The ILAsm syntax for field declaration in types with sequential layout is similar to the case of the explicit layout, except the integer value in square brackets represents the field's ordinal rather than the offset:

```
.class public value sealed sequential OneTwoThreeFour
{
    .field [0] public uint8 one
    .field [1] public uint8 two
    .field [2] public uint8 three
    .field [3] public uint8 four
}
```

Global Fields

Fields declared outside the scope of any class are known as *global* fields. They don't belong to a class but instead belong to the module in which they are declared. A module is represented by a special TypeDef record with RID=1 under the name <Module>, so all the formalities that govern how field records are identified by reference from their parent TypeDef records are observed.

Global fields must be static. Since only one instance of the module exists when the assembly is loaded and because it is impossible to create alternative instances of the module, this limitation seems obvious.

Global fields can have public, private, or privatescope accessibility flags—at least that's what the metadata validity rules say. As you saw in Chapter 1, however, a global item (a field or a method) can have any accessibility flag, and the loader interprets this flag only as assembly, private, or privatescope. The public, assembly, and famorassem flags are all interpreted as assembly, while the family, famandassem, and private flags are all interpreted as private. The global fields cannot be accessed from outside the assembly, so they don't have true public accessibility. And as no type can be derived from <Module>, the question about family-related accessibility is moot.

Global fields can be accessed from anywhere within the module, regardless of their declared accessibility. In this regard, the classes that are declared within a module and use the global fields have the same access rights as if they were nested in the module. The metadata contains no indications of such nesting, of course.

A reference to a global field declared in the same module has no <class_ref>:: part:

<global_field_ref> ::= [**field**] <field_type> <field_name>

The keyword field is used in particular cases when the nature of the reference cannot be inferred from the context, for example in the ldtoken instruction.

A reference to a global field declared in a different module of the assembly also lacks the class name but has resolution scope:

<global_field_ref> ::= [**field**] [**.module** <mod_name>]::<field_ name>

The following are two examples of such declarations:

```
ldsfld int32 globalInt
// field globalInt from this module
ldtoken field int32 [.module supporting.dll]::globalInt
// globalInt from other module
```

Since the global fields are static, we cannot explicitly specify their layout except by mapping them to data. Thus, our 4-2-1-byte union MultiDword would look like this if we implemented it with global fields:

```
.field public static uint32 dw at D_00
.field public static uint16 w1 at D_00
.field public static uint16 w2 at D_02
.field public static uint8 b1 at D_00
.field public static uint8 b2 at D_01
.field public static uint8 b3 at D_02
.field public static uint8 b4 at D_03
.data D_00 = int8(0)
.data D_01 = int8(0)
.data D_02 = int8(0)
.data D_03 = int8(0)
...
ldc.i1.1
stsfld uint8 b3 // Set value of third byte
```

Fortunately, we don't have to do that every time we need a global union. Instead, we can declare the value type MultiDword exactly as before and then declare a global field of this type:

```
.field public static valuetype MultiDword multi_dword
...
ldc.i1.1
ldsflda valuetype MultiDword multi_dword
// Load reference to the field
// As instance of MultiDword
stfld uint8 MultiDword::b3 // Set value of third byte
```

Constructors vs. Data Constants

You've already taken a look at field mapping as a technique of field initialization, and I've listed the drawbacks and limitations of this technique. Field mapping has this distinct "unmanaged" scent about it, but the compilers routinely use it for field initialization nevertheless. Is there a way to get the fields initialized without mapping them? Yes, there is.

The common language runtime object model provides two special methods, the instance constructor (.ctor) and the class constructor (.cctor), a.k.a. the type initializer. We're getting ahead of ourselves a bit here; Chapter 10 discusses methods in general and constructors in particular, so I won't concentrate on the details here. For now, all we need to know about .ctor and .cctor is that .ctor is executed when a new instance of a type is created, and .cctor is executed after the type is loaded and before any one of the type members is accessed. The class constructors are static and can deal with static members of the type only, so we have a perfect setup for field initialization: .cctors take care of static fields, and .ctors take care of instance fields.

But how about global fields? The good news is that we can define a global .cctor. Field initialization by constructors is vastly superior to field mapping, with none of its limitations, as described earlier in the section "Mapped Fields." The catch? Unfortunately, initialization by constructors must be executed at run time, burning processor cycles, whereas mapped fields simply "are there" after the module has been loaded. The mapped fields don't require additional operations for the initialization. Whether this price is worth the increased freedom and safety regarding field initialization depends on the concrete situation, but in general I think it is.

Let me illustrate the point by building an alternative enumeration. Since all the values of an enumeration are stored in literal fields, which are inaccessible from IL directly, the compilers replace references to these fields with the respective values at compile time. We can use a very simple enum as a model:

```
.class public enum sealed MagicNumber
{
    .field private specialname int32 value__
    .field public static literal valuetype
        MagicNumber MagicOne = int32(123)
    .field public static literal valuetype
        MagicNumber MagicTwo = int32(456)
    .field public static literal valuetype
        MagicNumber MagicThree = int32(789)
}
```

Let's suppose that our code uses the symbolic constants of an enumeration declared in a third-party assembly. We compile the code, and the symbolic constants are replaced with their values. Forget for a moment that we must have that third-party assembly available at compile time. But we will need to recompile the code every time the enumeration changes, and we have no control over the enumeration because it is defined outside our jurisdiction. In another scenario, when we declare an enumeration in one of our own modules, we must recompile all the modules that reference this enumeration once it is changed.

Let's suppose also—for the sake of an argument—that we don't like this situation, so we decide to devise our own enumeration:

```
.class public value sealed MagicNumber
{
    .field public int32 _value_ // Specialname value_ is
                                // reserved for enums
    .field public static valuetype MagicNumber MagicOne at D_00
    .field public static valuetype MagicNumber MagicTwo at D_04
    .field public static valuetype MagicNumber MagicThree at D_08
}
.data D_00 = int32(123)
.data D_04 = int32(456)
.data D_08 = int32(789)
```

This solution looks good, except in the platform-independence department. We conquered the recompilation problem and can at last address the symbolic constants by their symbols (names), through field access instructions. This approach presents a problem, though: the fields representing the symbolic constants can be written to.

Let's try again with a class constructor; refer to the sample MyEnums.il on the Apress Web site:

```
.class public value sealed MagicNumber
{
    .field private int32 _value_ // Specialname value_ is
                                 // reserved for enums
    .field public static initonly valuetype MagicNumber MagicOne
    .field public static initonly valuetype MagicNumber MagicTwo
    .field public static initonly valuetype MagicNumber MagicThree
    .method public static specialname void .cctor()
    {
        ldsflda valuetype MagicNumber MagicNumber::MagicOne
        ldc.i4 123
        stfld int32 MagicNumber::_value_

        ldsflda valuetype MagicNumber MagicNumber::MagicTwo
        ldc.i4 456
        stfld int32 MagicNumber::_value_

        ldsflda valuetype MagicNumber MagicNumber::MagicThree
        ldc.i4 789
        stfld int32 MagicNumber::_value_
```

```
    ret
  }
  .method public int32 ToBase()
  {
    ldarg.0 // Instance pointer
    ldfld int32 MagicNumber::_value_
    ret
  }
}
```

This seems to solve all the remaining problems. The `initonly` flag on the static fields protects them from being overwritten outside the class constructor. Embedding the numeric values of symbolic constants in the IL stream takes care of platform dependence. We are not mapping the fields, so we are free to use any type as the underlying type of our enumeration. And, of course, declaring the `_value_` field private protects it from having arbitrary values assigned to it.

Alas, this solution does have a hidden problem: the `initonly` flag does not provide full protection against arbitrary field overwriting. The operations `ldflda` (`ldsflda`) and `stfld` (`stsfld`) on `initonly` fields are unverifiable outside the constructors. They're unverifiable but not impossible, which means that if the verification procedures are disabled, the `initonly` fields can be overwritten in any method.

It looks like my attempts to devise a "nice" equivalent of an enum failed. If you have any fresh ideas in this regard, let me know.

Summary of Metadata Validity Rules

The field-related metadata tables are Field, FieldLayout, FieldRVA, FieldMarshal, Constant, and MemberRef. The records of these tables have the following entries:

- The Field table contains the `Flags`, `Name`, and `Signature` entries.

- The FieldLayout table contains the `OffSet` and `Field` entries.

- The FieldRVA table contains the `RVA` and `Field` entries.

- The FieldMarshal table contains the `Parent` and `NativeType` (native signature) entries.

- The Constant table contains the `Type`, `Parent`, and `Value` entries.

- The MemberRef table contains the `Class`, `Name`, and `Signature` entries.

Field Table Validity Rules

- The `Flags` entry can have only those bits set that are defined in the enumeration `CorFieldAttrEnum` in CorHdr.h (validity mask 0xB7F7).

- [run time] The accessibility flag (mask 0x0007) must be one of the following: `privatescope`, `private`, `famandassem`, `assembly`, `family`, `famorassem`, or `public`.

- The `literal` and `initonly` flags are mutually exclusive.

- If the literal flag is set, the static flag must also be set.

- If the rtspecialname flag is set, the specialname flag must also be set.

- [run time] If the flag 0x1000 (fdHasFieldMarshal) is set, the FieldMarshal table must contain a record referencing this Field record, and vice versa.

- [run time] If the flag 0x8000 (fdHasDefault) is set, the Constant table must contain a record referencing this Field record, and vice versa.

- [run time] If the flag 0x0100 (fdHasFieldRVA) is set, the FieldRVA table must contain a record referencing this Field record, and vice versa.

- [run time] Global fields, owned by the TypeDef <Module>, must have the static flag set.

- [run time] The Name entry must hold a valid reference to the #Strings stream, indexing a nonempty string no more than 1,023 bytes long in UTF-8 encoding.

- [run time] The Signature entry must hold a valid reference to the #Blob stream, indexing a valid field signature. Chapter 8 discusses validity rules for field signatures.

- No duplicate records—attributed to the same TypeDef and having the same Name and Signature values—can exist unless the accessibility flag is privatescope.

- Fields attributed to enumerations must comply with additional rules, described in Chapter 7.

FieldLayout Table Validity Rules

- The Field entry must hold a valid reference to the Field table.

- The field referenced in the Field entry must not have the static flag set.

- [run time] If the referenced field is an object reference type and belongs to TypeDefs that have an explicit layout, the Offset entry must hold a value that is a multiple of sizeof(void*).

- [run time] If the referenced field is an object reference type and belongs to TypeDefs that have an explicit layout, this field must not overlap with any other field.

FieldRVA Table Validity Rules

- [run time] The RVA entry must hold a valid nonzero relative virtual address.

- The Field entry must hold a valid index to the Field table.

- No duplicate records referencing the same field can exist.

FieldMarshal Table Validity Rules

- The Parent entry must hold a valid reference to the Field or Param table.

- No duplicate records that contain the same Parent value can exist.

- The NativeType entry must hold a valid reference to the #Blob stream, indexing a valid marshaling signature. Chapter 7 describes native types that make up the marshaling signatures.

Constant Table Validity Rules

- The Type entry must hold a valid ELEMENT_TYPE_* code, one of the following: bool, char, a signed or unsigned integer of 1 to 8 bytes, string, or object.

- The Value entry must hold a valid offset in the #Blob stream.

- The Parent entry must hold a valid reference to the Field, Property, or Param table.

- No duplicate records that contain the same Parent value can exist.

MemberRef Table Validity Rules

- [run time] The Class entry must hold a valid reference to one of the following tables: TypeRef, TypeSpec, ModuleRef, MemberRef, or Method.

- [run time] The Class entry of a MemberRef record referencing a field must hold a valid reference to the TypeRef or ModuleRef table.

- [run time] The Name entry must hold a valid offset in the #Strings stream, indexing a nonempty string no longer than 1,023 bytes in UTF-8 encoding.

- [run time] The name defined by the Name entry must not match the common language runtime reserved names _Deleted* or _VtblGap*.

- [run time] The Signature entry must hold a valid offset in the #Blob stream, indexing a valid MemberRef signature. Chapter 7 discusses validity rules for MemberRef signatures.

- No duplicate records with all three entries matching can exist.

- An item (field or method) that a MemberRef record references must not have the accessibility flag privatescope.

CHAPTER 10

■ ■ ■

Methods

Methods are the third and last leg of the tripod supporting the entire concept of managed programming, the first two being types and fields. When it comes down to execution, types, fields, and methods are the central players, with the rest of the metadata simply providing additional information about this triad.

Method items can appear in three contexts: a method definition, a method reference (for example, when a method is called), and a method implementation (when a method provides the implementation of another method).

Method Metadata

Similar to field-related metadata, method-related metadata involves definition-specific and reference-specific metadata. In addition, method-related metadata includes the method implementation, discussed later in this chapter, as well as method semantics, method interoperability, and security metadata. (Chapter 15 describes method semantics, Chapter 18 examines method interoperability, and Chapter 17 includes method security.) Figure 10-1 shows the metadata tables involved in the method definition and referencing implementation and their mutual dependencies. To avoid cluttering the illustration, I have not included metadata tables involved in the other three method-related aspects: method semantics, method interoperability, and security metadata. The MethodSpec table, introduced in version 2.0 of the CLR, is used to define the generic method instantiations. This table will be discussed in Chapter 12.

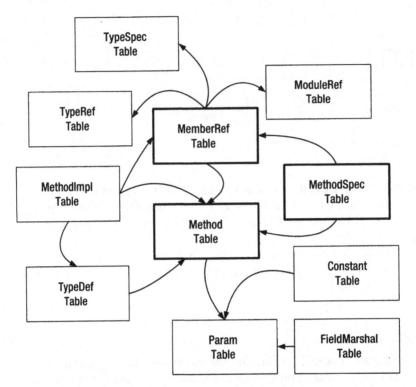

Figure 10-1. *Metadata tables related to method definition and referencing*

Method Table Record Entries

The central table for method definition is the Method table, which has the associated token type mdtMethodDef (0x06000000). A record in the Method table has six entries:

- RVA (4-byte unsigned integer). The RVA of the method body in the module. The method body consists of the header, IL code, and managed exception handling descriptors. The RVA must point to a read-only section of the PE file.

- ImplFlags (2-byte unsigned integer). Implementation binary flags indicating the specifics of the method implementation.

- Flags (2-byte unsigned integer). Binary flags indicating the method's accessibility and other characteristics.

- Name (offset in the #Strings stream). The name of the method (not including the name of the class to which the method belongs). This entry must index a string of nonzero length no longer than 1,023 bytes in UTF-8 encoding.

- Signature (offset in the #Blob stream). The method signature. This entry must index a blob of nonzero size and must comply with the method definition signature rules described in Chapter 8.

- ParamList (RID in the Param table). The record index of the start of the parameter list belonging to this method. The end of the parameter list is defined by the start of the next method's parameter list or by the end of the Param table (the same pattern as in method and field lists belonging to a TypeDef).

As in the case of field definition, Method records carry no information regarding the parent class of the method. Instead, the Method table is referenced in the MethodList entries of TypeDef records, indexing the start of Method records belonging to each particular TypeDef.

The RVA entry must be 0 or must hold a valid relative virtual address pointing to a read-only section of the image file. If the RVA value points to a read/write section, the loader will reject the method unless the application is run from a local drive with all security checks disabled. If the RVA entry holds 0, it means this method is implemented somewhere else (imported from a COM library, platform-invoked from an unmanaged DLL, or simply implemented by descendants of the class owning this method). All these cases are described by special combinations of method flags and implementation flags.

The ILAsm syntax for method definition is the following:

```
<method_def> ::=
.method <flags> <call_conv> <ret_type> <name>(<arg_list>) < impl> {
   <method_body> }
```

where <call_conv>, <ret_type>, and <arg_list> are the method calling convention, the return type, and the argument list defining the method signature.

For example:

```
.method public instance void set_X(int32 value) cil managed
{
  ldarg.0
  ldarg.1
  stfld int32 .this::x
  ret
}
```

Method Flags

The nonterminal symbol <flags> identifies the method binary flags, which are defined in the enumeration CorMethodAttr in CorHdr.h and are described in the following list:

- Accessibility flags (mask 0x0007), which are similar to the accessibility flags of fields:

  - privatescope (0x0000). This is the default accessibility. A private scope method is exempt from the requirement of having a unique triad of owner, name, and signature and hence must always be referenced by a MethodDef token and never by a MemberRef token. The privatescope methods are accessible (callable) from anywhere within current module.

  - private (0x0001). The method is accessible from its owner class and from classes nested in the method's owner.

- `famandassem` (0x0002). The method is accessible from types belonging to the owner's family—that is, the owner itself and all its descendants—defined in the current assembly.

- `assembly` (0x0003). The method is accessible from types defined in the current assembly.

- `family` (0x0004). The method is accessible from the owner's family.

- `famorassem` (0x0005). The method is accessible from the owner's family and from all types defined in the current assembly.

- `public` (0x0006). The method is accessible from any type.

- Contract flags (mask 0x00F0):

  - `static` (0x0010). The method is static, shared by all instances of the type.

  - `final` (0x0020). The method cannot be overridden. This flag must be paired with the `virtual` flag; otherwise, it is meaningless and is ignored.

  - `virtual` (0x0040). The method is virtual. This flag cannot be paired with the `static` flag.

  - `hidebysig` (0x0080). The method hides all methods of the parent classes that have a matching signature and name (as opposed to having a matching name only). This flag is ignored by the common language runtime and is provided for the use of compilers only. The IL assembler recognizes this flag but does not use it.

- Virtual method table (v-table) control flags (mask 0x0300):

  - `newslot` (0x0100). A new slot is created in the class's v-table for this virtual method so that it does not override the virtual method of the same name and signature this class inherited from its base class. This flag can be used only in conjunction with the `virtual` flag.

  - `strict` (0x0200). This virtual method can be overridden only if it is accessible from the overriding class. This flag can be used only in conjunction with the `virtual` flag.

- Implementation flags (mask 0x2C08):

  - `abstract` (0x0400). The method is abstract; no implementation is provided. This method must be overridden by the nonabstract descendants of the class owning the abstract method. Any class owning an abstract method must have its own abstract flag set. The RVA entry of an abstract method record must be 0.

  - `specialname` (0x0800). The method is special in some way, as described by the name.

  - `pinvokeimpl( <pinvoke_spec> )` (0x2000). The method has an unmanaged implementation and is called through the platform invocation mechanism P/Invoke, discussed in Chapter 18. `<pinvoke_spec>` in parentheses defines the implementation map, which is a record in the ImplMap metadata table specifying the unmanaged DLL exporting the method and the method's unmanaged calling convention. If the DLL name in <pinvoke_spec> is provided, the method's RVA must be 0, because the method is implemented externally. If the DLL name is not specified or the <pinvoke_spec> itself is not provided—that is, the parentheses are empty—the defined method is a local P/Invoke, implemented in unmanaged native code embedded in the current PE file; in this case, its RVA must not be 0 and must point to the location, in the current PE file, of the native method's body.

- unmanagedexp (0x0008). The managed method is exposed as an unmanaged export. This flag is not currently used by the common language runtime.

- Reserved flags (cannot be set explicitly; mask 0xD000):

  - rtspecialname (0x1000). The method has a special name reserved for the internal use of the runtime. Four method names are reserved: .ctor for instance constructors, .cctor for class constructors, _VtblGap* for v-table placeholders, and _Deleted* for methods marked for deletion but not actually removed from metadata. The keyword rtspecialname is ignored by the IL assembler and is displayed by the IL disassembler for informational purposes only. This flag must be accompanied by a specialname flag.

  - [no ILAsm keyword] (0x4000). The method either has an associated DeclSecurity metadata record that holds security details concerning access to the method or has the associated custom attribute System.Security.SuppressUnmanagedCodeSecurityAttribute.

  - reqsecobj (0x8000). This method calls another method containing security code, so it requires an additional stack slot for a security object. This flag is formally under the Reserved mask, so it cannot be set explicitly. Setting this flag requires emitting the pseudocustom attribute System.Security.DynamicSecurityMethodAttribute. When the IL assembler encounters the keyword reqsecobj, it does exactly that: emits the pseudocustom attribute and thus sets this "reserved" flag. Since anybody can set this flag by emitting the pseudocustom attribute, I wonder what the reason was for putting this flag under the Reserved mask. This flag could just as well been left as assignable.

I've used the word *implementation* here and there rather extensively; perhaps some clarification is in order, to avoid confusion. First, note that *method implementation* in the sense of one method providing the implementation for another is discussed later in this chapter. Implementation-specific flags of a method are not related to that topic; rather, they indicate the features of implementation of the current method. Second, a Method record contains two binary flag entries: Flags and ImplFlags (implementation flags). It so happens that part of Flags (mask 0x2C08) is also implementation related. That's a lot of implementations. Thus far, I have been talking about the implementation part of Flags. For information about ImplFlags, see "Method Implementation Flags" later in this chapter.

Method Name

A method name in ILAsm either is a simple name or (in version 2.0 only) a dotted name or is one of the two keywords .ctor or .cctor. As you already know, .ctor is the reserved name for instance constructors, while .cctor is reserved for class constructors, or type initializers. In ILAsm, .ctor and .cctor are keywords, so they should not be single quoted as any other irregular simple name.

The general requirements for a method name are straightforward: the name must contain 1 to 1,023 bytes in UTF-8 encoding plus a zero terminator, and it should not match one of the four reserved method names—unless you really mean it. If you give a method one of these reserved names, the common language runtime treats the method according to this name.

Method Implementation Flags

The nonterminal symbol <impl> in the method definition form denotes the implementation flags of the method (the ImplFlags entry of a Method record). The implementation flags are defined in the enumeration CorMethodImpl in CorHdr.h and are described in the following list:

- Code type (mask 0x0003):

  - cil (0x0000). The default. The method is implemented in common intermediate language (CIL, a.k.a. IL or MSIL). Yes, I realize that CIL does not sound like a good abbreviation for those familiar with the innards of the Visual C++ compiler, because in that area it traditionally means "C intermediate language." You can use the il keyword if you don't like cil. Or don't use either of them; it is a default flag anyway.

  - native (0x0001). The method is implemented in native platform-specific code.

  - optil (0x0002). The method is implemented in optimized IL. The optimized IL is not supported in existing releases of the common language runtime, so this flag should not be set.

  - runtime (0x0003). The method implementation is automatically generated by the runtime itself. Only certain methods from the base class library (Mscorlib.dll) carry this flag. If this flag is set, the RVA of the method must be 0.

- Code management (mask 0x0004):

  - managed (0x0000). The default. The code is managed. In the existing releases of the runtime, this flag cannot be paired with the native flag.

  - unmanaged (0x0004). The code is unmanaged. This flag must be paired with the native flag.

- Implementation and interoperability (mask 0x10D8):

  - forwardref (0x0010). The method is defined, but the IL code of the method is not supplied. This flag is used primarily in edit-and-continue scenarios and in managed object files, produced by the Visual C++ compiler. This flag should not be set for any of the methods in a managed PE file.

- `preservesig` (0x0080). The method signature must not be mangled during the interoperation with classic COM code, which is discussed in Chapter 18.

- `internalcall` (0x1000). Reserved for internal use. This flag indicates that the method is internal to the runtime and must be called in a special way. If this flag is set, the RVA of the method must be 0.

- `synchronized` (0x0020). Instruct the JIT compiler to automatically insert code to take a lock on entry to the method and release the lock on exit from the method. When an instance synchronized method is called, the lock is taken on the instance reference (the this parameter). For static methods, the lock is taken on the System.Type object associated with the class of the method. Methods belonging to value types cannot have this flag set.

- `noinlining` (0x0008). The runtime is not allowed to inline the method—that is, to replace the method call with explicit insertion of the method's IL code.

Take a look at the examples shown here:

```
.method public static int32 Diff(int32,int32) cil managed
{
    ...
}
.method public void .ctor( ) runtime managed {}
```

Method Parameters

Method parameters reside in the Param metadata table, whose records have three entries:

- `Flags` (2-byte unsigned integer). Binary flags characterizing the parameter.

- `Sequence` (2-byte unsigned integer). The sequence number of the parameter, with 0 corresponding to the method return.

- `Name` (offset in the #Strings stream). The name of the parameter, which can be zero length (because the parameter name is used solely for Reflection and is not involved in any resolution by name). For the method return, it must be zero length.

Parameter flags are defined in the enumeration CorParamAttr in CorHdr.h and are described in the following list:

- Input/output flags (mask 0x0013):
  - `in` (0x0001). Input parameter.
  - `out` (0x0002). Output parameter.
  - `opt` (0x0010). Optional parameter.

- Reserved flags (cannot be set explicitly; mask 0xF000):
  - [no ILAsm keyword] (0x1000). The parameter has an associated Constant record. The flag is set by the metadata emission API when the respective Constant record is emitted.

- marshal(<native_type>) (0x2000). The parameter has an associated FieldMarshal record specifying how the parameter must be marshaled when consumed by unmanaged code.

To describe the ILAsm syntax of parameter definition, let me remind you of the method definition form:

```
<method_def> ::=
.method <flags> <call_conv> <ret_type> <name>(<arg_list>) < impl> {
   <method_body> }
```

where

```
<ret_type> ::=  <type> [marshal(<native_type>)];
<arg_list> ::= [ <arg> [,<arg>*] ];
<arg> ::= [ [<in_out_flag>]* ] <type> [marshal(<native_typ e>)]
         [<p_name>];
<in_out_flag> ::= in | out | opt
```

Obviously, <p_name> is the name of the parameter, which, if provided, must be a simple name.

Here is an example of parameter definitions:

```
.method public static int32 marshal(int) Diff(
[in] int32 marshal(int) First,
[in] int32 marshal(int) Second)
{
   ...
}
```

The syntax just shown takes care of all the entries of a Param record (Flags, Sequence, Name) and, if needed, those of the associated FieldMarshal record (Parent, NativeType). To set the default values for the parameters, which are records in the Constant table, we need to add parameter specifications within the method scope:

```
<param_const_def> ::= .param [<sequence>] = <const_type> [ (<value>) ]
```

<sequence> is the parameter's sequence number. This number should not be 0, because a 0 sequence number corresponds to the return type, and a "default return value" does not make sense. <const_type> and <value> are the same as for field default value definitions, described in Chapter 9. For example:

```
.method public static int32 marshal(int) Diff(
[in] int32 marshal(int) First,
[opt] int32 marshal(int) Second)
{
   .param [2] = int32(0)
   ...
}
```

According to the common language runtime metadata model, it is not necessary to emit a Param record for each return or argument of a method. Rather, it must be done only if we want to specify the name, flags, marshaling, or default value. The IL assembler emits Param records for all arguments unconditionally and for a method return only if marshaling is specified. The name, flags, and default value are not applicable to a method return.

Referencing the Methods

Method references, like field references, translate into either MethodDef tokens or MemberRef tokens. As a rule, a reference to a locally defined method translates into a MethodDef token. However, even a locally defined method can be represented by a MemberRef token; and in certain cases, such as references to vararg methods, it *must* be represented by a MemberRef token.

The ILAsm syntax for method referencing is as follows:

```
<method_ref> ::=
[method] <call_conv> <ret_type> <class_ref>::<name>(<arg_list>)
```

The method keyword, with no leading dot, is used in the following two cases in which the kind of metadata item being referenced is not clear from the context:

- When a method is referenced as an argument of the ldtoken instruction

- When a method is referenced in an explicit specification of a custom attribute's owner (see Chapter 16 for more information)

The same rules apply to the use of the field keyword in field references. The method keyword is used in one additional context: when specifying a function pointer as a type of field, variable, or parameter (see Chapter 8). That case, however, involves not a method reference but a signature definition.

Flags, implementation flags, and parameter-related information (names, marshaling, and so on) are not specified in a method reference. As you know, a MemberRef record holds only the member parent's token, name, and signature—the three elements needed to identify a method or a field unambiguously. Here are a few examples of method references:

```
call instance void Foo::Bar(int32,int32)
ldtoken method instance void Foo::Bar(int32,int32)
```

In the case of method references, the nonterminal symbol <class_ref> can be a TypeDef, TypeRef, TypeSpec, or ModuleRef:

```
call instance void Foo::Bar(int32,int32) // TypeDef
call instance void [OtherAssembly]Foo::Bar(int32,int32) // TypeRef
call instance void class Foo[]::Bar(int32,int32) // TypeSpec
call void [.module Other.dll]::Bar(int32,int32) // ModuleRef
```

Method Implementation Metadata

Method implementations represent specific metadata describing method overriding, in which one virtual method's implementation is substituted for another virtual method's implementation. The method implementation metadata is held in the MethodImpl table, which has the following structure:

- Class (RID in the TypeDef table). The record index of the TypeDef implementing a method—in other words, replacing the method's implementation with that of another method.

- MethodBody (coded token of type MethodDefOrRef). A token indexing a record in the Method table that corresponds to the implementing method—that is, to the method whose implementation substitutes for another method's implementation. A coded token of this type can point to the MemberRef table as well, but this is illegal in the existing releases of the common language runtime. The method indexed by MethodBody must be virtual. In the existing releases of the runtime, the method indexed by Method-Body must belong to the class indexed by the Class entry.

- MethodDecl (coded token of type MethodDefOrRef). A token indexing a record in the Method table or the MemberRef table that corresponds to the implemented method—that is, to the method whose implementation is being replaced by another method's implementation. The method indexed by MethodDecl must be virtual.

Static, Instance, Virtual Methods

We can classify methods in many ways: global methods vs. member methods, variable argument lists vs. fixed argument lists, and so on. Global and vararg methods are discussed in later sections. In this section, we'll focus on static vs. instance methods. Take a look at Figure 10-2.

Static methods are shared by all instances of a type. They don't require an instance reference (this) and cannot access instance members unless the instance reference is provided explicitly. When a type is loaded, static methods are placed in a separate typewide table.

The signature of a static method is exactly as it is specified, with the first specified argument being number 0:

```
.method public static void Bar(int32 i, float32 r)
{
    ldarg.0 // Load int32 i on stack
    ...
}
```

Instance methods are instance specific and have the this instance reference as an unlisted first (number 0) argument of the signature:

```
.method public instance void Bar(int32 i, float32 r)
{
    ldarg.0 // Load instance pointer on stack
    ldarg.1 // Load int32 i on stack
    ...
}
```

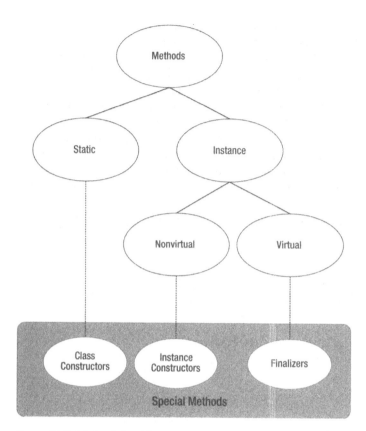

Figure 10-2. *Method classification*

■Note Be careful about the use of the keyword instance in specifying the method calling convention. When a method is defined, its flags—including the static flag—are explicitly specified. Because of this, at definition time it's not necessary to specify the instance calling convention—it can be inferred from the presence or absence of the static flag. When a method is referenced, however, its flags are not specified, so in this case the instance keyword *must* be specified explicitly for instance methods; otherwise, the referenced method is presumed static. This creates a seeming contradiction: a method when declared is instance by default (no static flag specified), and the same method when referenced is static by default (no instance specified). But static is a flag and instance is a calling convention, so in fact we're dealing with two different default options here.

Instance methods are divided into virtual and nonvirtual methods, identified by the presence or absence of the virtual flag. The virtual methods of a class can be called through the virtual method table (v-table) of this class, which adds a level of indirection to implement so-called late binding. Method calling through the v-table (virtual dispatch) is performed by a special virtual call instruction (callvirt). Virtual methods can be overridden in derived classes by these classes' own virtual methods of the same signature and name—and even of a different name, although such overriding requires an explicit declaration, as described later in this chapter. Virtual methods can be abstract or might offer some implementation.

If you have a nonvirtual method declared in a class, it does not mean you can't declare another nonvirtual method with the same name and signature in a class derived from the first one. You can, but it will be a different method, having nothing to do with the method declared in the base class. Such a method in the derived class hides the respective method in the base class, but the hidden method can still be called if you explicitly specify the owning class.

If you do the same with virtual methods, however, the method declared in the derived class actually overrides (replaces in the v-table) the method declared in the base class. This is true unless, of course, you specify the newslot flag on the overriding method, in which case the overriding method will occupy a new entry of the v-table and hence will not really be overriding anything.

To illustrate this point, take a look at the following code from the sample file Virt_not.il on the Apress Web site:

```
.class public A
{
    .method public specialname void .ctor()
    {
        ldarg.0
        call instance void [mscorlib]System.Object::.ctor()
        ret
    }
    .method public void Foo()
    {
        ldstr "A::Foo"
        call void [mscorlib]System.Console::WriteLine(string)
        ret
    }
    .method public virtual void Bar()
    {
        ldstr "A::Bar"
        call void [mscorlib]System.Console::WriteLine(string)
        ret
    }
    .method public virtual void Baz()
    {
        ldstr "A::Baz"
        call void [mscorlib]System.Console::WriteLine(string)
        ret
    }

}
```

```
.class public B extends A
{
   .method public specialname void .ctor()
   {
      ldarg.0
      call instance void A::.ctor()
      ret
   }
   .method public void Foo()
   {
      ldstr "B::Foo"
      call void [mscorlib]System.Console::WriteLine(string)
      ret
   }
   .method public virtual void Bar()
   {
      ldstr "B::Bar"
      call void [mscorlib]System.Console::WriteLine(string)
      ret
   }
   .method public virtual newslot void Baz()
   {
      ldstr "B::Baz"
      call void [mscorlib]System.Console::WriteLine(string)
      ret
   }
}

.method public static void Exec()
{
   .entrypoint
   newobj instance void B::.ctor() // Create instance of derived class
   castclass class A               // Cast it to base class

   dup                    // We need 3 instance pointers
   dup                    // On stack for 3 calls

   call instance void A::Foo()
   callvirt instance void A::Bar()
   callvirt instance void A::Baz()
   ret
}
```

If we compile and run the sample, we'll receive this output:

```
A:Foo
B:Bar
A:Baz
```

The method A::Foo is nonvirtual; hence, declaring B::Foo does not affect A::Foo in any way. So when we cast B to A and call A::Foo, B::Foo does not enter the picture—it's a different method.

The A::Bar method is virtual, as is B::Bar, so when we create an instance of B, B::Bar replaces A::Bar in the v-table. Casting B to A after that does not change anything: B::Bar is sitting in the v-table of the class instance, and A::Bar is gone. Hence, when we call A::Bar using virtual dispatch, the "usurper" B::Bar is called instead.

Both the A::Baz and B::Baz methods are virtual, but B::Baz is marked newslot. Thus, instead of replacing A::Baz in the v-table, B::Baz takes a new entry and peacefully coexists with A::Baz. Since A::Baz is still present in the v-table of the instance, the situation is practically (oops, almost wrote "virtually"; I should watch it; we can't have puns in such a serious book) identical to the situation with A::Foo and B::Foo, except that the calls are done through the v-table. The Visual Basic .NET compiler likes this concept and uses it rather extensively.

If we don't want a virtual method to be overridden in the class descendants, we can mark it with the final flag. If you try to override a final method, the loader fails and throws a TypeLoad exception.

Instances of unboxed value types don't have pointers to v-tables. It is perfectly legal to declare the virtual methods as members of a value type, but these methods can be virtually called only from a boxed instance of the value type:

```
.class public value XXX
{
    .method public void YYY( )
    {
        ...
    }
    .method public virtual void ZZZ( )
    {
        ...
    }
}
.method public static void Exec( )
{
    .entrypoint
    .locals init(valuetype XXX xxx) // Variable xxx is an
                                    // Instance of XXX
    ldloca xxx                      // Load managed ptr to xxx
    call instance void XXX::YYY( )  // Legal: access to value
                                    // type member
                                    // by managed ptr

    ldloca xxx
```

```
        callvirt instance void XXX::ZZZ( ) // Illegal: virtual call of
                                           //   methods possible only
                                           //   by object reference.
        ldloca xxx
        call instance void XXX::ZZZ( )  // Legal: nonvirtual call,
                                        //   access to value type member
                                        //   by managed ptr.
        ldloc xxx                       //   Load instance of XXX.
        box valuetype XXX               //   Convert it to object reference.
        callvirt instance void XXX::ZZZ( ) // Legal
        ...
}
```

Explicit Method Overriding

Thus far, I've discussed implicit virtual method overriding—that is, a virtual method defined in a class overriding another virtual method of the same name and signature, defined in the class's ancestor or an interface the class implements. But implicit overriding covers only the simplest case.

Consider the following problem: class A implements interfaces IX and IY, and each of these interfaces defines its own virtual method int32 Foo(int32). It is known that these methods are different and must be implemented separately. Implicit overriding can't help in this situation. It's time to use the MethodImpl metadata table.

The MethodImpl metadata table contains descriptors of explicit method overrides. An explicit override states which method overrides which other method. To define an explicit override in ILAsm, the following directive is used within the scope of the overriding method:

.override <class_ref>::<method_name>

The signature of the method need not be specified because the signature of the overriding method must match the signature of the overridden method, and the signature of the overriding method is known: it's the signature of the current method. For example:

```
.class public interface IX {
    .method public abstract virtual int32 Foo(int32) { }
}
.class public interface IY {
.method public abstract virtual int32 Foo(int32) { }
}
.class public A implements IX,IY {
    .method public virtual int32 XFoo(int32) {
    .override IX::Foo
    ...
    }
    .method public virtual int32 YFoo(int32) {
    .override IY::Foo
    ...
    }
}
```

Not surprisingly, we can't override the same method with two different methods within the same class: there is only one slot in the v-table to be overridden. However, we can use the same method to override several virtual methods. Let's have a look at the following code from the sample file Override.il on the Apress Web site:

```
.class public A
{
    .method public specialname void .ctor()
    {
        ldarg.0
        call instance void [mscorlib]System.Object::.ctor()
        ret
    }
    .method public void Foo()
    {
        ldstr "A::Foo"
        call void [mscorlib]System.Console::WriteLine(string)
        ret
    }
    .method public virtual void Bar()
    {
        ldstr "A::Bar"
        call void [mscorlib]System.Console::WriteLine(string)
        ret
    }
    .method public virtual void Baz()
    {
        ldstr "A::Baz"
        call void [mscorlib]System.Console::WriteLine(string)
        ret
    }
}
.class public B extends A
{
    .method public specialname void .ctor()
    {
        ldarg.0
        call instance void A::.ctor()
        ret
    }
    .method public void Foo()
    {
        ldstr "B::Foo"
        call void [mscorlib]System.Console::WriteLine(string)
        ret
    }
    .method public virtual void BarBaz()
    {
```

```
        .override A::Bar
        .override A::Baz
        ldstr "B::BarBaz"
        call void [mscorlib]System.Console::WriteLine(string)
        ret
    }
}
...
.method public static void Exec()
{
    .entrypoint
    newobj instance void B::.ctor() // Create instance of derived class
    castclass class A            // Cast it to base class

    dup                  // We need 3 instance pointers
    dup                  // On stack for 3 calls

    call instance void A::Foo()
    callvirt instance void A::Bar()
    callvirt instance void A::Baz()
    ...
    ret
}
```

The output of this code demonstrates that the method B::BarBaz overrides both A::Bar and A::Baz:

```
A::Foo
B::BarBaz
B::BarBaz
```

Virtual method overriding, both implicit and explicit, is propagated to the descendants of the overriding class, unless the descendants themselves override those methods. The second half of the sample file Override.il demonstrates this:

```
...
.class public C extends B
{
    .method public specialname void .ctor()
    {
        ldarg.0
        call instance void B::.ctor()
        ret
    }
    // No overrides; let's inherit everything from B
}
.method public static void Exec()
{
```

```
.entrypoint
...
newobj instance void C::.ctor() // Create instance of derived class
castclass class A            // Cast it to "grandparent"

dup                    // We need 3 instance pointers
dup                    // On stack for 3 calls

call instance void A::Foo()
callvirt instance void A::Bar()
callvirt instance void A::Baz()
ret
}
```

The output is the same, which proves that class C has inherited the overridden methods from class B:

```
A::Foo
B::BarBaz
B::BarBaz
```

ILAsm supports an extended form of the explicit override directive, placed within the class scope:

.override <class_ref>::<method_name> with <method_ref>

For example, the overriding effect would be the same in the preceding code if we defined class B like so:

```
.class public B extends A
{
   .method public specialname void .ctor()
   {
      ldarg.0
      call instance void A::.ctor()
      ret
   }
   .method public void Foo()
   {
      ldstr "B::Foo"
      call void [mscorlib]System.Console::WriteLine(string)
      ret
   }
   .method public virtual void BarBaz()
   {
      ldstr "B::BarBaz"
      call void [mscorlib]System.Console::WriteLine(string)
      ret
```

```
      }
    .override A::Bar with instance void B::BarBaz()
    .override A::Baz with instance void B::BarBaz()
}
```

In the extended form of the .override directive, the overriding method must be fully specified because the extended form is used within the overriding class scope, not within the overriding method scope.

To tell the truth, the extended form of the .override directive is not very useful in the existing versions of the common language runtime because the overriding methods are restricted to those of the overriding class. Under these circumstances, the short form of the directive is sufficient, and I doubt that anyone would want to use the more cumbersome extended form. But I've noticed that in this industry the circumstances tend to change.

One more note: you probably have noticed that the sample Override.il looks tedious and repetitive: similar constructors of the classes and multiple calls to [mscorlib]System. Console::WriteLine(string). As was discussed in Chapter 3, version 2.0 of the ILAsm allows you to streamline the programming by means of defines, typedefs, and the special keywords .this, .base, and .nester. Have a look at the sample Override_v2.il on the Apress Web site:

```
#define DEFLT_CTOR
".method public specialname void .ctor()
  {ldarg.0; call instance void .base::.ctor(); ret}"


.typedef method void [mscorlib]System.Console::WriteLine(string) as PrintString

.class public A
{
  DEFLT_CTOR
  .method public void Foo()
  {
    ldstr "A::Foo"
    call PrintString
    ret
  }
  .method public virtual void Bar()
  {
    ldstr "A::Bar"
    call PrintString
    ret
  }
  .method public virtual void Baz()
  {
    ldstr "A::Baz"
    call PrintString
    ret
  }


}
```

```
.class public B extends A
{
   DEFLT_CTOR
   .method public void Foo()
   {
      ldstr "B::Foo"
      call PrintString
      ret
   }
   .method public virtual void BarBaz()
   {
      .override .base::Bar
      .override .base::Baz
      ldstr "B::BarBaz"
      call PrintString
      ret
   }
}
...
.class public C extends B
{
   DEFLT_CTOR
   // No overrides; let's inherit everything from B
}
.method public static void Exec()
{
   .entrypoint
   ...
   newobj instance void C::.ctor() //  Create instance of derived class
   castclass class A          // Cast it to "grandparent"

   dup                // We need 3 instance pointers
   dup                // On stack for 3 calls

   call instance void A::Foo()
   callvirt instance void A::Bar()
   callvirt instance void A::Baz()
   ret
}
```

Not only is sample Override_v2.il easier to read and to type, it is compiled faster (only marginally; you will not notice any effect compiling such small sample). I will leave it to you to modify the Virt_not.il sample in the same way. Just don't forget that these syntax enhancements are specific to version 2.0 and are not supported in versions 1.0 and 1.1.

Method Overriding and Accessibility

Can I override an inaccessible virtual method? For example, if class A has private virtual method Foo, can I derive class B from A and override Foo? I know I cannot call A::Foo, but I don't want to call it; I want to override it and call my own B::Foo. Can I?

"Yes you can," says C++, "exactly because you are not calling the private method Foo of A."

"No you cannot," says C#, "because you have no access whatsoever to the private method Foo of A."

"Eh?" says Visual Basic…. No, no, I'm just kidding, of course. Actually, VB sides with C#.

So what should the *common* language runtime say in this regard? As usual, it finds some common ground that is acceptable to all languages.

There is the special flag strict (0x0200), which controls the "overridability" of a virtual method. If the method is declared strict virtual, then it can be overridden only by classes that have access to it. A private strict virtual method, for example, cannot be overridden in principle, so it just as well might have been marked final.

If the flag strict is not specified, then the method can be overridden without any regard to its accessibility.

So C# and VB declare their methods strict virtual, C++ declares its methods virtual, and everyone is happy.

An interesting thing about this situation is that the explicit overrides are *always* bound to the accessibility, as if all virtual methods were strict virtual. This creates a regrettable asymmetry between implicit and explicit overriding.

One more note about overriding and accessibility: you cannot override a virtual method with a method that has more restricted accessibility. For example, you cannot override a public method with a family method, but you can override a family method with a public method. This rule works for both implicit and explicit overrides. I leave it to you to figure out the reasoning behind this rule.

Method Header Attributes

The RVA value (if it is nonzero) of a Method record points to the method body. The managed method body consists of a method header, IL code, and an optional managed exception handling (EH) table, as shown in Figure 10-3.

Two types of method headers—fat and tiny—are defined in CorHdr.h. The first two bits of the header indicate its type: bits 10 stand for the tiny format, and bits 11 stand for the fat format. Why do we need two bits for a simple dichotomy? Speaking hypothetically, the day might come when more method header types are introduced.

A tiny method header is only 1 byte in size, with the first two (least significant) bits holding the type—10—and the six remaining bits holding the method IL code size in bytes. A method is given a tiny header if it has neither local variables nor managed exception handling, if it works fine with the default evaluation stack depth of 8 slots, and if its code size is less than 64 bytes. A fat header is 12 bytes in size and has the structure described in Table 10-1. The fat headers must begin at 4-byte boundaries. Figure 10-4 shows the structures of both tiny and fat method headers.

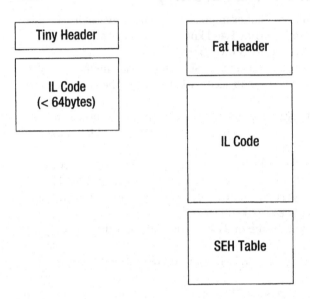

Figure 10-3. *Managed method body structure*

Table 10-1. *The Fat Header Structure*

Entry Size	Description
WORD	The lower 2 bits hold the fat header type code (0x3); the next 10 bits hold Flags. The upper 4 bits hold the size of the header in DWORDs and must be set to 3. Currently used flags are 0x2, which indicates that more sections follow the IL code—that is, an exception handling table is present—and 0x4, which indicates that local variables will be initialized to 0 automatically on entry to method.
WORD	MaxStack is the maximal evaluation stack depth in slots. Stack size in IL is measured not in bytes but in slots, with each slot able to accept one item regardless of the item's size. The default value is 8 slots, and the stack depth can be set explicitly in ILAsm by the directive .maxstack <integer> used inside the method scope. Be careful about trying to economize the method run-time footprint by specifying .maxstack lower than the default: if the specified stack depth differs from the default depth, the IL assembler has no choice but to give the method a fat header even if the method has neither local variables nor exception handling table, and its code size is less than 64 bytes.
DWORD	CodeSize is the size of the IL code in bytes.
DWORD	LocalVarSigTok is the token of the local variables signature (token type 0x11000000). Chapter 8 discusses the structure of the local variables signature. If the method has no local variables, this entry is set to 0.

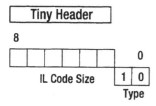

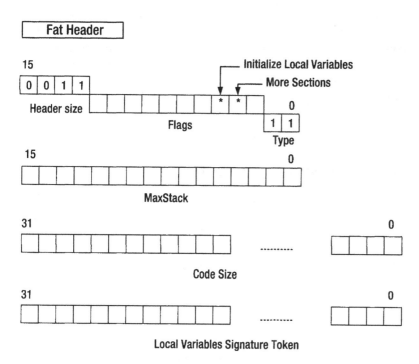

Figure 10-4. *The structures of tiny and fat method headers*

Local Variables

Local variables are the typed data items that are declared within the method scope and exist from the moment the method is called until it returns. ILAsm allows us to assign names to local variables and reference them by name, but IL instructions address the local variables by their zero-based ordinals.

When the source code is compiled in debug mode, the local variable names are stored in the PDB file accompanying the module, and in this case the local variable names might survive round-tripping. In general, however, these names are not preserved because they, unlike the names of fields and method parameters, are not part of the metadata.

All the local variables, no matter when they are declared within the method scope, form a single signature, kept in the StandAloneSig metadata table (token type 0x11000000). The token referencing respective signature is part of the method header.

Local variables are declared in ILAsm as follows:

```
.method public void Foo(int32 ii, int32 jj)
{
    .locals init (float32 ff, float64 dd, object oo, string ss)
    ...
}
```

The init keyword sets the flag 0x4 in the method header, indicating that the JIT compiler must inject the code initializing all local variables before commencing the method execution. Initialization means that for all variables of value types, which are allocated upon declaration, the corresponding memory is zeroed, and all variables of object reference types are set to null. Code that contains methods without a local variable initialization flag set is deemed unverifiable and can be run only with verification disabled.

ILAsm does not require that all local variables be declared in one place; the following is perfectly legal:

```
.method public void Foo(int32 ii, int32 jj)
{
    .locals init (float32 ff, float64 dd, object oo, string ss)
    ...
    {
        .locals (int32 kk, bool bb)
        ...
    }
    ...
    {
        .locals (int32 mm, float32 f)
        ...
    }
    ...
}
```

In this case, the summary local variables signature will contain the types float32, float64, object, string, int32, bool, int32, and float32. Repeating init in subsequent local variable declarations of the same method is not necessary because any one of the .locals init directives sets the local variable initialization flag.

It's obvious enough that we have a redundant local variable slot in the composite signature: by the time we need mm, we don't need kk any more, so we could reuse the slot and reduce the composite signature. In ILAsm, we can do that by explicitly specifying the zero-based slot numbers for local variables:

```
.method public void Foo(int32 ii, int32 jj)
{
   .locals init ([0]float32 ff, [1]float64 dd,
                 [2]object oo, [3]string ss)
   ...
   {
     .locals ([4]int32 kk, [5]bool bb)
     ...
   }
   ...
   {
     .locals ([4]int32 mm, [6]float32 f)
     ...
   }
   ...

}
```

Could we also reuse slot 5 for variable f? No, because the type of slot 5 is bool, and we need a slot of type float32 for f. Only the slots holding local variables of the same type and used within nonoverlapping scopes can be reused.

Note The number of local variables declared in a method is completely unrelated to the .maxstack value, which depends only on how many items you might have to load simultaneously for computational purposes. For example, if you declare 20 local variables, you don't need to declare .maxstack 20; but if your method is calling another method that takes 20 arguments, you need to ensure that the stack has sufficient depth, because you will need at least to load all 20 arguments on the stack to make the call.

The number of local variables for any given method cannot exceed 65535 (0xFFFF), because the local variable ordinals are represented in the CLR by unsigned short integers. The same limitation is imposed on the number of method parameters (including the return), for the same reason.

Class Constructors

Class constructors, or type initializers, are the methods specific to a type as a whole that run after the type is loaded and before any of the type's members are accessed. You've already encountered class constructors in the preceding chapter, which discussed approaches to static field initialization. That is exactly what class constructors are most often used for: static field initialization.

Class constructors are static, have specialname and rtspecialname flags, cannot use the vararg calling convention, have neither parameters nor a return value (that is, the return type is void), and have the name .cctor, which in ILAsm is a keyword rather than a name. Because of this, only one class constructor per type can be declared. Normally, class constructors are never called from the IL code. If a type has a class constructor, this constructor is executed automatically after the type is loaded. However, a class constructor, like any other static method, can be called explicitly. As a result of such a call, the global fields of the type are reset to their initial values. Calling .cctor explicitly does not lead to type reloading.

Class Constructors and the beforefieldinit Flag

The class constructors are executed before any members (static or instance) of the classes are accessed. Normally, it means that a .cctor is executed right before first access to a static member of the class or before the first class instantiation, whichever comes first.

However, if the class has the beforefieldinit flag set (see Chapter 7), the invocation of .cctor happens on "relaxed" (as it is called in the Ecma International/ISO standard) schedule—the .cctor is supposed to be called any time, at CLR discretion, prior to the first access to a static field of the class.

In fact, the .cctor invocation schedule in presence of the beforefieldinit flag is anything but "relaxed": the .cctor is invoked right when the class is referenced, *even if no members of the class are ever accessed*.

Take a look at the following code (sample Cctors.il on the Apress Web site):

```
.assembly extern mscorlib { auto }
.assembly cctors {}
.module cctors.exe

.typedef [mscorlib]System.Console as TTY

#define DEFLT_CTOR
  ".method public specialname void .ctor()
  {ldarg.0; call instance void .base::.ctor(); ret;}"

.class public Base
{
    DEFLT_CTOR
    .method public void DoSomething()
    {
        ldarg.0
        pop
        ldstr "Base::DoSomething()"
        call void TTY::WriteLine(string)
        ret
    }
}
.class public /*beforefieldinit*/ A extends Base
{
```

```
    DEFLT_CTOR
    .method public static specialname void .cctor()
    {
        ldstr "A::.cctor()"
        call void TTY::WriteLine(string)
        ret
    }
}
.class public /*beforefieldinit*/ B extends Base
{
    DEFLT_CTOR
    .method public static specialname void .cctor()
    {
        ldstr "B::.cctor()"
        call void TTY::WriteLine(string)
        ret
    }
}


.method public static void Exec()
{
    .entrypoint
    .locals init(class Base b1)

    ldstr "Enter string"
    call void TTY::WriteLine(string)
    call string TTY::ReadLine()
    call bool string::IsNullOrEmpty(string)
    brtrue L1 // use result of IsNullOrEmpty

    // Instantiate class A with .cctor
    newobj instance void A::.ctor()
    stloc.s b1
    br L2
L1:
    // Instantiate class B with .cctor
    newobj instance void B::.ctor()
    stloc.s b1
L2:
    // Use the instance
    ldloc.s b1
    call instance void Base::DoSomething()

    ret
}
```

This code instantiates either class A or class B, depending on whether you input a non-empty or empty string. The output shows that the class constructor of respective class is executed right before the instantiation of the class:

```
>cctors.exe
```

```
Enter string

B::.cctor()
Base::DoSomething()
```

or

```
>cctors.exe
```

```
Enter string
aaa
A::.cctor()
Base::DoSomething()
```

But if we uncomment the beforefieldinit flags on declarations of classes A and B and reassemble the code, the output changes:

```
>cctors.exe
```

```
A::.cctor()
B::.cctor()
Enter string

Base::DoSomething()
```

As you see, the class constructors of both A and B are executed even before the program requests the input string, let alone before either class is accessed. It's a good thing our class constructors are so harmless—imagine what would happen if the class constructors of A and B were mutually exclusive in some respect. Besides, the class constructors are very expensive to run: the instantiation of a class with .cctor takes about 50 times longer than the instantiation of a class without .cctor, given that in both cases .cctor and .ctor summarily do the same work.

The moral of the story is this: avoid using the beforefieldinit flag if you want to run only relevant class constructors. To do so in C#, always explicitly specify static constructors for classes that have initialized static fields.

Module Constructors

What happens if I declare a type initializer (.cctor) outside any type scope? What type will it initialize and when?

The answer is simple: as you already know, the global static methods and fields belong to special type (always the first record in the TypeDef table), usually named `<Module>` and representing current managed module (PE file). Thus, the globally declared type initializer is the module initializer, or module constructor. It is executed upon module load, before any contents of this module are accessed. In this regard, a module constructor is functionally similar to `DllMain`, called with reason `DLL_PROCESS_ATTACH`. The most common use of the module constructors is the initialization of global fields, but far it be from me to stifle your imagination.

Instance Constructors

Instance constructors, unlike class constructors, are specific to an instance of a type and are used to initialize both static and instance fields of the type. Functionally, instance constructors in IL are a direct analog of C++ constructors. Instance constructors can have parameters but must return `void`, must be `instance`, must have `specialname` and `rtspecialname` flags, and must have the name `.ctor`, which is an ILAsm keyword. In the existing releases of the common language runtime, instance constructors are not allowed to be virtual. A type can have multiple instance constructors, but they must have different parameter lists because the name (`.ctor`) and the return type (`void`) are fixed.

Note that it is impossible to instantiate a reference type if it does not have an instance constructor. As an exercise, devise a technique to instantiate a reference type that has only private instance constructor(s). If you don't feel like exercising right now, take a look at sample Privatector.il on the Apress Web site.

Usually, instance constructors are called during the execution of the `newobj` instruction, when a new type instance is created:

```
.class public Foo
{
    .field private int32 tally
    .method public void .ctor( int32 tally_init)
    {
        ldarg.0  // Load the instance reference
        dup      // Need two instance references on the stack
        call instance void [mscorlib]System.Object::.ctor
                 // Call the base constructor
        ldarg.1 // Load the initializing value tally_init
        stfld int32 Foo::tally // this->tally = tally_init;
        ret
    }
    ...
}
.method public static void Exec( )
{
    .entrypoint
    .locals init (class Foo foo)
    // foo is a null reference at this point
    ldc.i4   128 //  Put 128 on stack as Foo's constructor argument
    newobj instance void Foo::.ctor(int32)
```

```
// Instance of Foo is created
stloc.0 // foo = new Foo(128);
...
```
}

But, as is the case for class constructors, an instance constructor can be called explicitly. Calling the instance constructor resets the fields of the type instance and does not create a new instance. The only problem with calling class or instance constructors explicitly is that sometimes the constructors include type instantiations, if some of the fields to be initialized are of object reference type. In this case, additional care should be taken to avoid multiple type instantiations.

Please note that before calling any instance methods, an instance constructor must call its parent's instance constructor. This is called *instance initialization*, and without it any further instance method calls on the created instance of this type are unverifiable. Accessing the instance fields of an uninitialized instance is, however, verifiable.

Caution Calling the class and instance constructors explicitly, however possible in principle, renders the code unverifiable. This limitation is imposed on the constructors of the reference types (classes) only and does not concern those of the value types. The CLR does not execute the instance constructors of value types when an instance of the value type is created (for example, when a local variable of some value type is declared), so the only way to invoke a value type instance constructor is to call it explicitly. The only place where an instance constructor of a reference type can be verifiably called explicitly is within an instance constructor of the class's direct descendant.

Constructors of the classes cannot be the arguments of the ldftn instruction. In other words, you can't obtain a function pointer to a .ctor or .cctor of a class.

Class and instance constructors are the only methods allowed to set the values of the static and instance (respectively) fields marked initonly. Methods belonging to some other class, including .ctor and .cctor, cannot modify the initonly field, even if the field accessibility permits. Subsequent explicit calls to .ctor and .cctor can modify the initonly fields as well as the first, implicit initializing calls. Modification of initonly fields by methods other than the type's constructors renders the code unverifiable.

The value types are not instantiated using the newobj instruction, so an instance constructor of a value type (if specified) should be called explicitly by using the call instruction, even though declaring a variable of a value type creates an instance of this value type.

Interfaces cannot have instance constructors at all; there is no such thing as an interface instance.

Instance Finalizers

Another special method characteristic of a class instance is a finalizer, which is in many aspects similar to a C++ destructor. The finalizer must have the following signature:

```
.method family virtual instance void Finalize( )
{
    ...
}
```

Unlike instance constructors, which cannot be virtual, instance destructors—sorry, I mean finalizers—*must* be virtual. This requirement and the strict limitations imposed on the finalizer signature and name result from the fact that any particular finalizer is an override of the virtual method Finalize of the inheritance root of the class system, the [mscorlib]System.Object class, the ultimate ancestor of all classes in the Microsoft .NET universe. To tell the truth, the Object's finalizer does exactly nothing. But Object, full of fatherly care, declares this virtual method anyway, so Object's descendants could override it, should they desire to do something meaningful at the inevitable moment of their instances' demise. And at this sad moment, the instances of Object's descendants must have their own finalizers executed, even if they (instances) are cast to Object. This explains the requirement for the finalizers to be virtual.

The finalizer is executed by the garbage collection (GC) subsystem of the runtime when that subsystem decides that a class instance should be disposed of. No one knows exactly when this happens; the only solid fact is that it occurs after the instance is no longer used and has become inaccessible—but how soon after is anybody's guess.

If you prefer to execute the instance's last will and testament—that is, call the finalizer—when *you* think you don't need the instance any more, you can do exactly that by calling the finalizer explicitly. But then you should notify the GC subsystem that it does not need to call the finalizer again when in due time it decides to dispose of the abandoned class instance. You can do this by calling the .NET Framework class library method [mscorlib]System.GC::SuppressFinalize, which takes the object (a reference to the instance) as its sole argument—the instance is still there; you simply called its finalizer but did not destroy it—and returns void.

If for some reason you change your mind afterward, you can notify the GC subsystem that the finalizer must be run after all by calling the [mscorlib]System.GC::ReRegisterForFinalize method with the same signature, void(object). You needn't fear that the GC subsystem might destroy your long-suffering instance without finalization before you call ReRegisterForFinalize— as long as you can still reference this instance, the GC will not touch it. Both methods for controlling finalization are public and static, so they can be called from anywhere.

Variable Argument Lists

Encounters with variable argument list (vararg) methods in earlier chapters revealed the following information:

- The calling convention of these methods is vararg.

- Only mandatory parameters are specified in the vararg method declaration:

```
.method public static vararg void Print(string Format)
{ ... }
```

- If and only if optional parameters are specified in a vararg method reference at the call site, they are preceded by a sentinel—an ellipsis in ILAsm notation—and a comma:

```
call vararg void Print(string, ..., int32, float32, string)
```

I'm not sure that requiring the sentinel to appear as an independent comma-separated argument was a good idea. After all, a sentinel is not a true element type but is a modifier of the element type immediately following. Nevertheless, such was ILAsm notation in the first release of the common language runtime, and we had to live with it for a while. Version 2.0 of ILAsm takes care of this, and the following notations are considered equivalent:

```
call vararg void Print(string, ..., int32, float32, string)
                                            // works for all versions
call vararg void Print(string, ... int32, float32, string) // works for v2.0 only
```

The vararg method signature at the call site obviously differs from the signature specified when the method is defined, because the call site signature carries information about optional parameters. That's why vararg methods are always referenced by MemberRef tokens and never by MethodDef tokens, even if the method is defined in the current module. (In that case, the MemberRef record corresponding to the vararg call site will have the respective MethodDef as its parent, which is slightly disturbing, but only at first sight.)

Now let's see how the vararg methods are implemented. IL offers no specific instructions for argument list parsing beyond the arglist instruction, which merely creates the argument list structure. To work with this structure and iterate through the argument list, you need to work with the .NET Framework class library value type [mscorlib]System.ArgIterator. This value type should be initialized with the argument list structure, which is an instance of the value type [mscorlib]System.RuntimeArgumentHandle, returned by the arglist instruction. ArgIterator offers such useful methods as GetRemainingCount and GetNextArg.

To make a long story short, let's review the following code snippet from the sample file Vararg.il on the Apress Web site:

```
// Compute sum of undefined number of arguments
.method public static vararg unsigned int64
    Sum(/* all arguments optional */)
{
    .locals init(value class [mscorlib]System.ArgIterator Args,
                 unsigned int64 Sum,
                 int32 NumArgs)
    ldc.i8 0
    stloc Sum
```

```
    ldloca Args
    arglist // Create argument list structure
    // Initialize ArgIterator with this structure:
    call instance void [mscorlib]System.ArgIterator::.ctor(
        valuetype [mscorlib]System.RuntimeArgumentHandle)

    // Get the optional argument count:
    ldloca Args
    call instance int32 System.ArgIterator::GetRemainingCount()
    stloc NumArgs

    // Main cycle:
  LOOP:
    ldloc NumArgs
    brfalse RETURN // if(NumArgs == 0) goto RETURN;

    // Get next argument:
    ldloca Args
    call instance typedref [mscorlib]System.ArgIterator::GetNextArg()

    // Interpret it as unsigned int64:
    refanyval [mscorlib]System.UInt64
    ldind.u8

    // Add it to Sum:
    ldloc Sum
    add
    stloc Sum // Sum += *((int64*)&next_arg)
    // Decrease NumArgs and go for next argument:
    ldloc NumArgs
    ldc.i4.m1
    add
    stloc NumArgs
    br LOOP

  RETURN:
    ldloc Sum
    ret
}
```

In this code, we did not specify any mandatory arguments and thus took the return value of GetRemainingCount for the argument count. Actually, GetRemainingCount returns only the number of optional arguments, which means that if we had specified N mandatory arguments, the total argument count would have been greater by N.

The GetNextArg method returns a typed reference, typedref, which is cast to a managed pointer to an 8-byte unsigned integer by the instruction refanyval [mscorlib]System.UInt64. If the type of the argument cannot be converted to the required type, the JIT compiler throws an InvalidCast exception. The refanyval instruction is discussed in detail in Chapter 13.

Method Overloading

High-level languages such as C# and C++ allow method overload on parameters only. This means you can declare several methods with the same name within the same class only if the parameter lists of these methods are different. However, you know by now that the methods are uniquely identified by the triad {name, signature, parent} (let's forget about privatescope methods for now) and that the signature of a method includes the calling convention and the return type. The conclusion we are coming to is…yes! The common language runtime allows you to overload the methods on the return type and even on the calling convention. And, naturally, so does ILAsm.

Take a look at the following code from sample Overloads.il on the Apress Web site:

```
#define DEFLT_CTOR
".method public specialname void .ctor()
    {ldarg.0; call instance void .base::.ctor(); ret}"

.typedef method void [mscorlib]System.Console::WriteLine(string) as PrintString

.class public A
{
    DEFLT_CTOR
    .method public void Foo()
    {
        ldstr "instance void Foo"
        call PrintString
        ret
    }
    .method public static void Foo()
    {
        ldstr "static void Foo"
        call PrintString
        ret
    }
    .method public vararg void Foo()
    {
        ldstr "instance vararg void Foo"
        call PrintString
        ret
    }
    .method public static vararg void Foo()
    {
        ldstr "static vararg void Foo"
        call PrintString
        ret
    }
    .method public int32 Foo()
    {
        ldstr "instance int32 Foo"
        call PrintString
```

```
        ldc.i4.1
        ret
    }
    .method public static int32 Foo()
    {
        ldstr "static int32 Foo"
        call PrintString
        ldc.i4.1
        ret
    }

}
.method public static void Exec()
{
    .entrypoint
    newobj instance void A::.ctor() // Create instance of A

    dup                 // We need 3 instance pointers
    dup                 // On stack for 3 calls

    call instance void A::Foo()
    call instance vararg void A::Foo()
    call instance int32 A::Foo()
    pop
    call void A::Foo()
    call vararg void A::Foo()
    call int32 A::Foo()
    pop
    ret
}
```

The output proves that all overloads are successfully recognized by the runtime:

```
instance void Foo
instance vararg void Foo
instance int32 Foo
static void Foo
static vararg void Foo
static int32 Foo
```

As you probably deduced, the same principle applies to the fields: the fields can be overloaded on type, so you can have fields int32 foo and int16 foo in the same class. Unlike methods, the fields cannot be overloaded on the calling convention, because all field signatures have the same calling convention (IMAGE_CEE_CS_CALLCONV_FIELD).

No high-level language (I know of), including C# and C++, supports method overloading on return type or field overloading on type. ILAsm does, because in ILAsm the return type of a method and the type of a field must be explicitly specified when the method or the field is referenced.

Let me reformulate the last statement: the CLR supports overloading on return type/field type and on the method's calling convention, so ILAsm *has* to support it also; that's why in ILAsm the calling convention and return type must be explicitly specified.

Why don't C# and C++ support method overloading on return type? Don't they have linguistic means to specify the type? Yes, they have and use these means for distinguishing methods overloaded on parameters. I'm talking about casts. Why can C# or C++ distinguish which method Foo to call between

```
int i = Foo((int)j);
int i = Foo((short)j);
```

but can't distinguish between

```
int i = (int)Foo();
int i = (int)(short)Foo();
```

with the rightmost cast on the method's return serving as specification of the method's return type? I don't know why.

Global Methods

Global methods, similar to global fields, are defined outside any class scope. Most of the features of global fields and global methods are also similar: global methods are all static, and the accessibility flags for both global fields and methods mean the same.

Of course, one global method worth a special mention is the global class constructor, .cctor. As the preceding chapter discussed, a global .cctor is the best way to initialize global fields. The following code snippet from the sample file Gcctor.il on the Apress Web site provides an example:

```
.field private static string Hello
.method private static void .cctor( )
{
    ldstr "Hi there! What's up?"
    stsfld string Hello
    ret
}
.method public static void Exec( )
{
    .entrypoint
    ldsfld string Hello // Global fields are accessible
                        // within the module
    call void [mscorlib]System.Console::WriteLine(string)
    ret
}
```

Summary of Metadata Validity Rules

Method-related metadata tables discussed in this chapter include the Method, Param, FieldMarshal, Constant, MemberRef, and MethodImpl tables. The records in these tables have the following entries:

- The Method table: RVA, ImplFlags, Flags, Name, Signature, and ParamList

- The Param table: Flags, Sequence, and Names

- The FieldMarshal table: Parent and NativeType (native signature)

- The Constant table: Type, Parent, and Value

- The MemberRef table: Class, Name, and Signature

- The MethodImpl table: Class, MethodBody, and MethodDecl

Chapter 9 summarized the validity rules for the FieldMarshal, Constant, and Member Ref tables. The only point to mention here regarding the MemberRef table is that, unlike field-referencing MemberRef records, method-referencing records can have the Method table referenced in the Parent entry. The Method table can be referenced exclusively by the MemberRef records representing vararg call sites.

Method Table Validity Rules

- The Flags entry can have only those bits set that are defined in the enumeration CorMethodAttr in CorHdr.h (validity mask 0xFDF7).

- [run time] The accessibility flag (mask 0x0007) must be one of the following: privatescope, private, famandassem, assembly, family, famorassem, or public.

- The static flag must not be combined with any of the following flags: final, virtual, newslot, or abstract.

- The pinvokeimpl flag must be paired with the static flag (but not vice versa).

- Methods having privatescope accessibility must not have the virtual, final, newslot, specialname, or rtspecialname flag set.

- The abstract, newslot, and final flags must be paired with the virtual flag.

- The abstract flag and the implementation flag forwardref are mutually exclusive.

- [run time] If the flag 0x4000 is set, the method must either have an associated DeclSecurity metadata record that holds security information concerning access to the method or have the associated custom attribute System.Security. SuppressUnmanagedCodeSecurityAttribute. The inverse is true as well.

- [run time] Methods belonging to interfaces must have either the static flag set or the virtual flag set.

- [run time] Global methods must have the static flag set.

- If the rtspecialname flag is set, the specialname flag must also be set.

- The ImplFlags entry must have only those bits set that are defined in the enumeration CorMethodImplAttr in CorHdr.h (validity mask 0x10BF).

- The implementation flag forwardref is used only during in-memory edit-and-continue scenarios and in object files (generated by the MC++ compiler) and must not be set for any method in a managed PE file.

- [run time] The implementation flags cil and unmanaged are mutually exclusive.

- [run time] The implementation flags native and managed are mutually exclusive.

- The implementation flag native must be paired with the unmanaged flag.

- [run time] The implementation flag synchronized must not be set for methods belonging to value types.

- [run time] The implementation flags runtime and internalcall are for internal use only and must not be set for methods defined outside .NET Framework system assemblies.

- [run time] The Name entry must hold a valid reference to the #Strings stream, indexing a nonempty string no more than 1,023 bytes long in UTF-8 encoding.

- [run time] If the method name is .ctor, .cctor, _VtblGap*, or _Deleted*, the rtspecialname flag must be set, and vice versa.

- [run time] A method named .ctor—an instance constructor—must not have the static flag or the virtual flag set.

- [run time] A method named .cctor—a class constructor—must have the static flag set.

- [run time] The Signature entry must hold a valid reference to the #Blob stream, indexing a valid method signature. Chapter 8 discusses validity rules for method signatures.

- [run time] A method named .ctor—an instance constructor—must return void and must have the default calling convention.

- [run time] A method named .cctor—a class constructor—must return void, can take no parameters, and must have the default calling convention.

- No duplicate records—attributed to the same TypeDef and having the same name and signature—should exist unless the accessibility flag is privatescope.

- [run time] The RVA entry must hold 0 or a valid relative virtual address pointing to a read-only section of the PE file.

- [run time] The RVA entry holds 0 if and only if

    - the abstract flag is set, or

    - the implementation flag runtime is set, or

- the implementation flag `internalcall` is set, or

- the class owning the method has the `import` flag set, or

- the `pinvokeimpl` flag is set, the implementation flags `native` and `unmanaged` are not set, and the ImplMap table contains a record referencing the current `Method` record, and this record contains valid ModuleRef reference.

Param Table Validity Rules

- The `Flags` entry can have only those bits set that are defined in the enumeration `CorParamAttr` in CorHdr.h (validity mask 0x3013).

- [run time] If the flag 0x2000 (`pdHasFieldMarshal`) is set, the FieldMarshal table must contain a record referencing this `Param` record, and vice versa.

- [run time] If the flag 0x1000 (`pdHasDefault`) is set, the Constant table must contain a record referencing this `Param` record, and vice versa.

- [run time] The `Sequence` entry must hold a value no larger than the number of mandatory parameters of the method owning the `Param` record.

- If the method owning the `Param` record returns `void`, the `Sequence` entry must not hold 0.

- The `Name` entry must hold 0 or a valid reference to the #Strings stream, indexing a nonempty string no more than 1,023 bytes long in UTF-8 encoding.

MethodImpl Table Validity Rules

- [run time] The `Class` entry must hold a valid index to the TypeDef table.

- [run time] The `MethodDecl` entry must index a record in the Method or MemberRef table.

- [run time] The method indexed by `MethodDecl` must be virtual.

- [run time] The method indexed by `MethodDecl` must not be final.

- [run time] If the parent of the method indexed by `MethodDecl` is not the `TypeDef` indexed by `Class`, the method indexed by `MethodDecl` must not be private.

- [run time] The parent of the method indexed by `MethodDecl` must not be sealed.

- [run time] The signatures of the methods indexed by `MethodDecl` and `MethodBody` must match.

- [run time] The `MethodBody` entry must index a record in the Method table.

- [run time] The method indexed by `MethodBody` must be virtual.

- [run time] The parent of the method indexed by `MethodBody` must be the `TypeDef` indexed by `Class`.

CHAPTER 11

■■■

Generic Types

Generic types, introduced in version 2.0 of the CLR, differ from "normal" (nongeneric) types in one major aspect: "normal" types, even the abstract ones, are fully defined, while generic types represent pure abstractions—templates for the generation (or instantiation) of "normal" types. Generic types are pure abstractions because they describe types constructed not from other types but from abstract type parameters, or *type variables*. Thus, a generic type has one or more type parameters and hence belongs to *parameterized types*. You are already familiar with one generic type implemented in versions 1.0 and 1.1 of the CLR—a vector (single-dimensional, zero lower-bound array). A vector doesn't exist per se—it's always a vector "of something," such as a vector of 32-bit integers, a vector of strings, or a vector of objects, and so on. The vector was (and still is) an intrinsic generic type in the sense it is implemented by the CLR but has no representation as a separate class.

My reference to the templates is not an error. The C++ templates, another representative of parameterized types, are probably the most-known vehicle of generic programming, so C++ templates and generics (generic types and generic functions, discussed in Chapter 12) play similar roles. There, however, the similarity ends and the differences begin, including the two most important:

- C++ templates can have various parameters (type parameters, integer parameters, and so on), whilst generics can have only type parameters. For example, you can define a template of a stack of a specific predefined depth, but you can't define a generic stack of a specific predefined depth.

- The type parameters of generics can be constrained, meaning you can demand that such-and-such type parameter meet such-and-such requirements, while C++ doesn't have the linguistic means to specify constraints of template parameters.

In general, the set of parameters of a parameterized type is often referred to as the type's *parameter list*, and the set of actual arguments used for the parameterized type instantiation is known as the instantiation *environment*. The parameter list may be homogenous (all parameters are of the same kind, say, type) or heterogeneous. The parameter list may also be constrained, meaning some limitations may be imposed on the instantiation contexts (for example, this type argument must be derived from type X, or that integer argument must be a prime number). So, the .NET generics are parameterized types with homogenous constrained parameter lists, while C++ templates represent parameterized types with heterogeneous unconstrained parameter lists.

The generics in .NET were introduced by the outstanding work of Don Syme and Andrew Kennedy from Microsoft Research (Cambridge, United Kingdom). Don and Andrew started their work on .NET generics shortly before version 1.0 of the CLR was released. The way to the final implementation was long and not without turns, but now version 2.0 of the CLR boasts advanced, completely functional support of generics.

Being template-like abstractions for building the concrete types, generic types don't change the .NET type hierarchy discussed in Chapter 7 (refer to Figure 7-1). Rather, the generic types add a "genericity" dimension to the type hierarchy: there can be generic and nongeneric classes, interfaces, and value types, and for example, a generic interface is as much an interface as a nongeneric one.

All concepts of inheritance (from a base class) and implementation (of the interfaces) defined for nongeneric types are valid for generic types. Both generic and nongeneric types can extend and implement only nongeneric types or instantiations of generic types, for obvious reasons: the instantiations of generic types are true types and can be used anywhere, while the generic types are the templates of true types and cannot be used anywhere but in instantiations.

Generic Type Metadata

As I mentioned in Chapter 7, the nongeneric type metadata is grouped around the concepts of type definition (TypeDef) and type reference (TypeRef). The generic type metadata uses one more basic concept—type specification (TypeSpec), representing the instantiations of generic types.

The definition of a nongeneric type involves the following information:

- The full name of the type being defined

- Flags indicating special features the type should have

- The type from which this type is derived

- The interfaces this type implements

- How the loader should lay out objects of this type in memory

- Whether this type is nested in another type—and if so, in which one

- Where fields and methods of this type (if any) can be found

To define a generic type, you should also supply the list of type parameters and define the constraints of each type parameter.

Referencing a generic type is a tricky question. Strictly speaking, you cannot reference a generic type per se; you can reference only an instantiation of a generic type, providing in addition to the type's name and resolution scope the list of type arguments.

Saving you a trip four chapters back, I'm repeating the figure here that shows the metadata tables participating in type definition and referencing (see Figure 11-1). The arrows indicate cross-table referencing by means of metadata tokens.

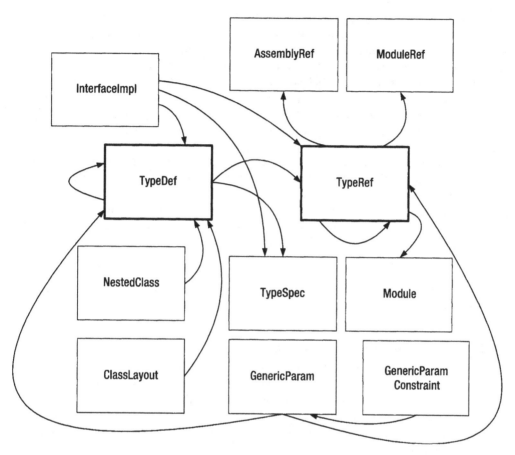

Figure 11-1. *Metadata tables participating in type definition and referencing*

Three tables in the lower part of Figure 11-1 (TypeSpec, GenericParam, and Generic-ParamConstraint) and their associated links are related to generic types and will be discussed in this chapter.

The rest of the tables shown in Figure 11-1 are common to generic and nongeneric types, so everything I said about these tables in Chapter 7 holds true for the case of generic types. This means, in particular, that looking at a TypeDef or TypeRef record, you cannot say whether the type represented by this record is generic (for a TypeDef you need to look in the Generic-Param table and see whether it contains generic parameters associated with this type). This in turn means that the genericity of the type (list of its type parameters, if any) cannot be used for type identification, and the type identification is still based on the type's full name and res-olution scope. In other words, you cannot have types G (nongeneric) and G<T> (generic with one type parameter) defined in the same module. This is rather restrictive and can be likened to the prohibition of method overloads (this design was chosen because it allowed for the introduction of generics via incremental changes in the metadata scheme; an alternative would be the complete overhaul of the metadata structure and of the ways the types are recognized in the CLR).

The high-level languages bypass this limitation and allow you to define types G and G<T> (and G<T,U>, and so on) in the same module by mangling the names of generic types, usually adding the generic *arity* (the number of type parameters) to the type name. For example, VB and C# emit type G as G, type G<T> as G`1, type G<T,U> as G`2, and so on (now you probably have guessed why the backtick symbol was added as a legal identifier symbol in ILAsm 2.0).

Since the generic parameters can represent only types, mangling the type name with generic arity is enough to simulate the "type overload on genericity." If you had to deal with C++ templates rather than generics, you would probably have to use a more sophisticated name-mangling scheme, reflecting the "generic signature" of the type.

The negative side effect (rather minor) of the name mangling is that the generic types are emitted under names different from those specified in the high-level language code. The positive effect is that you can identify a generic type and its arity by looking at the type's name (however, this doesn't work for nested types, as I will show you later in this chapter).

The IL assembler does not do the type name mangling automatically, leaving it to the programmer or to the tool (for example, a compiler) generating ILAsm code. I will follow the C#/VB name-mangling convention in the samples, but you should remember it is in no way mandatory.

Having agreed on this, let's proceed to the discussion of the metadata tables specific to generic types.

GenericParam Metadata Table

The GenericParam table contains the information about generic parameters. You might wonder why this table is needed; if the generic parameters can be only types, their number (arity of a generic type) should be sufficient. The main reasons for the existence of the Generic-Param table are the need to be able to tell a generic type from a nongeneric one (generic types have associated generic parameters) and the need to be able to define constraints of each generic parameter.

Each record in this table has four entries:

- Number (2-byte unsigned integer). Zero-based ordinal of the generic parameter in the generic type's parameter list.

- Flags (2-byte bit field). The binary flags indicating certain kinds of constraints imposed on this generic parameter. I discuss the values of the flags and the constraints they represent in the section "Constraint Flags" later in this chapter.

- Owner (coded token of type TypeOrMethodDef). A token of the generic type or method definition to which this generic parameter belongs. I discuss generic methods in Chapter 12. Note that TypeRefs and MemberRefs, even those of generic types and methods, don't have their generic parameters represented in the GenericParam table; the generic parameters and their constraints are always defined together with their owners, in the metadata of the same module. This doesn't mean you cannot reference a generic type from another module; it means only that since constraints are defined when the generic type is defined and the role of GenericParams is to carry the constraints, associating GenericParams with type references would be meaningless.

- Name (offset in the #Strings stream). The name of the generic parameter. This entry may be zero (unnamed parameter).

In the optimized metadata model, the GenericParam records must be sorted by their Owner field.

GenericParamConstraint Metadata Table

The GenericParamConstraint metadata table contains inheritance and implementation constraints imposed on the generic parameters. An inheritance constraint imposed on a generic parameter means that the type substituting for the parameter in a generic instantiation must be derived from the specified type. An implementation constraint means that the type substituting for this parameter must implement the specified interface.

Each record in this table has two entries:

- Owner (RID in the GenericParam table). The index of the GenericParam record describing the generic parameter to which this constraint is attributed.

- Constraint (coded token of type TypeDefOrRef). A token of the constraining type, which can reside in the TypeDef, TypeRef, or TypeSpec table. The nature of the constraint (inheritance or implementation) is defined by the constraining type: if it is an interface, then it's an implementation constraint; otherwise it's an inheritance constraint. (This reminds me of an old Navy adage: "Salute all that moves and paint all that doesn't.") Since the CLR supports only single inheritance, no more than one GenericParamConstraint record pertaining to a certain generic parameter can have its Constraint entry referencing a noninterface type.

In the optimized metadata model, the GenericParamConstraint records must be sorted by their Owner field.

TypeSpec Metadata Table

The TypeSpec metadata table, which you already encountered in Chapter 8, represents the constructed types—in versions 1.0 and 1.1 it represented vectors and arrays, and in version 2.0 it represents also instantiations of the generic types. The TypeSpec table has only one entry in each record: Signature (offset in the #Blob stream), representing the signature of the constructed type. Chapter 8 discussed the signatures of vectors and arrays, and I will describe the signatures of generic type instantiations in the section "Generic Type Instantiations" of this chapter.

I still don't understand what was the purpose of introducing the TypeSpec metadata table (and the StandAloneSig table as well) in the first place. These tables serve as simple redirectors to the #Blob stream. It would make more sense to do the same trick as with mdtString tokens—interpret the RID part of an mdtTypeSpec or mdtStandAloneSig token as the offset in the #Blob stream. Maybe the concerns about the 16MB offset limit (the RID part of the token is 24-bits wide) were the reason? But I digress.

Constraint Flags

The constraint flags describe the constraints imposed on a generic parameter that are not of an inheritance or implementation nature. Table 11-1 describes the constraint flags defined in version 2.0 of the CLR (see also enumeration CorGenericParamAttr in file CorHdr.h):

Table 11-1. *Constraint Flags*

Flag	Constant Name	ILAsm Notation	Comments
0x01	gpCovariant	+	The type argument must be covariant. In other words, G<T> must be assignable to G<U> if T is assignable to U (the assignability of T to U means that the value of type T can be assigned to a location, say, a variable, of type U; Chapter 13 lists the assignability rules). This constraint is applicable only to type parameters of generic interfaces or delegates.
0x02	gpContravariant	-	The type argument must be contravariant. In other words, G<T> must be assignable to G<U> if U is assignable to T. This constraint is applicable only to type parameters of generic interfaces or delegates.
0x04	gpReferenceTypeConstraint	class	The type argument must be a reference type (not a value type).
0x08	gpNotNullableValueTypeConstraint	valuetype	The type argument must be a value type but not an instantiation of the generic value type [mscorlib]System.Nullable`1<T>.
0x10	gpDefaultConstructorConstraint	.ctor	The type argument must have a default instance constructor (a public instance constructor without arguments) or must be a value type.

Defining Generic Types in ILAsm

The ILAsm syntax for defining a generic type is as follows:

```
.class <flags> <dotted_name> < <gen_params> >
            [extends <class_ref>]
            [implements <class_refs>]
{
    ...
}
```

As you can see, the only difference between the generic type definition and nongeneric type definition is the presence of the <gen_params> clause (enclosed in angular brackets):

<gen_params> ::= <gen_param> [, <gen_param>]*

where

<gen_param> ::= [<constraint_flags>] [(<constraints>)] <gen_param_name>

where

<constraint_flags> ::= + | - | **class** | **valuetype** | **.ctor**
<constraints> ::= <class_ref> [, <class_ref>]*
<gen_param_name> ::= <simple_name>

For example:

```
.class public EventHandler`1< - class ([mscorlib]System.IAsyncResult) T>
            extends [mscorlib]System.MulticastDelegate
{
  // T must be a contravariant reference type implementing IAsyncResult
  ...
}
```

The types specified as constraints cannot be less visible than the generic type itself. The reasoning is obvious enough: if you define a public generic type and constrain its type parameter with a private type, what will happen if somebody tries to instantiate your generic type in his own assembly?

The types specified as constraints can be nongeneric types (as in the previous example), generic instantiations, and even references to other type parameters of the same type. If you don't need to put any constraints on a generic type, just declare it as G`1<T>. Don't declare it as G`1<([mscorlib]System.Object) T>. That's just plain silly: since any type is derived eventually from System.Object, "constraining" a generic parameter like that just bloats the GenericParamConstraint table and increases the type load time. I'm saying this because I've seen people and even compilers doing exactly that.

Addressing the Type Parameters

The type parameters of a generic type are referenced within the type as !<name> or !<ordinal>, where <name> is the name of the type parameter and <ordinal> is the parameter's number (zero-based) in the type parameter list. For example:

```
.class public value Pair`1<T>
{
  .field public !T x
  .field public !0 y    // fields x and y have the same type T
}
```

Both notations translate into the single encoded types {E_T_VAR, <compressed_ordinal>}, so both fields x and y in the previous sample have the signatures {CALLCONV_FIELD, E_T_VAR, <compressed_ordinal>} = {0x06, 0x13, 0x00}.

Type parameters are referenced in the same way in the method signatures of generic types:

```
.class public List`1<T>
{
  .method public void Append(!T val) { ... }
  .method public !T GetLast() { ... }
  ...
}
```

Generic Type Instantiations

An instantiation of a generic type involves two items—the generic type itself and the instantiation context, representing the list of actual type arguments substituting for the generic type's parameters.

The ILAsm syntax representing a generic instantiation is as follows:

```
class <type_name> < <type> [, <type>]* >
```

or as follows:

```
valuetype <type_name> < <type> [, <type>]* >
```

where <type_name> is a fully qualified name of the generic type and the <type> sequence in angular brackets represents the type argument list. For example:

```
.field private class List`1<string> nameList
.field private class List`1<[mscorlib]System.Type> typeList
```

The keyword class or valuetype is necessary in specifications of generic type instantiations because generic type instantiations are represented in the metadata by TypeSpecs, and these keywords signal the IL assembler to produce a TypeSpec rather than a TypeRef or a TypeDef. This is a general rule of ILAsm, not specific to the generic type instantiations. For example, the notation [mscorlib]System.Type translates into a TypeRef, while the notation class [mscorlib]System.Type translates into a TypeSpec with the signature {E_T_CLASS, <token>}, where <token> is a TypeRef token of [mscorlib]System.Type.

The signatures of TypeSpecs representing the generic instantiations have the following form: {E_T_GENERICINST, E_T_CLASS, <gen_type_token>, <arity>, <arg_token>[, <arg_token>]*}, where <gen_type_token> is a TypeRef or TypeDef token representing the generic type, <arity> is a compressed number of type arguments, and the sequence of <arg_token> is a sequence of TypeRef, TypeDef, or TypeSpec tokens (or element type codes) representing the type arguments (the instantiation context). For example, the generic instantiation class List`1<string> is represented by a TypeSpec with the signature {E_T_GENERICINST, E_T_CLASS, <token_of_List`1>, 1, E_T_STRING} = {0x15, 0x12, <token_of_List`1>, 0x01, 0x0E}.

In general, any type satisfying the constraints (if any) can be used as a type argument of a generic instantiation. There are three exceptions: a managed pointer to some type, void, and a value type that contains references to the IL evaluation stack, such as [mscorlib]System. RuntimeArgumentHandle. All three are unsuitable as the type of a field, and this is the main reason they are not allowed as type arguments. The CLR doesn't want you to declare a field of type T in class A<T> and then instantiate A<void>. It would be embarrassing.

Within the scope of a generic type its type parameters are considered regular types, so the generic instantiations can use these type parameters as type arguments:

```
.class public List`1<T> // Generic type
{
...
}
.class public Stack`1<T> // Generic type
{
  .field private class List`1<!T> stackList // Generic type instantiated with
                                            // parameter of host generic type
...
}
```

So, the instantiation context of a generic type within the scope of another generic type can itself be generic (type parameterized).

The instantiation context can also contain instantiations of other generic types, for example:

```
.class public StackSet`1<T>
{
  .field private class List`1<class Stack`1<!T>> stackList
...
}
```

Having said that, let's return to the generic class declaration, where we have unfinished business.

Defining Generic Types: Inheritance, Implementation, Constraints

When I talked about generic type definition, I purposefully avoided elaborating on such important aspects of type definition as inheritance and interface implementation. The reason for that is all these aspects of a type can be generic instantiations. With a generic type, all these aspects (and the generic parameter constraints as well) are considered to be in the scope of the generic type, so their instantiation contexts can be parameterized:

```
.class public A`2<T,U> extends class B`1<!T>
                        implements class IX`1<!T>, class IY`1<!U>
{
...
}
```

Only the declaration of a generic class itself has a type parameter list; all references to a generic type can be only generic instantiations. For example, the following notation of the previous example is wrong because it presumes the parent type and implemented interfaces have type parameters, when in fact they are instantiations with parameterized context:

```
.class public A`2<T,U> extends B`1<T> implements IX`1<T>, IY`1<U> // Illegal
{
...
}
```

The same rule applies to the specification of the constraints of generic parameters. For example:

```
.class public SortedList`1<(class [mscorlib]System.IComparable`1<!T>) T>
                    extends class List`1<!T>
{
...
}
```

Here I declare a generic sorted list, the type parameter of which must implement the interface System.IComparable`1 of itself (otherwise how could I possibly sort the list?).

One important note: the type parameters of a generic type are indeed considered rightful types within the generic type's scope, but they are *not* instantiations. So, you cannot use the "naked" type parameters in the extends or implements clause. The following code example is wrong:

```
.class public AnyonesChild`1<T> extends !T // Illegal
{
...
}
```

This restriction allows the runtime to check the generic type validity at declaration time rather than at instantiation time. The latter is possible in principle but might be very expensive.

At the same time you can use "naked" type parameters as constraints of other type parameters. For example, the following declaration is perfectly legal:

```
.class public ParentChild`2<T, (!T)U> // U must be descendant of T
{
...
}
```

Defining Generic Types: Cyclic Dependencies

As you know from Chapter 7, cyclic dependencies in type inheritance and interface implementation are illegal. A cyclic dependence means that, for example, class A extends class B, and B extends C, and C extends A. The cyclic dependencies of nongeneric types are easily detected by the CLR loader, which throws the Type Load exception and aborts the loading.

The question of cyclic dependencies becomes more complex in the case of generic types, which use instantiations with parameterized contexts in extends and implements clauses, given that these contexts may contain other instantiations, and so on.

When loading a generic type, the loader must suspend processing this type when it encounters a generic instantiation as the base or one of the implemented interfaces of this type, load this instantiation, and then return to loading this type. As you can see, this process is recursive and can lead to a stack overflow if mutual dependencies of the instantiations are cyclic.

For example, the following three type declarations have a cyclic inheritance dependency of the instantiations:

```
.class public A`1<T> extends class C`1<class B`1<!T>>
{
...
}
.class public B`1<U> extends class A`1<class C`1<!U>>
{
...
}
.class public C`1<V>
{
...
}
```

The following algorithm is used to identify a cyclic dependency in the inheritance and implementation of a generic type declaration.

First, list all generic types that have mutual dependency (in this example, A`1, B`1, and C`1) and their type parameters.

Then list all generic instantiations used in the extends and implements clauses of these types, including the instantiations used as type arguments of other instantiations (as in C`1<B`1<!T>>).

Then build a graph that has an edge from each type parameter mentioned in an instantiation to the respective type parameter of a generic type being instantiated. Use the edges of two kinds: *nonexpanding* edge means a type parameter is replaced with a "naked" parameter of another type, and *expanding* edge means a type parameter is replaced with an instantiation involving parameter of another type. For example, the instantiation class C`1<!U> of class C`1<V> creates a nonexpanding edge from U to V, because "naked" !U is substituting for V; at the same time, the instantiation class C`1<class B`1<!T>> of the same class C`1<V> creates an expanding edge from T to V, because the instantiation involving !T (class B`1<!T>) is substituting for V.

If the resulting graph contains a loop having at least one expanding edge in it, you have a cyclic dependency of instantiations, because each expanding edge means "suspend loading this type and load the referenced instantiation first" for the CLR loader.

Table 11-2 illustrates the instantiation dependency analysis of the discussed example. A single-line arrow indicates a nonexpanding edge, and a double-line arrow indicates an expanding edge.

Table 11-2. *Instantiation Dependency Analysis*

Generic Type	Instantiation	Substitution Edge
A`1<T>	A`1<C`1<!U>>	U ⇒ T
B`1<U>	B`1<!T>	T → U
C`1<V>	C`1<!U>	U → V
C`1<V>	C`1<B`1<!T>>	T ⇒ V

Figure 11-2 shows the resulting graph; expanding edges are represented by solid arrows and nonexpanding edges are represented by dashed arrows. As you can see, the graph contains a loop with an expanding edge in it.

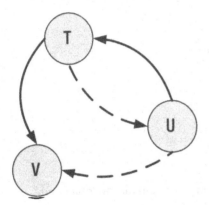

Figure 11-2. *Instantiation dependency graph*

The ECMA/ISO standard specification illustrates the circular instantiation dependencies with a sample that is probably the simplest instantiation dependency with an expanding loop:

```
.class public A`1<T> extends class B`1<class A`1<class A`1<!T>>>
{
...
}
.class public B`1<U>
{
...
}
```

This sample has the instantiation dependency graph where the node representing type parameter T is connected to itself with an expanding edge.

If the instantiation dependency graph has no loops or has loops consisting only of nonexpanding edges, such instantiation dependency is noncyclic and can be loaded.

The inheritance and implementation constraints imposed on the type parameters of the generic types don't affect the type loading in the same way as the generic instantiations, which the type itself extends and implements, so the instantiations representing these constraints are not included in the instantiation dependency analysis.

The Members of Generic Types

Declaring the members of generic types is more or less straightforward: the types of the members can be nongeneric types, type parameters of the generic type, or generic instantiations (or constructions thereof):

```
.class public Container`1<T>
{
  .field private int32 count
  .field private !T[] arr
  .method public int32 Count()
  {
    ...
  }
  .method public !T Element(int32 idx)
  {
    ...
  }
...
}
```

There is an interesting limitation imposed on the methods of generic types: they cannot have the vararg calling convention.

Referencing the members of a generic type is a bit trickier than declaring them: their resolution scope must always be the instantiation of the parent type *even if the members are referenced inside the parent type*:

```
.class public Container`1<T>
{
  .field private int32 count
  .field private !T[] arr
  .method public int32 Count()
  {
    ldarg.0
    ldfld int32 class Container`1<!T>::count
    ret
  }
  .method public !T Element(int32 idx)
  {
    ldarg.0
    ldfld !T[] class Container`1<!T>::arr
    ldarg.1
    ldelem !T
    ret
  }
...
}
```

You cannot use the .this, .base, or .nester keywords within a generic type's scope the same way you do within nongeneric types, because the reference to a generic type must always be an instantiation. However, you can use these keywords to form instantiations. For example:

```
...
ldfld int32 class .this<!T>::count
...
ldfld !T[] class .this<!T>::arr
...
```

When addressing the members of generic instantiations outside the defining class's scope, you need to specify their signatures as they were defined, not as they became in the instantiation. For example:

```
...
call instance !0 class Container`1<string>::Element(int32) // Correct
...
call instance string class Container`1<string>::Element(int32) // Incorrect
...
```

The return type of method Element was defined as the "type parameter number 0 of Container`1," and it must be the same at the method call site, even though the method is called on the instantiation of Container`1 with string substituting for the type parameter number 0. You cannot use !T instead of !0 either, because !T does indeed mean the "type parameter number 0 of Container`1" but only within the lexical scope of the Container`1 declaration.

This means you can't inadvertently create a duplicate member declaration when instantiating the generic type. For example:

```
.class public Pair`2<T,U>
{
  .field private !T t
  .field private !U u
  .method public void Set(!T newT)
  {
    ...
  }
  .method public void Set(!U newU)
  {
    ...
  }
  ...
}
```

Everything seems in order: method Set is overloaded on its parameter type, which is completely legal. Now, try to instantiate Pair`2<string, string>. Do you have a problem distinguishing one Set from another? Not at all. The methods will be called as follows:

```
...
ldstr "ABCD"
call instance void class Pair`2<string,string>::Set(!0) // first Set called
...
ldstr "EFGH"
call instance void class Pair`2<string,string>::Set(!1) // second Set called
...
```

Virtual Methods in Generic Types

Declaring virtual methods in generic types is not different in principle from declaring nonvirtual methods:

```
.class interface public abstract System.IComparable`1<T>
{
  .method public abstract virtual int32 CompareTo(!T other) {}
}
```

Implicitly overriding a virtual method is also relatively straightforward: the name of the overriding method must match the name of the overridden method, and the signature of the overriding method must match the signature of the overridden method with instantiation type arguments substituting for the type parameters of the overridden method:

```
.class public serializable sealed beforefieldinit System.String
              implements ...
                          class System.IComparable`1<string>,
                          ...
{
...
  .method public virtual final int32 CompareTo(string strB)
  {
  ...
  }
...
}
```

or in the case of a generic class overriding a virtual method from another generic class:

```
.class public Element`1<T> implements class [mscorlib]System.IComparable`1<!T>
{
...
  .method public virtual int32 CompareTo(!T other)
  {
  ...
  }
...
}
```

And of course you cannot override a method that doesn't have the type parameters in its signature with a method that does have them:

```
.class interface public abstract System.IComparable
{
  .method public abstract virtual int32 CompareTo(object obj) {}
}
...
.class public Element`1<T> implements [mscorlib]System.IComparable
{
...
  .method public virtual int32 CompareTo(!T other) // Invalid override
  {
    ...
  }
...
}
```

When dealing with implicit overriding, however, you should watch for possible duplicate overrides upon instantiation (yes, in the same vein as inadvertent duplicate member declarations, which I said are not a problem). For example:

```
.class interface public abstract IX<T,U>
{
  .method public abstract virtual int32 XX(!T t) {}
  .method public abstract virtual int32 XX(!U u) {}
}
...
.class public A implements class IX<string,string>
{
...
  .method public virtual int32 XX(string s) // Which XX does it override?
  {
    ...
  }
...
}
```

If some evil person (not you, of course) declared an interface (or a class) such as IX<T,U> in the previous sample and you need to override its methods, your only option is to give the overriding methods other names and use explicit override.

Just to save you a trip back to Chapter 10, let me remind you of the short form of an explicit override directive in a nongeneric case:

```
.class public Element implements [mscorlib]System.IComparable
{
...
  .method public virtual int32 Comp(object other)
  {
```

```
    .override [mscorlib]System.IComparable::CompareTo
    ...
  }
  ...
}
```

Explicitly overriding virtual methods of generic types is more complicated: you have to supply the signature of the overridden method. So, the short form of an explicit override directive used within the overriding method's body looks as follows:

```
.class public Element`1<T> implements class [mscorlib]System.IComparable`1<!T>
{
...
  .method public virtual int32 Comp(!T other)
  {
    .override method instance int32
            class [mscorlib]System.IComparable`1<!T>::CompareTo(!0)
    ...
  }
  ...
}
```

Note the keyword method followed by the overridden method's calling convention and return type.

It is necessary to specify the overridden method's signature because the overriding method's signature is different: the original signature of CompareTo has a single argument of type "type parameter number 0 of IComparable`1." That's why, by the way, the argument type in the signature of CompareTo has the form !0 instead of !T—!T means the "type parameter T of Element`1."

To illustrate this point, the following is an example of a method of a nongeneric class overriding a method of a generic class:

```
.class public EStr implements class [mscorlib]System.IComparable`1<string>
{
...
  .method public virtual int32 Comp(string other)
  {
    .override method instance int32
            class [mscorlib]System.IComparable`1<string>::CompareTo(!0)
    ...
  }
  ...
}
```

The long form of the explicit override directive follows the pattern of the short form. First, let me remind you of the long form of an explicit override directive in a nongeneric case:

```
.class public Element implements [mscorlib]System.IComparable
{
  .override [mscorlib]System.IComparable::CompareTo with
```

```
        instance int32 .this::Comp(object)
...
   .method public virtual int32 Comp(object other)
   {
   ...
   }
...
}
```

The long form of the explicit override directive in the case of a generic class overriding a method of another generic class looks as follows:

```
.class public Element`1<T> implements class [mscorlib]System.IComparable`1<!T>
{
   .override method instance int32
           class [mscorlib]System.IComparable`1<!T>::CompareTo(!0)
       with method instance int32 class .this<!T>::Comp(!0)
...
   .method public virtual int32 Comp(!T other)
   {
   ...
   }
...
}
```

Note that when explicitly overriding a method of a generic class, you need to specify the overriding method the same way as the overridden method, and it does not matter whether the overriding class is generic:

```
.class public EStr implements class [mscorlib]System.IComparable`1<string>
{
   .override method instance int32
           class [mscorlib]System.IComparable`1<string>::CompareTo(!0)
       with method instance int32 .this::Comp(string)
...
   .method public virtual int32 Comp(string other)
   {
   ...
   }
...
}
```

As you can see, the long form of the .override directive is even more cumbersome in the case of generic types, and strictly speaking this form is not necessary: the short form is fully sufficient for explicit overriding.

Nested Generic Types

As you know, the nested types have full access to the members, even private ones, of their immediate enclosers. But the types nested in generic types don't have any access to the type parameters of their enclosers. This means if a nongeneric type is nested in a generic type, this nested type must not use the encloser's environment:

```
.class public A`1<T>
{
  .class nested public B
  {
    ... // Cannot use !T here
  }
  ... // Can use !T here
}
```

When a generic type is nested in another (generic or nongeneric) type, its encloser, naturally, has no access to the nested type's generic environment. In short, the generic environments (if any) of the nested and the enclosing types are completely independent:

```
.class public A`1<T>
{
  .class nested public B
  {
    ... // Cannot use !T or !U here
  }
  .class nested public C`1<U>
  {
    ... // Cannot use !T here
  }
  ... // Can use !T but not !U here
}
```

The reason for this independence is that the nested and enclosed types are instantiated separately. When you instantiate an enclosing type, the nested types are not instantiated automatically, and you don't need to instantiate the encloser to instantiate the nested type. This goes for both meanings of *instantiate*—the creation of a generic instantiation of the type and the creation of an instance of it.

As you know, the nested types are referenced in ILAsm as `<encloser_ref>/<nested_type_name>`, where `<encloser_ref>` is a fully qualified name of the enclosing type, for example, `[mscorlib]System.RuntimeTypeHandle/DispatchWrapperType`. This is true for the types nested in generic types, because of the generic environment independence. For example, the nested class B described earlier is referenced as `A`1/B`. There is no such thing as a type nested in a generic instantiation, so the notation `class A`1<string>/B` makes no sense. But an instantiation of a nested generic type is a very real thing, and the notation `class A`1/C<string>` is completely legal.

I must warn you about one helpful feature of the C# compiler. When you declare a class nested in a generic class, the compiler presumes that the nested class needs "access" to the type parameters of the encloser and makes the nested type generic. So, you can't possibly define a nongeneric type nested in a generic type using C#. For example, the following C# code:

```
public class A<T>
{
    public class B
    {
        ...
    }
    ...
}
```

translates into the following ILAsm code:

```
.class public A`1<T>
{
  .class nested public B<T> // Note: no `1 added to B's name
  {
    ...
  }
  ...
}
```

And if you declare the nested class as generic, the C# compiler concatenates the declared type parameter lists of the encloser and the nested type and assigns the result to the nested type.

Note that the C# compiler mangles the nested type's name according to its own declared generic arity, not according to the summary encloser's and nested type's arity, probably because the nested type's name must be unique only within its encloser:

```
public class A<T>
{
    public class B<U>
    {
        ...
    }
    ...
}
```

which in ILAsm looks as follows:

```
.class public A`1<T>
{
  .class nested public B`1<T,U> // Note: `1 instead of `2 added to B's name
  {
    ...
  }
  ...
}
```

An interesting thing happens if you declare a generic nested type with the same type parameter name as the encloser's:

```
public class A<T>
{
    public class B<T>
    {
        ... // Here T means B's type parameter
    }
    ... // Here T means A's type parameter
}
```

which produces the following ILAsm code:

```
.class public A`1<T>
{
  .class nested public B`1<T,T>
  {
    ... // Here !0 means A's type parameter
    ... // And !1 or !T means B's type parameter
  }
  ... // Here !0 or !T means A's type parameter
}
```

Of course, after such a declaration, the encloser's type parameter T cannot be accessed inside the nested type in C#, because in C# the type parameters are referenced only by their names, and T inside the nested type means the nested type's T. The C# compiler doesn't diagnose this declaration as an error, but, of course, it issues a warning.

ILAsm can reference the type parameters by ordinal as well as by name, so duplicate names of type parameters don't prevent these parameters from being addressed.

Summary of the Metadata Validity Rules

The metadata tables specific to the generic types (other type-related tables were discussed in Chapter 7) include TypeSpec, GenericParam, and GenericParamConstraint. The records of these tables contain the following entries:

- The TypeSpec record contains the single entry Signature, which must hold a valid offset in the #Blob stream.

- The GenericParam record contains four entries: Number (2-byte zero-based ordinal of the type parameter), Flags (2-byte bit field containing the constraint flags of the type parameter), Owner (coded token of type TypeOrMethodDef, which must be a valid reference to the TypeDef or Method table), and Name (must be a valid offset in the #Strings stream, can be zero); there must be no duplicate records in the table with identical Number and Owner values.

- The GenericParamConstraint record contains two entries: Owner (must be a valid RID in the GenericParam table) and Constraint (coded token of type TypeDefOrRef, which must be a valid reference to the TypeDef, TypeRef, or TypeSpec table).

CHAPTER 12

■■■

Generic Methods

Generic methods are methods that carry type parameters in addition to their "normal" method parameters. These type parameters are subject to all the rules governing the type parameters of generic types, discussed in Chapter 11. This simplifies the discussion of generic methods significantly; therefore, this chapter will be brief.

The generic parameters of generic methods, as in the case of generic types, are limited to representing only types and can be constrained in the same way. The scope of the generic method's type parameters is the scope of the method itself, which includes the method's signature and body. Methods don't have members or inheritance attributes, which simplifies the discussion even further.

Like in the case of generic types, the introduction of genericity does not affect the classification of the methods proposed in Chapter 10. We still deal with static and instance methods (independent and dependent of the parent type's instance, respectively) and with virtual and nonvirtual instance methods, only now any method can be generic or not.

The genericity of methods is in no way related to the genericity of their owner types. You can have a nongeneric method of a generic type or a generic method of a nongeneric type. The fact that a method's signature and body reference the type parameters of the parent type doesn't make the method generic. What makes a method generic is the presence of its own type parameter list.

Generic Method Metadata

Recall, to define a nongeneric method, you need to supply its name, its parent, its signature, and its flags—and, of course, the method's body, unless the method is abstract, internal to the CLR, CLR generated, or P/Invoked from an unmanaged module.

To define a generic method, as in the case of generic types, you need also to supply the list of type parameters and define the constraints of each type parameter.

Again as in the case of generic types, the generic methods can be referenced only in the form of their instantiations.

Figure 12-1 shows the full mutual reference graph between the metadata tables involved in method defining and referencing. This figure is similar to Figure 10-1, except I omitted the tables GenericParam and GenericParamConstraint in Figure 10-1 because these tables are irrelevant to the nongeneric methods. The arrows indicate cross-table referencing by means of metadata tokens and RIDs.

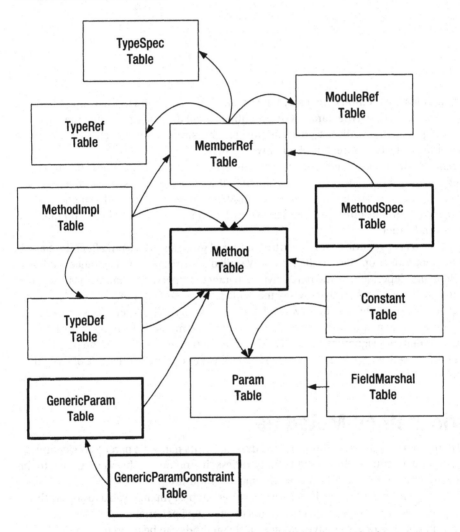

Figure 12-1. *Metadata tables participating in method definition and referencing*

The tables specific to the representation of generic methods are GenericParam, Generic-ParamConstraint, and MethodSpec. I discussed the first two tables in Chapter 11, so I won't repeat this discussion here. This leaves the MethodSpec table.

MethodSpec Metadata Table

The MethodSpec table carries the information about generic method instantiations. Unlike generic type instantiations represented by instantiation signatures stored as TypeSpecs, the instantiations of generic methods have to be represented by two signatures, because the method itself, generic or not, has a signature describing its calling convention, return type, and parameter types. This signature is referenced from the Method and MemberRef tables (as offset in the #Blob stream). The MethodSpec table provides the link of a generic method to the second signature—the instantiation signature.

Each record in the MethodSpec table has two entries:

- Method (coded token of type MethodDefOrRef). A token of the generic method definition being instantiated (references the Method or MemberRef table).

- Instantiation (offset in the #Blob stream). The instantiation signature, described in the next section of this chapter, cannot be 0.

The MethodSpec records don't need to be sorted in any metadata model.

Signatures of Generic Methods

The signature of a generic method differs from the signature of a nongeneric method, described in Chapter 8, and has the following structure:

```
<gen_method_sig> ::= <callconv_gen_method> <num_of_type_pars> <num_of_args>
                     <return_type> [<arg_type>[, <arg_type>]*]
```

where <callconv_gen_method> is the method's calling convention ORed with IMAGE_CEE_CS_CALLCONV_GENERIC (0x10) and where <num_of_type_pars> is a compressed number of type parameters of this generic method.

The method calling conventions acceptable for generic methods are limited to CALLCONV_GENERIC possibly in combination with CALLCONV_HASTHIS and CALLCONV_EXPLICITTHIS. The vararg generic methods are not supported, and the nongeneric vararg methods in generic types are not either.

The <return_type> and <arg_type> items of a generic method signature can be (or can contain) references to the method's type parameters. Such references have the form {E_T_MVAR, <ordinal>}, where E_T_MVAR = 0x1E and <ordinal> is a compressed zero-based ordinal of the method's type parameter. As you may recall from Chapter 11, the references to the type parameters of generic types in signatures have the form {E_T_VAR, <ordinal>}, where E_T_VAR = 0x13. So, you can declare a generic method of a generic class and easily tell a reference to the class's type parameter number N from a reference to the method's type parameter number N.

The ILAsm notation for referencing the method's type parameters is !!<ordinal> or !!<name>, where <name> is the name of the type parameter and <ordinal> is the parameter's number (zero-based) in the type parameter list. The generic type's type parameters, as you remember, are referenced in ILAsm as !<ordinal> or !<name>.

There is no need for a special ILAsm keyword denoting `IMAGE_CEE_CS_CALLCONV_GENERIC`, because the definitions and references to generic methods have specific syntax. I'll come to that in a moment, but now, while on the subject of signatures, let me show you what the instantiation signatures look like.

An instantiation signature of a generic method carries only information about the types the method is instantiated with, so its structure is relatively simple:

```
<gen_method_inst_sig> ::= <callconv_inst> <num_of_type_args>
                          <type_arg_type>[,<type_arg_type>]*
```

where `<callconv_inst>` is `IMAGE_CEE_CS_CALLCONV_GENERICINST` (0x0A), `<num_of_type_args>` is a compressed number of type arguments (cannot be 0), and `<type_arg_type>` is a single encoded type representing the respective type argument.

Defining Generic Methods in ILAsm

The ILAsm syntax for defining a generic type is as follows:

```
<gen_method_def> ::=
.method <flags> <call_conv> <ret_type> <name>< <gen_params> > (<arg_list>) <impl>
    { <method_body> }
```

For example:

```
.method public static !!T GetMedian<T>(!!T[] tarray)
{
  ldarg.0
  dup
  ldlen
  ldc.i4.1
  shr
  ldelem !!T
  ret
}
```

As in the case of generic types, the only difference between a generic method definition and nongeneric method definition is the presence of the `<gen_params>` clause (enclosed in angular brackets). I described this clause in detail in Chapter 11, and the only difference between generic types and generic methods in this regard is that the constraint flags + (covariance) and – (contravariance) are not applicable to the type parameters of a generic method.

The implementation flags `<impl>` of a generic method definition cannot be native, unmanaged, `internalcall`, or `runtime`, which leaves cil and managed, and as you know, cil and managed are default flags and do not need to be specified.

The `<flags>` clause of a generic method definition cannot contain the `pinvokeimpl` flag. And you know already, that `<call_conv>` of a generic method cannot be vararg.

Class constructors (.cctor) cannot be generic, because they are not called explicitly, so there is no way to specify a type argument for a .cctor. The instance constructors (.ctor), which are called explicitly (in the newobj directive) can be generic.

Calling Generic Methods

Strictly speaking, you cannot call (or otherwise reference) a generic method; you can call only an *instantiation* of a generic method. It is the same story as with the generic types.

When calling (or otherwise referencing) a generic method instantiation directly, you need to specify its signature as it was defined, not as it became in the instantiation. It is the same rule that applies to calling nongeneric methods of generic types: if a parameter or return type of the method is declared as a "type parameter (of class or method) number 0," it should be specified as such at the call site, no matter what type substitutes for the type parameter number 0. For example:

```
.method public static void Exec()
{
  .entrypoint
  ldc.i4.3
  newarr string
  ... // Fill in the string array here
  call !!0 GetMedian<string>(!!0[])  // Execute direct call
  call [mscorlib]System.Console::WriteLine(string)
  ret
}
```

Calling a generic method instantiation indirectly is a different story. To call a method (generic or not) indirectly, you need to load a function pointer to this method and then execute an indirect call on this function pointer. You reference the generic method instantiation only when you load the function pointer to it; after that you work with the pointer and not with the instantiation. The function pointer itself and the indirect call instruction carry the signature of the method *as it became an instantiation.* They have to, because they carry no reference to the method instantiation. The following example illustrates my point:

```
.method public static void Exec()
{
  .entrypoint
  .locals init (string[] sarr, method string*(string[]) fptr)
  ldc.i4.3
  newarr string
  stloc.0 // Store string vector
  ... // Fill in the string array here
  ldftn !!0 GetMedian<string>(!!0[])  // Load ptr to instantiation
  stloc.1 // Store function pointer
  ...
  ldloc.0 // Load string vector
  ldloc.1 // Load function pointer
  calli string(string[])  // Execute indirect call. Note the signature
  call [mscorlib]System.Console::WriteLine(string)
  ret
}
```

The previous code snippets are slightly modified parts of the sample Genfptr.il, which you can download from the Apress Web site:

```
.assembly extern mscorlib { auto }
.assembly genfptr {}
.module genfptr.exe

.typedef method void [mscorlib]System.Console::WriteLine(string) as PrintString

.method public static !!T GetMedian<T>(!!T[] tarray)
{
  ldstr "GetMedian<T> called"
  call PrintString
  ldarg.0
  dup
  ldlen
  ldc.i4.1
  shr
  ldelem !!T
  ret
}
.method public static !!T Invoke<T>(method !!T*(!!T[]) medFunc, !!T[] tarr)
{
  ldstr "Invoke<T> called"
  call PrintString
  ldarg.1
  ldarg.0
  calli !!T (!!T[])
  ret
}

#define CALL_VIA_INVOKE

.method public static void Exec()
{
  .entrypoint
#ifdef CALL_VIA_INVOKE
  ldftn !!0 GetMedian<string>(!!0[])
#endif
  ldc.i4.3
  newarr string
  dup
  dup
  dup
  ldc.i4.0
  ldstr "One"
  stelem.ref
  ldc.i4.1
```

```
      ldstr "Two"
      stelem.ref
      ldc.i4.2
      ldstr "Three"
      stelem.ref
#ifdef CALL_VIA_INVOKE
      call !!0 Invoke<string>(method !!0*(!!0[]), !!0[])
#else
      ldftn !!0 GetMedian<string>(!!0[])
      calli string(string[])
#endif
      call PrintString
      ret
}
```

Overriding Virtual Generic Methods

Declaring generic virtual methods is similar to declaring nonvirtual methods (just add type parameters!):

```
.class interface public abstract IX
{
   .method public abstract virtual int32 Do<T>(!!T theT) {}
}
```

Overriding the generic virtual methods, however, is severely limited compared to non-generic virtual methods (including those of generic types): a generic virtual method can override (or can be overridden by) only a generic method of the same generic arity—not a (or by a) nongeneric method and not by an instantiation of a generic method. This goes for both implicit and explicit overriding.

Think about the meaning of a virtual generic method. Let's consider the "most virtual" case—an abstract virtual method. An abstract virtual method is a contract between the super-class and all possible subclasses requiring all subclasses to supply an implementation of that method. By making the virtual abstract method generic, the superclass is requiring subclasses to provide an infinite number of implementations (one for each possible instantiation with various type arguments). The only mechanism that a subclass can use to provide an infinite number of implementations is by providing the method implementation as a generic "template."

For example, the following implicit override of IX::Do is acceptable:

```
.class public A implements IX
{
...
   .method public virtual final int32 Do<T>(!!T argT)   // Implicit override
   {
   ...
   }
...
}
```

Explicitly overriding generic virtual methods is slightly more complex than even explicitly overriding virtual methods of generic classes: you have to supply the signature of the overridden method *and* the generic arity of the overridden method itself (not the generic arity of the overridden method's class). So, the explicit override directives for generic virtual methods look as follows (the construct `<[1]>` following the overridden method's name is the method's generic arity):

```
.class public B implements IX
{
...
    .method public virtual final int32 DoIt<T>(!!T argT)  //Explicit override
    {
        .override method instance int32 IX::Do<[1]>(!!0) // !!0 is type arg of Do
        ...
    }
...
}

.class public C implements IX
{
    // Explicit override, long form:
    .override method instance int32 IX::Do<[1]>(!!0) // !!0 is type arg of Do
        with method instance int32 .this::DoIt<[1]>(!!0) // !!0 is type arg of DoIt
    .method public virtual final int32 DoIt<T>(!!T argT)
    {
        ...
    }
...
}
```

To reiterate, overrides of generic methods by generic methods of different arity (including nongeneric methods) or by instantiations of generic methods are illegal.

The type parameters of the overriding method cannot be constrained more restrictively than the type parameters of the overridden method. The reason for this requirement is simple. Suppose you override the method void $A<T>()$ with the method void $B<U>()$ and constrain U more restrictively than T. Constraining a type parameter means narrowing the possible choices of instantiation arguments, which means there will be types $\{X_i\}$ that can substitute for T but not for U. When you call virtually the instantiation of the overridden method, the CLR checks the type argument compliance with the overridden method's constraints, because it's the method that is called. So, you can call virtually void $A<X_i>()$, which means you will be calling in fact void $B<X_i>()$, violating the constraints of U.

For example, the following code is wrong:

```
.class interface public abstract IX
{
    .method public abstract virtual int32 Do<T>(!!T) {} // T unconstrained
}
...
```

```
.class public A implements IX
{
...
  .method public virtual int32 Do<.ctor T>(!!T t) // T constrained
  {
  ...
  }
...
}
```

The previous code snippets are slightly modified fragments of the sample Gen_virt.il, which you can download from the Apress Web site. The sample also shows the definition and usage of a generic .ctor:

```
.assembly extern mscorlib { auto }
.assembly gen_virt{}
.module gen_virt.exe

#define DEFLT_CTOR ".method public specialname void .ctor()
                       {ldarg.0; call instance void .base::.ctor(); ret;}"

.typedef method void [mscorlib]System.Console::WriteLine(string) as PrintString
.typedef method void [mscorlib]System.Console::WriteLine(int32) as PrintInt
.typedef [mscorlib]System.Type as SysType

// Non-generic interface with generic method
.class public interface IX
{
  .method public virtual abstract int32 Do<T>(!!T theT){}
}

// Implicit override of generic virtual method
.class public A implements IX
{
  DEFLT_CTOR
  .method public virtual int32 Do<T>(!!T theT)
  {
    ldarga.s theT
    constrained. !!T
    callvirt instance string object::ToString()
    call PrintString
    ldc.i4.2
    ret
  }
}

// Explicit override of generic method, short form
.class public B implements IX
```

```
{
  DEFLT_CTOR
  .method public virtual int32 DoIt<T>(!!T theT)
  {
    .override method instance int32 IX::Do<[1]>(!!0)
    ldarga.s theT
    constrained. !!T
    callvirt instance string object::ToString()
    call PrintString
    ldc.i4.3
    ret
  }
}

// Generic instance constructor and
// Explicit override of generic method, long form
.class public C implements IX
{
  .method public specialname void .ctor<U>(!!U u)
  {
    ldarg.0
    call instance void .base::.ctor()

    ldtoken !!U
    call class SysType SysType::GetTypeFromHandle(
                valuetype [mscorlib]System.RuntimeTypeHandle)
    callvirt instance string SysType::ToString()
    call PrintString

    ldarga.s u
    constrained. !!U
    callvirt instance string object::ToString()
    call PrintString

    ret
  }
  .override method instance int32 IX::Do<[1]>(!!0)
    with method instance int32 .this::DoIt<[1]>(!!0)

  .method public virtual int32 DoIt<T>(!!T theT)
  {
    ldarga.s theT
    constrained. !!T
    callvirt instance string object::ToString()
    call PrintString
    ldc.i4.4
    ret
```

```
  }
}

// The executing method
.method public static void Exec()
{
  .entrypoint

  newobj instance void A::.ctor()
  ldstr "Hehe"
  callvirt instance int32 IX::Do<string>(!!0)
  call PrintInt

  newobj instance void B::.ctor()
  ldstr "Haha"
  callvirt instance int32 IX::Do<string>(!!0)
  call PrintInt

  ldstr "Huhu"
  newobj instance void C::.ctor<string>(!!0)
  ldstr "Hoho"
  callvirt instance int32 IX::Do<string>(!!0)
  call PrintInt

  ret
}
```

Summary of the Metadata Validity Rules

One metadata table is specific to the generic methods—the MethodSpec table. The records of this table contain two entries:

- Method (coded token of type MethodDefOrRef). A token of the instantiated generic method definition. Must be a valid reference to the Method or MemberRef table.

- Instantiation (offset in the #Blob stream). The instantiation signature must be a valid nonzero offset.

The signature of a generic method has the calling convention bit IMAGE_CEE_CS_CALLCONV_GENERIC (0x10) set.

The generic methods cannot have a vararg calling convention.

The type parameters of a generic method should not have the constraint flags + (covariance) and – (contravariance). These constraints are not applicable to the type parameters of generic methods.

The flags of a generic method definition cannot contain the pinvokeimpl flag.

The implementation flags of a generic method definition cannot be native, unmanaged, internalcall, or runtime.

Class constructors (.cctor) cannot be generic.

PART 4

Inside the Execution Engine

CHAPTER 13

■■■

IL Instructions

When a method is executed, three categories of memory local to the method plus one category of external memory are involved. All these categories represent typed data slots, not simply an address interval as is the case in the unmanaged world. The external memory manipulated from the method is the community of the fields the method accesses (except the fields of value types belonging to the local categories). The local memory categories include an argument table, a local variable table, and an evaluation stack. Figure 13-1 describes data transitions between these categories. As you can see, all IL instructions resulting in data transfer have the evaluation stack as a source or a destination, or both.

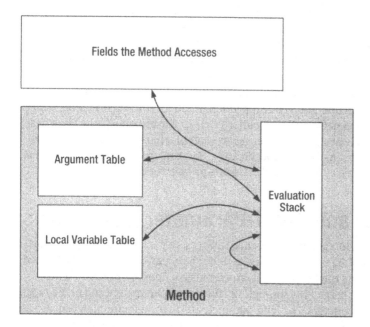

Figure 13-1. *Method memory categories*

The number of slots in the argument table is inferred from the method signature at the call site (not from the method signature specified when the method is defined—remember vararg methods). The number of slots in the local variable table is inferred from the local variable signature whose token is specified in the method header. The number of slots in the evaluation stack is defined by the MaxStack value of the method header, specified in ILAsm by the .maxstack directive.

The slots of the argument and local variable tables have static types, which can be any of the types defined in the .NET Framework and the application. The slots of the evaluation stack hold different types at different times during the course of the method execution. The types of slots change as the computations progress, and the same stack slots are used for different values. The execution engine of the common language runtime implements a coarser type system for the evaluation stack: the only types a stack slot can have at a given moment are int32, native int, int64, Float (the current implementation uses 64-bit floating-point representation, which covers both float32 and float64 types), & (a managed pointer), ObjectRef (an object reference, which is an instance pointer to an object), or an instance of a value type.

The IL instruction sequences that make up the IL code of a method can be valid or verifiable, or both, or neither. The concept of validity is easy to grasp: invalid instruction sequences are rejected by the JIT compiler, so nothing really bad can happen if you emit an invalid sequence—except that your code won't run.

Verifiability of the code is a security issue, not a compilation issue. The verifiable code is guaranteed to access only the memory it is allowed to access and hence is not capable of any malice or hidden hacks, so you can download a verifiable component from a remote location and run it without fear. If the code is deemed unverifiable—that is, if the code contains segments that just *might* contain a hack—the runtime security system will not allow it to be run except from a local disk. (I'll discuss the verifiability of IL code in the "Code Verifiability" section.) Generally, it's a good idea to check your executables with the PEVerify utility, distributed with the Microsoft .NET Framework SDK. This utility provides metadata validation and IL code verification, which includes checking both aspects—code validity and verifiability.

IL instructions consist of an operation code (opcode), which for some instructions is followed by an instruction parameter. Opcodes are either 1 byte or 2 bytes long; in the latter case, the first byte of the opcode is always 0xFE. In later sections of this chapter, opcodes are specified in parentheses following the instruction specification. Some instructions have synonyms, which I've also listed in parentheses immediately after the principal instruction name.

Long-Parameter and Short-Parameter Instructions

Many instructions that take an integer or an unsigned integer as a parameter have two forms. The long-parameter form requires a 4-byte integer, and the short-parameter form, recognized by the suffix .s, requires a 1-byte integer. Short-parameter instructions are used when the value of the parameter is in the range –128 through 127 for signed parameters and in the range 0 through 255 for unsigned parameters. The long-parameter form of an instruction can also be used for parameters within these ranges, but it leads to unnecessary bloating of the IL code.

Instructions that take a metadata token as a parameter don't have short forms: metadata tokens are always used in the IL stream in uncompressed and uncoded form, as 4-byte unsigned integers.

The byte order of the integers embedded in the IL stream must be little endian—that is, the least significant byte comes first.

Labels and Flow Control Instructions

Flow control instructions include branching instructions, the switch instruction, exiting and ending instructions used with managed EH blocks, and a return instruction.

All these instructions, except the return instruction, use integer offsets (in bytes) from the current position within the method IL code to specify the target instruction. The "current position" in this case is the offset of the beginning of the next instruction—the one following the flow control instruction. The target offset (which is the sum of the current position and the offset specified in the branching instruction) must point at the beginning of some instruction *of this method*. In other words, the target offset cannot be less than zero, cannot be larger than the method's code size, and cannot point at the middle of an instruction. If the target instruction is prefixed (the prefix instructions are discussed later in this chapter), the target offset cannot point at the prefixed instruction directly and must point at the prefix instruction. From the flow control point of view, a combination of a prefix instruction and a prefixed instruction is a single instruction.

Unconditional Branching Instructions

Unconditional branching instructions take no arguments from the stack and have a signed integer parameter. The parameter specifies the offset in bytes from the current position (which is the beginning of the next instruction—the one following the branching instruction) within the IL stream. The ILAsm notation does allow you to specify the offset explicitly (for example, br -234), but this practice is not recommended for an obvious reason: it's difficult to calculate the offset correctly when you're writing in a programming language.

It is much safer and less troublesome to use labels instead, letting the ILAsm compiler calculate the correct offsets. Labels, which you've already encountered many times, are simple names followed by a colon:

```
...
Loop:
...
br   Loop
...
```

By default, the IL assembler does not automatically choose between long-parameter and short-parameter forms. Thus, if you specify a short-parameter instruction and put the target label farther away than the short parameter permits, the calculated offset is truncated to 1 byte, and the IL assembler issues an error message. Version 2.0 of the IL assembler features the command-line option */OPT*, which turns on the automatic replacement of long-parameter instructions by the short-parameter instructions whenever the parameter size permits.

Unconditional branching instructions take nothing from the evaluation stack and put nothing on it.

- br <int32> (0x38). Branch <int32> bytes from the current position.

- br.s <int8> (0x2B). The short-parameter form of br.

Conditional Branching Instructions

Conditional branching instructions differ from the unconditional instructions in one aspect only: they branch only if the condition (<value>, which they take from the evaluation stack) is true (nonzero) or false (zero):

- brfalse (brnull, brzero) <int32> (0x39). Branch if <value> is 0.

- brfalse.s (brnull.s, brzero.s) <int8> (0x2C). The short-parameter form of brfalse.

- brtrue (brinst) <int32> (0x3A). Branch if <value> is nonzero.

- brtrue.s (brinst.s) <int8> (0x2D). The short-parameter form of brtrue.

Comparative Branching Instructions

Comparative branching instructions take two values (<value1>, <value2>) from the evaluation stack and compare them according to the <condition> specified by the opcode. Not all combinations of types of <value1> and <value2> are valid; Table 13-1 lists the valid combinations.

Table 13-1. *Valid Type Combinations in Comparison Instructions*

Type of <value₁>	Can Be Compared with Type
int32	int32, native int.
int64	int64.
native int	int32, native int, & (equality or nonequality comparisons only).
Float	Float. Without exception, all floating-point comparisons are formulated as "<condition> or unordered". Unordered is true when at least one of the operands is NaN.
& (managed pointer)	native int (equality or nonequality comparisons only), &. Unless the compared values are pointers to the same array or value type or pointers to pinned variables, comparing two managed pointers should be limited to equality or nonequality comparisons, because the garbage collection subsystem might move the managed pointers in an unpredictable way at unpredictable moments.
ObjectRef	ObjectRef (equality or nonequality comparisons only). "Greater-than" unsigned comparison is also admissible and is used to compare an object reference to null, because objects are subject to garbage collection, and their references can be changed by the GC at will.

- beq <int32> (0x3B). Branch if <value1> is equal to <value2>.

- beq.s <int8> (0x2E). The short-parameter form of beq.

- bne.un <int32> (0x40). Branch if the two values are not equal. Integer values are interpreted as unsigned; floating-point values are compared unordered.

- bne.un.s <int8> (0x33). The short-parameter form of bne.un.

- bge <int32> (0x3C). Branch if <value1> is greater or equal to <value2>.

- `bge.s <int8>` (0x2F). The short-parameter form of `bge`.

- `bge.un <int32>` (0x41). Branch if greater or equal. Integer values are interpreted as unsigned; floating-point values are compared unordered.

- `bge.un.s <int8>` (0x34). The short-parameter form of `bge.un`.

- `bgt <int32>` (0x3D). Branch if greater.

- `bgt.s <int8>` (0x30). The short-parameter form of `bgt`.

- `bgt.un <int32>` (0x42). Branch if greater. Integer values are interpreted as unsigned; floating-point values are compared unordered.

- `bgt.un.s <int8>` (0x35). The short-parameter form of `bgt.un`.

- `ble <int32>`(0x3E). Branch if less or equal.

- `ble.s <int8>` (0x31). The short-parameter form of `ble`.

- `ble.un <int32>` (0x43). Branch if less or equal. Integer values are interpreted as unsigned; floating-point values are compared unordered.

- `ble.un.s <int8>` (0x36). The short-parameter form of `ble.un`.

- `blt <int32>` (0x3F). Branch if less.

- `blt.s <int8>` (0x32). The short-parameter form of `blt`.

- `blt.un <int32>` (0x44). Branch if less. Integer values are interpreted as unsigned; floating-point values are compared unordered.

- `blt.un.s <int8>` (0x37). The short-parameter form of `blt.un`.

The switch Instruction

The `switch` instruction implements a jump table. This instruction is unique in the sense that it has not one, not two, but $N+1$ parameters following it, where N is the number of cases in the switch. The first parameter is a 4-byte unsigned integer specifying the number of cases, and the following N parameters are 4-byte signed integers specifying offsets to the targets (cases). There is no short-parameter form of this instruction. The ILAsm notation is as follows:

```
switch(Label1, Label2,...,LabelN)
...                 // Default case
Label1:
...
Label2:
...
...
LabelN:
...
```

As in the case of branching instructions, ILAsm syntax allows you to replace the labels in a switch(...) instruction with explicit offsets, but I definitely do not recommend this.

The instruction takes one value from the stack and converts it to an unsigned integer. It then switches to the target according to the value of this unsigned integer. A 0 value corresponds to the first target offset on the list. If the value is greater than or equal to the number of targets, the switch instruction is ignored, and control is passed to the instruction immediately following it. In this sense, the default case in ILAsm is always the first (lexically) case of the switch.

- switch <unsigned int32> <int32>...<int32> (0x45). Branch to one of the <unsigned int32> offsets.

The break Instruction

This break instruction is *not* equivalent to the break statement in C, which is used as an exit from the switch cases or loops. The break instruction in IL inserts a breakpoint into the IL stream and is used to indicate that if a debugger is attached, execution will stop and control will be given to the debugger. If a debugger is not present, the instruction does nothing. This instruction does not have parameters and does not touch the evaluation stack.

- break (0x01). Debugging breakpoint.

Managed EH Block Exiting Instructions

The blocks of code involved in managed exception handling cannot be entered or exited by simple branching because of the strict stack state requirements imposed on them. The leave instruction, or its short-parameter form, is used to exit a guarded block (a try block) or an exception handler block. You cannot use this instruction, however, to exit a filter, finally, or fault block. (For more details about these blocks, see Chapter 14.)

The instruction has one integer parameter specifying the offset of the target and works the same way as an unconditional branching instruction except that it empties the evaluation stack before the branching. The ILAsm notation for this instruction is similar to the notation for unconditional branching instructions: leave <label> or leave <int32>; the latter one is highly unrecommended.

- leave <int32> (0xDD). Clear the stack, and branch <int32> bytes from the current point.

- leave.s <int8> (0xDE). The short-parameter form of leave.

EH Block Ending Instructions

IL has two specific instructions to mark the end of filter, finally, and fault blocks. Unlike leave, these instructions mark the lexical end of a block (the instruction that has the highest offset in the block) rather than an algorithmic end or point of exit (which may just as well be located in the middle of the block). These instructions have no parameters.

- endfilter (0xFE 0x11). The lexical end of a filter block. The instruction takes one 4-byte integer value from the evaluation stack and signals the execution engine whether the associated exception handler should be engaged (a value of 1) or whether the search for the handler for this particular exception should be continued (a value other than 1), because this filter doesn't know what to do with this particular exception.

- endfinally (endfault) (0xDC). The lexical end of a finally or fault block. This instruction clears the evaluation stack.

The ret Instruction

The return instruction—ret—returns from a called method to the call site (immediately *after* the call site, to be precise). It has no parameters. If the called method should return a value of a certain type, exactly one value of the required type must be on the evaluation stack at the moment of return. The ret instruction causes this value to be removed from the evaluation stack of the called method and put on the evaluation stack of the calling method. If the called method returns void, its evaluation stack must be empty at the moment of return.

- ret (0x2A). Return from a method.

Arithmetical Instructions

Arithmetical operations deal with numeric data processing and include stack manipulation instructions, constant loading instructions, indirect (by pointer) loading and storing instructions, arithmetical operations, bitwise operations, data conversion operations, logical condition check operations, and block operations.

Stack Manipulation

Stack manipulation instructions work with the evaluation stack and have no parameters.

- nop (0x00). No operation; a placeholder only. The nop instruction is not exactly a stack manipulation instruction, since it does not touch the stack, but I've included it here rather than creating a separate category for it. The nop instruction is somewhat useful only in that, as it is a distinct opcode, a line of source code can be bound to it in the PDB file containing the debug information. The Visual Basic compiler introduces a lot of nop instructions because it wants to bind each and every line of the source code to the IL code. The reasoning behind this is not clear; perhaps the Visual Basic programmers want to be able to put breakpoints on comment lines.

  Another useful application of the nop instructions is specific to version 2.0 of the common language runtime (or, more exactly, its JIT compiler). Compilers, emitting the debug information into the PDB files, specify so-called code points, which bind source code lines and columns to offsets in the method code. In versions 1.0 and 1.1, the JIT compiler provided the ability to set the breakpoints at any code point specified in the PDB file. In version 2.0, an "optimized" mode was introduced, in which the JIT compiler effectively ignores the code points specified in the PDB and allows setting the breakpoints only according to some "heuristics." These heuristics include, for example, the moments when the evaluation stack is empty or when nop is encountered. Empty evaluation stack heuristics work for most imperative high-level languages, because, as a rule, each completed statement in these languages translates into code that begins and ends with the evaluation stack empty. This does not work, of course, for ILAsm, so in "optimized" mode you cannot set a breakpoint on an arbitrary instruction, and you cannot "walk" the ILAsm code instruction by instruction under a debugger. Inserting nop instructions after each meaningful instruction would probably help, but it is not a feasible option. Fortunately, the traditional mode, which allows setting the breakpoints according to PDB code points, is also supported in version 2.0. But I had to fight for preserving it and explain at lengths why it is important. You can find more details of debug modes in Chapter 16.

- dup (0x25). Duplicate the value on the top of the stack. If the stack is empty, the JIT compiler fails because of the stack underflow.

- pop (0x26). Remove the value from the top of the stack. The value is lost. If the stack is empty, the JIT compiler fails. It's not healthy to invoke dup or pop on an empty stack.

Constant Loading

Constant loading instructions take at most one parameter (the constant to load) and load it on the evaluation stack. The ILAsm syntax requires explicit specification of the constants (in other words, you cannot use a variable or argument name), in decimal or hexadecimal form:

```
ldc.i4 -1
ldc.i4 0xFFFFFFFF
```

Some instructions have no parameters because the value to be loaded is specified by the opcode itself.

Note that for integer and floating-point values, the slots of the evaluation stack are either 4- or 8-bytes wide, so the constants being loaded are converted to the suitable size.

- ldc.i4 <int32> (0x20). Load <int32> on the stack.

- ldc.i4.s <int8> (0x1F). Load <int8> on the stack.

- ldc.i4.m1 (ldc.i4.M1) (0x15). Load –1 on the stack.

- ldc.i4.0 (0x16). Load 0.

- ldc.i4.1 (0x17). Load 1.

- ldc.i4.2 (0x18). Load 2.

- ldc.i4.3 (0x19). Load 3.

- ldc.i4.4 (0x1A). Load 4.

- ldc.i4.5 (0x1B). Load 5.

- ldc.i4.6 (0x1C). Load 6.

- ldc.i4.7 (0x1D). Load 7.

- ldc.i4.8 (0x1E). Load 8. (I should have listed these in reverse order so then we could imagine ourselves on Cape Canaveral.)

- ldc.i8 <int64> (0x21). Load <int64> on the stack.

- `ldc.r4 <float32>` (0x22). Load `<float32>` (single-precision) on the stack.

- `ldc.r8 <float64>` (0x23). Load `<float64>` (double-precision) on the stack. ILAsm permits the use of integer parameters or byte arrays in both the `ldc.r4` and `ldc.r8` instructions; this is useful when you need to load special floating-point codes denoting positive or negative infinity or NaN. In such cases, the integers are either converted to floating-point numbers or interpreted as binary images of the floating-point numbers; the byte arrays are always interpreted as such binary images:

  - `ldc.r4 1078530000` loads floating-point number 1078530000.0.

  - `ldc.r4 float32(1078530000)` loads 3.1415901184082.

  - `ldc.r4 (D0 0F 49 40)` loads 3.1415901184082.

Indirect Loading

An indirect loading instruction takes a managed pointer (&) or an unmanaged pointer (`native int`) from the stack, retrieves the value at this pointer, and puts the value on the stack. The type of the value to be retrieved is defined by the opcode. The indirect loading instructions have no parameters.

- `ldind.i1` (0x46). Load a signed 1-byte integer from the location specified by the pointer taken from the stack.

- `ldind.u1` (0x47). Load an unsigned 1-byte integer.

- `ldind.i2` (0x48). Load a signed 2-byte integer.

- `ldind.u2` (0x49). Load an unsigned 2-byte integer.

- `ldind.i4` (0x4A). Load a signed 4-byte integer.

- `ldind.u4` (0x4B). Load an unsigned 4-byte integer.

- `ldind.i8` (`ldind.u8`) (0x4C). Load an 8-byte integer, signed or unsigned.

- `ldind.i` (0x4D). Load `native int`, an integer the size of a pointer.

- `ldind.r4` (0x4E). Load a single-precision floating-point value.

- `ldind.r8` (0x4F). Load a double-precision floating-point value.

- `ldind.ref` (0x50). Load an object reference.

Indirect Storing

Indirect storing instructions take a value and an address, in that order, from the stack and store the value at the location specified by the address. Since we are copying the memory (stack slot to specified location) without the need to interpret it, all we care about really is the size of the value to be stored. That's why the indirect storing instructions for integers don't have "unsigned" modifications. The address can be a managed or an unmanaged pointer. The type of the value to be stored is specified in the opcode. These instructions have no parameters.

- stind.ref (0x51). Store an object reference.

- stind.i1 (0x52). Store a 1-byte integer.

- stind.i2 (0x53). Store a 2-byte integer.

- stind.i4 (0x54). Store a 4-byte integer.

- stind.i8 (0x55). Store an 8-byte integer.

- stind.i (0xDF). Store a pointer-size integer.

- stind.r4 (0x56). Store a single-precision floating-point value.

- stind.r8 (0x57). Store a double-precision floating-point value.

Arithmetical Operations

All instructions performing the arithmetical operations except the negation operation take two operands from the stack and put the result on the stack. If the result value does not fit the result type, the value is truncated. Table 13-2 lists the admissible type combinations of operands and their corresponding result types.

Table 13-2. *Admissible Operand Types and Their Result Types in Arithmetical Operations*

Operand Type	Operand Type	Result Type
int32	int32	int32
native int	native int	native int
int32	native int	native int
int64	int64	int64
int32, native int	& (addition only, unverifiable)	&
&	int32, native int (addition or subtraction only, unverifiable)	&
Float	Float (except unsigned division)	Float
&	& (addition only, unverifiable)	native int

The arithmetical operation instructions are as follows:

- add (0x58). Addition.

- sub (0x59). Subtraction.

- mul (0x5A). Multiplication. For floating-point numbers, which have the special values infinity and NaN, the following rule applies:

    0 * infinity = NaN

- div (0x5B). Division. For integers, division by 0 results in a DivideByZero exception. For floating-point numbers, the following rule applies:

    0 / 0 = NaN, infinity / infinity = NaN, x / infinity = 0

- div.un (0x5C). Division of operands treated as unsigned (integer operands only).

- rem (0x5D). Remainder, modulo. For integers, modulo 0 results in a DivideByZero exception. For floating-point numbers, the following rule applies:

  infinity rem x = NaN, x rem 0 = NaN, x rem infinity = x

- rem.un (0x5E). The remainder of unsigned operands (integer operands only).

- neg (0x65). Negate—that is, invert the sign. This is the only unary arithmetical operation. It takes one operand rather than two from the evaluation stack and puts the result back. This operation is not applicable to managed pointers or object references but is applicable to unmanaged pointers. With integers, a peculiar situation can occur in which the maximum negative number does not change after negation because of the overflow condition during the operation, as shown in this example:

```
ldc.i4 0x80000000 // Max. negative number for int32,
                  //-2147483648
neg
call void [mscorlib]System.Console::WriteLine(int32)
// Output: -2147483648;
// The same effect with subtraction:
ldc.i4.0
ldc.i4 0x80000000
sub
call void [mscorlib]System.Console::WriteLine(int32)
// Output: -2147483648;
```

The previous problem is not in any way IL specific; it stems from the binary representation of integer numbers. Floating-point numbers don't have this problem. Negating NaN returns NaN because NaN, which is not a number, has no sign.

If an arithmetical operation is applied to integer operands and the result overflows the target, the result is bit truncated to fit the target type, with most significant bits thrown away:

```
ldc.i4 0xFFFFFFF0 // 4294967280
ldc.i4 0x000000FF // 255
add
call void [mscorlib]System.Console::WriteLine(int32)
// Output: 239 (0xEF);
```

When int32 and native int are used as operands of arithmetic instructions on a 64-bit platform, int32 operand is sign extended to native int.

Overflow Arithmetical Operations

Overflow arithmetical operations are similar to the arithmetical operations described in the preceding section except that they work with integer operands only and generate an Overflow exception if the result does not fit the target type. The ILAsm notation for the overflow arithmetical operations contains the suffix .ovf following the operation kind. The type compatibility list, shown in Table 13-3, is similar to the list shown in Table 13-2.

Table 13-3. *Acceptable Operand Types and Their Result Types in Overflow Arithmetical Operations*

Operand Type	Operand Type	Result Type
int32	int32	int32
native int	native int	native int
int32	native int	native int
int64	int64	int64
int32, native int	& (unsigned addition only, unverifiable)	&
&	int32, native int (unsigned addition or subtraction only, unverifiable)	&
&	& (unsigned subtraction, unverifiable)	native int

- add.ovf (0xD6). Addition.

- add.ovf.un (0xD7). Addition of unsigned operands.

- sub.ovf (0xDA). Subtraction.

- sub.ovf.un (0xDB). Subtraction of unsigned operands.

- mul.ovf (0xD8). Multiplication.

- mul.ovf.un (0xD9). Multiplication of unsigned operands.

Bitwise Operations

Bitwise operations have no parameters and are defined for integer types only; floating-point, pointer, and object reference operands are not allowed. As a result, the related operand type compatibility list, shown in Table 13-4, is pretty simple.

Table 13-4. *Acceptable Operand Types and Their Result Types in Bitwise Operations*

Operand Type	Operand Type	Result Type
int32	int32	int32
int32	native int	native int
int64	int64	int64

Three of the bitwise operations are binary, taking two operands from the stack and placing one result on the stack; and one is unary, taking one operand from the stack and placing one result on the stack:

- and (0x5F). Bitwise AND (binary).

- or (0x60). Bitwise OR (binary).

- xor (0x61). Bitwise exclusive OR (binary).

- not (0x66). Bitwise inversion (unary). This operation (which is the equivalent of ldc.i4.1; add; neg;), rather than neg, can be used (to some extent) for the integer sign inversion of the maximum negative integer:

```
ldc.i4 0x80000000 // Max. negative number for int32,
                  // -2147483648
not
call void [mscorlib]System.Console::WriteLine(int32)
// Output: 2147483647 (0x7FFFFFFF);
// Of course, it's not +2147483648,
// which cannot be with int32,
// but at least we have the max. positive number
```

When int32 and native int are used as operands of bitwise instructions on a 64-bit platform, int32 operand is sign-extended to native int.

Shift Operations

Shift operations have no parameters and are defined for integer operands only. The shift operations are binary: they take from the stack the shift count and the value being shifted, in that order, and put the shifted value on the stack. The result always has the same type as the operand being shifted, which can be of any integer type. The type of the shift count cannot be int64 and is limited to int32 or native int.

- shl (0x62). Shift left.

- shr (0x63). Shift right (the most significant bits of the result assume the value of the sign bit of the value being shifted).

- shr.un (0x64). Shift right, treating the shifted value as unsigned (the most significant bits of the result assume the zero value).

It is interesting that, as you can see, there are no rotational shift operations in the IL, and it is not obvious how these operations could be implemented through shl and shr.un, because rotational shift operations are size specific: rol(i, n) == (shl(i, n%sizeof(i)) | shr.un(i, sizeof(i)-n%sizeof(i))), where i is the operand being shifted and n is the shift count.

Conversion Operations

The conversion operations have no parameters. They take a value from the stack, convert it to the type specified by the opcode, and put the result back on the stack. The specifics of the conversion obviously depend on the type of the converted value and the target type (the type to which the value is converted). If the type of the value on the stack is the same as the target type, no conversion is necessary, and the operation itself is doing nothing more than bloating the IL code.

For integer source and target types, several rules apply. If the target integer type is narrower than the source type (for example, int32 to int16, or int64 to int32), the value is truncated—that is, the most significant bytes are thrown away. If the situation is the opposite—if the target integer type is wider than the source—the result is either sign-extended or zero-extended, depending on the type of conversion. Conversions to signed integers use sign-extension, and conversions to unsigned integers use zero-extension.

If the source type is a pointer, it can be converted to either unsigned int64 or native unsigned int. In either case, if the converted pointer was managed, it is dropped from the GC tracking and is not automatically updated when the GC rearranges the memory layout. A pointer cannot be used as a target type.

If both source and target types are floating point, the conversion merely results in a change of precision. In float-to-integer conversions, the values are truncated toward 0—for example, the value 1.1 is converted to 1, and the value –2.3 is converted to –2. In integer-to-float conversions, the integer value is simply converted to floating point, possibly losing less significant mantissa bits.

Object references cannot be subject to conversion operations either as a source or as a target.

- conv.i1 (0x67). Convert the value to int8.

- conv.u1 (0xD2). Convert the value to unsigned int8.

- conv.i2 (0x68). Convert the value to int16.

- conv.u2 (0xD1). Convert the value to unsigned int16.

- conv.i4 (0x69). Convert the value to int32.

- conv.u4 (0x6D). Convert the value to unsigned int32.

- conv.i8 (0x6A). Convert the value to int64.

- conv.u8 (0x6E). Convert the value to unsigned int64. This operation can be applied to pointers.

- conv.i (0xD3). Convert the value to native int.

- conv.u (0xE0). Convert the value to native unsigned int. This operation can be applied to pointers.

- conv.r4 (0x6B). Convert the value to float32.

- conv.r8 (0x6C). Convert the value to float64.

- conv.r.un (0x76). Convert an unsigned integer value to floating point.

Overflow Conversion Operations

Overflow conversion operations differ from the conversion operations described in the preceding section in two aspects: the target types are exclusively integer types, and an Overflow exception is thrown whenever the value must be truncated to fit the target type. In short, the story is the same as it is with overflow arithmetical operations and arithmetical operations.

- conv.ovf.i1 (0xB3). Convert the value to int8.

- conv.ovf.u1 (0xB4). Convert the value to unsigned int8.

- conv.ovf.i1.un (0x82). Convert an unsigned integer to int8.

- conv.ovf.u1.un (0x86). Convert an unsigned integer to unsigned int8.

- conv.ovf.i2 (0xB5). Convert the value to int16.

- conv.ovf.u2 (0xB6). Convert the value to unsigned int16.

- conv.ovf.i2.un (0x83). Convert an unsigned integer to int16.

- conv.ovf.u2.un (0x87). Convert an unsigned integer to unsigned int16.

- conv.ovf.i4 (0xB7). Convert the value to int32.

- conv.ovf.u4 (0xB8). Convert the value to unsigned int32.

- conv.ovf.i4.un (0x84). Convert an unsigned integer to int32.

- conv.ovf.u4.un (0x88). Convert an unsigned integer to unsigned int32.

- conv.ovf.i8 (0xB9). Convert the value to int64.

- conv.ovf.u8 (0xBA). Convert the value to unsigned int64.

- conv.ovf.i8.un (0x85). Convert an unsigned integer to int64.

- conv.ovf.u8.un (0x89). Convert an unsigned integer to unsigned int64.

- conv.ovf.i (0xD4). Convert the value to native int.

- conv.ovf.u (0xD5). Convert the value to native unsigned int.

- conv.ovf.i.un (0x8A). Convert an unsigned integer to native int.

- conv.ovf.u.un (0x8B). Convert an unsigned integer to native unsigned int.

Logical Condition Check Instructions

Logical condition check operations are similar to comparative branching instructions except that they result not in branching but in putting the condition check result on the stack. The result type is int32, and its value is equal to 1 if the condition checks and 0 otherwise; in other words, logically the result is a Boolean value. The two operands being compared are taken from the stack, and since no branching is performed, the condition check instructions have no parameters.

The logical condition check instructions are useful when you want to store the result of the condition check for multiple use or for later use. If you need the condition check to decide only once and on the spot whether you need to branch, you would be better off using a comparative branching instruction.

The admissible combinations of operand types are the same as for comparative branching instructions (see Table 13-1). There are, however, fewer condition check instructions than conditional branching operations: some conditions are just logical negations of other conditions ("not equal" is not "equal," "less or equal" is not "greater," and so on), so it would be redundant to introduce special check instructions for such conditions.

- ceq (0xFE 0x01). Check whether the two values on the stack are equal.

- cgt (0xFE 0x02). Check whether the first value is greater than the second value. It's the stack we are working with, so the "second" value is the one on the top of the stack.

- cgt.un (0xFE 0x03). Check whether the first value is greater than the second; integer values are compared as unsigned, and floating-point values are compared as unordered.

- clt (0xFE 0x04). Check whether the first value is less than the second value.

- clt.un (0xFE 0x05). Check whether the first value is less than the second; integer values are compared as unsigned, and floating-point values are compared as unordered.

- ckfinite (0xC3). This unary operation, which takes only one value from the stack, is applicable to floating-point values only. It throws an Arithmetic exception if the value is +infinity, -infinity, or NaN. Otherwise, the operation puts the same value back on the stack.

Block Operations

Two IL instructions deal with blocks of memory regardless of the type or types that make up this memory. Because of their type blindness, both instructions are unverifiable.

- cpblk (0xFE 0x17). Copy a block of memory. The instruction has no parameters and takes three operands from the stack in the following order: the size (in bytes) of the block to be copied (unsigned int32), the source address (a pointer or native int), and the destination address (a pointer or native int). The source and destination addresses must be aligned on the size of native int unless the instruction is prefixed with the unaligned. instruction, described in "Prefix Instructions," later in this chapter. The cpblk instruction does not deduce the right direction of byte copying when the source and destination areas overlap, so there is no guarantee in such case. The cpblk instruction puts nothing on the stack.

- initblk (0xFE 0x18). Initialize a block of memory. The instruction has no parameters and takes three operands from the evaluation stack: the size of the block in bytes (unsigned int32), the initialization value (int8), and the block start address (a pointer or native int). The alignment rules mentioned apply to the block start address. The initblk instruction puts nothing on the stack. As a result of this operation, each byte within the specified block is assigned the initialization value.

Addressing Arguments and Local Variables

A special group of IL instructions is dedicated to loading the values of method arguments and local variables on the evaluation stack and storing the values taken from the stack in local variables and method arguments. It is to be noted that in the case of vararg methods, the argument-addressing instructions described in the following sections cannot target the arguments of the variable part of the signature.

Method Argument Loading

The following instructions are used for loading method argument values on the evaluation stack:

- `ldarg <unsigned int16>` (0xFE 0x09). Load the argument number `<unsigned int16>` on the stack. The argument enumeration is zero based, but it's important to remember that instance methods have an "invisible" argument not specified in the method signature: the class instance pointer, `this`, which is always argument number 0. The static methods don't have such an "invisible" argument, so for them the argument number 0 is the first argument specified in the method signature. The total number of arguments cannot exceed 65535 (0xFFFF), which means the argument ordinal cannot exceed 65534. This limitation stems from the fact that the Sequence entry of the Parameter metadata table is only 2 bytes wide.

- `ldarg.s <unsigned int8>` (0x0E). The short-parameter form of `ldarg`.

- `ldarg.0` (0x02). Load argument number 0 on the stack.

- `ldarg.1` (0x03). Load argument number 1 on the stack.

- `ldarg.2` (0x04). Load argument number 2 on the stack.

- `ldarg.3` (0x05). Load argument number 3 on the stack.

Method Argument Address Loading

These two instructions are used for loading method argument addresses on the evaluation stack:

- `ldarga <unsigned int16>` (0xFE 0x0A). Load the address of argument number `<unsigned int16>` on the stack.

- `ldarga.s <unsigned int8>` (0x0F). The short-parameter form of `ldarga`.

Method Argument Storing

These two instructions are used for storing a value from the stack in a method argument slot:

- `starg <unsigned int16>` (0xFE 0x0B). Take a value from the stack and store it in argument slot number `<unsigned int16>`. The value on the stack must be of the same type as the argument slot or must be convertible to the type of the argument slot. The convertibility rules and effects are the same as those for conversion operations, discussed earlier in this chapter.

- `starg.s <unsigned int8>` (0x10). The short-parameter form of `starg`.

Method Argument List

The following instruction is used exclusively in vararg methods to retrieve the method argument list and put an instance of the value type [mscorlib]System.RuntimeArgumentHandle on the stack. Chapter 10 discusses the application of this instruction.

- arglist (0xFE 0x00). Get the argument list handle.

Local Variable Loading

Local variable loading instructions are similar to argument loading instructions except that no "invisible" items appear among the local variables, so local variable number 0 is always the first one specified in the local variable signature.

- ldloc <unsigned int16> (0xFE 0x0C). Load the value of local variable number <unsigned int16> on the stack. Like the argument numbers, local variable numbers can range from 0 to 65534 (0xFFFE). The value 65535, also admissible for unsigned 2-byte integers, is excluded because otherwise the *counter* of local variables would have to be 4 bytes wide. Limiting the number of the local variables, however standardized, seems arbitrary and implementation specific, because the number of the local variables of a method is not stored in the metadata or in the method header, so this limitation comes purely from one particular implementation of the JIT compiler.

- ldloc.s <unsigned int8> (0x11). The short-parameter form of ldloc.

- ldloc.0 (0x06). Load the value of local variable number 0 on the stack.

- ldloc.1 (0x07). Load the value of local variable number 1 on the stack.

- ldloc.2 (0x08). Load the value of local variable number 2 on the stack.

- ldloc.3 (0x09). Load the value of local variable number 3 on the stack.

Local Variable Reference Loading

The following instructions load references (managed pointers) to the local variables on the evaluation stack:

- ldloca <unsigned int16> (0xFE 0x0D). Load the address of local variable number <unsigned int16> on the stack. The local variable number can vary from 0 to 0xFFFE.

- ldloca.s <unsigned int8> (0x12). The short-parameter form of ldloca.

Local Variable Storing

It would be strange to have local variables and be unable to assign values to them. The following two instructions take care of this aspect of our life:

- stloc <unsigned int16> (0xFE 0x0E). Take the value from the stack, and store it in local variable slot number <unsigned int16>. The value on the stack must be of the same type as the local variable slot or must be convertible to the type of the local variable slot. The convertibility rules and effects are the same as those for the conversion operations discussed earlier in this chapter.

- `stloc.s <unsigned int8>` (0x13). The short-parameter form of `stloc`. You've probably noticed that using short-parameter forms of argument and local variable manipulation instructions results in a double gain against the standard form: not only is the parameter 1 byte instead of 2, but also the opcode is shorter.

Local Block Allocation

With all due respect to the object-oriented approach, sometimes it is necessary (or just convenient) to obtain a plain, C-style chunk of memory. The IL instruction set provides an instruction for such allocation. It is to be noted, however, that this memory is available only while the method is executing and is deallocated on the method exit (via `ret` or an exception). Only the allocating method itself and the methods it calls can access this memory.

- `localloc` (0xFE 0x0F). Allocate a block of memory for the duration of the method execution. The instruction takes the block size (`native unsigned int`) from the evaluation stack and puts a managed pointer (&) to the allocated block on the evaluation stack. If not enough space is available on the native thread stack, a `StackOverflow` exception is thrown. This instruction must not appear within any exception handling block. Like any other block instruction, `localloc` is unverifiable.

Prefix Instructions

The prefix instructions listed in this section have no meaning per se but are used as prefixes for the pointer-consuming instructions—that is, the instructions that take a pointer value from the stack, such as `ldind.*`, `stind.*`, `ldfld`, `stfld`, `ldobj`, `stobj`, `initblk`, and `stblk`—that immediately follow them. When used as prefixes of instructions that don't consume pointers, the prefix instructions are ignored and do *not* carry on to the nearest pointer-consuming instruction.

- `unaligned. <unsigned int8>` (0xFE 0x12). Indicates that the pointer(s) on the stack are aligned on `<unsigned int8>` rather than on the pointer size. The `<unsigned int8>` parameter must be 1, 2, or 4.

- `volatile.` (0xFE 0x13). Indicates that the pointer on the stack is volatile—that is, the value it points at can be modified from another thread of execution and the results of its dereferencing therefore cannot be cached for performance considerations.

A prefix instruction affects only the immediately following instruction and does not mark the respective pointer as unaligned or volatile throughout the entire method. Both prefixes can be used with the same instruction—in other words, the pointer on the stack can be marked as both unaligned and volatile; in such a case, the order of appearance of the prefixes does not matter.

The ILAsm syntax requires the prefix instructions to be separated from the next instruction by at least a space symbol:

```
volatile. ldind.i4 // Correct
```

```
volatile.
ldind.i4 // Correct
```

```
volatile.ldind.i4 // Syntax error
```

Such a mistake is unlikely with the unaligned. instruction because it requires an integer parameter:

unaligned. 4 **ldind.i4**

The prefix instructions tail. and constrained. are specific to method calling, and the prefix instruction readonly. is specific to array manipulation. These prefix instructions are discussed in respective sections of this chapter.

Addressing Fields

Six instructions can be used to load a field value or an address on the stack or to store a value from the stack in a field. A field signature does not indicate whether the field is static or instance, so the IL instruction set defines separate instructions for dealing with instance and static fields. Instructions dealing with instance fields take the instance pointer—an object reference if the field addressed belongs to a class and a managed pointer if the field belongs to a value type—from the stack.

- ldfld <token> (0x7B). Take the instance from the stack, and load the value of an instance field on the stack. <token> specifies the field being loaded and must be a valid FieldDef or MemberRef token, uncompressed and uncoded. The "instance" may be an object reference, a managed pointer to instance of a value type, or an instance of a value type itself. An unmanaged pointer to an instance of a value type can also be used, but it renders the code unverifiable.

- ldsfld <token> (0x7E). Load the value of a static field on the stack.

- ldflda <token> (0x7C). Take the instance pointer from the stack, and load a managed pointer to the instance field on the stack. Unlike ldfld, this instruction cannot use an instance of a value type and takes only an object reference or a pointer (managed or unmanaged) to an instance of a value type. Using an unmanaged pointer renders the code unverifiable.

- ldsflda <token> (0x7F). Load a managed pointer to the static field on the stack.

- stfld <token> (0x7D). Take the value from the stack, take the instance pointer from the stack, and store the value in the instance field. "The instance pointer" in this case, like in ldflda instruction, is either an object reference or a pointer to an instance of a value type. In this respect, stfld is asymmetric to ldfld.

- stsfld <token> (0x80). Store the value from the stack in the static field.

The ILAsm notation requires full field specification, which is resolved to <token> at compile time:

ldfld int32 Foo.Bar::ii

The applicable conversion rules when loading and storing values are the same as those discussed earlier. Note also that the fields cannot be of managed pointer type, as was discussed in Chapter 8.

Calling Methods

Methods can be called directly or indirectly. In addition, you can also use the special case of a so-called tail call, discussed in this section. The method signature indicates whether the method is instance or static, so separate instructions for instance and static methods are unnecessary. What the method signature *doesn't* hold, however, is information about whether the method is virtual. As a result, separate instructions are used for calling virtual and nonvirtual methods. Besides, even a virtual method may be called as nonvirtual. In this case, the call is not dispatched through the class's virtual table, and all our nice overrides have no effect. Because of that, the nonvirtual calls of the virtual methods have been declared unverifiable in version 2.0 except in some specific contexts (see "Direct Calls").

Method call instructions have one parameter: the token of the method being called, either a MethodDef or a MemberRef. The arguments of the method call should be loaded on the stack in order of their appearance in the method signature, with the last signature parameter being loaded last, which is exactly the opposite of what you would normally expect. Instance methods have an "invisible" first argument (an instance pointer, which is an object reference for reference types or a managed pointer for value types) not present in the signature; when an instance method is called, this instance pointer should be loaded on the stack first, preceding all arguments corresponding to the method signature.

Unless the called method returns void, the return value is left on the stack by the callee when the call is completed.

Direct Calls

The IL instruction set contains three instructions intended for the direct method calls (well, "direct" in the sense that all these instructions directly specify the method being called; some purists would not consider a virtual call "direct," because under the hood it is done via the v-table):

- jmp <token> (0x27). Abandon the current method and jump to the target method, specified by <token>, transferring the current arguments in their present state (which may be different from the original state, because the calling method could change the argument values before the jump). Everything else of the current method, including local variables and locally allocated memory, is abandoned. At the moment jmp is invoked, the evaluation stack must be empty, and the arguments are transferred automatically. Because of this, the signature of the target method must exactly match the signature of the method invoking jmp. This instruction should not be used within EH blocks—.try, catch, filter, fault, or finally blocks, discussed in Chapter 14—or within a synchronized region (the code segment protected by a thread lock, such as a mutex). The jmp instruction is unverifiable.

- call <token> (0x28). Call an instance or static method nonvirtually. You can also call a virtual method, but in this case it is called not through the type's v-table. (If this sounds somehow vague to you, you might want to return to Chapter 10 and, more precisely, to the sample file Virt_not.il.) The real difference between virtual and nonvirtual instance methods becomes obvious when you create an instance of a class, cast it to the parent type of the class, and then call instance methods on this "child-posing-as-parent" instance. The nonvirtual methods are called directly, bypassing the child type's v-table, so the parent's methods will be called in this case. Virtual methods are called through the v-table, and hence the overriding child's methods will be called. To confirm this, carry out a simple experiment: open the sample file Virt_not.il in a text editor, and change `callvirt instance void A::Bar( )` to `call instance void A::Bar( )`. Then recompile the sample, and run it.

- `callvirt <token>` (0x6F). Call the virtual method specified by `<token>`. This type of method call is conducted through the instance's v-table. It is possible to call a nonvirtual instance method using `callvirt`. In this case, the method is called directly simply because the method cannot be found in the v-table. But unlike `call`, the `callvirt` instruction first checks the validity of the object reference (`this` pointer) before doing anything else, which is a very useful feature. The C# compiler exploits it shamelessly, emitting `callvirt` to call both virtual and nonvirtual instance methods of classes. I say "of classes" because `callvirt` requires an object reference as the `this` pointer and will not accept a managed pointer to a value type instance. To use `callvirt` with an instance of a value type, you need to box the instance first, thus converting it to a class instance carrying the v-table.

CLR 2.0 considers nonvirtual calls of virtual methods unverifiable except in the following cases:

- If the called method is final (cannot be overridden)

- If the instance reference is that of a boxed value type

- If the parent class of the called method is sealed

- If the calling method and the called method are instance methods of the same class

- If the instance pointer is a managed pointer to a value type

These exceptions cover almost all cases when the called virtual method is guaranteed not to be overridden. I say "almost" because there is at least one such case not covered—when the type of the object reference is reliably traceable and the called method belongs to this type:

```
.class public A
{
    ...
    .method public virtual void f() { ... }
}
.class public B extends A
{
    ...
    .method public virtual void f() { ... }
}
...
newobj instance void B::.ctor()
dup
// The objects on the stack are known to be B (not B's descendants cast to B)
call instance void B::f() // should be verifiable, the type matches the object
call instance void A::f() // unverifiable - the type doesn't match the object
...
```

Indirect Calls

Methods in IL can be called indirectly through the function pointer loaded on the evaluation stack. This allows us to make calls to computed targets—for example, to call a method by a function pointer returned by another method. Function pointers used in indirect calls are unmanaged pointers represented by native int. Two instructions load a function pointer to a specified method on the stack, and one other instruction calls a method indirectly:

- ldftn <token> (0xFE 0x06). Load the function pointer to the method specified by <token> of MethodDef or MemberRef type.

- ldvirtftn <token> (0xFE 0x07). Take the object reference (the instance pointer) from the stack, and load the function pointer to the method specified by <token>. The method is looked up in the instance's v-table.

- calli <token> (0x29). Take the function pointer from the stack, take all the arguments from the stack, and make an indirect method call according to the method signature specified by <token>. <token> must be a valid StandAloneSig token. The function pointer must be on the top of the stack. If the method returns a value, it is pushed on the stack at the completion of the call, just like in direct calls. The calli instruction is unverifiable, which is not surprising, considering that the call is made via an unmanaged pointer, which is itself unverifiable.

It's easy enough to see that the combination ldftn/calli is equivalent to call, as long as we don't consider verifiability, and the combination ldvirtftn/calli is equivalent to callvirt.

The ILAsm notation requires full specification of the method in the ldftn and ldvirtftn instructions, similar to the call and callvirt instructions. The method signature accompanying the calli instruction is specified as <call_conv> <ret_type>(<arg_list>). For example:

```
.locals init (native int fnptr)
...
ldftn void [mscorlib]System.Console::WriteLine(int32)
stloc.0 // Store function pointer in local variable
...
ldc.i4 12345 // Load argument
ldloc.0 // Load function pointer
calli void(int32)
...
```

Tail Calls

Tail calls are similar to method jumps (jmp) in the sense that both lead to abandoning the current method and passing the arguments to the tail-called (jumped-at) method. However, since the arguments of a tail call have to be loaded on the evaluation stack explicitly (a tail call discards the stack frame of the current method, unlike a jump, which preserves the stack frame and can use the arguments already loaded), a tail call—unlike a jump—does not require the entire signature of the called method to match the signature of the calling method; only the return types must be the same or compatible. The tail calls are very useful in implementing massively recursive methods: the caller's stack frame is discarded in the process of a tail call, so there is no risk of overflowing the stack, no matter how deep the recursion is. This is important for the functional languages, which use recursion instead of loops.

Tail calls are distinguished by the prefix instruction `tail.` immediately preceding a `call`, `callvirt`, or `calli` instruction:

- `tail.` (0xFE 0x14). Mark the following call instruction as a tail call. This instruction has no parameters and does not work with the stack. In ILAsm, this instruction—like the other prefix instructions `unaligned.` and `volatile.`, discussed earlier—must be separated from the call instruction that follows it by at least a space symbol.

The difference between a method jump and a tail call is that the tail call instruction pair is verifiable in principle, subject to the verifiability of the call arguments, as long as it is immediately followed (in the caller instruction stream) by the `ret` instruction. As is the case with other prefix instructions, it is illegal to bypass the prefix and branch directly to the prefixed instruction, in this case, `call`, `callvirt`, or `calli`.

Constrained Virtual Calls

Constrained virtual calls were introduced in version 2.0 of the common language runtime in order to deal with instantiations of generic types or methods when the type w

hose method is called is represented by a type parameter and hence equally might be a reference type or a value type:

```
.class public G<(IFoo)T> // Interface IFoo specifies method void Foo(int32)
{
    .method public static void CallVirtFoo(!T t, int32 val)
    {
        // How do I get the object ref?
        // If T is a reference type, I just need ldarg.0
        // If T is a value type, I need ldarga.s 0 and then box
        ldarg.1
        callvirt instance void IFoo::Foo(int32)
        ...
```

Obviously, the applicable calling mechanism must be identified "on the spot," when the virtual call is about to be executed and the nature of the type instance becomes known. This is not good—the IL code of the method becomes dependent on the nature of the generic parameter.

The constrained virtual calls, unlike unconstrained calls and virtual calls, require a managed pointer (&) to the type instance (`this` pointer), whether this instance is an object reference or a value type instance. In unconstrained calls, as you know, the `this` pointer must be an object reference (0) or a managed pointer (&) to a value type instance. Uniform usage of a managed pointer in constrained calls allows us to use the same IL instructions, "preparing" the instance pointer for the virtual call:

```
.class public G<(IFoo)T> // Interface IFoo specifies method void Foo(int32)
{
    .method public static void CallVirtFoo(!T t, int32 val)
```

```
{
    ldarga.s 0 // load managed pointer to t
    ldarg.1
    constrained. !T
    callvirt instance void IFoo::Foo(int32)
...
```

The applicable calling mechanism is identified as follows:

- If the type is a reference type (and hence the this pointer is a managed pointer to object reference), then the this pointer is dereferenced yielding the object reference, and the virtual call is executed on this object reference.

- If the type is a value type (and hence the this pointer is a managed pointer to a value type instance) and the type implements the specified method, then the nonvirtual call is executed on the this pointer; it is safe to do, because value types are sealed, and the virtual methods implemented by them cannot be possibly overridden.

- If the type is a value type and it does not implement the specified method (must have inherited it from its ancestors System.Object, System.ValueType and maybe System.Enum), then the this pointer is dereferenced yielding a value type instance, which is then boxed yielding an object reference, and the virtual call is executed on this object reference. We cannot use the same trick here and call the method nonvirtually, because the value type doesn't implement it; but at least one of its ancestors does, so the method is present in the (boxed) value type's v-table.

Constrained calls are distinguished by the prefix instruction constrained. immediately preceding a callvirt or ldvirtftn instruction:

- constrained. <token> (0xFE 0x16). Mark the following virtual call instruction as a constrained call. The <token> usually is a TypeSpec token representing a generic type variable ({E_T_VAR <ordinal>} or {E_T_MVAR <ordinal>}). However, <token> may be a TypeRef or TypeDef token as well, which means that constrained virtual calls can be used with nongeneric types.

The mechanism of constrained virtual calls unifies the way the methods can be called on reference and value types and hence is very useful to compilers, which now don't have to figure out whether the instance is an object reference or a value type instance. Considering that some languages don't even make a distinction between reference types and value types and treat all types as objects, the constrained virtual call mechanism is indeed a good addition to the IL instruction set.

Addressing Classes and Value Types

Being object oriented in its base, IL offers quite a few instructions dedicated specifically to manipulating class and value type instances:

- ldnull (0x14). Load a null object reference on the stack. This is *not* the same as ldc.i4.0! The resulting bits are the same (all zero), but the type of the top slot of the evaluation stack becomes an object reference (0).

- ldobj <token> (0x71). Load an instance of value type specified by <token> on the stack. This instruction takes from the stack the managed pointer to the value type instance to be loaded (obtained via the ldarga, ldloca, or ldflda/ldsflda instruction). <token> must be a valid TypeDef, TypeRef, or TypeSpec token. The name of the instruction is somewhat misleading, for it deals with value type instances rather than objects (class instances). The ILAsm notation requires full specification of the value type so that it can be resolved to the token. For example:

ldobj [.**module** other.dll]Foo.Bar

- stobj <token> (0x81). Take the value type value—no, that's not a typo—from the stack, take the managed pointer to the value type instance from the stack, and store the value type value in the instance referenced by the pointer. <token> indicates the value type and must be a valid TypeDef, TypeRef, or TypeSpec token. The ILAsm notation is similar to that used for ldobj.

- ldstr <token> (0x72). Load a string reference on the stack. <token> is a token of a user-defined string, whose RID portion is actually an offset in the #US blob stream. This instruction performs a lot of work: by the token, the Unicode string is retrieved from the #US stream, an instance of the [mscorlib]System.String class is created from the retrieved string, and the object reference is pushed on the stack. In ILAsm, the string is specified explicitly either as a composite quoted string:

ldstr "Hello"+" World!"

or as a byte array:

ldstr bytearray(A1 00 A2 00 A3 00 A4 00 A5 00 00 00)

In the first case, at compile time the composite quoted string is converted to Unicode before being stored in the #US stream. In the second case, the byte array is stored "as is" without conversion. It can be padded with one 0 byte to make the byte count even (if you forget to do it, the IL assembler will do it as a courtesy). Storing a string in the #US stream gives the compiler the string token, which it puts into the IL stream.

- cpobj <token> (0x70). Copy the value of one value type instance to another instance. This instruction pops the source and the target instance pointers and pushes nothing on the stack. Both instances must be of the value type specified by <token>, either a TypeDef token or a TypeRef token. The ILAsm notation for this instruction is similar to that used for ldobj or stobj.

- newobj <token> (0x73). Allocate memory for a new instance of a class—not a value type—and call the instance constructor method specified by <token>. The object reference to newly created class instance is pushed on the stack. <token> must be a valid MethodDef or MemberRef token of a .ctor. The instruction takes from the stack all the arguments explicitly specified in the constructor signature but does not take the instance pointer (no instance exists yet; it's being created):

newobj instance void [mscorlib]System.Object::.**ctor**( )

The newobj instruction is also used for array creation:

newobj instance void int32[0...,0...]::.**ctor**(**int32, int32**)

An array constructor takes as many parameters as there are undefined lower bounds and sizes of the array being created. (Hence, the same number of integer values must be loaded on the stack before newobj is invoked.) In the example just shown, both lower bounds of the two-dimensional array are specified in the array type, so we need to specify only two sizes.

- initobj <token> (0xFE 0x15). Initialize the value type instance. This instruction takes an instance pointer—a managed pointer to a value type instance—from the stack. <token> specifies the value type and must be a valid TypeDef, TypeRef, or TypeSpec token. The initobj instruction zeroes all the fields of the value type instance, so if you need more sophisticated initialization, you might want to define .ctor and call it instead.

- castclass <token> (0x74). Cast a class instance to the class specified by <token>. This instruction takes the object reference to the original instance from the stack and pushes the object reference to the cast instance on the stack. <token> must be a valid TypeDef, TypeRef, or TypeSpec token. If the specified cast is illegal, the instruction throws InvalidCast exception.

- isinst <token> (0x75). Check to see whether the object reference on the stack is an instance of the class specified by <token>. <token> must be a valid TypeDef, TypeRef, or TypeSpec token. This instruction takes the object reference from the stack and pushes the result on the stack. If the check succeeds, the result is an object reference, as if castclass had been invoked; otherwise, the result is a null reference, as if ldnull had been invoked. This instruction does not throw exceptions. The check succeeds under the following conditions:

  - If <token> indicates a class and the object reference on the stack is an instance of this class or of any class derived from it

  - If <token> indicates an interface and the object reference is an instance of the class implementing this interface

  - If <token> indicates a value type and the object reference is a boxed instance of this value type

- box <token> (0x8C). Convert a value type instance to an object reference. <token> specifies the value type being converted and must be a valid TypeDef, TypeRef, or TypeSpec token. This instruction takes the value type instance from the stack, creates a new instance of the type as an object, and pushes the object reference to this instance on the stack. Since a copy of the instance is created, all further changes of the original instance of the value type have no effect on the boxed instance.

- unbox <token> (0x79). Revert a boxed value type instance from the object form to its value type form. <token> specifies the value type being converted and must be a valid TypeDef, TypeRef, or TypeSpec token. This instruction takes an object reference from the stack and pushes back a managed pointer to the value type instance. As you can see, unbox is asymmetric to the box instruction: box takes an instance of value type, and unbox returns a managed pointer to such instance; box creates a copy of the instance, and unbox returns a pointer to the value part of the existing instance.

- unbox.any <token> (0xA5). Introduced in version 2.0 of the CLR, this unboxing instruction is symmetric to the box instruction, because it returns an instance of the value type.

- mkrefany <token> (0xC6). Take a pointer—either managed or unmanaged—from the stack, convert it to a typed reference (typedref), and push the typed reference back on the stack. The typed reference is an opaque handle that carries both type information and an instance pointer. The type of the created typedref is specified by <token>, which must be a valid TypeDef, TypeRef, or TypeSpec token. Typically, this instruction is used to create the typedref values to be passed as arguments to methods that expect typedref parameters. These methods split the typed references into type information and instance pointers using the refanytype and refanyval instructions.

- refanytype <token> (0xFE 0x1D). Take a typed reference from the stack, retrieve the type information, and push the internal type handle on the stack. This instruction has no parameters.

- refanyval <token> (0xC2). Take a typed reference from the stack, retrieve the instance pointer (& or native int), and push it on the stack. This instruction has one parameter <token>, which must be a valid TypeDef, TypeRef, or TypeSpec token and must match the type of the typed reference or be its ancestor. In other words, the type of the typed reference must be castable to the type specified by <token>; otherwise, the instruction throws an exception. Why do we need to specify the type by <token> when the type is already present in the typed reference? Well, the type is indeed present, but we need to specify it explicitly for the sake of the verifier, which performs static analysis of the IL code. Without explicit specification of the type, the result of the refanyval instruction would have "whatever type was encoded in the typed reference," unidentifiable in static analysis. And we don't want refanyval instruction to be absolutely unverifiable, now do we?

- ldtoken <token> (0xD0). Convert <token> to an internal handle to be used in calls to the [mscorlib]System.Reflection methods in the .NET Framework class library. The admissible token types are MethodDef, MemberRef, TypeDef, TypeRef, and FieldDef. The handle pushed on the stack is an instance of one of the following value types: [mscorlib]System.RuntimeMethodHandle, [mscorlib]System.RuntimeTypeHandle, or [mscorlib]System.RuntimeFieldHandle.

The ILAsm notation requires full specification for classes (value types), methods, and fields used in ldtoken. This instruction is the only IL instruction that is not specific to methods only or fields only, and thus the keyword method or field must be used:

```
ldtoken [mscorlib]System.String
ldtoken method instance void [mscorlib]System.Object::.ctor( )
ldtoken field int32 Foo.Bar::ff
```

- sizeof <token> (0xFE 0x1C). Load the size in bytes of the value type specified by <token> on the stack. <token> must be a valid TypeDef, TypeRef, or TypeSpec token. This instruction can be applied to the reference types as well, but the usefulness of such an application is questionable: for reference types, sizeof always returns pointer size (4 or 8, depending on the underlying platform).

- throw (0x7A). Take the object reference from the stack and throw it as a managed exception. See Chapter 14 for details about exception handling.

- rethrow (0xFE 0x1A). Throw the caught exception again. This instruction can be used exclusively within exception handlers. This instruction does not take anything from the stack. The rethrown exception is whatever was last thrown on the corresponding thread.

Vector Instructions

Arrays and vectors are the only true generics implemented in the first release of the common language runtime. Vectors are "elementary" arrays, with one dimension and a zero lower bound. In signatures, vectors are represented by type ELEMENT_TYPE_SZARRAY, whereas "true" arrays are represented by ELEMENT_TYPE_ARRAY. The two different array types have different layouts and are for the most part unrelated to each other. We can, of course, declare a single-dimensional, zero-lower-bound array (whose ILAsm notation is <type>[0...]), which will be a true array, as opposed to a vector (whose ILAsm notation is <type>[ ]).

The IL instruction set defines specific instructions dealing with vectors but not with arrays. To handle array elements and arrays themselves, you need to call the methods of the .NET Framework class [mscorlib]System.Array, from which all arrays are derived. However, don't look in vain among the System.Array's methods to find the most useful ones—Get, Set, and Address. These methods are provided by the runtime, and unlike other runtime-provided methods, they are not reflected in the metadata of Mscorlib.dll. The Get method takes N (where N is the rank of the array) arguments (all int32) representing indexes in respective array dimensions and returns the value of the indexed element. The Address method takes the same arguments and returns the managed pointer to the indexed element. The Set method takes N indexes and the element value to be assigned, assigns the specified value to the indexed element, and returns void.

Now let's get back to the vectors.

Vector Creation

In order to work with a vector, it is necessary to create one. The IL instruction set contains special instructions for vector creation and vector length querying:

- newarr <token> (0x8D). Create a vector. <token> specifies the type of vector elements and must be a valid TypeDef, TypeRef, or TypeSpec token. This instruction pops the number of vector elements (native int or int32) from the stack and pushes an object reference to the created vector on the stack. If the operation fails, an OutOfMemory exception is thrown. If the number of elements happens to be negative, an Overflow exception is thrown. The elements of the newly created vector are zero initialized. For example:

```
.locals init (int32[] arr)
ldc.i4 123
newarr [mscorlib]System.Int32 // newarr int32 would work too
stloc.0
```

For specific details about array creation, see the description of the newobj instruction.

- ldlen (0x8E). Get the element count of a vector. This instruction takes an object reference to the vector instance from the stack and puts the element count (native int) on the stack.

Element Address Loading

You can obtain a managed pointer to a single vector element by using the following instruction:

- ldelema <token> (0x8F). Get the address (a managed pointer) of a vector element. <token> specifies the type of the element and must be a valid TypeDef, TypeRef, or TypeSpec token. This instruction takes the element index (native int) and the vector reference (an object reference) from the stack and pushes the managed pointer to the element on the stack.

- readonly. (0xFE 0x1E). Prefix instruction, introduced in version 2.0 of the CLR, to be used with the ldelema instruction. With this prefix, ldelema yields not a managed pointer to the element but a *controlled mutability* managed pointer, which can be used only as a source pointer but not as a destination pointer. For example, you can use a controlled mutability pointer as an instance pointer when accessing instance fields or methods, as a source pointer in cpobj instruction, or as a pointer in an ldind or ldobj instruction. But it cannot be used in any instruction that would change the instance it points to, such as initobj, stind, stobj, or mkrefany. The main reason for introducing this prefix instruction is to avoid the type check ldelema must execute when the type specified might be a reference class. If the ldelema instruction is preceded by the readonly. prefix, the type check is suppressed, because it is known that the obtained pointer cannot be used for writing purposes (the referent type instance cannot be mutated). Of course, the type might have a method that mutates the instance, and the controlled mutability pointer can be used to call this method and thus mutate the instance. Also, you can use this pointer for the stfld instruction, and if it doesn't mutate the instance, I don't know what does. So, a controlled mutability pointer is not exactly a read-only pointer. However, you can only fiddle with this very instance (pointed at by the controlled mutability pointer); you cannot replace it with another instance, and in this sense the pointer is read-only.

Element Loading

Element loading instructions load a vector element of an elementary type on the stack. All these instructions take the element index (native int) and the vector reference (an object reference) from the stack and put the value of the element on the stack. If the vector reference is null, the instructions throw a NullReference exception. If the index is negative or greater than or equal to the element count of the vector, an IndexOutOfRange exception is thrown.

- ldelem.i1 (0x90). Load a vector element of type int8.

- ldelem.u1 (0x91). Load a vector element of type unsigned int8.

- ldelem.i2 (0x92). Load a vector element of type int16.

- ldelem.u2 (0x93). Load a vector element of type unsigned int16.

- ldelem.i4 (0x94). Load a vector element of type int32.

- ldelem.u4 (0x95). Load a vector element of type unsigned int32.

- ldelem.i8 (ldelem.u8) (0x96). Load a vector element of type int64.

- ldelem.i (0x97). Load a vector element of type native int.

- ldelem.r4 (0x98). Load a vector element of type float32.

- ldelem.r8 (0x99). Load a vector element of type float64.

- ldelem.ref (0x9A). Load a vector element of object reference type.

- ldelem (ldelem.any) <token> (0xA3). Load a vector element of the type specified by <token>, which must be a valid TypeDef, TypeRef, or TypeSpec token. This instruction was introduced in version 2.0 of the CLR to deal with, as you probably guessed, vectors and arrays of a type defined by a generic type variable. The good thing about this instruction (and its sister instruction stelem described next) is that it allows you to load elements of vectors of an arbitrary value type.

Element Storing

Element storing instructions store a value from the stack in a vector element of an elementary type. All these instructions take the value to be stored, the element index (native int), and the vector reference (an object reference) from the stack and put nothing on the stack. Generally, the instructions can throw the same exceptions as the ldelem.* instructions described in the preceding section.

- stelem.i (0x9B). Store a value in a vector element of type native int.

- stelem.i1 (0x9C). Store a value in a vector element of type int8.

- stelem.i2 (0x9D). Store a value in a vector element of type int16.

- stelem.i4 (0x9E). Store a value in a vector element of type int32.

- stelem.i8 (0x9F). Store a value in a vector element of type int64.

- stelem.r4 (0xA0). Store a value in a vector element of type float32.

- stelem.r8 (0xA1). Store a value in a vector element of type float64.

- stelem.ref (0xA2). Store a value in a vector element of the object reference type. This instruction involves the casting of the object on the stack to the type of the vector element, so an InvalidCast exception can be thrown.

- stelem (stelem.any) <token> (0xA4). Store a value in a vector element of the type specified by <token>, which must be a valid TypeDef, TypeRef, or TypeSpec token. This instruction was introduced in version 2.0 of the CLR to support vectors and arrays of the type defined by a generic type variable.

Special stelem.* instructions for unsigned integer types are missing for an obvious reason: the stelem.i* instructions are equally applicable to signed and unsigned integer types.

Code Verifiability

The verification algorithm associates IL instructions with the number of stack slots occupied and available at each moment and with valid evaluation stack states. Stack overflows and underflows render the code not only unverifiable but invalid as well. The verification algorithm also requires that all local variables are zero initialized before the method execution begins. As a result, the .locals directive—at least one, if several of these are used throughout the method—must have the init clause in order for the method to be verifiable.

The verification algorithm simulates all possible control flow paths and branchings, checking to see whether the stack state corresponding to every reachable instruction is legal for this instruction. It is impossible, of course, to predict the actual values stored on the evaluation stack at every moment, but the number of stack slots occupied and the types of the slots can be analyzed.

As mentioned, the evaluation stack type system is coarser than the metadata type system used for field, argument, and local variable types. Hence, the type validity of instructions transferring data between the stack and other typed memory categories depends on the type conversion performed during such transfers. Table 13-5 lists type conversions between different type systems (for example, a value of a local variable of type int8 loaded on the stack becomes int32, and the managed pointer to the same local variable is int8&).

Table 13-5. *Evaluation Stack Type Conversions*

Metadata Type	Stack Type	Managed Pointer to Type
[unsigned] int8, bool	int32	int8&
[unsigned] int16, char	int32	int16&
[unsigned] int32	int32	int32&
[unsigned] int64	int64	int64&
native [unsigned] int, function pointer	native int	native int&
float32	Float	float32&
float64	Float	float64&
Value type	Same type (see substitution rules in this section)	Same type&
Object	Same type (see substitution rules in this section)	Same type&

According to verification rules, if top-of-stack has type A, then the current instruction, expecting to find a type B, is verifiable in the following cases only:

- If A is a class and B is the same class or any class derived from A

- If A an interface and B is a class implementing this interface

- If both A and B are interfaces and the implementation of B requires the implementation of A

- If A is a class or an interface and B is a null reference

- If both A and B are function pointers and the signatures of their respective methods match

- If both A and B are vectors and their element types can be respectively substituted as outlined previously

- If both A and B are arrays of the same rank and their element types can be respectively substituted

- If both A and B are vectors or both are arrays of the same rank and their element types are identically sized integers (for example, int32[] and uint32[])

These substitution rules set the limits of "type leeway" allowed for the IL code to remain verifiable. As the verification algorithm proceeds from one instruction to another along every possible path, it checks the simulated stack types against the types expected by the next instruction. Failure to comply with the substitution rules results in verification failure and possibly indicates invalid IL code.

A few verification rules, rather heuristic than formal, are based on the question "Is it possible in principle to do something unpredictable using this construct?"

- Any code containing embedded native code is unverifiable.

- Any code using unmanaged pointers is unverifiable.

- Any code containing calls to methods that return managed pointers is unverifiable, unless the managed pointers are to instances of reference types or their parts. The reason is that, theoretically, the called method might return a managed pointer to one of its local variables or another "perishable" item. The instances of reference types reside in the GC heap and cannot be considered "perishable."

- An instance constructor of a class must call the instance constructor of the base class. The reason is that until the base class .ctor is called, the instance pointer (this) is considered uninitialized; and until this is initialized, no instance methods should be called.

- When a delegate is being instantiated—its constructor takes a function pointer as the last argument—the newobj instruction must be immediately preceded by the ldftn or ldvirtftn instruction, which loads the function pointer. If anything appears between these two instructions, the code becomes unverifiable.

A great many additional rules regulate exception handling, but the place to discuss them is the next chapter.

CHAPTER 14

■ ■ ■

Managed Exception Handling

Usually the exception handling model of a programming language is considered the domain of that particular language's runtime. Under the hood, each language has its own way of detecting exceptions and locating an appropriate exception handler. Some languages perform exception handling completely within the language runtime, whereas others rely on the structured exception handling (SEH) mechanism provided by the operating system—which in our case is Win32 or Win64.

In the world of managed code, exception handling is a fundamental feature of the common language runtime execution engine. The execution engine is fully capable of handling exceptions without regard to language, allowing exceptions to be raised in one language and caught in another. At that, the runtime does not dictate any particular syntax for handling exceptions. The exception mechanism is language neutral in that it is equally efficient for all languages.

No special metadata is captured for exceptions other than the metadata for the exception classes themselves. No association exists between a method of a class and the exceptions that the method might throw. Any method is permitted to throw any exception at any time.

Although we talk about managed exceptions thrown and caught within managed code, a common scenario involves a mix of both managed and unmanaged code. Execution threads routinely traverse managed and unmanaged blocks of code through the use of the common language runtime's platform invocation mechanism (P/Invoke) and other interoperability mechanisms. (See Chapter 18.) Consequently, during execution, exceptions can be thrown or caught in either managed code or unmanaged code.

The runtime exception handling mechanism integrates seamlessly with the Win32/Win64 SEH mechanism so that exceptions can be thrown and caught within and between the two exception handling systems.

EH Clause Internal Representation

Managed exception handling tables are located immediately after a method's IL code, with the beginning of the table aligned on a double word boundary. It would be more accurate to say that "additional sections" are located after the method IL code, but the existing releases of the common language runtime allow only one kind of additional section—the exception handling section.

This additional section begins with the section header, which comes in two varieties (small and fat) and contains two entries, Kind and DataSize. In a *small* header, DataSize is represented by 1 byte, whereas in a *fat* header, DataSize is 3 bytes long. A Kind entry can contain the following binary flags:

- Reserved (0x00). This should not be used.

- EHTable (0x01). The section contains an exception handling table. This bit must be set.

- OptILTable (0x02). Not used in the current releases of the runtime. This bit must not be set.

- FatFormat (0x40). The section header has a fat format—that is, DataSize is represented by 3 bytes.

- MoreSects (0x80). More sections follow this one.

The section header—padded with 2 bytes if small, which makes one wonder what the reason was to introduce the small header at all—is followed by a sequence of EH clauses, which can also have a small or fat format. Each EH clause describes a single triad made up of a guarded block, an exception identification, and an exception handler. The entries of small and fat EH clauses have the same names and meanings but different sizes, as shown in Table 14-1.

Table 14-1. *EH Clause Entries*

EH Clause Entry	Size in Small Clause (Bytes)	Size in Fat Clause (Bytes)	Description
Flags	2	4	Binary flags specifying the type of the EH clause, which is the type of the exception identification method.
TryOffset	2	4	Offset, in bytes, of the beginning of the guarded code block from the beginning of the method IL code. The guarded block can begin only at code points where the evaluation stack is empty.
TryLength	1	4	Length, in bytes, of the guarded block.
HandlerOffset	2	4	Offset of the exception handler block.
HandlerLength	1	4	Length of the exception handler block.
ClassToken/ FilterOffset	4	4	Exception type token or offset of the exception filtering block, depending on the type of the EH clause.

Branching into or out of guarded blocks and handler blocks is illegal. A guarded block must be entered "through the top"—that is, through the instruction located at TryOffset—and handler blocks are entered only when they are engaged by the exception handling subsystem of the execution engine. To exit guarded and handler blocks, you must use the instruction leave (or leave.s). You might recall that in Chapter 2, this principle was formulated as "leave only by leave." Another way to leave any block is to throw an exception using the throw or rethrow instruction.

Types of EH Clauses

Exception handling clauses are classified by the algorithm of the handler engagement. Four mutually exclusive EH clause types are available, and because of that, the Flags entry must hold one of the following values:

0x0000: The handler must be engaged if the type of the exception object matches the type identified by the token specified in the ClassToken entry or any of this type's descendants. Theoretically, any object can be thrown as an exception, but it's strongly recommended that all exception types be derived from the [mscorlib]System.Exception class. This is because throughout Microsoft .NET Framework classes the construct catch [mscorlib]System.Exception is used in the sense of "catch any exception"—it is an analog of catch(...) in C++. In other words, [mscorlib]System.Exception is presumed to be the ultimate base class for all exceptions. This type of EH clause is called a catch type.

0x0001: A dedicated block of the IL code, called a *filter*, will process the exception and define whether the handler should be engaged. The offset of the filter block is specified in the FilterOffset entry. Since we cannot specify the filter block length—the EH clause structure contains no entry for it—a positioning limitation is associated with the filter block: the respective handler block must immediately follow the filter block, allowing the length of the filter block to be inferred from the offset of the handler. The filter block must end with the endfilter instruction, described in Chapter 13. At the moment endfilter is executed, the evaluation stack must hold a single int32 value, equal to 1 if the handler is to be engaged and equal to 0 otherwise. This EH clause type is called a filter type. Branching into or out of the filter block is illegal. Falling through into the filter block is also illegal.

0x0002: The handler will be engaged whether or not an exception has occurred. The EH clause entry ClassToken/FilterOffset is ignored. This EH clause type is called a finally type. The finally handlers are not meant to process an exception but rather to perform any cleanup that might be needed when leaving the guarded block. The finally handlers must end with the endfinally instruction. If no exception has occurred within the guarded block, the finally handler is executed at the moment of leaving that block. If an exception has been thrown within the guarded block, the finally handler is executed after any preceding handler (of a nested guarded block) is executed or, if no preceding handler was engaged, before any following handler is executed. If no catch or filter handlers are engaged—that is, the exception is uncaught—the finally handler is engaged when the CLR registers the uncaught exception, right before the application execution is aborted.

Figure 14-1 illustrates this process. If an exception of type A is thrown within the innermost guarded block, it is caught and processed by the first handler (catch A), and the finally handler is engaged after the first handler executes the leave instruction. If an exception of type B is thrown, it is caught by the third handler (catch B); this fact is registered by the runtime, and the finally handler is executed before the third handler. If no exception is thrown within the guarded block, the finally handler is engaged when the guarded block executes the leave instruction.

0x0004: The handler will be engaged if any exception occurs. This type of EH clause is called a fault type. A fault handler is similar to a finally handler in all aspects except one: the fault handler is not engaged if no exception has been thrown within the guarded block and everything is nice and quiet. The fault handler must also end with the endfinally instruction, which for this specific purpose has been given the synonym endfault.

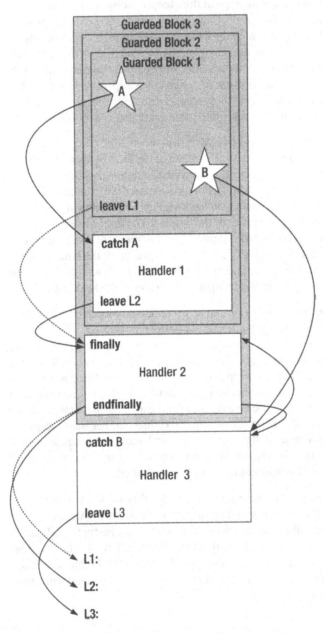

Figure 14-1. *Engagement of the finally exception handler*

Label Form of EH Clause Declaration

The most generic form of ILAsm notation of an EH clause is as follows:

.try <label> **to** <label> <EH_type_specific> **handler** <label> **to** <label>

where <EH_type_specific> ::=

catch <class_ref> |
filter *<label>* |
finally |
fault

Take a look at this example:

```
BeginTry:
    ...
    leave KeepGoing
BeginHandler:
    ...
    leave KeepGoing
KeepGoing:
    ...
    ret
    .try BeginTry to BeginHandler catch [mscorlib]System.Exception
        handler BeginHandler to KeepGoing
```

In the final lines of the example, the code .try <label> to <label> defines the guarded block, and handler <label> to <label> defines the handler block. In both cases, the second <label> is exclusive, pointing at the first instruction after the respective block. ILAsm imposes a limitation on the positioning of the EH clause declaration directives: all labels used in the directives must have already been defined. Thus, the best place for EH clause declarations in the label form is at the end of the method scope.

In the case just presented, the handler block immediately follows the guarded block, but we could put the handler block anywhere within the method, provided it does not overlap with the guarded block or other handlers:

```
    ...
    br AfterHandler //  Can't enter the handler block on our own
BeginHandler:
    ...
    leave KeepGoing
AfterHandler:
    ...
BeginTry:
    ...
    leave KeepGoing
KeepGoing:
    ...
    ret
    .try BeginTry to KeepGoing catch [mscorlib]System.Exception
        handler BeginHandler to AfterHandler
```

A single guarded block can have several catch or filter handlers:

```
    ...
    br AfterHandler2 //  Can't enter the handler block(s) on our own
BeginHandler1:
    ...
    leave KeepGoing
AfterHandler1:
    ...
BeginHandler2:
    ...
    leave KeepGoing
AfterHandler2:
    ...
BeginTry:
    ...
    leave KeepGoing
KeepGoing:
    ...
    ret
    .try BeginTry to KeepGoing
        catch [mscorlib]System.StackOverflowException
            handler BeginHandler1 to AfterHandler1
    .try BeginTry to KeepGoing catch [mscorlib]System.Exception
        handler BeginHandler2 to AfterHandler2
```

In the case of multiple handlers—catch or filter but not finally or fault, as explained next—the guarded block declaration need not be repeated:

```
.try BeginTry to KeepGoing
    catch [mscorlib]System.StackOverflowException
        handler BeginHandler1 to AfterHandler1
    catch [mscorlib]System.Exception
        handler BeginHandler2 to AfterHandler2
```

The lexical order of handlers belonging to the same guarded block is the order in which the IL assembler emits the EH clauses and is the same order in which the execution engine of the runtime processes these clauses. You must be careful about ordering the handlers. For instance, if you swap the handlers in the preceding example, the handler for [mscorlib]System.Exception will always be executed, and the handler for [mscorlib]System.StackOverflowException will never be executed. This is because all standard exceptions are (and user-defined should be) derived, eventually, from [mscorlib]System.Exception, and hence all exceptions are caught by the first handler, leaving the other handlers unemployed.

The finally and fault handlers cannot peacefully coexist with other handlers, so if a guarded block has a finally or fault handler, it cannot have anything else. To combine a finally or fault handler with other handlers, you need to nest the guarded and handler blocks within other guarded blocks, as shown in Figure 14-1, so that each finally or fault handler has its own personal guarded block.

Scope Form of EH Clause Declaration

The label form of the EH clause declaration is universal, ubiquitous, and close to the actual representation of the EH clauses in the EH table. The only quality the label form lacks is convenience. In view of that, ILAsm offers an alternative form of EH clause description: a scope form. You've already encountered the scope form in Chapter 2, which discussed protecting the code against possible surprises in the unmanaged code being invoked. Just to remind you, here's what the protected part of the method (from the sample file Simple2.il on the Apress Web site) looks like:

```
...
.try {
    // Guarded block begins
    call string [mscorlib]System.Console::ReadLine()
    // pop
    // ldnull
    ldstr "%d"
    ldsflda int32 Odd.or.Even::val
    call vararg int32 sscanf(string,string,...,int32*)
    stloc.0
    leave.s DidntBlowUp
    // Guarded block ends
}
catch [mscorlib]System.Exception
{ // Exception handler begins
    pop
    ldstr "KABOOM!"
    call void [mscorlib]System.Console::WriteLine(string)
    leave.s Return
} // Exception handler ends
DidntBlowUp:
...
```

The scope form can be used only for a limited subset of all possible EH clause configurations: the handler blocks must immediately follow the previous handler block or the guarded block. If the EH clause configuration is different, we must resort to the label form or a mixed form in which the guarded block is scoped but the catch handler is specified by IL offsets, or vice versa:

```
...
br AfterHandler
HandlerBegins:
    // The exception handler code
    ...
    leave KeepGoing
AfterHandler:
    ...
.try {
    // Guarded code
```

```
    ...
    leave KeepGoing
}
catch [mscorlib]System.Exception
    handler HandlerBegins to AfterHandler
    ...
KeepGoing:
    ...
```

The IL disassembler by default outputs the EH clauses in the scope form—at least those clauses that can be represented in this form. However, we have the option to suppress the scope form and output all EH clauses in their label form (command-line option /RAW). But let's suppose for the sake of convenience that we can shape the code in such a way that the contiguity condition is satisfied, allowing us to use the scope form. A single guarded block with multiple handlers in scope form will look like this:

```
.try {
    // Guarded code
    ...
    leave KeepGoing
}
catch [mscorlib]System.StackOverflowException {
    // The exception handler #1 code
    ...
    leave KeepGoing
}
catch [mscorlib]System.Exception {
    // The exception handler #2 code
    ...
    leave KeepGoing
}
    ...
KeepGoing:
    ...
```

Much more readable, isn't it? The nested EH configuration shown earlier in Figure 14-1 is easily understandable when written in scope form:

```
.try {
    .try {
        .try {
            // Guarded code
            ...
            leave L1
        }
        catch A {
            // This code works when exception A is thrown
            ...
            leave L2
```

```
      }
   } // No need for leave here!
   finally {
      // This code works in any case
      ...
      endfinally
   }
} // No need for leave here either!
catch B {
   //  This code works when exception B is thrown in guarded  code
   ...
   leave L3
}
```

The filter EH clauses in scope form are subject to the same limitation: the handler block must immediately follow the guarded block. But in a filter clause the handler block includes first the filter block and then, immediately following it, the actual handler, so the scope form of a filter clause looks like this:

```
.try {
   // Guarded code
   ...
   leave KeepGoing
}
filter {
   //  Here we decide whether we should invoke the actual handler
   ...
   ldc.i4.1 // OK, let's invoke the handler
   endfilter
} {
   // Actual handler code
   ...
   leave KeepGoing
}
```

And, of course, we can easily switch between scope form and label form within a single EH clause declaration. The general ILAsm syntax for an EH clause declaration is as follows:

```
<EH_clause> ::= .try <guarded_block>
                    <EH_type_specific> <handler_block>
Where
<guarded_block> ::= <label> to <label> | <scope>
<EH_type_specific> ::= catch <class_ref> |
        filter <label> | filter <scope> |
        finally |
        fault
<handler_block> ::= handler <label> to <label> | <scope >
```

The nonterminals <label> and <class_ref> must be familiar by now, and the meaning of <scope> is obvious: "code enclosed in curly braces."

Processing the Exceptions

The execution engine of the CLR processes an exception in two passes. The first pass determines which, if any, of the managed handlers will process the exception. Starting at the top of the EH table for the current method frame, the execution engine compares the address where the exception occurred to the TryOffset and TryLength entries of each EH clause. If it finds that the exception happened in a guarded block, the execution engine checks to see whether the handler specified in this clause will process the exception. (The "rules of engagement" for catch and filter handlers were discussed in previous sections.) If this particular handler can't be engaged—for example, the wrong type of exception has been thrown—the execution engine continues traversing the EH table in search of other clauses that have guarded blocks covering the exception locus. The finally and fault handlers are ignored during the first pass.

If none of the clauses in the EH table for the current method is suited to handling the exception, the execution engine steps up the call stack and starts checking the exception against EH tables of the method that called the method where the exception occurred. In these checks, the call site address serves as the exception locus. This process continues from method frame to method frame up the call stack, until the execution engine finds a handler to be engaged or until it exhausts the call stack. The latter case is the end of the story: the execution engine cannot continue with an unhandled exception on its conscience, and the runtime executes all finally and fault handlers and then either aborts the application execution or offers the user a choice between aborting the execution and invoking the debugger, depending on the runtime configuration.

If a suitable handler is found, the execution engine swings into the second pass. The execution engine again walks the EH tables it worked with during the first pass and invokes all relevant finally and fault handlers. Each of these handlers ends with the endfinally instruction (or endfault, its synonym), signaling the execution engine that the handler has finished and that it can proceed with browsing the EH tables. Once the execution engine reaches the catch or filter handler it found on its first pass, it engages the actual handler.

What happens to the method's evaluation stack? When a guarded block is exited in any way, the evaluation stack is discarded. If the guarded block is exited peacefully, without raising an exception, the leave instruction discards the stack; otherwise, the evaluation stack is discarded the moment the exception is thrown.

During the first pass, the execution engine puts the exception object on the evaluation stack every time it invokes a filter block. The filter block pops the exception object from the stack and analyzes it, deciding whether this is a job for its actual handler block. The decision, in the form of int32 having the value 1 or 0 (engage the handler or don't, respectively), is the only thing that must be on the evaluation stack when the endfilter instruction is reached; otherwise, the IL verification will fail. The endfilter instruction takes this value from the stack and passes it to the execution engine.

During the second pass, the finally and fault handlers are invoked with an empty evaluation stack. These handlers do nothing about the exception itself and work only with method arguments and local variables, so the execution engine doesn't bother providing the exception object. If anything is left on the evaluation stack by the time the endfinally (or endfault) instruction is reached, it is discarded by endfinally (or endfault).

When the actual handler is invoked, the execution engine puts the exception object on the evaluation stack. The handler pops this object from the stack and handles it to the best of its abilities. When the handler is exited by using the leave instruction, the evaluation stack is discarded.

Table 14-2 summarizes the stack evolutions.

Table 14-2. *Changes in the Evaluation Stack*

When the Block	Is Entered, the Stack...	Is Exited, the Stack...
try	Must be empty	Is discarded
filter	Holds the exception object	Must hold a single int32 value, equal to 1 or 0, consumed by endfilter
handler	Holds the exception object	Is discarded
finally, fault	Is empty	Is discarded

Two IL instructions are used for raising an exception explicitly: throw and rethrow. The throw instruction takes the exception object (ObjectRef) from the stack and raises the exception. This instruction can be used anywhere, within or outside any EH block.

The rethrow instruction can be used within catch handlers only (*not* within the filter block), and it does not work with the evaluation stack. This instruction signals the execution engine that the handler that was supposed to take care of the caught exception has for some reason changed its mind and that the exception should therefore be offered to the higher-level EH clauses. The only blocks where the words "caught exception" mean something are the catch handler block and the filter block, but invoking rethrow within a filter block, though theoretically possible, is illegal. It is legal to throw the caught exception from the filter block, but it doesn't make much sense to do so: the effect is the same as if the filter simply refused to handle the exception, by loading 0 on the stack and invoking endfilter.

Rethrowing an exception is not the same as throwing the caught exception, which we have on the evaluation stack upon entering a catch handler. The rethrow instruction preserves the call stack trace of the original exception so that the exception can be tracked down to its point of origin. The throw instruction starts the call stack trace anew, giving us no way to determine where the original exception came from.

Exception Types

Chapter 13 mentioned some of the exception types that can be thrown during the execution of IL instructions. Earlier chapters mentioned some of the exceptions thrown by the loader and the JIT compiler. Now it's time to review all these exceptions in an orderly manner.

All managed exceptions defined in the .NET Framework classes are descendants of the [mscorlib]System.Exception class. This base exception type, however, is never thrown by the common language runtime. In the following sections, I've listed the exceptions the runtime *does* throw, classifying them by major runtime subsystems. Enjoying the monotonous repetition no more than you do, I've omitted the [mscorlib]System. part of the names, common to all exception types. As you can see, many of the exception type names are self-explanatory.

Loader Exceptions

The loader represents the first line of defense against erroneous applications, and the exceptions it throws are related to the file presence and integrity:

- AppDomainUnloadedException.

- CannotUnloadAppDomainException.

- BadImageFormatException. Corrupt file headers or segments that belong in read-only sections (such as the runtime header, metadata, and IL code) are located in writable sections of the PE file.

- ArgumentException. This exception is also thrown by the JIT compiler and the interoperability services.

- Security.Cryptography.CryptographicException.

- FileLoadException.

- MissingFieldException.

- MissingMethodException.

- TypeLoadException. This exception, which is most frequently thrown by the loader, indicates that the type metadata is illegal.

- UnauthorizedAccessException. A user application is attempting to directly manipulate the system assembly Mscorlib.dll.

- OutOfMemoryException. This exception, which is also thrown by the execution engine, indicates memory allocation failure.

JIT Compiler Exceptions

The JIT compiler throws only two exceptions. The second one can be thrown only when the code is not fully trusted (for example, comes from the Internet):

- InvalidProgramException. This exception, which is also thrown by the execution engine, indicates an error in IL code.

- VerificationException. This exception, which is also thrown by the execution engine, indicates that IL code verification has failed.

Execution Engine Exceptions

The execution engine throws a wide variety of exceptions, most of them related to the operations on the evaluation stack. A few exceptions are thrown by the thread control subsystem of the engine.

- ArithmeticException. Base class for DivideByZeroException, OverflowException, and NotFiniteNumberException.

- ArgumentOutOfRangeException.

- ArrayTypeMismatchException. This exception is also thrown by the interoperability services.

- DivideByZeroException.

- DuplicateWaitObjectException.

- ExecutionEngineException. This is the generic exception, indicating that some sequence of IL instructions has brought the execution engine into a state of complete perplexity—as a rule, by corrupting the memory. Verifiable code cannot corrupt the memory and hence does not raise exceptions of this type.

- FieldAccessException. This exception indicates, for example, an attempt to load from or store to a private field of another class.

- FormatException.

- IndexOutOfRangeException.

- InvalidCastException.

- InvalidOperationException.

- MethodAccessException. This exception indicates an attempt to call a method to which the caller does not have access—for example, a private method of another class.

- NotSupportedException.

- NullReferenceException. This exception indicates an attempt to dereference a null pointer (a managed or unmanaged pointer or an object reference).

- OverflowException. This exception is thrown when a checked conversion fails because the target data type is too small.

- RankException. This exception is thrown when a method specific to an array is being called on a vector instance.

- RemotingException.

- Security.SecurityException.

- StackOverflowException.

- Threading.SynchronizationLockException. This exception is thrown when an application tries to manipulate or release a lock it has not acquired—for example, by calling the Wait, Pulse, or Exit method before calling the Enter method of the [mscorlib]System.Threading.Monitor class.

- Threading.ThreadAbortException.

- Threading.ThreadInterruptedException.

- Threading.ThreadStateException.

- Threading.ThreadStopException.

- TypeInitializationException. This exception is thrown when a type—a class or a value type—failed to initialize.

Interoperability Exceptions

The following exceptions are thrown by the interoperability services of the common language runtime, which are responsible for managed and unmanaged code interoperation:

- DllNotFoundException. This exception is thrown when an unmanaged DLL specified as a location of the unmanaged method being called cannot be found.

- ApplicationException.

- EntryPointNotFoundException.

- InvalidComObjectException.

- Runtime.InteropServices.InvalidOleVariantTypeException.

- MarshalDirectiveException. This exception is thrown when data cannot be marshaled between managed and unmanaged code in the specified way.

- Runtime.InteropServices.SafeArrayRankMismatchException.

- Runtime.InteropServices.SafeArrayTypeMismatchException.

- Runtime.InteropServices.COMException.

- Runtime.InteropServices.SEHException. This is the generic managed exception type for unmanaged exceptions.

Subclassing the Exceptions

In addition to the plethora of exception types already defined in the .NET Framework classes, you can always devise your own types tailored to your needs. The best way to do this is to derive your exception types from the "standard" types listed in the preceding sections.

The following exception types are sealed and can't be subclassed. Again, I've omitted the [mscorlib]System. portion of the names.

- InvalidProgramException

- TypeInitializationException

- Threading.ThreadAbortException

- StackOverflowException

■**Caution** As mentioned earlier, I must warn you against devising your own exception types not derived from [mscorlib]System.Exception or some other exception type of the .NET Framework classes.

Unmanaged Exception Mapping

When an unmanaged exception occurs within a native code segment, the execution engine maps it to a managed exception that is thrown in its stead. The different types of unmanaged exceptions, identified by their status code, are mapped to the managed exceptions as described in Table 14-3.

Table 14-3. *Mapping Between the Managed and Unmanaged Exceptions*

Unmanaged Exception Status Code	Mapped to Managed Exception
STATUS_FLOAT_INEXACT_RESULT	ArithmeticException
STATUS_FLOAT_INVALID_OPERATION	ArithmeticException
STATUS_FLOAT_STACK_CHECK	ArithmeticException
STATUS_FLOAT_UNDERFLOW	ArithmeticException
STATUS_FLOAT_OVERFLOW	OverflowException
STATUS_INTEGER_OVERFLOW	OverflowException
STATUS_FLOAT_DIVIDE_BY_ZERO	DivideByZeroException
STATUS_INTEGER_DIVIDE_BY_ZERO	DivideByZeroException
STATUS_FLOAT_DENORMAL_OPERAND	FormatException
STATUS_ACCESS_VIOLATION	NullReferenceException
STATUS_ARRAY_BOUNDS_EXCEEDED	IndexOutOfRangeException
STATUS_NO_MEMORY	OutOfMemoryException
STATUS_STACK_OVERFLOW	StackOverflowException
All other status codes	Runtime.InteropServices.SEHException

Summary of EH Clause Structuring Rules

The rules for structuring EH clauses within a method are neither numerous nor overly complex.

All the blocks—try, filter, handler, finally, and fault—of each EH clause must be fully contained within the method code. No block can protrude from the method.

The guarded blocks and the handler blocks belonging to the same EH clause or different EH clauses can't partially overlap. A block either is fully contained within another block or is completely outside it. If one guarded block (A) is contained within another guarded block (B) but is not equal to it, all handlers assigned to A must also be fully contained within B.

A handler block of an EH clause can't be contained within a guarded block of the same clause, and vice versa. And a handler block can't be contained in another handler block that is assigned to the same guarded block.

A filter block can't contain any guarded blocks or handler blocks.

All blocks must start and end on instruction boundaries—that is, at offsets corresponding to the first byte of an instruction. Prefixed instructions must not be split, meaning that you can't have constructs such as tail. .try { call ... }.

A guarded block must start at a code point where the evaluation stack is empty.

The same handler block can't be associated with different guarded blocks:

```
.try Label1 to Label2 catch A handler Label3 to Label4
.try Label4 to Label5 catch B handler Label3 to Label4  // Illegal!
```

If the EH clause is a filter type, the filter's actual handler must immediately follow the filter block. Since the filter block must end with the endfilter instruction, this rule can be formulated as "the actual handler starts with the instruction after endfilter."

If a guarded block has a finally or fault handler, the same block can have no other handler. If you need other handlers, you must declare another guarded block, encompassing the original guarded block and the handler:

```
.try {
   .try {
      .try {
         // Code that needs finally, catch, and fault handlers
         ...
         leave KeepGoing
      }
      finally {
         ...
         endfinally
      }
   }
   catch [mscorlib]System.StackOverflowException
   {
      ...
      leave KeepGoing
   }
}
fault {
   ...
   endfault
}
```

PART 5

■ ■ ■

Special Components

CHAPTER 15

■ ■ ■

Events and Properties

Events and properties are special metadata components that are intended to make life easier for the high-level language compilers. The most intriguing feature of events and properties is that the JIT compiler and the execution engine are completely unaware of them. Can you recall any IL instruction that deals with an event or a property? That's because none exist.

To understand the indifference of the JIT compiler and the execution engine toward events and properties, you need to understand the way these items are implemented.

Events and Delegates

The managed events I'm talking about here are not synchronization elements, similar to Win32/Win64 event objects. Rather, they more closely resemble Visual Basic events and On<event> functions. Managed events provide a means to describe the asynchronous execution of methods, initiated by certain other methods.

Figure 15-1 illustrates the general sequence of activities. A program unit—known as the *publisher*, or *source*, of an event—defines the event. We can think of this program unit as a class, for the sake of simplicity. Other program units (classes)—known as *subscribers*, *event listeners*, or *event sinks*—define the methods to be executed when the event occurs and pass this information to the event publisher. When the event publisher *raises*, or *fires*, the event by calling a special method, all the subscriber's methods associated with this event are executed.

In a nutshell, to implement a managed event, we need an entity that can collect the callback methods (event handlers) from the event subscribers and execute these methods when the publisher executes a method that signifies the event.

We have a type (a class) designed to do exactly that: the delegate type, which is discussed in Chapter 7. As you might remember, delegates are classes derived from the class [mscorlib] System.MulticastDelegate and play the role of "politically correct" type-safe function pointers in the managed world. The actual function pointer to a delegated method is passed to the delegate as an argument of its constructor, and the delegated method can subsequently be executed by calling the delegate's Invoke method.

What Chapter 7 doesn't mention is that several delegates can be aggregated into one delegate. Calling the Invoke method of such an aggregated delegate invokes all the delegated methods that make up the aggregate—which is exactly what we need to implement an event.

The [mscorlib]System.MulticastDelegate class defines the virtual methods CombineImpl and RemoveImpl, adding a delegate (more exactly, the callback function pointer it carries) to the aggregate (more exactly, to the list of callback function pointers the aggregate carries) and removing a delegate from the aggregate, respectively. These methods are defined in Mscorlib.dll as follows. (I have omitted the resolution scope [mscorlib] of delegate types here because the methods are defined in the same assembly; this doesn't mean you can omit the resolution scope when you refer to these types in your assemblies.)

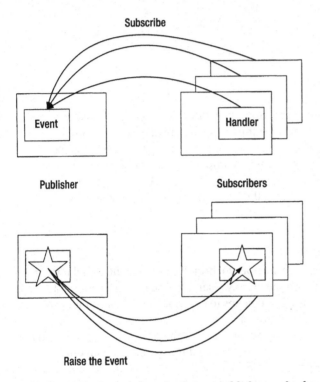

Figure 15-1. *The interaction of an event publisher and subscribers*

```
.method family hidebysig final virtual
    instance class System.Delegate
    CombineImpl(class System.Delegate follow)  cil managed
{ ... }
.method family hidebysig final virtual
    instance class System.Delegate
    RemoveImpl(class System.Delegate 'value')  cil managed
{ ... }
```

The methods take the object reference to the delegate being added (or removed) as the argument and return the object reference to the aggregated delegate. The parameter and return type of both methods is System.Delegate rather than System.MulticastDelegate, but this isn't contradictory: System.MulticastDelegate is derived from System.Delegate and hence can be used in its stead.

The principle of the delegate-based implementation of an event is more or less clear. Each event subscriber creates a delegate representing its event handler and then subscribes to the event by combining the handler delegate with the aggregate delegate, held by the event publisher. To raise the event, the publisher simply needs to call the Invoke method of the aggregate delegate, and everybody is happy.

One question remains, though: what does the publisher's aggregate delegate look like before any event subscriber has subscribed to the event? The answer is, it doesn't exist at all. The aggregate delegate is a result of combining the subscribers' handler delegates. As long as there are no subscribers, the publisher's aggregate delegate does not exist. This poses a certain problem: CombineImpl is an instance method, which has to be called on the instance of the aggregated delegate, and hence each subscriber must worry about whether it is the first in line (in other words, whether the aggregated delegate exists yet). That's why the subscribers usually use the static methods Combine and Remove, inherited by System.MulticastDelegate from System.Delegate:

```
.method public hidebysig static class System.Delegate
    Combine(class System.Delegate a,
        class System.Delegate b)
{ ... }
.method public hidebysig static class System.Delegate
    Remove(class System.Delegate source,
        class System.Delegate 'value')
{ ... }
```

If one of the arguments of these methods is a null reference, the methods simply return the non-null argument. If both arguments are null references, the methods return a null reference. If the arguments are incompatible—that is, if the delegated methods have different signatures—Combine, which internally calls CombineImpl, throws an Argument exception, and Remove, which internally calls RemoveImpl, simply returns the aggregated delegate unchanged.

In general, delegates are fascinating types with more features than this book can discuss. The best way to learn more about delegates first-hand is to disassemble Mscorlib.dll and have a look at how System.Delegate and System.MulticastDelegate are implemented and used. The same advice is applicable to other Microsoft .NET Framework classes you happen to be interested in: when in doubt, disassemble the respective DLL, and see for yourself.

Events, of course, can be implemented without delegates. But given the functionality needed to implement events, I don't see why anyone would waste time on an alternative implementation when the delegates offer a complete and elegant solution.

MANAGED SYNCHRONIZATION ELEMENTS

You're probably wondering whether managed code has any elements equivalent to the synchronization events and APIs of the unmanaged world. It does, although this aspect is unrelated to the events discussed in this chapter. The synchronization elements of the managed world are implemented as classes of the .NET Framework class library. You can learn a lot about them by disassembling Mscorlib.dll and looking at the namespace System.Threading—and especially at the WaitHandle class of this namespace. (You've already encountered the System.Threading.WaitHandle class in the discussion of asynchronous invocation of delegates in Chapter 7.) The WaitHandle class is central to the entire class system of the System.Threading namespace and implements such methods as WaitOne, WaitAll, and WaitAny. Sounds familiar, doesn't it? The AutoResetEvent, ManualResetEvent, and Mutex classes, derived from the WaitHandle class, are also worth a glance.

Event Metadata

To define an event, we need to know the event type, which, as a rule, is derived from [mscorlib]System.MulticastDelegate; the methods associated with the event (methods to subscribe to the event, to unsubscribe, to fire the event, and perhaps to carry out other tasks we might define); and, of course, the class defining the event. The events are never referenced in IL instructions, so we needn't worry about the syntax for referencing the events.

The event metadata group includes the Event, EventMap, TypeDef, TypeRef, Method, and MethodSemantics tables. Figure 15-2 shows the mutual references between the tables of this group.

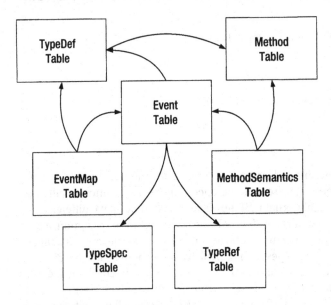

Figure 15-2. *The event metadata group*

The Event Table

The Event table has the associated token type mdtEvent (0x14000000). An Event record has three entries:

- EventFlags (2-byte unsigned integer). Binary flags of the event characteristics.

- Name (offset in the #Strings stream). The name of the event, which must be a simple name no longer than 1,023 bytes in UTF-8 encoding.

- EventType (coded token of type TypeDefOrRef). The type associated with the event. The coded token indexes a TypeDef, TypeRef, or TypeSpec record. The class indexed by this token is either a delegate or a class providing the necessary functionality similar to that of a delegate.

Only two flag values are defined for events, and only one of them can be set explicitly:

- specialname (0x0200). The event is special in some way, as specified by the name.

- rtspecialname (0x0400). The event has a special name reserved for the internal use of the common language runtime. This flag can't be set explicitly. The IL disassembler outputs this flag for information purposes, but the IL assembler ignores the keyword.

To my knowledge, the primary use of these event flags is to mark deleted events in edit-and-continue scenarios. When an event record is marked as deleted, both flags are set, and its name is changed to _Deleted. Some compilers, however, might find certain uses for the specialname flag. After all, an event as a metadata item exists solely for the benefit of the compilers.

The EventMap Table

The EventMap table provides mapping between the classes defining the events (the TypeDef table) and the events themselves (the Event table). An EventMap record has two entries:

- Parent (record index [RID] in the TypeDef table). The type declaring the events.

- EventList (RID in the Event table). The beginning of the events declared by the type indexed by the Parent entry. The mechanism of addressing the events in this case is identical to the mechanism used by TypeDef records to address the Method and Field records belonging to a certain TypeDef. In the optimized metadata model (the #~ stream), the records in the Event table are ordered by the declaring type. In the unoptimized model (the #- stream), the event records are not so ordered, and an intermediate lookup metadata table, EventPtr, is used. (Chapter 5 describes the metadata models and intermediate tables.)

The MethodSemantics Table

The MethodSemantics metadata table connects events and properties with their associated methods and provides information regarding the type of this association. A record in this table has three entries:

- Semantic (2-byte unsigned integer). The kind of method association.

- Method (RID in the Method table). The index of the associated method.

- Association (coded token of type HasSemantics). A token indexing an event or a property the method is associated with.

The Semantic entry can have the following values, which look like binary flags but in fact are mutually exclusive:

- msSetter (0x0001). The method sets a value of a property.

- msGetter (0x0002). The method retrieves a value of a property.

- msOther (0x0004). The method has another meaning for a property or an event

- msAddOn (0x0008). The method subscribes to an event.

- msRemoveOn (0x0010). The method removes the subscription to an event.

- msFire (0x0020). The method fires an event.

The same method can be associated in different capacities with different events or properties. An event must have one subscribing method and one unsubscribing method. These methods return void and have one parameter of the same type as the event's associated type (the EventType entry of the respective Event record). The Visual C# and Visual Basic compilers use uniform naming for subscribing and unsubscribing methods: add_<event_name> and remove_<event_name>, respectively. In addition, these compilers mark these methods with the specialname flag.

An event can have at most one firing method. The firing method usually boils down to an invocation of the delegate implementing the event. The Visual C# and Visual Basic compilers, for example, never bother to define a firing method for an event—that is, the method invoking the delegate is there, but it is never associated with the event as a firing method. Such an approach contains certain logic: the firing method is a purely internal affair of the event publisher and need not be exposed to the event subscribers. And since the compilers, as a rule, use the event metadata to facilitate subscription and unsubscription, associating a firing method with an event is not necessary. If an event does have an associated firing method, however, this method must return void.

Event Declaration

In ILAsm, the syntax for an event declaration is as follows:

```
.event <class_ref> <name> { <method_semantics_decl>* }
```

where <class_ref> represents the type associated with the event, <name> is a simple name, and

```
<method_semantics_decl> ::= <semantics> <method_ref>
<semantics> ::= .addon | .removeon | .fire | .other
```

The following is an example of an event declaration:

```
// The delegate implementing the event
.class public sealed MyEventImpl
    extends [mscorlib]System.MulticastDelegate
{
    .method public specialname
        void   .ctor(object obj,
                native int 'method') runtime { }
      .method public virtual void
        Invoke(int32 EventCode, string Msg) runtime
        { }
}
// The event publisher
.typedef class [mscorlib]System.Delegate as delegate
.class public A
{
```

```
.field private class MyEventImpl evImpl
          // Aggregate delegate
.method public specialname void .ctor()
{
    ldarg.0
    dup
    call instance void .base::.ctor()
    ldnull
    stfld class MyEventImpl A::evImpl
    ret
}
.method public void Subscribe(class MyEventImpl aHandler)
{
    ldarg.0
    dup
    ldfld class MyEventImpl A::evImpl
    ldarg.1
    call delegate
         A::Combine( delegate,
         delegate )
    stfld class MyEventImpl A::evImpl
    ret
}
.method public void Unsubscribe(class MyEventImpl aHandler)
{
    ldarg.0
    dup
    ldfld class MyEventImpl A::evImpl
    ldarg.1
    call delegate
         A::Remove( delegate,
         delegate )
    stfld class MyEventImpl A::evImpl
    ret
}
.method public void Raise(int32 EventCode, string Msg)
{
    ldarg.0
    ldfld class MyEventImpl A::evImpl
    ldarg.1
    ldarg.2
    call void MyEventImpl::Invoke(int32, string)
    ret
}
.method public bool HasSubscribers()
{
    ldc.i1.0
```

```
        ldarg.0
        ldfld class MyEventImpl A::evImpl
        brnull L1
        pop
        ldc.i1.1
      L1:    ret
    }
    .event MyEventImpl MyEvent
    {
      .addon instance void A::Subscribe(class MyEventImpl)
      .removeon instance void A::Unsubscribe(class MyEventImpl)
      .fire instance void A::Raise(int32, string)
      .other instance bool A::HasSubscribers()
    }
    // Other class members
    ...
} // The end of the publisher class
// The event subscriber
.class public B
{
    .method public void MyEvtHandler(int32 EventCode, string Msg)
    {
      //  If EventCode > 100, print the message
      ldarg.1
      ldc.i4 100
      ble.s Return
      ldarg.2
      call void [mscorlib]System.Console::WriteLine(string)
    Return:
      ret
    }
    .method private void SubscribeToMyEvent(class A Publisher)
    {
      // Publisher->Subscribe(new MyEventImpl
      // (this,(int)(this->MyEvtHandler)))
      ldarg.1
      ldarg.0
      dup
      ldftn instance void MyEvtHandler(int32, string)
      newobj instance void MyEventImpl::.ctor(object, native int)
      call instance void A::Subscribe(class MyEventImpl)
      ret
    }
    // Other class members
    ...
} // The end of the subscriber class
```

Property Metadata

Properties are considerably less fascinating than events. Typically, a property is some characteristic of the class that declares it—for example, the value of a private field—accessible only through the so-called accessor methods. Because of this, the only aspects of a property the common language runtime is concerned with are the property's accessors.

Let's suppose that a property is based on a private field (you might also have heard the phrase *backed by a private field*). Let's also suppose that both read and write accessors are defined. What is the sense in declaring such a property, when we could simply make the field public and be done with it? At least two reasons argue for declaring it: the accessors can run additional checks to ensure that the field has valid values at all times, and the accessors can fire events signaling that the property has been changed or accessed. I'm sure you can think of other reasons for implementing properties, even leaving aside cases in which the property has no backing field or has only a read accessor or only a write accessor.

A property's read and write accessors are referred to as *getters* and *setters*, respectively. The Visual C# and Visual Basic compilers follow these naming conventions for the property accessors: setters are named set_<property_name>, and getters are named get_<property_name>. Both methods are marked with the specialname flag.

The property metadata group includes the following tables: Property, PropertyMap, TypeDef, Method, MethodSemantics, and Constant. Figure 15-3 shows the structure of the property metadata group. The following sections describe the Property and PropertyMap tables. I discussed the MethodSemantics table in the preceding section of this chapter, and Chapter 9 contains information about the Constant table.

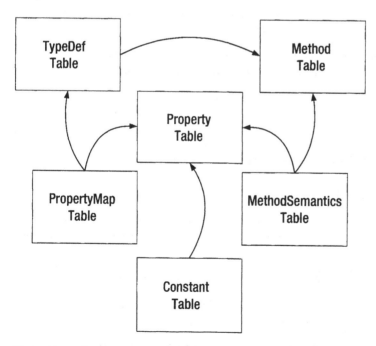

Figure 15-3. *The property metadata group*

The Property Table

The Property table has the associated token type mdtProperty (0x17000000), and its records have three entries:

- PropFlags (2-byte unsigned integer). Binary flags of the property characteristics.

- Name (offset in the #Strings stream). The name of the property, which must be a simple name no longer than 1,023 bytes in UTF-8 encoding.

- Type (offset in the #Blob stream). The property signature. It's about the only occurrence in the metadata when an entry named Type has nothing to do with type (TypeDef, TypeRef, or TypeSpec). Why this entry couldn't be called Signature (which it is) remains mystery to me.

So then, the Type entry holds an offset to the property signature residing in the #Blob metadata stream. The structure of the property signature is similar to that of the method signature, except that the calling convention is IMAGE_CEE_CS_CALLCONV_PROPERTY (0x08). The return type and the parameter types of the property should correspond to those of the getter and setter, respectively. The runtime, of course, pays no attention to what the property signature looks like, but the compilers do care.

Three flag values are defined for properties, and as in the case of events, only one of them can be set explicitly:

- specialname (0x0200). The property is special in some way, as specified by the name.

- rtspecialname (0x0400). The event has a special name reserved for the internal use of the common language runtime. This flag can't be set explicitly.

- [no ILAsm keyword] (0x1000). The property has a default value, which resides in the Constant table; that is, the Constant table contains a record, the Parent entry of which refers to this property.

Like the event flags, the specialname and rtspecialname flags are used by the runtime for marking deleted properties in edit-and-continue scenarios. The deleted property name is changed to _Deleted*. The flag 0x1000 is set by the metadata emission API when a Constant record is emitted for this property, signifying the property's default value.

The PropertyMap Table

The PropertyMap table serves the same purpose for properties as the EventMap table does for events: it provides mapping between the TypeDef table and the Property table. A PropertyMap record has two entries:

- Parent (RID in the TypeDef table). The type declaring the properties.

- PropertyList (RID in the Property table). The beginning of the properties declared by the type referenced by the Parent entry.

In the unoptimized model (the #- stream), an intermediate lookup metadata table, PropertyPtr, is used to remap the properties so that they look as if they were ordered by parent.

Property Declaration

The ILAsm syntax for a property declaration is as follows:

```
.property <flags> <ret_type> <name>(<param_type>[,<param _type>*] )
    [ <const_decl> ] { <method_semantics_decl >* }
```

where

```
<method_semantics_decl> ::= <semantics> <method_ref>
<semantics> ::= .set | .get | .other
<const_decl> ::=  = <const_type> [ ( <value> ) ]
```

The <ret_type> and the sequence of <param_type> nonterminals define the property's signature. <semantics> defines the kind of the associated methods: .set for the setter, .get for the getter, and .other for any other method defined for this property. The optional <const_decl> is the declaration of the property's default value, similar to that of a field or a method parameter. The parent of the property is the class in whose scope the property is declared, as is the case for other class members (fields, methods, and events).

Now, as an exercise, let's declare a simple property:

```
.class public A
{
    // theTally is the backing field of the property Tally
    .field private uint32 theTally = int32(0xFFFFFFFF)
    // Constructor: set theTally to 0xFFFFFFFF (not used yet)
    .method public void .ctor()
    {
        ldarg.0
        dup
        call instance void .base::.ctor()
        ldc.i4 0xFFFFFFFF
        stfld uint32 A::theTally
        ret
    }
    // Setter: set Tally to Val if Val is not 0xFFFFFFFF
    .method public void set_Tally(uint32 Val)
    {
        ldarg.1
        ldc.i4 0xFFFFFFFF
        beq.s Return
        ldarg.0
        ldarg.1
        stfld uint32 A::theTally // set the backing field
    Return:
        ret
    }
    // Getter: return the value of Tally
    .method public uint32 get_Tally()
    {
```

```
    ldarg.0
    ldfld uint32 A::theTally // get the backing field
    ret
}
//  Other method: reset the value of Tally to 0xFFFFFFFF
.method public void reset_Tally()
{
    ldarg.0
    ldc.i4 0xFFFFFFFF
    stfld uint32 A::theTally
    ret
}
.property uint32 Tally(uint32)
  = int32(0xFFFFFFFF)
{
    .set instance void A::set_Tally(uint32)
    .get instance uint32 A::get_Tally()
    .other instance void A::reset_Tally()
}
} // The end of class A
```

Summary of Metadata Validity Rules

The event-related and property-related metadata tables are Event, EventMap, Property, PropertyMap, Method, MethodSemantics, TypeDef, TypeRef, TypeSpec, and Constant. Earlier chapters have discussed the validity rules for Method, TypeDef, TypeRef, TypeSpec, and Constant tables. The records of the remaining tables have the following entries:

- The Event table: EventFlags, Name, and EventType

- The EventMap table: Parent and EventList

- The Property table: PropFlags, Name, and Type

- The PropertyMap table: Parent and PropertyList

- The MethodSemantics table: Semantic, Method, and Association

Event Table Validity Rules

- The EventFlags entry must contain 0, must have the specialname flag set (0x0200), or must have both the specialname and rtspecialname flags set (0x0600).

- The Name entry must contain a valid offset in the #Strings stream, indexing a string no longer than 1,023 bytes in UTF-8 encoding.

- If the specialname and rtspecialname flags are set, the event name must be _Deleted*.

- No duplicate records—those with the same name belonging to the same class—can exist unless the event name is _Deleted*.

- The EventType entry must contain a valid reference to the TypeDef, TypeRef, or TypeSpec table.

EventMap Table Validity Rules

- The Parent entry must hold a valid reference to the TypeDef table.

- The EventList entry must hold a valid reference to the Event table.

Property Table Validity Rules

- The PropFlags entry must contain 0 or a combination of the binary flags specialname (0x0200), rtspecialname (0x0400), and 0x1000.

- If the rtspecialname flag is set, the specialname flag must also be set.

- If the 0x1000 flag is set, the Constant table must contain a valid record whose Parent entry holds the reference to this Property record, and vice versa.

- The Name entry must contain a valid offset in the #Strings stream, indexing a string no longer than 1,023 bytes in UTF-8 encoding.

- If the specialname and rtspecialname flags are set, the property name must be _Deleted*.

- No duplicate records—those with the same name and signature belonging to the same class—can exist unless the property name is _Deleted*.

- The Type entry must contain a valid offset in the #Blob stream, indexing a valid property signature. Chapter 7 discussed the validity rules for property signatures.

PropertyMap Table Validity Rules

- The Parent entry must hold a valid reference to the TypeDef table.

- The PropertyList entry must hold a valid reference to the Property table.

MethodSemantics Table Validity Rules

- The Semantic entry must contain one of the following values: msSetter (0x0001), msGetter (0x0002), msOther (0x0004), msAddOn (0x0008), msRemoveOn (0x0010), and msFire (0x0020).

- The Method entry must contain a valid index to the Method table.

- The Association entry must contain a valid reference to the Event or Property table.

- If the Semantic entry contains msSetter or msGetter, the Association entry must reference the Property table.

- If the Semantic entry contains msAddOn, msRemoveOn, or msFire, the Association entry must reference the Event table.

- No duplicate records that have the same Method and Association entries can exist.

- No duplicate records that have the same Association and Semantic entries can exist unless the Semantic entry contains msOther.

- For each Event record referenced in the Association entry, the table can contain one and only one MethodSemantics record with a Semantic entry equal to msAddOn.

- For each Event record referenced in the Association entry, the table can contain one and only one MethodSemantics record with a Semantic entry equal to msRemoveOn.

- For each Event record referenced in the Association entry, the table can contain no more than one MethodSemantics record with a Semantic entry equal to msFire.

CHAPTER 16

■■■

Custom Attributes

Every system worth its salt needs extensibility. The languages that describe an extensible system and their compilers need extensibility as well; otherwise, they are describing not the system but rather its glorious past.

A system and the associated languages can be extended in three ways. The first way is to tinker with the system itself, changing its inner structure and changing the languages accordingly. This approach is good as long as the system has a negligible number of users, because each new version of the system (and hence the languages) is basically different from the previous version. This approach is characteristic of the early stages of the life cycle of a complex system.

The second way is to leave the system and the languages as they are and build a parallel system (and parallel languages and their compilers), providing additional functionality. A classic example of this approach was the introduction of the remote procedure call (RPC) standard and the interface description language (IDL) in parallel with existing C runtime and C/C++ compilers.

The third way is to build into the system (and the languages) some formal means of extensibility and then employ these means when needed. This approach allows the system developers to sneak in new features and subsystems without changing the basic characteristics of the system. The only challenge is to devise means of extensibility that are both efficient and universal—efficient because we need productivity, and universal because we don't know what we'll need tomorrow or a year from now. These requirements are contradictory, and usually universality wins out. If efficiency wins at universality's expense, sooner or later the designers run out of options and must switch to the second way.

The Microsoft .NET platform, including the common language runtime, the .NET Framework, and the compilers, has an extensibility mechanism built in. This mechanism employs the metadata entities known as *custom attributes*.

Concept of a Custom Attribute

A *custom attribute* is a metadata item specifically designed as a universal tool for metadata extension. Custom attributes do not, of course, change the metadata schema, which is hardcoded and a sacrosanct part of the common language runtime. Custom attributes also don't play any role similar to the generics, which create new types based on some "templates." Rather, custom attributes provide a way to specify additional information about metadata items—information not represented by a metadata item itself.

The information carried by custom attributes is intended mostly for various tools such as compilers, linkers, and debuggers. The runtime recognizes only a small subset of custom attributes.

Custom attributes are also lifesavers for compilers. If the designers of compilers and languages discover, to their surprise, that more features are required to describe a problem area than were initially built into a language or its compiler, they can easily extend the descriptive power of the language by introducing new custom attributes. Of course, the language and its compiler must recognize the concept of a custom attribute to begin with, but that's hardly a problem—all managed languages and their compilers do this.

I've heard some slanderous statements to the effect that the number of custom attributes used by a tool is in direct proportion to the degree of wisdom acquired by the tool designers after the fact. But of course this can't be true.

Jokes aside, custom attributes are extremely useful tools. Think of the following simple example. If we want managed code to interoperate with classic COM applications, we need to play by the classic COM rules. One of these rules is that every exported interface must have a globally unique identifier (GUID) assigned to it. The runtime generates GUIDs on the fly, but we might need not just *any* GUID but rather a specific GUID assigned to a class. What do we do? Add another field to the TypeDef record to store an offset in the #GUID stream? This would surely not help reduce the size of the metadata tables, especially when we consider that only a small fraction of all TypeDefs might ever be used in COM interoperation. To solve the problem, we can introduce a GUID-carrying custom attribute—actually, we have one already, System.Runtime.InteropServices.GuidAttribute—and assign this attribute to any TypeDef participating in the COM interoperation.

The problem with custom attributes is that they are very expensive in terms of resources. They bloat the metadata. Because they represent metadata add-ons, the IL code has no means of accessing them directly. As a result, custom attributes must be resolved through Reflection methods, an approach that approximates having a lively chat by means of mailing letters written in Morse code—fun if you have an eternity at your disposal.

There's bad news regarding custom attributes, and there's also good news. The bad news is that custom attributes keep breeding at an astonishing rate as new tools and new features are introduced. And sometimes custom attributes are invented not because of need but because "I can" or because someone wonders, "Why should I do it the hard way?" It's so easy to use, no wonder…. Ahem! The good news, however, is that most custom attributes are specific to certain tools and only a small fraction are actually used at run time.

CustomAttribute Metadata Table

The CustomAttribute table contains data that can be used to instantiate custom attributes at run time. A record in this CustomAttribute table has three entries:

- Parent (coded token of type HasCustomAttribute). This entry references the metadata item to which the attribute is assigned.

- Type (coded token of type CustomAttributeType). This entry defines the type of the custom attribute itself.

- Value (offset in the #Blob stream). This entry is the binary representation of the custom attribute's parameters.

Given their nature as informational add-ons to other metadata items, custom attributes can be attached to any metadata item that has a specific token type assigned to it. The one exception is that custom attributes cannot be attached to another custom attribute. Chapter 5 described the 23 token types. The token type mdtCustomAttribute (0x0C000000) belongs to the custom attributes themselves. This leaves 22 tables providing potential owners of custom attributes: Module, TypeRef, TypeDef, Field, Method, Param, InterfaceImpl, MemberRef, DeclSecurity, StandAloneSig, Event, Property, ModuleRef, TypeSpec, Assembly, AssemblyRef, File, ExportedType, ManifestResource, GenericParam, GenericParamConstraint, and Method-Spec. No metadata table references the CustomAttribute table. Note that a custom attribute can be assigned to a specific type (TypeRef, TypeDef), but not to an instance of the type.

The Type entry of a custom attribute is a coded token of type CustomAttributeType and hence theoretically can be one of the following: TypeRef, TypeDef, Method, MemberRef, or String. (See Chapter 5.) In fact, in the existing releases of the common language runtime, the choice is limited to Method or MemberRef because of the requirement that the type of a custom attribute must be an instance constructor and nothing else. The class whose instance constructor represents the custom attribute type should be derived from the abstract class [mscorlib]System.Attribute.

The Value entry of a custom attribute is a blob whose contents depend on the nature of the custom attribute. If we were allowed to use a user-defined string as the custom attribute type, Value would contain the Unicode text. But because the custom attribute type is limited to instance constructors, the Value blob contains the encoded arguments of the constructor and (possibly) encoded name/value pairs, setting the fields and properties of the custom attribute's class. If the constructor has no parameters, because the mere presence of the custom attribute is considered sufficiently informational, the Value entry can hold 0.

Custom Attribute Value Encoding

The Value blob of a custom attribute might contain two categories of data: encoded argument values of the instance constructor and additional encoded name/value pairs specifying the initialization values of the fields and properties of the custom attribute class.

The Value blob encoding is based on serialization type codes enumerated in CorSerializationType in the CorHdr.h file. The serialization codes for the primitive types, strings, and vectors are the same as the respective ELEMENT_TYPE_* codes—that is, ELEMENT_TYPE_BOOLEAN, and so on, as described in Chapter 8. Additional serialization codes include TYPE (0x50), TAGGED_OBJECT (0x51), FIELD (0x53), PROPERTY (0x54), and ENUM (0x55). All the constant names include the prefix SERIALIZATION_TYPE_, which I omit because of my inherent laziness.

The encoded blob begins with the prolog, which is always the 2-byte value 0x0001. This is actually the version of the custom attribute blob encoding scheme, which hasn't changed since its introduction, so the prolog is the same for all existing versions of the runtime. The prolog is followed by the values of the constructor arguments. The size and byte layout of these values are inferred from the constructor's signature. For example, the value 0x1234 supplied as an argument of type int32 is encoded simply as a little-endian 4-byte integer, that is, as the following sequence of bytes:

0x34 0x12 0x00 0x00

If the argument is a vector, its encoding begins with a 4-byte element count, followed by the element values. For example, a vector of the three unsigned int16 values 0x1122, 0x3344, and 0x5566 is encoded as follows:

```
0x03 0x00 0x00 0x00 0x22 0x11 0x44 0x33 0x66 0x55
```

If the argument is a string, its encoding begins with the compressed string length, followed by the string itself in UTF-8 encoding, without the terminating 0 byte. The length compression formula was discussed in Table 5-1. For example, the string Common Language Runtime is encoded as the following byte sequence, with the leading byte (0x17) representing the string length (23 bytes):

```
0x17 0x43 0x6F 0x6D 0x6D 0x6F 0x6E 0x20 0x4C 0x61 0x6E 0x67 0x75 0x61
0x67 0x65 0x20 0x52 0x75 0x6E 0x74 0x69 0x6D 0x65
```

If the argument is an object reference to a boxed primitive value type—bool, char, one of the integer types, or one of the floating-point types—the encoding consists of SERIALIZATION_TYPE_TAGGED_OBJECT (0x51), followed by 1-byte primitive type encoding, by the value of the primitive value type. The encoding does not support object references to boxed nonprimitive value types.

Finally, if the argument is of type System.Type, its encoding is similar to that of a string, with the type's fully qualified name playing the role of the string constant. The rules of the fully qualified type name formatting applied in the custom attribute blob encoding are those of Reflection, which differ from ILAsm conventions. The full class name is formed in Reflection and ILAsm almost identically, except for the separator symbols that denote the class nesting. ILAsm notation uses a forward slash:

```
MyNamespace.MyEnclosingClass/MyNestedClass
```

whereas the Reflection standard uses a plus sign:

```
MyNamespace.MyEnclosingClass+MyNestedClass
```

We find greater difference, however, in the way resolution scope is designated. In ILAsm, the resolution scope is expressed as the external assembly's alias (see Chapter 6) in square brackets preceding the full class name. In Reflection notation, the resolution scope is specified after the full class name, separated by a comma. In addition, the concept of the external assembly alias is specific to ILAsm, and Reflection does not recognize it. Thus, if the version, public key token, or culture must be specified, it is done explicitly as part of the resolution scope specification. The following is an ILAsm example:

```
.assembly extern OtherAssembly as OtherAsm2
{
    .ver 1:2:3:4
    .publickeytoken = (01 02 03 04 05 06 07 08)
    .locale "fr-CA"
}
...
[OtherAsm2]MyNamespace.MyEnclosingClass/MyNestedClass
```

In contrast, here is a Reflection example:

```
MyNamespace.MyEnclosingClass+MyNestedClass, OtherAssembly,
    Version=1.2.3.4, PublicKeyToken=0102030405060708, Culture=fr-CA
```

According to Reflection conventions, the resolution scope specification can be omitted if the referenced class is defined in the current assembly or in Mscorlib.dll. In ILAsm, as you know, the resolution scope is omitted only if the class is defined in the current module.

The byte sequence representing the prolog and the constructor arguments is followed by the 2-byte count of the name/value pairs. A name/value pair specifies which particular field or property must be initialized to a certain value.

The name/value pair encoding begins with the serialization code of the target: FIELD or PROPERTY. The next byte is the serialization code of the target type, which is limited to the primitive types, enums, STRING, and TYPE. After the target type comes the name of the target, encoded the same way a string argument would be: the compressed length, followed by the string itself in UTF-8 encoding, without the 0 terminator. Immediately after the target name is the target initialization value, encoded similarly to the arguments. For example, the name/value pair initializing a field (0x53) of type bool (0x02) named Inherited (length 0x09) to true (0x01) is encoded as this byte sequence:

```
0x53 0x02 0x09 0x49 0x6E 0x68 0x65 0x72 0x69 0x74 0x65 0x64 0x01
```

There is a specific way to encode the enumerations in name/value pairs. If the type of a field or property is an enum, the target type encoding starts with SERIALIZATION_TYPE_ENUM (0x55) rather than with ELEMENT_TYPE_VALUETYPE, as you would expect. The SERIALIZATION_TYPE_ENUM byte is followed by the compressed length of the full enum's name in Reflection notation and the name itself without the zero terminator.

Verbal Description of Custom Attribute Value

Version 2.0 of the ILAsm compiler supports the verbal description of the custom attribute value blob. This makes reading and writing the custom attribute values quite a lot easier.

The definition of a serialized primitive type is similar to the definition of the fields' and properties' initialization values (see Chapter 9). For example, the value 0x1234 of an int32 parameter from the previous section is expressed as int32(0x1234). The values of Boolean parameters are expressed as bool(true) or bool(false).

The definition of a string begins with the keyword string, followed by the single-quoted string value in parentheses. For example, the string Common Language Runtime from the previous section would be represented as string('Common Language Runtime'). To express a null-reference string, the construct string(nullref) is used.

The definition of the serialized types (instances of [mscorlib]System.Type) begins with the keyword type, followed either by the type name in ILAsm notation or by keyword class and the single-quoted class name in Reflection notation:

```
type([OtherAsm2]MyNamespace.MyEnclosingClass/MyNestedClass)
```

or

```
type(class 'MyNamespace.MyEnclosingClass+MyNestedClass, OtherAssembly,
Version=1.2.3.4,PublicKeyToken=0102030405060708, Culture=fr-CA')
```

To express a null-reference type, the construct type(nullref) is used.

The definition of a boxed value of a primitive value type begins with the keyword object, followed by the definition of the primitive type in parentheses, such as object(int32(0x1234)).

The definition of an array contains the element count in square brackets and the space-delimited sequence of values in parentheses, such as int32[3](123 456 789) or string[4]('One' 'Two' 'Three' 'Four').

The definition of a name/value pair, denoting the initialization of a field or a property, begins with the keyword field or property, respectively, followed by the type of the field (property) and its name, followed by the equality symbol and the definition of the serialized initialization value as described previously. For example:

```
field int32[] xxx = int32[3](1 2 3)
property string yyy = string('Hello World!')
property enum MyEnum yyy = int32(2)
```

All definitions of the serialized initialization values comprising the custom attribute value blob are written in space-delimited sequence and enclosed in curly braces.

Custom Attribute Declaration

The ILAsm syntax for declaring a custom attribute is as follows:

```
.custom <attribute_type> [ = ( <hexbytes> ) ]
```

or, considering the limitation imposed on <attribute_type> in the existing releases of the common language runtime that the only legal <attribute_type> is an instance constructor, is as follows:

```
.custom instance void <class_ref>::.ctor(<arg_list>)
    [ = ( <hexbytes> ) ]
```

where <class_ref> is a fully qualified class reference, <arg_list> is an argument list of the instance constructor, and <hexbytes> is the sequence of two-digit hexadecimal numbers representing the bytes in the custom attribute's blob.

The ILAsm v2.0 syntax for declaring a custom attribute with a verbal value description is as follows:

```
.custom <attribute_type> [ = { <serialized values> } ]
```

or

```
.custom instance void <class_ref>::.ctor(<arg_list>)
    [ = { <serialized values> } ]
```

To appreciate the difference between verbal and byte-array representations of a custom attribute value, consider the following definition of a hypothetical custom attribute:

```
.custom instance void [System]System.SomeAttribute::.ctor(bool,object)
   = {  bool(true)
        object(int32(1234))
```

```
    field type XXX = type([mscorlib]System.MulticastDelegate)
    field int32[] YYY = int32[3](1 2 3)
    field string[] ZZZ = string[3]('abc' 'def' 'ghe')
    property enum MyEnum PPP = int32(2) }
```

versus the following:

```
.custom instance void [System]System.SomeAttribute::.ctor(bool,object)
= ( 01 00 01 08 D2 04 00 00 04 00 53 50 03 58 58 58
    65 53 79 73 74 65 6D 2E 4D 75 6C 74 69 63 61 73
    74 44 65 6C 65 67 61 74 65 2C 20 6D 73 63 6F 72
    6C 69 62 2C 20 56 65 72 73 69 6F 6E 3D 32 2E 30
    2E 30 2E 30 2C 20 43 75 6C 74 75 72 65 3D 6E 65
    75 74 72 61 6C 2C 20 50 75 62 6C 69 63 6B 65 79
    74 6F 6B 65 6E 3D 62 37 37 61 35 63 35 36 31 39
    33 34 65 30 38 39 53 1D 08 03 59 59 59 03 00 00
    00 01 00 00 00 02 00 00 00 03 00 00 00 53 1D 0E
    03 5A 5A 5A 03 00 00 00 03 61 62 63 03 64 65 66
    03 67 68 65 54 55 06 4D 79 45 6E 75 6D 03 50 50
    50 02 00 00 00 )
```

The owner of the custom attribute, or the metadata item to which the attribute is attached, is defined by the positioning of the custom attribute declaration. At first glance, the rule regarding the declaration of metadata items is simple: if the item declaration has a scope (for example, an assembly, a class, or a method), the custom attributes of the item are declared within this scope. Otherwise—that is, if the item declaration has no scope (such items as a file, a module, or a field)—the custom attributes of the item are declared immediately *after* the item declaration. For example, take a look at these excerpts from the disassembly of Mscorlib.dll:

```
.assembly mscorlib
{
    // Assembly's custom attributes
    .custom instance void System.CLSCompliantAttribute::.ctor(bool)
        = ( 01 00 01 00 00 )
    .custom instance void
        System.Resources.NeutralResourcesLanguageAttribute::.ctor(string)
        = ( 01 00 05 65 6E 2D 55 53 00 00 )    // ...en-US..
    ...
}
...
.module CommonLanguageRuntimeLibrary
// Module's custom attribute
.custom instance void
    System.Security.UnverifiableCodeAttribute::.ctor()
    = ( 01 00 00 00 )
...
.class interface public abstract auto ansi IEnumerable
{
```

```
// Class's custom attribute
.custom instance void
    System.Runtime.InteropServices.GuidAttribute::.ctor(string)
    = ( 01 00 24 34 39 36 42 30 41 42 45 2D 43 44 45  45
        2D 31 31 64 33 2D 38 38 45 38 2D 30 30 39 30  32
        37 35 34 43 34 33 41 00 00 )
.method public hidebysig newslot virtual abstract
    instance class System.Collections.IEnumerator
    GetEnumerator()
{
    // Method's custom attribute
    .custom instance void
        System.Runtime.InteropServices.DispIdAttribute::.ctor(int32)
        = ( 01 00 FC FF FF FF 00 00 )
    ...
} // End of method IEnumerable::GetEnumerator
    ...
} // End of class IEnumerable
...
```

This is in stark contrast to the way custom attributes are declared, for instance, in C# where a custom attribute belonging to an item immediately *precedes* the item declaration. For example, the following is an excerpt showing the C# declaration of the interface IEnumerable mentioned in the preceding code:

```
[Guid("496B0ABE-CDEE-11d3-88E8-00902754C43A")]
public interface IEnumerable
{
    [DispId(-4)]
    IEnumerator GetEnumerator();
}
```

The ILAsm rule specifying that custom attribute ownership is defined by the position of the attribute declaration can play tricks on you if you don't pay attention. Don't forget that when a declaration of a nonscoped item is encountered within the scope of another item, the custom attribute's ownership immediately switches to this newly declared item. Because of that, the custom attributes belonging to a scoped item cannot be declared just anywhere within the item's scope. The following code snippet illustrates the point:

```
.class public MyClass
{
    .custom instance void MyClassAttribute::.ctor()=(01 00 00 00)
    .field int32 MyField
    .custom instance void MyFieldAttribute::.ctor()=(01 00 00 00)
    .method public int32 MyMethod([opt]int32 J)
    {
        .custom instance void MyMethodAttribute::.ctor()=(01 00 00 00)
        .param[1] = int32(123456)
        .custom instance void MyParamAttribute::.ctor()=(01 00 00 00)
```

```
    ...
    }
}
```

To avoid possible confusion about the ownership of a custom attribute, it's better to declare an item's custom attributes as soon as the item's scope is opened, before any other items are declared within the scope.

The preceding discussion covers the rules for assigning custom attributes to items that are declared explicitly. Obviously, these rules cannot be applied to metadata items, which are declared implicitly, simply by their appearance in ILAsm directives and instructions. After all, such metadata items as TypeRefs, TypeSpecs, and MemberRefs might want their fair share of custom attributes, too.

To resolve this problem, ILAsm offers another (full) form of the custom attribute declaration, with the explicit specification of the custom attribute owner:

```
.custom ( <owner_spec> ) instance void <class_ref>::.ctor(<arg_list>)
        [ = ( <hexbytes> ) ]
```

where

```
<owner_spec> ::= <class_ref> | <type_spec>
                 | method <method_ref> | field <field_ref>
```

For example:

```
.custom ([mscorlib]System.String)
        instance void MyTypeRefAttribute::.ctor()=(01 00 00  00)
.custom ([mscorlib]System.String[])
        instance void MyTypeSpecAttribute::.ctor()=(01 00 0 0 00)
.custom (method instance void [OtherAssem]Foo::Bar(int32,int32))
        instance void MyMemberRefAttribute1::.ctor()=(01 00  00 00)
.custom (field int32 [.module OtherMod]Foo::Baz)
        instance void MyMemberRefAttribute2::.ctor()=(01 00  00 00)
```

Custom attribute declarations in their full form can appear anywhere within the ILAsm source code, because the owner of a custom attribute is specified explicitly and doesn't have to be inferred from the positioning of the custom attribute declaration. The IL disassembler puts the custom attribute declarations in full form at the end of the source code dump, before the data dump.

Note that version 2.0 of the IL assembler also supports the verbal description of custom attribute values in the full form of custom attribute declaration.

Two additional categories of metadata items can in principle own custom attributes: InterfaceImpls and StandAloneSigs. The existing releases of ILAsm offer no language means to define custom attributes belonging to these items, an omission to be corrected in future revisions of ILAsm and its compiler. Of course, so far no compiler or other tool has generated custom attributes for these items, but you never know. The tools develop quickly, and the custom attributes proliferate even more quickly, so sooner or later somebody will manage to assign a custom attribute to an interface implementation or a stand-alone signature.

Classification of Custom Attributes

Let's concentrate on the custom attributes recognized by the common language runtime or the tools dealing with managed PE files and see which custom attributes are intended for various subsystems of the runtime and tools.

Before proceeding, however, I must mention one custom attribute that stands apart from any classification and is truly unique. It is the attribute System.AttributeUsageAttribute, which can (and should) be owned only by the custom attribute types. Make no mistake—custom attributes can't own custom attributes, but as we have already found out, the Type entry of a custom attribute is always a reference to an instance constructor of some class. This class should own the custom attribute System.AttributeUsageAttribute, which identifies what kinds of metadata items can own the custom attributes typed after this class, whether these custom attributes are inheritable by the derived classes or overriding methods and whether multiple custom attributes of this type can be owned by a concrete metadata item. Because all operations concerning custom attributes are performed through Reflection, AttributeUsageAttribute can be considered the only custom attribute intended exclusively for Reflection itself. The instance constructor of the AttributeUsageAttribute type has one int32 parameter, representing the binary flags for various metadata items as potential owners of the custom attribute typed after the attributed class. The flags are defined in the enumeration System.AttributeTargets.

The following should save you the time of looking up this enumeration in the disassembly of Mscorlib.dll:

```
.class public auto ansi serializable sealed AttributeTargets
       extends System.Enum
{
    //  The following custom attribute is intended for the compilers
    //  And indicates that the values of the enum are binary flags
    //  And hence can be bitwise OR'ed
    .custom instance void System.FlagsAttribute::.ctor()
           = ( 01 00 00 00 )
    .field public specialname rtspecialname int32 value__
    .field public static literal valuetype System.AttributeTargets
           Assembly = int32(0x00000001)
    .field public static literal valuetype System.AttributeTargets
           Module = int32(0x00000002)
    .field public static literal valuetype System.AttributeTargets
           Class = int32(0x00000004)
    .field public static literal valuetype System.AttributeTargets
           Struct = int32(0x00000008) // Value type
    .field public static literal valuetype System.AttributeTargets
           Enum = int32(0x00000010)
    .field public static literal valuetype System.AttributeTargets
           Constructor = int32(0x00000020)
    .field public static literal valuetype System.AttributeTargets
           Method = int32(0x00000040)
    .field public static literal valuetype System.AttributeTargets
           Property = int32(0x00000080)
    .field public static literal valuetype System.AttributeTargets
           Field = int32(0x00000100)
```

```
.field public static literal valuetype System.AttributeTargets
      Event = int32(0x00000200)
.field public static literal valuetype System.AttributeTargets
      Interface = int32(0x00000400)
.field public static literal valuetype System.AttributeTargets
      Parameter = int32(0x00000800)
.field public static literal valuetype System.AttributeTargets
      Delegate = int32(0x00001000)
.field public static literal valuetype System.AttributeTargets
      ReturnValue = int32(0x00002000)
.field public static literal valuetype System.AttributeTargets
      GenericParameter = int32(0x00004000)
.field public static literal valuetype System.AttributeTargets
      All = int32(0x00007FFF)
} // End of class AttributeTargets
```

As you can see, Reflection's list of potential custom attribute owners is somewhat narrower than the metadata's list of 22 tables. Perhaps we needn't worry about the custom attributes of the interface implementations and stand-alone signatures just yet.

The remaining two characteristics of AttributeUsageAttribute—the Boolean properties Inherited and AllowMultiple—must be defined through the name/value pairs. The defaults are All for the potential custom attribute owners, true for Inherited, and false for AllowMultiple.

You'll find this information useful when (note that I'm not saying "if") you decide to invent your own custom attributes. And now, back to our classification scheme.

Execution Engine and JIT Compiler

The execution engine and the JIT compiler of the common language runtime recognize three custom attributes:

System.Diagnostics.DebuggableAttribute: This attribute, which can be owned by the assembly or the module, sets a special debug mode for the JIT compiler. There are two instance constructors: one, inherited from versions 1.0 and 1.1, has two Boolean parameters, the first enabling the JIT compiler tracking the extra information about the generated code (mapping of the IL instruction offsets to the generated native code offsets) and the second disabling JIT compiler optimizations. The second instance constructor, specific to version 2.0, has one integer parameter—OR combination of flags "default behavior" (0x1), "ignore sequence points defined in PDB" (0x2), "enable edit-and-continue mode" (0x4), and "disable JIT optimizations" (0x100). Chapter 19 discusses these flags and their effects in detail. The ILAsm compiler automatically emits this custom attribute when the /DEBUG command-line option is specified. The ILDASM outputs this attribute but comments it out.

Other debugging-related custom attributes (DebuggerStepThroughAttribute, DebuggerHiddenAttribute, DebuggerBrowsableAttribute, DebuggerTypeProxyAttribute, DebuggerDisplayAttribute, and DebuggerVisualizerAttribute) are debugger-specific and don't affect the operation of the JIT compiler or the execution engine.

System.Security.UnverifiableCodeAttribute: This attribute, which can be owned by the module, indicates that the module contains unverifiable code. Thus, because the result is known, IL code verification procedures don't have to be performed. The instance constructor has no parameters. A module owning this attribute can be executed only in full-trust mode.

`System.ThreadStaticAttribute`: This attribute, which can be owned by a field, indicates that the static field is not shared between threads. Instead, the common language runtime creates an individual copy of the static field for each thread. The effect is approximately the same as mapping the static field to the TLS data, but this effect is achieved on the level of the runtime rather than that of the operating system. The runtime-provided TLS is marginally slower but does not introduce the platform dependence.

Interoperation Subsystem

I discuss the interoperation between managed and unmanaged code in Chapter 18, and here I'm just listing the custom attributes related to this area. All the custom attribute types in this group belong to the namespace `System.Runtime.InteropServices`. The following list refers to them by their class names only:

`ClassInterfaceAttribute`: This attribute, which can be owned by an assembly or a `TypeDef` (class), specifies whether a COM class interface is generated for the attributed type. This attribute type has two instance constructors, each having a single parameter. The first constructor takes a value of enumeration `ClassInterfaceType`; the second takes an `int16` argument. The acceptable argument values are 0 (no automatic interface generation), 1 (automatic `IDispatch` interface generation), or 2 (automatic dual interface generation).

`ComAliasNameAttribute`: This attribute, which can be owned by a parameter (including the return value), a field, or a property, indicates the COM alias for the attributed item. The instance constructor has a single `string` parameter.

`ComConversionLossAttribute`: This attribute, which can be owned by any item, indicates that information about a class or an interface was lost when it was imported from a type library to an assembly. The instance constructor has no parameters.

`ComRegisterFunctionAttribute`: This attribute, which can be owned by a method, indicates that the method must be called when an assembly is registered for use from COM. This allows for the execution of user-defined code during the registration process. The instance constructor has no parameters.

`ComUnregisterFunctionAttribute`: This attribute, which can be owned by a method, indicates that the method must be called when an assembly is unregistered from COM. The instance constructor has no parameters.

`ComSourceInterfacesAttribute`: This attribute, which can be owned by a `TypeDef`, identifies a list of interfaces that are exposed as COM event sources for the attributed type. This attribute type has five instance constructors; the most useful one has a single `string` parameter, the value of which should contain a zero-separated list of all interface types in Reflection notation. (See "Custom Attribute Value Encoding" earlier in this chapter.)

ComVisibleAttribute: This attribute, which can be owned by an assembly, a TypeDef, a method, a field, or a property, indicates whether the attributed item is visible to classic COM. The instance constructor has one Boolean parameter with a value of true if the item is visible.

DispIdAttribute: This attribute, which can be owned by a method, a field, a property, or an event, specifies the COM DispId of the attributed item. The instance constructor has one int32 parameter, the value of the DispId.

GuidAttribute: This attribute, which can be owned by an assembly or a TypeDef, specifies an explicit GUID if the GUID automatically generated by the runtime is for some reason not guid—I mean, good—enough. The instance constructor has one string parameter, which should contain the GUID value in standard literal representation without the surrounding curly braces.

IDispatchImplAttribute: This attribute, which can be owned by the assembly or a TypeDef, indicates the kind of IDispatch interface implementation. The attribute is deemed obsolete and is not recommended for use. The instance constructor has one parameter of type IDispatchImplType (enum), indicating a system-defined implementation (0), internal implementation (1), or compatible implementation (2).

ImportedFromTypeLibAttribute: This attribute, which can be owned by the assembly, indicates that the types defined within the assembly were originally defined in a COM type library. The attribute is set automatically by the TlbImp.exe utility. The instance constructor has one string parameter, which should contain the filename of the imported type library.

InterfaceTypeAttribute: This attribute, which can be owned by a TypeDef (interface), indicates the COM-specific interface type this interface is exposed as. The instance constructor has one int16 parameter. A value of 0 indicates a dual interface, a value of 1 indicates IUnknown, and a value of 2 indicates IDispatch.

ProgIdAttribute: This attribute, which can be owned by a TypeDef (class), explicitly specifies the COM ProgId of the attributed class. Normally, the ProgId strings are generated automatically as a full class name (namespace plus name), but the ProgId length is limited to 39 bytes plus a 0 terminator. The namespaces and class names in .NET are rather long-winded, so there's a good chance 39 bytes won't even cover the namespace. The instance constructor has one string parameter, which should contain the ProgId string.

TypeLibFuncAttribute: This attribute, which can be owned by a method, specifies the COM function flags that were originally imported from the type library. (The COM function flags are described in COM literature and on the Microsoft Developer Network [MSDN].) This attribute is generated automatically by the TlbImp.exe utility. The instance constructor has one int16 parameter, the value of the flags.

TypeLibTypeAttribute: This attribute, which can be owned by a TypeDef, is similar to TypeLibFuncAttribute except that COM type flags are specified instead of COM function flags.

TypeLibVarAttribute: This attribute, which can be owned by a field, is similar to TypeLibFuncAttribute and TypeLibTypeAttribute except that the flags in question are COM variable flags.

Security

Security-related custom attributes are special attributes that are converted to DeclSecurity metadata records (discussed in the next chapter). Usually, the security custom attributes (except one, which is discussed in the next paragraph) don't make it past the compilation stage—the compiler uses them to create the DeclSecurity metadata and doesn't include the original custom attributes in the module's metadata. In one scenario, however, the security custom attributes do "survive" the compilation and are emitted into the PE file. This happens when the security attributes owned by the assembly are specified in the assembly modules, further linked to the assembly by the assembly linker tool. In this case, the assembly-owned security attributes are converted to DeclSecurity metadata records by the assembly linker, but they remain in the assembly modules, although they play no role.

One of the security custom attributes belongs to the namespace System.Security: SuppressUnmanagedCodeSecurityAttribute. This attribute, which can be owned by a method or a TypeDef, indicates that the security check of the unmanaged code invoked by the attribute owner through the P/Invoke mechanism must be suppressed. Only trusted code can call methods that have this attribute. The instance constructor has no parameters. This custom attribute differs from other security attributes in that it is not converted to DeclSecurity metadata and hence stays intact once emitted.

The rest of the security custom attributes belong to the namespace System.Security.Permissions. The ownership of all security custom attributes is limited to the assembly, a TypeDef (class or value type), or a method. The instance constructors of these attributes have one int16 parameter, the action type code. Chapter 17 discusses the security action types and their respective codes as well as various types of permissions.

The following list briefly describes the security custom attributes; you can find further details in Chapter 17:

SecurityAttribute: The abstract base class of all other security attributes.

CodeAccessSecurityAttribute: The abstract base class of the code access security attributes. Other attributes derived from this one are used to secure access to the resources or securable operations.

EnvironmentPermissionAttribute: This attribute sets the security action for the environment permissions that are to be applied to the code.

FileDialogPermissionAttribute: This attribute sets the security action for file open/save dialog box permissions.

FileIOPermissionAttribute: This attribute sets the security action for the file input/output permissions (read, write, append, and so on).

IsolatedStorageFilePermissionAttribute: This attribute sets the security action for the permissions related to the isolated storage files (available storage per user, the kind of isolated storage containment).

`KeyContainerPermissionAttribute`: This attribute sets the security action for the permissions related to the strong name key pair container.

`PermissionSetAttribute`: This attribute sets the security action not for one permission but for a whole permission set, specified in a string, an XML file, or a named permission set.

`PrincipalPermissionAttribute`: This attribute sets the security action for the principal security permissions (security checks against the active principal).

`PublisherIdentityPermissionAttribute`: This attribute sets the security action for the security permissions related to the software publisher's identity.

`ReflectionPermissionAttribute`: This attribute sets the security action for the Reflection permissions.

`RegistryPermissionAttribute`: This attribute sets the security action for the registry access permissions (read, write, create a key).

`SecurityPermissionAttribute`: This attribute sets the security action for the security permissions.

`SiteIdentityPermissionAttribute`: This attribute sets the security action for the site identity permissions.

`StrongNameIdentityPermissionAttribute`: This attribute sets the security action for the assembly's strong name manipulation permissions.

`UIPermissionAttribute`: This attribute sets the security action for the user interface permissions (window flags, Clipboard manipulation flags).

`UrlIdentityPermissionAttribute`: This attribute sets the security action for the URL permissions.

`ZoneIdentityPermissionAttribute`: This attribute sets the security action for the security zone (MyComputer, Intranet, Internet, Trusted, Untrusted).

All intricacies of the .NET security are described in an excellent book *.NET Framework Security* (Pearson, 2002), by Brian A. LaMacchia, Sebastian Lange, Matthew Lyons, Rudi Martin, and Kevin T. Price. These guys *created* the .NET security.

Remoting Subsystem

The following custom attributes are recognized by the remoting subsystem of the common language runtime and can be owned by a `TypeDef`:

`System.Runtime.Remoting.Contexts.ContextAttribute`: This custom attribute class, which sets the remoting context, is a base class of all context attribute classes. It provides the default implementations of the interfaces `IContextAttribute` and `IContextProperty`. The instance constructor has one `string` parameter, the attribute name.

`System.Runtime.Remoting.Contexts.SynchronizationAttribute`: This custom attribute specifies the synchronization requirement and the reentrance capability of the attributed class. It defines the class behavior in the synchronized contexts (contexts having the

Synchronization property). The presence of an instance of this property in a context enforces a synchronization domain for the context (and all contexts that share the same instance). This means that at any instant, at most one thread could be executing in all contexts that share this property instance. Table 16-1 describes the synchronization requirement flags. This attribute type has four instance constructors, as described in Table 16-2.

System.Runtime.Remoting.Activation.UrlAttribute: This attribute is used at the call site to specify the URL of the site where the activation will happen. The instance constructor has one string parameter, which contains the target URL.

Table 16-1. *Synchronization Requirement Flags of* SynchronizationAttribute

Value	Meaning
1	The class should not be instantiated in a context that has synchronization.
2	It is irrelevant to the class whether the context has synchronization.
4	The class should be instantiated in a context that has synchronization.
8	The class should be instantiated in a context with a new instance of the Synchronization property.

Table 16-2. *Instance Constructors of* SynchronizationAttribute

Constructor	Description
Constructor with no parameters	Defaults the synchronization requirement to 1 and the reentrancy flag to false
Constructor with one int32 parameter	Sets the synchronization requirement and defaults the reentrancy flag
Constructor with one Boolean parameter	Sets the reentrancy flag and defaults the synchronization requirement
Constructor with int32 and Boolean parameters	Sets both values

The information provided here is rather brief, but a protracted discussion of the topics related to remoting implementation goes far beyond the scope of this book. This is one of those occasions when one has to remember that modesty is a virtue. I'd rather refer you to the excellent book *Advanced .NET Remoting*, Second Edition (Apress, 2005), by Ingo Rammer.

Visual Studio Debugger

The following two custom attributes are recognized by the Microsoft Visual Studio debugger. They are not recognized by the .NET Framework debugger (Cordbg.exe). Both of these custom attributes belong to the namespace System.Diagnostics.

DebuggerHiddenAttribute: This attribute, which can be owned by a method or a property, signals the debugger not to stop in the attributed method and not to allow a breakpoint to be set in the method. The instance constructor has no parameters.

DebuggerStepThroughAttribute: This attribute is similar to DebuggerHiddenAttribute except that it *does* allow a breakpoint to be set in the method. The debugger won't stop in the attributed method (unless a breakpoint is set inside it).

Assembly Linker

The five custom attributes listed in this section are intended for the assembly linker tool (Al.exe). This tool takes a set of nonprime modules, analyzes them, and constructs an additional prime module, creating a multimodule assembly. The prime module of this assembly doesn't carry any functionality and serves as an "official spokesperson" for the assembly. The custom attributes I am about to discuss specify the characteristics of the multimodule assembly that the assembly linker is about to create from several modules.

The most fascinating aspect of these attributes is their ownership. Think about it: when the attributes are declared, no assembly exists yet; if it did, we wouldn't need these attributes in the first place. Hence, the attributes are declared in one or more of the modules that will make up the future assembly. What in a module might serve as an owner of these attributes? The solution is straightforward: the .NET Framework class library defines the System.Runtime. CompilerServices.AssemblyAttributesGoHere class (the prize for this class's name invention goes to Ronald Laeremans of Visual Studio), and the assembly-specific attributes are assigned to the TypeRef of this class. Ownership of the assembly-specific attributes is the only reason this class exists.

All of the assembly-specific attributes, described in the following list, belong to the namespace System.Reflection:

AssemblyCultureAttribute: This attribute specifies the culture of the assembly. The instance constructor has one string parameter, which contains the culture identification string.

AssemblyVersionAttribute: This attribute specifies the version of the assembly. The instance constructor has one string parameter, which contains the text representation of the version: dot-separated decimal values of the major version, the minor version, the build, and the revision. Everything beyond the major version can be omitted. If major and minor versions are specified, the build and/or the revision can be omitted or specified as an asterisk, which leads to automatic computation of these values at the assembly linker run time. The build number is computed as the current day's number counting since January 1, 2000. The revision number is computed as the number of seconds that have elapsed since midnight, local time, modulo 2.

AssemblyKeyFileAttribute: This attribute specifies the name of the file containing the key pair used to generate the strong name signature. The instance constructor has one string parameter.

AssemblyKeyNameAttribute: This attribute specifies the name of the key container holding the key pair used to generate the strong name signature. The instance constructor has one string parameter.

AssemblyDelaySignAttribute: This attribute specifies whether the assembly is signed immediately at the time of generation or delay signed—in other words, fully prepared to be signed later by the strong name signing utility (Sn.exe). The instance constructor has one Boolean parameter, true, indicating that the assembly is delay signed.

Common Language Specification (CLS) Compliance

The following two custom attributes are intended for the compilers and similar tools. Both custom attributes belong to the System namespace.

ObsoleteAttribute: This attribute, which can be owned by a TypeDef, a method, a field, a property, or an event, indicates that the item is not to be used anymore. The attribute holds two characteristics: a string message to be produced when the obsolete item is used and a Boolean flag indicating whether the use of the item should be treated as an error. This attribute type has three instance constructors, as described in Table 16-3.

CLSComplianceAttribute: This attribute, which can be owned by anything, indicates the (claimed) CLS compliance or noncompliance of the attributed item. The CLS is a subset of the .NET type system and IL code constructs, understandable by all CLS-compliant languages. If a compiler doesn't recognize something (and don't ask why it doesn't—that's impolite), this "something" is out of the CLS. For example, int32 is CLS compliant, and uint32 is not, because Visual Basic doesn't recognize this type. Global fields and methods are not CLS compliant, because C# doesn't recognize them. And so on, and so on. I wonder what happens to CLS if somebody writes a compiler that doesn't recognize System.Object. But I digress. Assigning this attribute to an assembly doesn't make the assembly CLS compliant or noncompliant; it's simply an expression of your opinion on the matter. The instance constructor has one Boolean parameter; a value of true indicates CLS compliance.

Table 16-3. *Instance Constructors of* ObsoleteAttribute

Constructor	Description
Constructor with no parameters	Produces no message and no error
Constructor with a string parameter	Produces a message but no error
Constructor with string and Boolean parameters	Produces a message and an error flag

Pseudocustom Attributes

As mentioned earlier, custom attributes are a lifesaver for compilers. Once a language is given the syntax to express a custom attribute, it's free to use this syntax to describe various metadata oddities its principal syntax can't express. The parallel evolution of the common language runtime and the managed compilers, with the runtime getting ahead now and then, created the concept of the so-called pseudocustom attributes. These attributes are perceived and treated by the compilers as other custom attributes are, but they are never emitted as such. Instead of emitting these attributes, the metadata emission API sets specific values of the metadata.

The following are the 13 pseudocustom attributes:

System.Runtime.InteropServices.ComImportAttribute: This attribute sets the import flag of a type definition. The instance constructor has no parameters.

System.Runtime.InteropServices.DllImportAttribute: This attribute sets the method flag pinvokeimpl, the implementation flag preservesig, and the name of the unmanaged library from which the method is imported. The instance constructor has one string parameter, the name of the unmanaged library. The entry point name and the marshaling flags are specified through the name/value pairs of the EntryPoint, CharSet, SetLastError, ExactSpelling, and CallingConvention properties.

System.SerializableAttribute: This attribute sets the serializable flag of a type definition. The instance constructor has no parameters.

System.NonSerializedAttribute: This attribute sets the notserialized field flag. The instance constructor has no parameters.

System.Runtime.InteropServices.InAttribute: This attribute sets the parameter flag in. The instance constructor has no parameters.

System.Runtime.InteropServices.OutAttribute: This attribute sets the parameter flag out. The instance constructor has no parameters.

System.Runtime.InteropServices.OptionalAttribute: This attribute sets the parameter flag opt. The instance constructor has no parameters.

System.Runtime.CompilerServices.MethodImplAttribute: This attribute sets the method implementation flags. The instance constructor has one int16 parameter, the implementation flags.

System.Runtime.InteropServices.MarshalAsAttribute: This attribute is used on fields and method parameters for managed/unmanaged marshaling. The instance constructor has one int16 parameter, the native type.

System.Runtime.InteropServices.PreserveSigAttribute: This attribute sets the preservesig method implementation flag. The instance constructor has no parameters.

System.Runtime.InteropServices.StructLayoutAttribute: This attribute sets the layout flags of a type definition (auto, sequential, or explicit), the string marshaling flags (ansi, unicode, or autochar), and the characteristics .pack and .size. The instance constructor has one int16 parameter, the layout flag. The .pack and .size characteristics and the string marshaling flags are specified through the name/value pairs of the Pack, Size, and CharSet properties, respectively.

System.Runtime.InteropServices.FieldOffsetAttribute: This attribute sets the field offset (ordinal) in explicit or sequential class layouts. The instance constructor has one int32 parameter, the offset or ordinal value.

System.Security.DynamicSecurityMethodAttribute: This attribute sets the method flag reqsecobj. The instance constructor has no parameters.

ILAsm syntax is adequate to describe all the parameters and characteristics listed here and does not use the pseudocustom attributes.

■**Caution** As a matter of fact, I should warn you against using the pseudocustom attributes instead of ILAsm keywords and constructs. Using pseudocustom attributes rather than keywords is not a bright idea in part because the keywords are shorter than the custom attribute declarations. In addition, you should not forget that the ILAsm compiler, which has no use for custom attributes, treats them with philosophical resignation—in other words, it emits them just as they are, without analysis. Hence, if you specify important flags through pseudocustom attributes, the compiler will not see these flags and as a result could come to the wrong conclusions.

Summary of Metadata Validity Rules

A record of the CustomAttribute table has three entries: Parent, Type, and Value. The metadata validity rules for the custom attributes are rather simple:

- The Parent entry (holding reference to the metadata item owning this custom attribute) must hold a valid index to one of the following tables: Module, TypeRef, TypcDef, Field, Method, Param, InterfaceImpl, MemberRef, DeclSecurity, StandAloneSig, Event, Property, ModuleRef, TypeSpec, Assembly, AssemblyRef, File, ExportedType, ManifestResource, GenericParam, GenericParamConstraint, or MethodSpec.

- The Type entry must hold a valid index to the Method or MemberRef table, and the indexed method must be an instance constructor of a type derived from [mscorlib]System.Attribute.

- The Value entry must hold either 0 or a valid offset in the #Blob stream.

- The blob indexed in the Value entry must be encoded according to the rules described earlier in this chapter; see "Custom Attribute Value Encoding."

- The fields and properties listed in the name/value pairs of the Value blob must be accessible from the custom attribute owner (referenced in the Parent entry).

CHAPTER 17

■ ■ ■

Security Attributes

As a platform for massively distributed operations, the Microsoft .NET Framework must have an adequate security mechanism. We all know that distributed platforms, especially those exposed to the Internet, are the favorite targets of all sorts of pranks and mischief, which can sometimes be very destructive.

The security system of the .NET Framework includes two major components: security policies and embedded security requirements. Security policies are part of the .NET Framework setup and reflect the opinions of the system administrator and the system user regarding what managed applications can and cannot do. Which policies are established can depend in part on the general origin of the application (for example, whether the application resides on the local drive of a machine, is taken from a closed intranet, or comes from the Internet), on the software publisher (for example, whether the system administrator feels differently about applications published by Microsoft or IBM and those published by Tailspintoys.com), on the URL specifying the application's origin, on a particular application, and so forth. Important as they are, these security policies and their definitions are beyond the scope of this book, so with regret, I will forgo a detailed discussion of this topic.

Embedded security requirements are embedded in the applications themselves. Effectively, the embedded security requirements tell the common language runtime which rights an application needs in order to execute. The runtime checks the application's security requirements against the policy under which the application is executed and decides whether it's a go or a no-go.

Embedded security requirements are of two kinds: imperative security, which is part of the application's code, and declarative security, which is part of the application's metadata. Imperative security explicitly describes the operations necessary to perform a security check—for example, calling a method to demand the right to write a file. Declarative security is a set of security attributes assigned to certain metadata items (the assembly as a whole or a certain class or method). Each of these attributes describes the rights that the corresponding item needs in order to be loaded and executed.

This chapter concentrates on declarative security because it is an important part of metadata and because you need to know how it is defined in ILAsm. Besides, I have a feeling that many aspects of imperative security, and even security policies, can be deduced from an analysis of declarative security.

All aspects of security (at least those applicable to versions 1.0 and 1.1 of the CLR and most of them applicable to version 2.0) are exhaustively analyzed in the excellent book *.NET Framework Security* (Pearson, 2002), by Brian A. LaMacchia, Sebastian Lange, Matthew Lyons, Rudi Martin, and Kevin T. Price. The book was written by the folks who created the .NET security, and I am happy to refer you to it.

Declarative Security

Compared to imperative security, declarative security has two main advantages:

- Being part of the metadata, declarative security can be identified and assessed without exhaustive analysis of the application's IL code.

- Declarative security can be developed and modified independent of the functional code. As a result, a division of labor is possible: developer X, the functionality guru, writes the application, and developer Y, the security guru, tinkers with the security attributes.

A disadvantage of declarative security is its coarse targeting. Declarative security can be attributed to a class as a whole but not to the parts of the class and not to specific instances. Declarative security can be attributed to a method as a whole, without the exact specification of when and under what circumstances the special rights might be needed. Imperative security, in contrast, allows the method to behave more flexibly: "Can I do this? No? OK, then I'll do it some other way. Let's see. Can I do that?"

Declarative Actions

A declarative security attribute has three characteristics: the target, the metadata item to which it is attributed; the permission, a description of the rights that interest the target; and the action, a description of the precise way the target is interested in these rights.

The nine declarative security actions are intended for different targets and take effect at different stages of the application execution. The earliest stage of execution is the initial loading of the assembly's prime module and analysis of its manifest. Three declarative actions, targeting the assembly, take effect at this stage:

Request Minimum: This action specifies that the permission is a minimum requirement for the assembly to be executed. If the minimal permissions are not specified, the assembly is granted all rights according to the existing security policy. These rights, however, might be reduced by other already running parts of the application, by means of a Deny or Permit Only action.

Request Optional: This action specifies that the permission is useful to have but is not vital for the assembly execution.

Request Refuse: This action specifies that the permission should not be granted even if the security policy is willing to grant it. This action might be used to ensure that the assembly does not have rights it does not need, thus providing a shield against possible bugs in the assembly itself and against malicious code that might try to coerce the assembly to do something it shouldn't.

The next stage of the application execution is the loading of its classes and their members. Only one declarative action, targeting classes and methods, plays a role at this stage:

Inheritance Demand: For classes, this action specifies the permission that all classes descending from this one must have. For methods, this action specifies the permission that all methods overriding this one must have. Obviously, this action makes sense for virtual methods only.

After the classes and their members have been loaded, the IL code of the invoked methods is JIT compiled. The declarative action targeting classes and methods takes effect at this stage:

Link Demand: This action specifies the permission that all callers of this method must have—or, if the target is a class, the permission that any method of this class must have. For example, if you have a method that formats the system drive, you want to ensure that this method cannot be successfully called from some rogue code that has no right to do so. This action is limited to the immediate caller only. If method A link-demands permission P and method B calling A has this permission but method C calling B does not, the call will go through.

The last stage of the application execution is the run time, when the JIT-compiled code is actually executed. The declarative actions taking effect at this last stage and targeting classes and methods are as follows:

Demand: This action is similar to Link Demand, but it demands that all callers in the call chain have the specified permission.

Assert: This action specifies the permission that the current method must have. Even if the callers of this method higher on the call stack don't have the specified permission, the security check succeeds. This action obviously weakens the declarative security model and should be applied with caution. You cannot apply this action unless the code has the access permission SecurityPermission, which is discussed in the next section.

Deny: This action specifies the permission that must be disabled for all callees down the call stack for the duration of the called method. If a callee never had the specified permission in the first place, the action has no effect on it.

Permit Only: This action specifies the permission that must *not* be disabled for all callees down the call stack, presuming that the rest of the permissions must be disabled. The action seems excessively cruel (to strip the poor callees of all their privileges except one), but you must not forget that the target might have multiple security attributes. Using a series of Permit Only actions, you can create a set of permissions that remain for the callees to enjoy while all other permissions are temporarily revoked. To clarify this, consider the following example. If the called method has security attributes Deny P and Deny Q, all methods it calls (and the methods those methods call, and so on) will have their permissions P and Q suspended. If the called method has security attributes Permit Only P and Permit Only Q, all permissions except P and Q of all callees will be suspended.

And now, let's see what these Ps and Qs stand for.

Security Permissions

Security permissions define the kinds of activities the code requests (or demands, or denies, and so on) the right to perform. The same permissions are used in security policy definitions, specifying what sorts of applications have the right to perform these activities and under what circumstances.

Special classes of the .NET Framework class library represent these permissions. Each permission class is accompanied by a permission attribute class, whose instance constructor is used as a type of security custom attribute. Applying a security custom attribute to a metadata item leads to instantiation of the security object targeting the associated metadata item.

In some sense, it's easier to describe the permissions in terms of the accompanying attribute classes, because the permission classes have instance constructors of different signatures, whereas the instance constructors of the security attribute classes invariably have one parameter—the security action code. All the parameters of the instance constructor(s) of the respective permission class are represented by the attribute's properties, set through name/value pairs.

The permissions form three groups. The first group includes the permissions related to access rights to certain resources. The second group consists of permissions related to identity characteristics of the code, including its origin. The third group represents custom permissions, invented by .NET Framework users for their particular purposes. It seems to be a general principle of the .NET Framework that if you can't find something satisfactory within the framework, it at least provides you with the means to build your own better mousetrap.

Most of the permission classes belong to the namespace System.Security.Permissions, of the Mscorlib.dll assembly, so I've specified the assembly and namespace in the following sections only when they are different.

Access Permissions

The access permissions control access rights to various resources. The group includes the following nine permissions:

- [System.DirectoryServices]System.DirectoryServices.DirectoryServicesPermission. This permission defines access to the Active Directory. The attribute class has two properties:

  - Path (type string) indicates the path for which the permission is specified.

  - PermissionAccess (type int32) specifies the type of access: a value of 0 indicates no access, a value of 2 indicates browse access, and a value of 6 indicates write access.

- [System]System.Net.DnsPermission. This permission defines the right to use the Domain Name System (DNS). The attribute class has no properties because there are no details to specify: either you can use DNS or you can't.

- EnvironmentPermission. This permission defines the right to access the environment variables. The attribute class has three properties, all of type string, which specify the names of the environment variables affected:

  - All specifies the name of the environment variable that can be accessed in any way.

- Read specifies the name of the environment variable that can be read.

- Write specifies the name of the environment variable that can be written to.

- FileDialogPermission. This permission defines the right to access a file selected through the standard Open or Save As dialog box. The attribute class has two properties, both of type bool, for which true indicates that the access is to be granted and false indicates that it is to be denied:

  - Open grants or denies the right to read the file.

  - Save grants or denies the right to write to the file.

- FileIOPermission. This permission defines the right to access specified directories or individual files. The attribute class has five properties, all of type string, which contain either a path or a file specification (with a full path). If the path is specified, the permission is propagated to the whole directory subtree starting at this path. The attribute class properties are as follows:

  - All indicates full access to the specified path or file.

  - Read indicates read access to the specified path or file.

  - Write indicates write access, including file overwriting and new file creation.

  - Append indicates append access—in other words, the existing file can be appended but not overwritten, and a new file can be created.

  - PathDiscovery indicates browse access—for example, querying the current directory, getting a filename back from the file dialog box, and so on.

- IsolatedStorageFilePermission. This permission defines the right to access the isolated storage. Briefly, the isolated storage is a storage space allocated specifically for the user's application, providing a data store independent of the structure of the local file system, a sort of "sandbox" for the application to play in without touching the rest of the file system. Data compartments within the isolated storage are defined by the identity of the application or component code. Thus, there's no need to work magic with the file paths to ensure that the data storages specific to different applications don't overlap. The attribute class has two properties:

  - UsageAllowed (int32-based enumeration IsolatedStorageContainment) indicates the isolated storage type. The UsageAllowed property can be assigned the following int32 values: None (0x00), DomainIsolationByUser (0x10), AssemblyIsolationByUser (0x20), DomainIsolationByRoamingUser (0x50), AssemblyIsolationByRoamingUser (0x60), AdministerIsolatedStorageByUser (0x70), and UnrestrictedIsolatedStorage (0xF0).

  - UserQuota (type int64) indicates the maximum size in bytes of the isolated storage that can be allocated for one user.

- ReflectionPermission. This permission defines the right to invoke Reflection methods on nonpublic class members and to create dynamic assemblies at run time using the methods of Reflection.Emit. The attribute class has four properties:

  - MemberAccess (type bool) grants or denies the right to access the nonpublic members through Reflection methods.

  - TypeInformation (type bool) grants or denies the right to invoke Reflection methods to retrieve information about the class, including information about the nonpublic members.

  - ReflectionEmit (type bool) grants or denies the right to invoke Reflection.Emit methods.

  - Flags (int32-based enumeration ReflectionPermissionFlag) summarizes the three preceding properties, using a binary OR combination of flags 0x01 for TypeInformation, 0x02 for MemberAccess, and 0x04 for ReflectionEmit.

- RegistryPermission. This permission defines the right to manipulate the registry keys and values. This permission is analogous in all ways to FileIOPermission except that it specifies the access rights to the registry rather than to the file system. The attribute class has four properties, all of type string, which contain the registry path:

  - Create grants the right to create the keys and values anywhere in the registry subtree, starting with the node specified in the property.

  - Read grants the right to read the keys and values.

  - Write grants the right to change the existing keys and values.

  - All grants all of the three preceding rights.

- SecurityPermission. This permission defines a set of 13 essential rights to modify the behavior of the common language runtime security subsystem itself. The attribute class has 13 properties of type bool (one for each right) plus one property (int32-based enumeration SecurityPermissionFlag) representing an OR combination of binary flags corresponding to the Boolean properties:

  - Assertion defines the right to override a security check for any granted permission. The respective binary flag is 0x0001.

  - UnmanagedCode defines the right to invoke the native unmanaged code, such as through P/Invoke or COM interoperation (flag 0x0002). If this right is granted, it is asserted every time the unmanaged code is invoked, which results in a significant performance hit. To avoid this, the custom attribute System.Security. SuppressUnmanagedCodeSecurityAttribute can be used. The presence of this attribute suppresses the repetitive security checks when the unmanaged code is invoked.

  - SkipVerification defines the right to run the code without the IL verification procedures at JIT compilation time (flag 0x0004). *This is an extremely dangerous right.* To avoid inviting trouble, this right should be granted only to code that is known to be safe and that comes from a trusted source.

- Execution defines the right to run the code (flag 0x0008). This right, which is granted to almost any code, is the opposite of SkipVerification. The right can be revoked by the administrator or by user security policies regarding specific applications or specific sources that are known for or suspected of being the purveyors of malicious code.

- ControlThread defines the right to perform thread control operations, such as suspending a thread, interrupting a thread, stopping a thread, changing the thread priority, and so on (flag 0x0010).

- ControlEvidence defines the right of the domain host to give evidence to the applications loaded in the domains created by this host (flag 0x0020). The evidence in question usually includes information about the origin and strong name signature of the loaded assembly. If the domain host does not have this right, it gives its own evidence instead.

- ControlPolicy defines the right to access and modify security policies, both user-specific and machinewide (flag 0x0040). *This is another extremely dangerous right that must be granted with great caution.*

- SerializationFormatter defines the right to perform the serialization formatting operations and to retrieve and change the characteristics of any nontransient members of the serializable types, regardless of the accessibility of these members (flag 0x0080). This permission resembles ReflectionPermission in the sense that both are of a very low opinion about the accessibility rules and allow you to access and invoke private class members at will.

- ControlDomainPolicy defines the right of the domain host to specify a domainwide security policy (flag 0x0100).

- ControlPrincipal defines the right to replace the Principal object (carrying the user's identity characteristics) for a given thread, such as in order to implement role-based security (flag 0x0200). In the role-based security model, the security actions depend on the identity (Principal object) of the "code runner" and the role in which the code runner operates.

- ControlAppDomain defines the right to create and manipulate the application domains (flag 0x0400).

- RemotingConfiguration defines the right to configure the remoting types and channels (flag 0x0800).

- Infrastructure defines the right to plug the code into the common language runtime infrastructure, such as adding remoting context sinks, envoy sinks, and dynamic sinks (flag 0x1000).

- Flags is a summary binary representation of the 13 rights just listed. The validity mask is 0x1FFF.

Identity Permissions

The access permissions discussed in the previous section describe the resources to be accessed and the actions to be performed. The identity permissions, in contrast, describe the identities of the agents that are accessing these resources and performing these actions. As a trivial example, suppose you've created a method or a component so atrocious that you want only components written by your company to be able to access it, because you can't trust anyone else to keep the beast in check.

It's a good practice to use identity permissions to extend rather than limit the rights granted to the code of a specific origin. Limiting the rights on the basis of the code's identity is a poor protection technique because the identity information of the code can easily be suppressed. A software publisher you particularly dislike could simply neglect to sign its malicious software, for instance, and you'd never know that this particular code must be treated with extra caution. Or the obnoxious snooping marketing site you'd love to block could start operating through a different Web server or spoof its IP address.

The five identity permissions all belong to the namespace System.Security.Permissions and are defined in the Mscorlib.dll assembly:

- ZoneIdentityPermission. This permission identifies the zone from which the calling code originates. The zones are defined and mapped from the URLs by APIs of IInternetSecurityManager and related interfaces. The zones are not overlapping, and any particular URL can belong to only one zone. The attribute class has one property, Zone (int32-based enumeration [mscorlib]System.Security.SecurityZone). The values of the enumeration are as follows:

  - MyComputer (0x0) means that the application runs from the local drive.

  - Intranet (0x1) means that the application runs from a closed intranet.

  - Trusted (0x2) means that the application runs from a trusted server.

  - Internet (0x3) means that the application originates from the Internet.

  - Untrusted (0x4) means that the application's origin is suspicious and that a high level of security is required.

  - NoZone (0xFFFFFFFF) means that no zone information is available.

- StrongNameIdentityPermission. This permission identifies an assembly by its strong name attributes—namely, by the assembly name, the assembly version, and the public encryption key. The public encryption key of the assembly must exactly match the one specified in the permission.

The assembly name, however, might only partially match the one specified in the permission because a wildcard character (*) can be used in the assembly name specification in the permission. The name of the assembly is usually a dotted name, such as System.DirectoryServices, and any right part of the name can be replaced with the wildcard character. Thus, System.DirectoryServices denotes this specific assembly only, System.* denotes any assembly whose name starts with System. (including the assembly System), and * denotes any assembly. If, for example, the permission includes the Microsoft private encryption key and the assembly name is given as `System.DirectoryServices`, the permission identifies the assembly `System.DirectoryServices` from the .NET Framework. If the assembly name included is `System.*`, the permission identifies it as any Microsoft assembly whose name begins with `System`. If the assembly name is given simply as `*`, the permission identifies it as any assembly produced and signed by Microsoft. It is illegal to replace the left part of the name with the wildcard character (for example, `*.DirectoryServices`).

The assembly version includes four components: the major version, the minor version, the build number, and the revision number. The fourth component or both the third and the fourth components can be omitted, but the first two components must be specified, unless the version is not specified at all. The attribute class has three properties, all of type `string`:

- `Name` is the name of the assembly, possibly with a wildcard character in the right part.

- `PublicKey` is the encoded hexadecimal representation of the public encryption key.

- `Version` is the literal representation of the version—for example, 1.12.123.1 or 1.12.

- `PublisherIdentityPermission`. This permission specifies the software publisher's identity, based on the public key defined by an X509v3 certificate. This certificate is issued by a trusted certification authority and contains encrypted information authenticating the publisher's public encryption key. The name of the publisher is ignored. The associated attribute class has three properties, all of type `string`. Only one of the properties can be set, because they represent alternate ways of obtaining the certificate:

  - `X509Certificate` contains the explicit X509v3 certificate in a coded form.

  - `CertFile` contains the name of the file containing the certificate.

  - `SignedFile` contains the name of the file strong name signed with this certificate so that the certificate can be obtained from the file's strong name signature.

- `SiteIdentityPermission`. This permission identifies the Web site from which the code originates. The attribute class has one property, `Site`, of type `string`, which contains part of the Web site's URL with a stripped protocol specification at the start and the filename at the end—for example, `www.microsoft.com` in the URL `http://www.microsoft.com/ms.htm`. The protocol is presumed to be HTTP, HTTPS, or FTP. The wildcard character (*) is allowed in the site specifications, this time as the left part of the specification.

- `UrlIdentityPermission`. This permission identifies the full URL of the site from which the code originates. The attribute class has one property, `Url`, of type `string`, which contains the full URL specification, including the protocol specification and file specification—for example, `http://oursite.microsoft.com/apps/foo/zzz.html`. The wildcard character is permitted, this time as the right part of the specification—for example, `http://oursite.microsoft.com/apps/foo/*`.

Custom Permissions

The custom permissions, similar to those already defined in the .NET Framework class library, describe access rights to various resources. Once defined, a custom permission can be used in the same way as any "standard" permission. Custom permissions are introduced, as a rule, when it's necessary to describe access to some new kind of resource not covered by existing permissions, such as a new input or output device.

Tip It's a bad practice to try to redefine existing permissions as custom permissions. It is possible to do so, but having multiple permissions pertaining to the same resource can only create pain for the system administrators, who must then keep an eye on all alternative "doors" leading to the resource. As a matter of practical advice, don't make system administrators any unhappier than they already are; it might cost you.

To define a custom permission, you'll need to do the following:

1. Define the new permission class.

2. Define constructors and methods of the permission class according to the permission semantics.

3. Define the methods implementing the [mscorlib]System.Security.IPermission interface: Copy, Intersect, Union, IsSubsetOf, and Demand.

4. If, in principle, full access to the resource can be granted, define the IsUnrestricted method implementing [mscorlib]System.Security.IUnrestrictedPermission.

5. Define the methods implementing the [mscorlib]System.Security.ISecurityEncodable interface that provide the XML encoding and decoding of the permission: FromXml and ToXml.

6. If necessary, define the GetObjectData method implementing the [mscorlib]System.Runtime.Serialization.ISerializable interface.

7. Define the accompanying attribute class.

8. Add support for declarative security.

9. Add the mechanism enforcing the permission wherever the associated resource is exposed.

10. Modify the security policies to take your new permission into account.

Needless to say, the preceding list is meant to discourage you from defining custom permissions.

The best way to define a custom permission is to pick a standard permission whose semantics resemble your intended semantics most closely and use it as an example. It's always a good idea to derive the custom permission classes from [mscorlib]System.Security.CodeAccessPermission and the accompanying attribute classes from [mscorlib]System.Security.Permissions.CodeAccessSecurityAttribute.

One of the major design problems in defining a custom permission is the question of the granularity of the resource access description. In other words, what level of detail is adequate to describe the protected resource? If you were designing RegistryPermission, for example, your choice of granularity could range from a 1-bit indication of whether full access to the registry is granted to a detailed description of a specific kind of access to a specific registry node.

Generally, four basic principles should guide your approach to permission granularity:

- Total Boolean, which grants or denies access to the resource

- Total enumerated, which grants one of the specified (enumerated) forms of access to the resource

- Listed Boolean, which grants or denies access to the resource components listed in the permission declaration

- Listed enumerated, which grants one of the specified forms of access to the resource components listed in the permission

Although additional questions might arise about the level of detail involved in the access form enumeration and the resource components list, the four basic principles, I think, stand. You are welcome to introduce a fifth and put me to shame.

A custom permission class must implement the ISecurityEncodable interface, with its methods ToXml and FromXml, to encode the permission in XML form and restore the permission object from the XML text. The outermost tag of the XML encoding is Permission:

```
<Permission  class="MyPermission,  MyOtherAssembly.dll"  version="1">
    ...
</Permission>
```

To support the declarative security mechanism built into the common language runtime, the custom permission class must be accompanied by the attribute class. The attribute class must have properties that correspond to the parameters of the permission class's constructors. The attribute class must also implement at least one variant of the CreatePermission method. The custom attribute System.AttributeUsageAttribute must be assigned to the attribute class, defining its possible targets, inheritance, and multiplicity, as described in Chapter 16.

Enforcing a newly created custom permission is the easy part; the items dealing with the new resource must create security objects from the custom permission and also security actions, such as Demand, Assert, and so on. The simplest way to do this is to assign the security custom attribute to the respective item.

The last step in creating a custom permission is updating the security policies to include the permission. This is done by writing an XML descriptor of the custom permission and invoking the code access security policy tool, Caspol.exe:

```
caspol  -addset  cust_perm.xml  cust_perm_name
```

Then, again by using the Caspol.exe utility, a new code group must be added, or the existing one changed, to specify the code identities that will be granted the custom permission. Operating the Caspol.exe utility is rather complicated and well beyond the scope of this book; for information, you can refer to the documentation on Caspol.exe and security administration included in the .NET Framework SDK.

Permission Sets

Individual permission objects (the instances of the permission classes) can be combined into permission sets. A permission set is an instance of the [mscorlib]System.Security.➡ PermissionSet class or of the [mscorlib]System.Security.NamedPermissionSet class, which is derived from the former. A permission set can be constructed, such as by combining all permissions relevant to a certain resource or to a certain metadata item (the assembly, a class, or a method).

The PermissionSet class, after its constituent permission classes, implements the interface IPermission with its methods Copy, Intersect, Union, IsSubsetOf, and Demand.

The declarative security is represented in the metadata by the unnamed permission sets, grouped by the security action. Each such permission set is attributed to one metadata item (assembly, class, or method).

Declarative Security Metadata

The declarative security metadata resides in the metadata table DeclSecurity. A record in this table has these three entries:

- Action (2-byte unsigned integer). The security action code.

- Parent (coded token of type HasDeclSecurity). The index to the Assembly, TypeDef, or Method metadata table, indicating the metadata item with which the DeclSecurity record is associated.

- PermissionSet (offset in the #Blob stream). Encoded representation of the permission set associated with a specific security action and a specific metadata item.

The following security action codes and their respective ILAsm keywords are defined for the security actions listed in the "Declarative Actions" section of this chapter and for special-purpose security actions:

Request: Code 0x0001. ILAsm keyword request.

Demand: Code 0x0002. ILAsm keyword demand.

Assert: Code 0x003. ILAsm keyword assert.

Deny: Code 0x0004. ILAsm keyword deny.

Permit Only: Code 0x0005. ILAsm keyword permitonly.

Link Demand: Code 0x0006. ILAsm keyword linkcheck.

Inheritance Demand: Code 0x0007. ILAsm keyword inheritcheck.

Request Minimum: Code 0x0008. ILAsm keyword reqmin.

Request Optional: Code 0x0009. ILAsm keyword reqopt.

Request Refuse: Code 0x000A. ILAsm keyword reqrefuse.

Pre-JIT Grant (persisted grant, set at pre-JIT compilation time by the Ngen.exe utility): Code 0x000B. ILAsm keyword `prejitgrant`.

Pre-JIT Deny (persisted denial, set at pre-JIT compilation time): Code 0x000C. ILAsm keyword `prejitdeny`.

Non-CAS Demand: Code 0x000D. ILAsm keyword `noncasdemand`. This action is similar to Demand, but the permission classes that make up the permission set must not be derived from `System.Security.Permissions.CodeAccessPermission`.

Non-CAS Link Demand: Code 0x000E. ILAsm keyword `noncaslinkdemand`. This action is similar to Link Demand but has the same limitation as Non-CAS Demand.

Non-CAS Inheritance Demand: Code 0x000F. ILAsm keyword `noncasinheritance`. This action is similar to Inheritance Demand but has the same limitation as Non-CAS Demand.

Permission Set Blob Encoding

The blob indexed in the `PermissionSet` entry of the `DeclSecurity` record contains an encoded representation of the permission set object. In versions 1.0 and 1.1 of the common language runtime, the blob contained simply a Unicode-encoded XML description of the permission set.

In version 2.0 of the CLR, new, more economical binary encoding has been introduced. The blob begins with byte 0x2E (character `.`), followed by a compressed number of permissions in the set, followed by the encoded permissions. An XML text cannot begin with a dot, so the system identifies the type of encoding (XML or binary) by the very first byte.

A permission encoding begins with the compressed length of the fully qualified class name in Reflection notation, followed by the name itself in UTF-8 encoding and without the zero terminator. After that comes the compressed size of the permission's blob, followed by the compressed number of properties to be set (can be 0), followed by the property encodings (if any). Unlike custom attributes in general, which allow both fields and properties to be initialized via name/value pairs, security attributes allow only properties to be set.

The property encoding follows the same pattern as the property name/value pair encoding in custom attributes: it begins with byte SERIALIZATION_TYPE_PROPERTY (0x54), followed by the property type, followed by the compressed length of the property name and the name itself, and followed by the encoded value.

To summarize:

- Permission set blob encoding:

  ```
  '.' // dot character
  <compressed_uint> // number of permissions in the set
  { <permission> } // set of permission encodings
  ```

- Permission blob encoding:

  ```
  <compressed_uint> // length of the class name (follows)
  <class_name> // fully qualified class name in Reflection notation
  <compressed_uint> // size of initialization blob
  <compressed_uint> // number of properties, can be 0
  [ { <property> } ] // set of properties, absent if num=0
  ```

- Permission property encoding:

```
SERIALIZATION_TYPE_PROPERTY // 1 byte, 0x54
<type_of_the_property> // property signature
<compressed_uint> // length of the property name (follows)
<property_name>
<encoded_value>
```

Security Attribute Declaration

ILAsm syntax offers two forms of security attribute declarations: separate permissions and permission sets. You can use the form you find more convenient; the IL assembler will automatically combine the separate permissions into permission sets. The owner of the security attribute is the item whose scope contains the security attribute declaration. The syntax for the permission declaration is as follows:

```
.permission <sec_action> <class_ref> [(<name_value_pairs>)]
```

where <sec_action> is one of the security action keywords listed in the preceding section, <class_ref> is a class reference to the attribute class associated with the permission class, and the optional <name_value_pairs> defines the values of the attribute class's properties, as shown here:

```
<name_value_pairs> ::= <nv_pair>[,<nv_pair>*]
<nv_pair> ::= <prop_name> = <prop_value>
```

<prop_name> is the property name of the attribute class, specified as a quoted string. The form of <prop_value> depends on the type of property:

```
<prop_value> ::= true | false // For Boolean properties
    | <int32> | int32(<int32>) // For integer properties
  | <class_ref> (<int32>) // For enumerated properties,
                    // <class_ref> specifies the enumerator
  | <class_ref>(<int_type> : <int32>) // <int_type>::=int8
                                    // | int16 | int32
  | <quoted_string> // For string properties
```

For example:

```
.method private void WriteToSystemDrive(string Str2BWritten )
{
    .permission demand
    [mscorlib]System.Security.Permissions.FileIOPermissionAttribute
        = ("Write"="C:\\")
    ...
}
```

The IL assembler combines separate .permission declarations into permission sets before emitting the DeclSecurity metadata. However, a permission set can be declared explicitly using

.permissionset <sec_action> = (<hexbytes>)

where <hexbytes> is a byte array representing the PermissionSet blob. This byte array is usually fairly long—a "live" example would take a couple of pages. To see such an example, you can simply disassemble any .NET Framework assembly (Mscorlib.dll or System.dll, for instance) and have a look.

The new form of the permission set blob encoding, specific to version 2.0, is expressed in ILAsm as follows:

.permissionset <sec_action> = {<class_ref> [= {<prop_value> [<prop_value>...]}]...}

For example:

.permissionset reqmin =
    {[mscorlib]System.Security.Permissions.SecurityPermissionAttribute
       = {**property bool** 'SkipVerification' = **bool**(**true**)}}

The IL disassembler always uses the .permissionset directive to reflect the DeclSecurity metadata records.

Summary of Metadata Validity Rules

A record of the DeclSecurity metadata table has three entries: Action, the security action code; Parent, the metadata item to which the security record is attached; and PermissionSet, the blob containing the XML descriptor of the permission set. The metadata validity rules for the DeclSecurity metadata records are as follows:

- [run time] The Action entry must hold a valid security action code in the range from 0x1 through 0xF.

- The Parent entry must hold a valid reference to the Assembly, TypeDef, or Method tables.

- If the Parent entry references a TypeDef record, this record must not define an interface.

- If the Parent entry references a TypeDef or Method record, the metadata item referenced in the Parent entry must have its respective HasSecurity flag set (0x00040000 for TypeDef records and 0x4000 for Method records).

- [run time] The PermissionSet entry must hold a valid offset in the #Blob heap. The blob at this offset must contain a legal XML representation of the permission set, Unicode-encoded, or a binary representation of the permission set, encoded according to the scheme described previously.

CHAPTER 18

■■■

Managed and Unmanaged Code Interoperation

There can be no question about the need to provide seamless interoperation between managed and unmanaged code, and I'm not going to waste time discussing this obvious point.

Depending on the kind and the role of the unmanaged code, managed and unmanaged code can interoperate in several scenarios. First, the unmanaged code participating in the interoperation can be either "traditional" code, exposed as a set of functions, or classic COM code, exposed as a set of COM interfaces. Second, the unmanaged code can play the role of either a server, with the managed code initiating the interaction, or a client, with the unmanaged code initiating the interaction. Third, the unmanaged code can reside in a separate executable file, or it can be embedded in the managed module. The embedding option exists only for a "traditional" unmanaged server and client, and its use is limited to the specifics of the Microsoft Visual C++ compiler implementation.

These three dichotomies result in the classification of the interoperation scenarios shown in Figure 18-1.

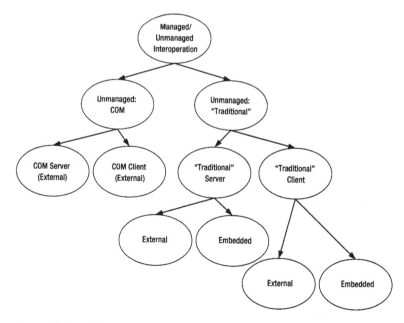

Figure 18-1. *A classification of interoperation scenarios*

We have six basic scenarios here; unmanaged code is acting as

- An external (separate executable file) COM server, implemented through the COM interoperability subsystem of the common language runtime and runtime callable wrappers (RCWs).

- An external COM client, implemented through the same subsystem and COM callable wrappers (CCWs).

- An external "traditional" server, implemented through the platform invocation (P/Invoke) subsystem of the runtime.

- An embedded "traditional" server, implemented through a special case of P/Invoke known as IJW ("it just works") or local P/Invoke.

- An external "traditional" client, implemented through the unmanaged export of the managed methods (inverse P/Invoke).

- An embedded "traditional" client, implemented through IJW (inverse local P/Invoke). In this case a managed module contains embedded unmanaged native code, and the entry point of the module is unmanaged, so the unmanaged code "takes the initiative" from the start and subsequently calls the managed methods.

Thunks and Wrappers

The interoperation between managed and unmanaged code requires the common language runtime to build special interface elements that provide the target identification and necessary data conversion, or marshaling. These runtime-generated interface elements are referred to as *thunks*, or *stubs*, in interoperation with "traditional" unmanaged code; in COM interoperation, they are referred to as *wrappers*.

For details on COM interoperation, which I describe in the next section rather briefly, please see the excellent and exhaustive book *.NET and COM: The Complete Interoperability Guide* (Sams, 2002), by Adam Nathan. Adam worked for many years on the CLR team in the COM interoperation area. If you cannot get Adam's book, try *COM and .NET Interoperability* (Apress, 2002), by Andrew Troelsen; it is a good book too.

P/Invoke Thunks

In order to build a client thunk for managed code to call unmanaged code, the common language runtime needs the following information:

- The name of the module exporting the unmanaged method—for example, Kernel32.dll

- The exported method's name or ordinal in the export table of this unmanaged module

- Binary flags reflecting specifics of how the unmanaged method is called and how its parameters are marshaled

All these items constitute the metadata item known as an *implementation map*, discussed in the following section.

In general cases, the referenced unmanaged module must be located somewhere on the path. However, there is a special case when it's desirable to consider the unmanaged module as part of the managed assembly and deploy them together. In this case, the unmanaged module resides in the application directory (which doesn't have to be on the path); the prime module of the assembly must carry a File record associated with this unmanaged module.

The binary flag values and the respective ILAsm keywords are as follows:

- nomangle (0x0001). The exported method's name must be matched literally.

- ansi (0x0002). The method parameters of type string must be marshaled as ANSI zero-terminated strings unless explicitly specified otherwise.

- unicode (0x0004). The method parameters of type string must be marshaled as Unicode strings.

- autochar (0x0006). The method parameters of type string must be marshaled as ANSI or Unicode strings, depending on the underlying platform.

- bestfit:on (0x0010). Allow "best fit" guessing when converting the strings.

- bestfit:off (0x0020). Disallow "best fit" guessing.

- lasterr (0x0040). The native method supports the last error querying by the Win32 API GetLastError.

- winapi (0x0100). The native method uses the calling convention standard for the underlying platform.

- cdecl (0x0200). The native method uses the C/C++-style calling convention; the call stack is cleaned up by the caller.

- stdcall (0x0300). The native method uses the standard Win32 API calling convention; the call stack is cleaned up by the callee.

- thiscall (0x0400). The native method uses the C++ member method (non-vararg) calling convention. The call stack is cleaned up by the callee, and the instance pointer (this) is pushed on the stack last.

- fastcall (0x0500). The native method uses the fastcall calling convention. This is much like stdcall where the first two parameters are passed in registers if possible.

- charmaperror:on (0x1000). Throw an exception when an unmappable character is encountered in a string.

- charmaperror:off (0x2000). Don't throw an exception when an unmappable character is encountered.

The flags ansi, unicode, and autochar are mutually exclusive and so are the flags defining the calling convention.

The name of the exported method can be replaced with the method's ordinal in the unmanaged module's export table. The ordinal is specified as a decimal number, preceded by the # character—for example, #10.

If the specified name is a regular name rather than an ordinal, it is matched to the entries of the Export Name table of the unmanaged module. If the nomangle flag is set, the name is matched literally. Otherwise, things get more interesting.

Let's suppose, for example, that the name is specified as Hello. If the strings are marshaled to ANSI and the Export Name table does not contain Hello, the P/Invoke mechanism tries to find HelloA. If the strings are marshaled as Unicode, the P/Invoke mechanism looks for HelloW; only if HelloW is not found does P/Invoke look for Hello. If it still can't find a match, it tries the mangled name Hello@N, where N is a decimal representation of the total size of the method's arguments in bytes. For example, if method Hello has two 4-byte parameters (either integer or floating point), the mangled name would be Hello@8. This kind of function name mangling is characteristic only of the stdcall functions, so if the calling convention is different and the name is mangled in some other way, the P/Invoke mechanism will not find the exported method.

You can see that the "name digging" methods employed by the P/Invoke mechanism are intended for Windows API naming conventions and name mangling schemes of the C/C++ compiler.

The thunk is perceived by the managed code as simply another method, and hence it must be declared as any method would be. The presence of the pinvokeimpl flag in the respective Method record signals the runtime that this method is indeed a client thunk and not a true managed method. You already encountered the following declaration of a P/Invoke thunk in Chapter 1:

```
.method public static pinvokeimpl("msvcrt.dll" cdecl)
    vararg int32 sscanf(string,int8*) cil managed { }
```

The parameters within the parentheses of the pinvokeimpl clause represent the implementation map data. The string marshaling flag is not specified, and the marshaling defaults to ANSI. The method name need not be specified because it is the same as the declared thunk name. If you want to use sscanf but would rather call it Foo (sscanf is such a reptilian name!), you could declare the thunk as follows:

```
.method public static pinvokeimpl("msvcrt.dll" as "sscanf" cdecl)
    vararg int32 Foo(string,int8*) cil managed { }
```

The unmanaged method resides somewhere else and the thunk is generated by the runtime, so the Method record of a "true" P/Invoke thunk has its RVA entry set to 0.

Implementation Map Metadata

The implementation map metadata resides in the ImplMap metadata table. A record in this table has four entries:

- MappingFlags (unsigned 2-byte integer). Binary flags, which were described in the previous section. The validity mask (bits that can be set) is 0x3777.

- MemberForwarded (coded token of type MemberForwarded). An index to the Method table, identifying the Method record of the P/Invoke thunk. This must be a valid index. The indexed method must have the pinvokeimpl and static flags set. The token of type MemberForwarded can, in principle, index the Field table as well; but the current releases of the common language runtime do not implement the P/Invoke mechanism for fields, and ILAsm syntax does not permit you to specify pinvokeimpl(...) in field definitions.

- ImportName (offset in the #Strings stream). The name of the unmanaged method as it is defined in the export table of the unmanaged module. The name must be nonempty and fewer than 1,024 bytes long in UTF-8 encoding.

- ImportScope (RID in the ModuleRef table). The index of the ModuleRef record containing the name of the unmanaged module. It must be a valid RID.

IJW Thunks

IJW thunks, similar in structure and function to "true" P/Invoke thunks, are created without the implementation map information or with an incomplete implementation map. The information regarding the identity of the target unmanaged method is not needed because the method is embedded in the same PE file and can be identified by its RVA. IJW thunks *cannot* have an RVA value of 0, as opposed to P/Invoke thunks, which *must* have an RVA value of 0.

The calling convention of the unmanaged method is defined by the thunk signature rather than by the binary flags of the implementation map. The IJW thunk signature usually has the modifier modopt or modreq on the thunk's return type—for example, modopt([mscorlib]System.Runtime.InteropServices.CallConvCdecl). The string marshaling default is ansi.

If, however, there is a need to specify some implementation flags for an IJW thunk, it may be assigned an incomplete implementation map. Such a map contains zero ImportName entry and either contains zero ImportScope entry or contains ImportScope entry pointing at a no-name ModuleRef. The last case is outright bizarre, but such is life in general in the IJW domain.

To distinguish IJW thunks from P/Invoke thunks, the loader first looks at the implementation flags; IJW thunk declarations should have the flags native and unmanaged set. If the loader doesn't see these flags, it presumes that this is a "true" P/Invoke thunk and tries to find its implementation map. If the map is not found, or the found map is incomplete, the loader realizes that this is an IJW thunk after all and proceeds accordingly. That's why I noted that the native and unmanaged flags *should* be set rather than specified that they *must* be set. The loader will discover the truth even without these flags, but not before it tries to find the implementation map and analyze it.

The following is a typical example of an IJW thunk declaration; it is a snippet from a disassembly of a VC++-generated mixed-code PE file:

```
.method public static pinvokeimpl(/* No map */)
    unsigned int32  _mainCRTStartup() native unmanaged preservesig
{
    .entrypoint
    .custom instance void [mscorlib]
        System.Security.SuppressUnmanagedCodeSecurityAttribute::.ctor()
        = ( 01 00 00 00 )
    // Embedded native code
    // Disassembly of native methods is not supported
    // Managed TargetRVA = 0x106f
} // End of global method _mainCRTStartup
```

As you can see, a thunk can be declared as an entry point, and custom attributes and security attributes can be assigned to it. In these respects, a thunk has the same privileges as any other method.

As you can also see, neither the IL disassembler nor ILAsm can handle the embedded native code. The mixed-code PE files, employing the IJW interoperation, cannot be round-tripped (disassembled and reassembled).

COM Callable Wrappers

Classic COM objects are allocated from the standard operating system heap and contain internal reference counters. The COM objects must self-destruct when they are not referenced anymore—in other words, when their reference counters reach 0.

Managed objects are allocated from the common language runtime internal heap, which is controlled by the garbage collection subsystem (the GC heap). Managed objects don't have internal reference counters. Instead, the runtime traces all the object references, and the GC automatically destroys unreferenced objects. But the references can be traced only if the objects are being referenced by managed code. Hence, it would be a bad idea to allow unmanaged COM clients to access managed objects directly.

Instead, for each managed object, the runtime creates a COM callable wrapper, which serves as a proxy for the object. A CCW is allocated outside the GC heap and is not subject to the GC mechanism, so it can be referenced from unmanaged code without causing any ill effects.

In addition to the lifetime control of the managed object, a CCW provides data marshaling for method calls and handles managed exceptions, converting them to HRESULT returns, which is standard for COM. If, however, a managed method is designed to return HRESULT (in the form of unsigned int32) rather than throw exceptions, it must have the implementation flag preservesig set. In this case, the method signature is exported exactly as defined.

The runtime carefully maintains a one-to-one relationship between a managed object and its CCW in any given application domain, not allowing an alternative CCW to be created. This guarantees that all interfaces of the same object relate to the same IUnknown and that the interface queries are consistent.

Any CCW generated by the runtime implements IDispatch for late binding. For early binding, which is done directly through the native v-table, the runtime must generate the type information in a form consumable by COM clients—namely, in the form of a COM type library. The Microsoft .NET Framework SDK includes the type library exporting the utility TlbExp.exe, which generates an accompanying COM type library for any specified assembly. Another tool, RegAsm.exe, also included in the .NET Framework SDK, registers the types exposed by an assembly as COM classes and generates the type library.

When managed classes and their members are exposed to COM, their exposed names might differ from the originals. First, the type library exporters consider all names that differ only in case to be the same—for example, Hello, hello, HELLO, and hEllo are exported as Hello. Second, classes are exported by name only, without the namespace part, except in the case of a name collision. If a collision exists—if, for example, an assembly has classes A.B.IHello and C.D.IHello defined—the classes are exported by their full names, with underscores replacing the dots: A_B_IHello, C_D_IHello.

Other COM parameters characterizing the CCW for each class are defined by the COM interoperability custom attributes, listed in Chapter 16. All information pertinent to exposing managed classes as COM servers is defined through custom attributes, so ILAsm does not have or need any linguistic constructs specific to this aspect of the interoperation.

Runtime Callable Wrappers

A runtime callable wrapper is created by the common language runtime as a proxy of a classic COM object that the managed code wants to consume. The reasons for creating an RCW are roughly the same as those for creating a CCW: the managed objects know nothing about reference counting and expect their counterparts to belong to the GC heap. An RCW is allocated from the GC heap and caches the reference-counted interface pointers to a single COM object. In short, from the runtime point of view, an RCW is a "normal" managed server; and from the COM point of view, an RCW is a "normal" COM client. So everyone is happy.

An RCW is created when a COM-exposed managed object is instantiated—for example, by a newobj instruction. There are two approaches to binding to the COM classes: early binding, which requires a so-called interop assembly, and late binding by name, which is performed through Reflection methods.

An *interop assembly* is a managed assembly either produced from a COM type library by means of running the utility TlbImp.exe (included in the .NET Framework SDK) or, at run time, produced by calling methods of the class [mscorlib]System.Runtime.InteropServices. TypeLibConverter. From the point of view of the managed code, the interop assembly is simply another assembly, all classes of which happen to carry the import flag. This flag is the signal for the runtime to instantiate an RCW every time it is commanded to instantiate such a class.

Late binding through Reflection works in much the same way as IDispatch does, but it has nothing to do with the interface itself. The COM classes that implement IDispatch can be early-bound as well. And late binding isn't restricted to imported classes only. "Normal" managed types can also be late-bound by using the same mechanism.

Instantiating a late-bound COM object is achieved by consecutive calls to the [mscorlib]System.Type::GetTypeFromProgID and [mscorlib]System.Activator:: CreateInstance methods, followed when necessary by calls to the [mscorlib]System.Type:: InvokeMember method. For example, if you want to instantiate a COM class Bar residing in the COM library Foo.dll and then call its Baz method, which takes no arguments and returns an integer, you could write the following code:

```
...
.locals init (class [mscorlib]System.Type Typ,
             object Obj,
             int32 Ret)
// Typ = Type::GetTypeFromProgID("Foo.Bar");
ldstr "Foo.Bar"
call class [mscorlib]System.Type
    [mscorlib]System.Type::GetTypeFromProgID(string)
stloc Typ
```

```
// Obj = Activator::CreateInstance(Typ);
ldloc Typ
call instance object [mscorlib]System.Activator::CreateInstance(
    class [mscorlib]System.Type)
stloc Obj
...
// Ret = (int)Typ->InvokeMember("Baz",BindingFlags::InvokeMethod,
//                              NULL,Obj,NULL);
ldloc Typ
ldstr "Baz"
ldc.i4 0x100  //  System.Reflection.BindingFlags::InvokeMethod
ldnull        // Reflection.Binder - don't need it
ldloc Obj
ldnull        // Parameter array - don't need it
call instance object [mscorlib]System.Type::InvokeMember(string,
            valuetype [mscorlib]System.Reflection.BindingFlags,
            class [mscorlib]System.Reflection.Binder,
            object,
            object[])
unbox valuetype [mscorlib]System.Int32
stloc Ret
...
```

An RCW converts the HRESULT returns of COM methods to managed exceptions. The only problem with this is that the RCW throws exceptions only for failing HRESULT values, so subtleties such as S_FALSE go unnoticed. The only way to deal with this situation is to set the implementation flag preservesig on the methods that might return S_FALSE and forgo the automated HRESULT to exception transformation.

Another problem arises when the COM method has a variable-length array as one parameter and the array length as another. The type library carries no information about which parameter is the length, and the runtime is thus unable to marshal the array correctly. In this case, the signature of the method must be modified to include explicit marshaling information.

Yet another problem requiring manual intervention involves unions with overlapped reference types. Perfectly legal in the unmanaged world, such unions are outlawed in managed code. Therefore, these unions are converted into value types with .pack and .size parameters specified but without the member fields.

The manual intervention mentioned usually involves disassembling the interop assembly, editing the text, and reassembling it. Since the interop assemblies don't contain embedded native code, this operation can easily be performed.

Data Marshaling

All thunks and wrappers provide data conversions between managed and unmanaged data types, which is referred to as *marshaling*. Marshaling information is kept in the FieldMarshal metadata table, which is described in Chapter 9. The marshaling information can be associated with Field and Param metadata records.

Blittable Types

One significant subset of managed data types directly corresponds to unmanaged types, requiring no data conversion across managed and unmanaged code boundaries. These types, which are referred to as *blittable*, include pointers (*not* references), function pointers, signed and unsigned integer types, and floating-point types. Formatted value types (the value types having sequential or explicit class layout) that contain only blittable elements are also blittable.

The nonblittable managed data types that might require conversion during marshaling because of different or ambiguous unmanaged representation are as follows:

- bool (1-byte, true = 1, false = 0) can be converted either to native type bool (4-byte, true = 1, false = 0) or to variant bool (2-byte, true = 0xFFFF, false = 0).

- char (Unicode character, unsigned 2-byte integer) can be converted either to int8 (an ANSI character) or to unsigned int16 (a Unicode character).

- string (class System.String) can be converted either to an ANSI or a Unicode zero-terminated string (an array of characters) or to bstr (a Unicode Visual Basic–style string).

- object (class System.Object) can be converted either to a structure or to a COM interface (CCW/RCW) pointer.

- class can be converted either to a COM interface pointer or, if the class is a delegate, to a function pointer.

- valuetype (nonblittable) is converted to a structure with a fixed layout.

- An array and a vector can be converted to a safe array or a C-style array.

The references (managed pointers) are marshaled as unmanaged pointers. The managed objects and interfaces are references in principle, so they are marshaled as unmanaged pointers as well. Consequently, references to the objects and interfaces (class IFoo&) are marshaled as double pointers (IFoo**). All object references passed to the unmanaged code must be pinned; otherwise, the GC subsystem might move them during the call to an unmanaged method.

In/Out Parameters

The method parameter flags in and out can be (but are not necessarily) taken into account by the marshaler. When that happens, the marshaler can optimize the process by abandoning the marshaling in one direction. By default, parameters passed by reference (including references to objects but excluding the objects) are presumed to be in/out parameters, whereas parameters passed by value (including the objects, even though managed objects are in principle references) are presumed to be in parameters. The exceptions to this rule are the [mscorlib]System.Text.StringBuilder class, which is always marshaled as in/out, and the classes and arrays containing the blittable types that can be pinned, which, if the in and out flags are explicitly specified, can be two-way marshaled even when passed by value. The StringBuilder class is used to represent a mutable string in the unmanaged world, that is, a string that might be changed within the unmanaged method (in C/C++ notation, char* as opposed to const char*); that's why StringBuilder is always marshaled as in/out.

Considering that managed objects don't necessarily stay in one place and can be moved any time the garbage collector does its job, it is vital to ensure that the arguments of an unmanaged call don't wander around while the call is in progress. This can be accomplished in the following two ways:

- Pin the object for the duration of the call, preventing the garbage collector from moving it. This is done for the instances of formatted, blittable classes that have fixed layout in memory, invariant to managed or unmanaged code.

- Allocate some unmovable memory, that is, a block of memory outside of the GC heap. If the parameter has an in flag, marshal the data from the argument to this unmovable memory. Call the method, passing this memory as the argument. If the parameter has an out flag, marshal this memory back to the original argument upon completion of the call.

Chapter 10 describes the ILAsm syntax for the explicit marshaling definition of method parameters. Chapter 8 discusses the native types used in explicit marshaling definitions. Rather than reviewing that information here, I'll discuss some interesting marshaling cases instead.

String Marshaling

String marshaling is defined in at least three places: in a string conversion flag of a TypeDef (ansi, unicode, or autochar), in a similar flag of a P/Invoke implementation map, and, explicitly, in marshal(...) clauses—for all parameters of all methods of a given class, for all parameters of a given method, and for one concrete parameter, respectively. Lower-level specifications override the higher-level specifications.

As method arguments, managed strings (instances of the System.String class) can be marshaled as the following native types:

- lpstr, a pointer to a zero-terminated ANSI string

- lpwstr, a pointer to a zero-terminated Unicode string

- lptstr, a pointer to a zero-terminated ANSI or Unicode string, depending on the platform

- bstr, a Unicode Visual Basic–style string with a prepended length

- ansi bstr, an ANSI Visual Basic–style string with a prepended length

- tbstr, an ANSI or Unicode Visual Basic–style string, depending on the platform

The COM wrappers marshal the string arguments as lpstr, lpwstr, or bstr only. Other unmanaged string types are not COM compatible.

At times, a string buffer must be passed to an unmanaged method in order to be filled with some particular contents. Passing a string by value does not work in this case because the called method cannot modify the string contents even if the string is passed as an in/out parameter (in the managed world, strings are immutable—once a string object is created, it cannot be changed). Passing the string by reference does not initialize the buffer to the required length. The solution, then, is to pass not a string (an instance of System.String) but rather an instance of System.Text.StringBuilder, initialized to the required length:

```
.typedef [mscorlib]System.Text.StringBuilder as StrB
.method public static pinvokeimpl("user32.dll" stdcall)
   int32 GetWindowText(int32 hndl,
                       class StrB s, // Default marshaling: ANSI
                       int32 nMaxLen) { }
.method public static string GetWText(int32 hndl)
{
   .locals init(class StrB sb )
   ldc.i4 1024 // Buffer size
   newobj instance void StrB::.ctor(int32)
   stloc.0
   ldarg.0    // Load hndl on stack
   ldloc.0    // Load StringBuilder instance on stack
   ldc.i4 1024 // Buffer size again
   call int32 GetWindowText(int32,
             class StrB,
             int32)
   pop        // Discard the return of GetWindowText
   ldloc.0    // Load StringBuilder instance (filled in) on stack
   call instance string StrB::ToString()
             // Resulting string has length less than 1024
   ret
}
```

The string fields of the value types are marshaled as lpstr, lpwstr, lptstr, bstr, or fixed sysstring[<size>], which is a fixed-length array of ANSI or Unicode characters, depending on the string conversion flag of the field's parent TypeDef and on the marshaling specification of the fields (if specified).

Object Marshaling

Objects (instances of reference types) are marshaled as struct (converted to a COM-style variant), interface (converted to IDispatch if possible and otherwise to IUnknown), iunknown (converted to IUnknown), or idispatch (converted to IDispatch). The default marshaling is as struct.

When an object is marshaled as struct to a COM variant, the type of the variant can be explicitly set by those object types that implement the [mscorlib]System.IConvertible interface. The types that do not implement this interface are marshaled to and from variants as shown in Table 18-1. All listed types belong to the System namespace.

Table 18-1. *Marshaling of Managed Objects to and from COM Variants*

Type of Object Marshaled To...	...COM Variant Type...	...Marshaled to Type of Object
Null reference	VT_EMPTY	Null reference
DBNull	VT_NULL	DBNull
Runtime.InteropServices.ErrorWrapper	VT_ERROR	UInt32
Reflection.Missing	VT_ERROR with E_PARAMNOTFOUND	UInt32
Runtime.InteropServices.IdispatchWrapper	VT_DISPATCH	___ComObject or null reference if the variant value is null
Runtime.InteropServices.IunknownWrapper	VT_UNKNOWN	___ComObject or null reference if the variant value is null
Runtime.InteropServices.CurrencyWrapper	VT_CY	Decimal
Boolean	VT_BOOL	Boolean
Sbyte	VT_I1	Sbyte
Byte	VT_UI1	Byte
Int16	VT_I2	Int16
UInt16	VT_UI2	UInt16
Int32	VT_I4	Int32
UInt32	VT_UI4	UInt32
Int64	VT_I8	Int64
UInt64	VT_UI8	UInt64
Single	VT_R4	Single
Double	VT_R8	Double
Decimal	VT_DECIMAL	Decimal
DateTime	VT_DATE	DateTime
String	VT_BSTR	String
IntPtr	VT_INT	Int32
UintPtr	VT_UINT	UInt32
Array	VT_ARRAY	Array

If you wonder why, for example, System.Int16 and System.Boolean should be used instead of int16 and bool, respectively, I should remind you that our discussion concerns the conversion of the *objects*.

When a managed object is passed to unmanaged code by reference, the marshaler creates a new variant and copies the contents of the object reference into this variant. The unmanaged code is free to tinker with the variant contents, and these changes are propagated back to the referenced object when the method call is completed. If the type of the variant has been changed within the unmanaged code, the back propagation of the changes can result in a change of the object type, so you might find yourself with a different type of object after the call. The same story happens (in reverse order) when unmanaged code calls a managed method, passing a variant by reference: the type of the variant can be changed during the call.

The variant can contain a pointer to its value rather than the value itself. (In this case, the variant has its type flag VT_BYREF set.) Such a "reference variant," passed to the managed code by value, is marshaled to a managed object, and the marshaler automatically dereferences the variant contents and retrieves the actual value. Despite its reference type, the variant is nonetheless passed by value, so any changes made to the object in the managed code are not propagated back to the original variant.

If a "reference variant" is passed to the managed code by reference, it is marshaled to an object reference, with the marshaler dereferencing the variant contents and copying the value into a newly constructed managed object. But in this case, the changes made in the managed code are propagated back to the unmanaged code only if they did not lead to a change in the variant type. If the changes did affect the variant type, the marshaler throws an InvalidCast exception.

More Object Marshaling

Objects are always marshaled by COM wrappers as COM interfaces. Every managed class can be seen as implementing an implicit interface that contains all nonprivate members of the class.

When a type library is generated from an assembly, a class interface and a coclass are produced for each accessible managed class. The class interface is marked as a default interface for the coclass.

A CCW generated by the common language runtime for each instance of the exposed managed class also implements other interfaces not explicitly implemented by the class. In particular, a CCW automatically implements IUnknown and IDispatch.

When an interop assembly is generated from a type library, the coclasses of the type library are converted to the managed classes. The member sets of these classes are defined by the default interfaces of the coclasses.

An RCW generated by the runtime for a specific instance of a COM class represents this instance and not a specific interface exposed by this instance. Hence, an RCW must implement all interfaces exposed by the COM object. This means that the identity of the COM object itself must be determined by one of its interfaces because COM objects are not passed as method arguments, but their interfaces are. In order to do this, the runtime queries the passed interface for IProvideClassInfo2. If this interface is unavailable, the runtime queries the passed interface for IProvideClassInfo. If either of the interfaces is available, the runtime obtains the class identifier (CLSID) of the COM class exposing the interface—by calling the IProvideClassInfo2::GetGUID() or IProvideClassInfo::GetClassInfo() method—and uses it to retrieve full information about the COM class from the registry. If this action sequence fails, the runtime instantiates a generic wrapper, System.ComObject.

Array Marshaling

Unmanaged arrays can be either C-style arrays of fixed or variable length or COM-style safe arrays. Both kinds of arrays are marshaled to managed vectors, with the unmanaged element type of the array marshaled to the respective managed element type of the vector. For example, a safe array of BSTR is marshaled to string[].

The rank and bound information carried by a safe array is lost in the transition. If this information is vital for correct interfacing, manual intervention is required again: the interop assembly produced from the COM type library must be disassembled, the array definitions must be manually edited, and the assembly must be reassembled. For example, if a three-dimensional safe array of BSTR is marshaled as string[], the respective type must be manually edited to string[0...,0...,0...] in order to restore the rank of the array.

C-style arrays can have a fixed length or a length specified by another parameter of the method or a combination thereof, the total length being a sum of fixed (base) length and the value of the length parameter. Both values, the base length and the length parameter's zero-based ordinal, can be specified for the marshaler so that a vector of appropriate size can be allocated. Chapter 8 describes the ILAsm syntax for specifying the array length. For example:

```
// Array length is fixed (128)
.method public static pinvokeimpl("unmanaged.dll" stdcall)
    void Foo(string[] marshal(bstr[128]) StrArray) {}
```

```
// Array length is specified by arrLen (parameter #1)
.method public static pinvokeimpl("unmanaged.dll" stdcall)
    void Boo(string[] marshal(bstr[+1]) StrArray, int32 arrLen) {}
```

```
// Base length is 128, additional length specified by moreLen
.method public static pinvokeimpl("unmanaged.dll" stdcall)
    void Goo(int32 moreLen, string[] marshal(bstr[128+0]) StrArray) {}
```

Managed vectors and arrays can be marshaled to unmanaged code as safe arrays or as C-style arrays. Marshaling as safe arrays preserves the rank and boundary information of the managed arrays. This information is lost when the managed arrays are marshaled as C-style arrays. Vectors of vectors—for example, int32[][]—cannot be marshaled.

Delegate Marshaling

Delegates are marshaled as interfaces by COM wrappers and as unmanaged function pointers by P/Invoke thunks. The type library Mscorlib.tlb defines the Delegate interface, which represents delegates in the COM world. This interface exposes the DynamicInvoke method, which allows the COM code to call a delegated managed method.

Marshaling a delegate as an unmanaged function pointer represents a certain risk. The unmanaged code may cache the received callback pointer "for future use." Such a reference cached on the unmanaged side does not count as a live reference to the delegate, so the garbage collector may destroy the delegate before the unmanaged side is done using it as a callback. The calling managed code must take steps to ensure the delegate's survival until interaction with the unmanaged code is complete, such as by storing the delegate reference in a field or in a pinned local variable.

Providing Managed Methods As Callbacks for Unmanaged Code

In a P/Invoke interaction, the initiative must come from the managed code's side. The process starts in managed mode and makes calls to the unmanaged functions. However, the exchange can't always go in only one direction; that model would be too simplistic to be usable.

Many unmanaged methods require callback functions, and the managed code must have the means to provide those functions. Thus, it's necessary to have a way to pass a managed method pointer to an unmanaged function, permitting the unmanaged function to call the managed method. The managed callback method might be simply a P/Invoke thunk of another unmanaged method, but that changes nothing—it's still a managed method.

The way to pass managed methods as callbacks to unmanaged functions involves the use of delegates. The delegates are marshaled by P/Invoke thunks as unmanaged function pointers, which makes them suitable for the task.

Let's look at a sample to review the way delegates are used for callback specifications. You can find this sample, Callback.il, on the Apress Web site. The sample implements a simple program that sorts 15 integer values in ascending order, employing the well-known C function qsort, called through P/Invoke. The difference between the P/Invoke calls you've encountered so far and this one is that qsort requires a callback function, which compares the two elements of the array being sorted, thus defining the sorting order.

I'll let the sample speak for itself:

```
// I can't pass the managed method pointer to the unmanaged function,
// and even the ldftn instruction will not help me.
// This delegate will serve as an appropriate vehicle.
.class public sealed CompareDelegate
      extends [mscorlib]System.MulticastDelegate
{
   .method public specialname
         void  .ctor(object Object,
                     native uint MethodPtr)
                     runtime {}
```

```
// Note the modopt modifier of the Invoke signature -- it's very
// important. Without it, the calling convention of the callback
// function is marshaled as stdcall (callee cleans the stack).
// But qsort expects the callback function to have the cdecl
// calling convention (caller clears the stack). If we supply the
// callback with the stdcall calling convention, qsort blows
// the stack away and causes a memory access violation. You are
// welcome to comment out the modopt line and see what happens.
// Note also that the modopt modifier is placed on the delegate's
// Invoke signature, not on the signature of the delegated method.
.method public virtual int32
    modopt([mscorlib]System.Runtime.CompilerServices.CallConvCdecl)
        Invoke(void*, void*) runtime {}


// Well, I don't really need asynchronous invocation here,
// but, you know, dura lex sed lex.
.method public newslot virtual
        class [mscorlib]System.IAsyncResult
            BeginInvoke(object,
                        class [mscorlib]System.AsyncCallback,
                        object) runtime {}


.method public newslot virtual
        void  EndInvoke(class [mscorlib]System.IAsyncResult)
            runtime {}
}


// The hero of the occasion: the qsort function.
.method public static pinvokeimpl("msvcrt.dll" ansi cdecl)
    void qsort(void*,int32,int32,class CompareDelegate) preservesig {}


// This is the comparison method I'm going to offer as
// a callback to qsort. What can be simpler than comparing
// two integers?
.method public static int32 compInt32(void* arg1,void* arg2)
{
    // return(*arg1 - *arg2);
    ldarg.0
    ldind.i4
    ldarg.1
    ldind.i4
    sub
    ret
}
```

```
// And now, let's get this show on the road.
.method public static void Exec()
{
   .entrypoint
   .locals init(class CompareDelegate)

   // Print the unsorted values.
   ldstr "Before Sorting:\n"
   call vararg int32 printf(string)
   pop
   ldsflda valuetype SixtyBytes DataToSort
   ldc.i4.s 15
   call void printInt32(void*, int32)

   // Create the delegate.
   // Null object ref indicates the global method.
   ldnull
   ldftn int32 compInt32(void*,void*)
   newobj instance void
      CompareDelegate::.ctor(object,native uint)
   stloc.0

   // Invoke qsort.
   ldsflda valuetype SixtyBytes DataToSort // Pointer to data
   ldc.i4.s 15 // Number of items to sort
   ldc.i4.4    // Size of an individual item
   ldloc.0    // Callback function pointer (delegate)
   call void qsort(void*,int32,int32,class CompareDelegate)

   // Print the sorted values.
   ldstr "After Sorting:\n"
   call vararg int32 printf(string)
   pop
   ldsflda valuetype SixtyBytes DataToSort
   ldc.i4.s 15
   call void printInt32(void*, int32)

   ret
}
```

Managed Methods As Unmanaged Exports

Exposing managed methods as unmanaged exports provides a way for unmanaged, non-COM clients to consume managed services. In fact, this technique opens the managed world in all its glory—with its secure and type-safe computing and with all the wealth of its class libraries—to unmanaged clients.

Of course, the managed methods are not exposed as such. Instead, inverse P/Invoke thunks, automatically created by the common language runtime, are exported. These thunks provide the same marshaling functions as "conventional" P/Invoke thunks, but in the opposite direction.

In order to expose managed methods as unmanaged exports, the IL assembler builds a v-table, a v-table fixup (VTableFixup) table, and a group of unmanaged export tables, which include the Export Address table, the Name Pointer table, the Ordinal table, the Export Name table, and the Export Directory table. Chapter 4 discusses all of these tables, their structures, and their positioning within a managed PE file. Now let's see how it all is done.

The VTableFixup table is an array of VTableFixup descriptors, with each descriptor carrying the RVA of a v-table entry, the number of slots in the entry, and the binary flags indicating the size of each slot (32-bit or 64-bit) and any special features of the entry. One special feature is the creation of the marshaling thunk to be exposed to the unmanaged client.

The v-table and the VTableFixup table of a managed module serve two purposes. One purpose—relevant only to the VC++ compiler, the only compiler that produces mixed-code modules—is to provide the intramodule managed/unmanaged code interoperation. Another purpose is to provide the means for the unmanaged export of managed methods.

Each slot of a v-table in a PE file carries the token of the managed method the slot represents. At run time, after respective methods have been compiled to native code, the v-table fixups are executed, replacing the method tokens with actual addresses of the compiled methods.

The ILAsm syntax for a v-table fixup definition is as follows:

.vtfixup [<num_slots>] <flags> **at** <data_label>

where square brackets are part of the definition and do not mean that <num_slots> is optional. <num_slots> is an integer constant, indicating the number of v-table slots grouped into one entry because their flags are identical. This grouping has no effect other than saving some space—you can emit a single slot per entry, but then you'll have to emit as many v-table fixups as there are slots.

The flags specified in the definition can be those that are described in the following list:

- int32. Each slot in this v-table entry is 4 bytes wide (32-bit target platform).

- int64. Each slot in this v-table entry is 8 bytes wide (64-bit target platform). The int32 and int64 flags are mutually exclusive.

- fromunmanaged. The entry is to be called from the unmanaged code, so the marshaling thunk must be created by the runtime.

- callmostderived. This flag is not currently used.

The order of appearance of .vtfixup declarations defines the order of the respective VTableFixup descriptors in the VTableFixup table.

The v-table entries are defined simply as data entries. Note that the v-table must be contiguous—in other words, the data definitions for the v-table entries must immediately follow one another.

For example:

```
...
.vtfixup [1] int32 fromunmanaged at VT_01
...
.vtfixup [1] int32 at VT_02
...
.data VT_01 = int32(0x0600001A)
.data VT_02 = int32(0x0600001B)
...
```

The actual data representing the method tokens is automatically generated by the IL assembler and placed in designated v-table slots. To achieve that, it is necessary to indicate which method is represented by which v-table slot. ILAsm provides the .vtentry directive for this purpose:

```
.vtentry <entry_number> : <slot_number>
```

where <entry_number> and <slot_number> are 1-based integer constants. The .vtentry directive is placed within the respective method's scope, as shown in the following code:

```
...
.vtfixup [1] int32 fromunmanaged at VT_01
...
.method public static void Foo()
{
    .vtentry 1:1 // Entry 1, slot 1
    ...
}
...
.data VT_01 = int32(0) // The slot will be filled automatically.
...
```

Export Table Group

The export table group (in managed and unmanaged modules) consists of five tables:

- The Export Address table (EAT), containing the RVA of the exported unmanaged functions.

- The Export Name table (ENT), containing the names of the exported functions.

- The Name Pointer table (NPT) and the Ordinal table (OT), together forming a lookup table that rearranges the exported functions in lexical order of their names. In special cases when an unmanaged module exports its methods exclusively by ordinal, ENT, NPT, and OT may be missing. Managed modules always export their methods by name.

- The Export Directory table, containing the location and size information about the other four tables.

Location and size information concerning the Export Directory table itself resides in the first of 16 data directories in the PE header. Figure 18-2 shows the structure of the export table group.

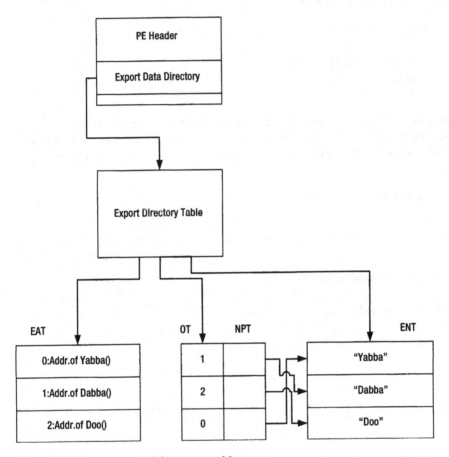

Figure 18-2. *The structure of the export table group*

In an unmanaged PE file, the EAT contains the RVA of the exported unmanaged methods. In a managed PE file, the picture is more complicated. The EAT cannot contain the RVA of the managed methods because it's not the managed methods that are exported—rather, it's their marshaling thunks, generated at run time.

The only way to address a yet-to-be-created thunk is to define a slot in a v-table entry for the exported managed method and a VTableFixup descriptor for this entry, carrying the fromunmanaged flag. In this case, the contents of the v-table slot (a token of the exported method) are replaced at run time with the address of the marshaling thunk. (If the fromunmanaged flag is not specified, the thunk is not created, and the method token is replaced with this method's address; but this is outside the scenario being discussed.)

For each exported method, the IL assembler creates a tiny native stub—yes, you've caught me: the IL assembler *does* produce embedded native code after all—consisting of the x86 command `jump indirect` (0x25FF) followed by the RVA of the v-table slot allocated for the exported method. The native stubs produced by version 2.0 of the IL assembler for X64 or Itanium targets look, of course, different but are functionally similar: they execute an indirect jump. The EAT contains the RVA of these tiny stubs.

The generation of the jump stubs renders the module strictly platform specific, but we've already made our module platform specific when we chose the width of the v-table slots (4 or 8 bytes).

The tiny stubs are necessary because the EAT must contain solid addresses of the exported methods as soon as the operating system loads the PE file. Otherwise, the unmanaged client won't be able to match the entries of its Import Address table (IAT) to the entries of the managed module's EAT. The addresses of the methods or their thunks don't exist at the moment the file is loaded. But the tiny stubs exist and have solid addresses. It's true that at that moment they cannot perform any meaningful jumps, because the v-table slots they are referencing contain method tokens instead of addresses. But by the time the stubs are called, the methods and thunks will have been generated and the v-table slots will be fixed up, with the method tokens replaced with thunk addresses.

Figure 18-3 illustrates this scenario.

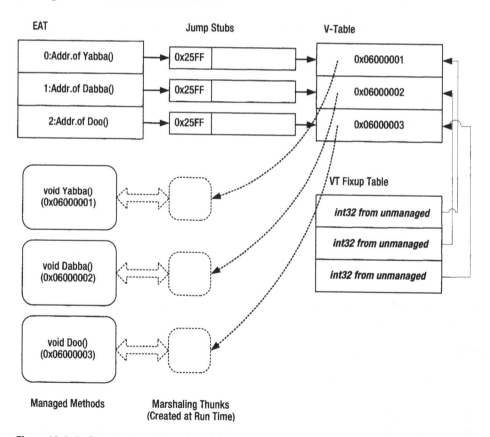

Figure 18-3. *Indirect referencing of v-table entries from the EAT*

The unmanaged exports require that relocation fixups are executed at the module load time. When a program runs under the Microsoft Windows XP operating system or later, this requirement can create a problem similar to those encountered with TLS data and data on data. As described in Chapter 4, if the common language runtime header flag COMIMAGE_FLAGS_ILONLY is set, the loader of Windows XP ignores the .reloc section, and the fixups are not executed. To avoid this, the IL assembler automatically replaces the COMIMAGE_FLAGS_ILONLY flag with COMIMAGE_FLAGS_32BITREQUIRED whenever the source code specifies TLS data or data on data. Unfortunately, the versions 1.0 and 1.1 of the compiler neglected to do this automatically when unmanaged exports were specified in the source code, and it was thus necessary to explicitly set the runtime header flags using the directive .corflags 0x00000002. Version 2.0 of the compiler is free of this deficiency, it automatically removes the ILONLY flag and then, if the target architecture is x86, sets the 32BITREQUIRED flag.

The ILAsm syntax for declaring a method as an unmanaged export is very simple:

```
.export [<ordinal>] as <export_name>
```

where <ordinal> is an integer constant. The <export_name> provides an alias for the exported method. In versions 1.0 and 1.1 of ILAsm, it was necessary to specify <export_name> even if the method is exported under its own name. In version 2.0, it is not necessary.

The .export directive is placed within the scope of the respective method together with the .vtentry directive, as shown in this example:

```
...
.corflags 0x00000002
...
.vtfixup [1] int32 fromunmanaged at VT_01
...
.method public static void Foo()
{
    .vtentry 1:1     // Entry 1, slot 1
    .export [1] as Bar // Export #1, Name="Bar"
    ...
}
...
.data VT_01 = int32(0) // The slot will be filled automatically.
...
```

The source code for the small sample described earlier in Figure 18-2 could look like the following, which was taken from the sample file YDD.il on the Apress Web site:

```
.assembly extern mscorlib { auto }
.assembly YDD { }
.module YDD.dll
.corflags 0x00000002
.vtfixup [1] int32 fromunmanaged at VT_01 // First v-table fixup
.vtfixup [1] int32 fromunmanaged at VT_02 // Second v-table fixup
.vtfixup [1] int32 fromunmanaged at VT_03 // Third v-table fixup
.data VT_01 = int32(0)         // First v-table entry
.data VT_02 = int32(0)         // Second v-table entry
.data VT_03 = int32(0)         // Third v-table entry
```

```
.method public static void Yabba()
{
    .vtentry 1:1
    .export [1]
    ldstr "Yabba"
    call void [mscorlib]System.Console::WriteLine(string)
    ret
}
.method public static void Dabba()
{
    .vtentry 2:1
    .export [2]
    ldstr "Dabba"
    call void [mscorlib]System.Console::WriteLine(string)
    ret
}
.method public static void Doo()
{
    .vtentry 3:1
    .export [3]
    ldstr "Doo!"
    call void [mscorlib]System.Console::WriteLine(string)
    ret
}
```

Now you can compile the sample to a managed DLL, remembering to use the /DLL command-line option of the IL assembler, and then write a small unmanaged program that calls the methods from this DLL. This unmanaged program can be built with any unmanaged compiler—for example, Microsoft Visual C++ 6—but don't forget that YDD.dll cannot run unless the .NET Framework is installed. It's still a managed assembly, even if your unmanaged program does not know about it.

As you've probably noticed, all .vtfixup directives of the sample sport identical flags. This means that three single-slot v-table entries can be grouped into one three-slot entry:

```
.vtfixup [3] int32 fromunmanaged at VT_01
.data VT_01 = int32(0)[3]
```

Then the .vtentry directives of the Dabba and Doo methods must be changed to .vtentry 1:2 and .vtentry 1:3, respectively.

It's worth making a few additional points about the sample. First, it's good practice to define all VTableFixup and v-table entries in the beginning of the source code, before any methods or other data constants are defined. This ensures that you will not attempt to assign a nonexistent v-table slot to a method and that the v-table will be contiguous.

Second, in the sample, the export ordinals correspond to v-table entry numbers. In fact, no such correspondence is necessary. But if you're using the v-table only for the purpose of unmanaged export, it might not be a bad idea to maintain this correspondence simply to keep track of your v-table slots. It won't do you any good to assign the same v-table slot or the same export ordinal to two different methods.

Third, you should remember that the export ordinals are relative. The Export Directory table has a Base entry, which contains the base value for the export ordinals. The IL assembler simply finds the lowest ordinal used in the .export directives throughout the source code and assigns this ordinal to the Base entry. If you start numbering your exports from 5, it does not mean that the first four entries in the EAT will be undefined. The common practice is to use 1-based export ordinals.

At this moment, if you were paying attention, you would say, "Wait a minute! You are talking about the v2.0 IL assembler targeting different platforms, and at the same you are suggesting to put the platform-specific details *right in the source code?!*"

But I'm not sure you were, so I'm saying it myself. Yes, if you look at the code of the sample YDD.il, you will see that the directives .corflags, .vtfixup, and .data are platform specific (in this case, x86 specific), so in order to generate YDD.DLL for, say, the X64 platform, you would need to change the source code. This is the bad news.

The good news is that version 2.0 of the IL assembler does not require these directives at all, as long as the v-table and VTFixup table are used for unmanaged exports only. Just specify the .export directives in the methods you want to export to the unmanaged world, and the flags, the v-table, and its fixups will be generated automatically by the compiler, with the slot size adjusted for the target platform:

```
.assembly extern mscorlib { auto }
.assembly YDD { }
.module YDD.dll
.method public static void Yabba()
{
    .export [1]
    ldstr "Yabba"
    call void [mscorlib]System.Console::WriteLine(string)
    ret
}
.method public static void Dabba()
{
    .export [2]
    ldstr "Dabba"
    call void [mscorlib]System.Console::WriteLine(string)
    ret
}
.method public static void Doo()
{
    .export [3]
    ldstr "Doo!"
    call void [mscorlib]System.Console::WriteLine(string)
    ret
}
```

In the case of an embedded "traditional" unmanaged client (that is, when the unmanaged code of a mixed-code module takes the initiative and calls the managed methods), the managed/unmanaged code interoperation is performed along the lines similar to the previously described case of external "traditional" unmanaged client. The embedded case is simpler because there is no need to involve the export tables (the calling code is embedded in this very module), and hence there is no need to generate the jump stubs. So in the case of the embedded unmanaged client, all interoperation is done via the module's v-table and VTFixup table, with the CLR automatically generating the marshaling thunks for inverse P/Invoke (unmanaged code calling the managed). Just in case, let me remind you that existing versions of the IL assembler cannot generate the mixed-code modules.

Summary

In this chapter, I discussed six possible scenarios of managed/unmanaged code interoperation, based on three dichotomies: COM interoperation vs. "traditional" interoperation, unmanaged code as client (calling) vs. unmanaged code as server (being called), and external unmanaged code (residing in different module) vs. embedded unmanaged code (residing in the same module). With three dichotomies, one would expect eight scenarios, but there are only six, because the COM interoperation always involves external unmanaged code.

COM interoperation involves the generation of RCWs for representing the COM objects in the managed world (COM as server) and of CCWs for exposing the managed objects to the COM world (COM as client). Both RCWs and CCWs are generated by the CLR at run time, and both serve two main purposes: marshaling the parameters across the managed/unmanaged boundaries and coordinating GC reference tracking on the managed side and COM-specific reference counting on the unmanaged side.

"Traditional" interoperation with unmanaged code posing as the server is based on the platform invocation mechanism (P/Invoke) and involves the generation of marshaling thunks. The marshaling thunks are automatically generated by the CLR at run time according to the implementation map metadata (ImplMap table) and to the called method's signature.

"Traditional" interoperation with unmanaged code posing as the client is based on the inverse P/Invoke mechanism and also involves the generation of marshaling thunks. This interoperation takes place via the module's v-table and VTFixup table, and the marshaling thunks are automatically generated by the CLR at run time according to data stored in these tables (which are not part of the metadata) and to the called method's signature. In case of external "traditional" unmanaged client, the unmanaged export tables and unmanaged jump stubs must be generated by the compiler and persisted in the managed module.

"Traditional" interoperation within mixed-code modules is known as IJW and is (so far) specific to the VC++ compiler, because no other compiler (so far) can produce the mixed-code modules.

CHAPTER 19

■■■

Multilanguage Projects

The Microsoft .NET paradigm is multilanguage by its very nature. You can derive your class from another class that has been declared in an assembly produced by someone else, and you don't need to worry about how the language you are using relates to the language used to write the other assembly. You can create a multimodule assembly, each module of which is written in a different language.

What you can't do so easily, however, is build a single-module assembly using different languages. This means once you've selected a development language for your single-module assembly, you must accept all the limitations of the selected language.

ILAsm offers a way to resolve this problem. ILAsm, as a platform-oriented and ideologically neutral language, provides a natural common base for the high-level, pure-IL languages. Because of this, ILAsm can be used as an intermediate stage for multilanguage projects. Most of the high-level language compilers don't actually use ILAsm as their base language, but this can be easily rectified by using the IL disassembler.

IL Disassembler

The IL disassembler tool, ILDASM.EXE, is distributed with the .NET Framework SDK and is one of the most popular tools among developers working on .NET-based programs. Virtually every book dedicated to .NET themes at least mentions ILDASM and briefly describes its features.

At least half of the ILAsm's power, I think, lies in the fact that the IL assembler and disassembler form a perfectly complementary pair and that the output of the IL disassembler can be fed to the IL assembler. Together, the IL disassembler and assembler form a toolset for serializing and deserializing managed PE files. What you can do with the serialized (text) representation of a managed PE file between disassembling and reassembling is limited by your imagination only.

ILDASM is a dual-mode application—that is, it can run either as a console or as a GUI application. Two ILDASM command-line options—/OUT:<file_name> and /TEXT—set the disassembler mode. If either /TEXT or /OUT:CON is specified, ILDASM outputs the disassembly text to the console window from which it was started. If /OUT:<file_name> is specified, ILDASM dumps the disassembly text into the specified file. If neither /TEXT nor /OUT is specified, ILDASM switches to graphical mode.

The graphical user interface of ILDASM is rather modest and strictly functional. The disassembled module is represented as a tree. The module itself is shown as the root, namespaces and classes as tree nodes, and members—methods, fields, events, and properties—as tree leaves. Double-clicking a tree leaf displays a disassembly window containing the ILAsm source text of the corresponding item of the module, as shown in Figure 19-1.

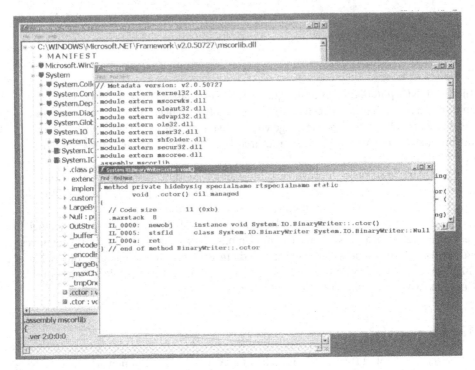

Figure 19-1. *The IL disassembler in graphical mode*

The tree leaf MANIFEST corresponds to all module-level information, including manifest metadata, module metadata, and v-table fixups.

Each tree node representing a type has special leaves providing information about the type: a class leaf, an extends leaf (if the type is derived from another type), and one implements leaf for each interface the type implements. Double-clicking a class leaf displays a disassembly window containing full class information except for the disassembly of the class members. Double-clicking an extends leaf or an implements leaf moves the cursor in the tree view to the respective class or interface if it is defined in the current module.

The disassembler provides numerous viewing options that allow you to control the disassembly text presentation. In graphical mode, these options appear in the View menu, as shown in Figure 19-2.

The module opened in ILDASM's graphical mode can be dumped to a file but not to a console window. To dump the module to a file, choose File ➤Dump, set the dump options as shown in Figure 19-3, and click OK. In the Save As dialog box displayed, specify a directory and the name of an output file. To dump a text representation of the fully expanded tree view to a specified file, choose File ➤DumpTree.

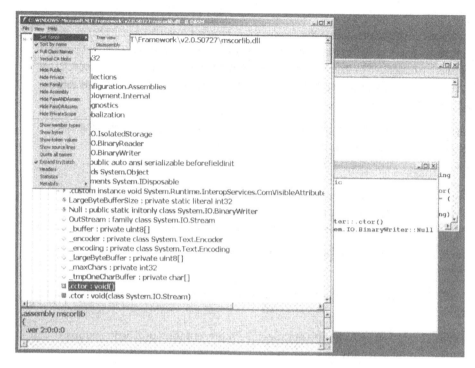

Figure 19-2. *Disassembler viewing options*

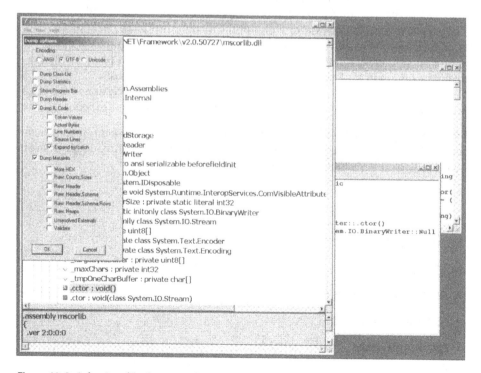

Figure 19-3. *Selecting file dump options*

▪**Note** For reasons I won't discuss here, the disassembler versions 1.0 and 1.1 do not offer all possible viewing options by default. To access all the options, you have to use the /ADVANCED (or /ADV, because ILDASM options are recognized by their first three characters) command-line option. Certain options are available only in advanced mode. Among them, the group of /METAINFO options, which provide various summaries of the module metadata, are very useful.

The disassembler version 2.0 offers all possible viewing (or dumping) options by default and does not require the /ADV command-line option.

All the disassembly options shown in Figure 19-3 are available as command-line options in ILDASM, but the inverse is not quite true. Appendix D contains a complete list of all the command-line options. The following list focuses only on the most important of these options:

- The /UTF8 and /UNICODE options set the encoding of the output file. The default encoding is ANSI.

- The /TOKENS option includes hexadecimal token values as comments in the disassembly text.

- The /BYTES option includes the hexadecimal representation of IL instructions as comments in the disassembly text.

- The /ITEM=<item_description> option limits the disassembly to the specified item: a class or a method. For example, /ITEM="Foo" dumps the Foo class and all its members, /ITEM="Foo::Bar" dumps all methods named Bar in the Foo class, and /ITEM="Foo::Bar(int32(int32, string))" dumps the method int32 Foo::Bar(int32, string). This option has no effect if the disassembler is invoked in graphical mode. Unfortunately, there is a problem with reading this option in version 2.0 of ILDASM, and for the option to work you need to omit the last closing parenthesis: /ITEM="Foo::Bar(int32(int32, string)". This problem did not exist in versions 1.0 and 1.1. In case you ever decide to use this option, I personally apologize for the inconvenience.

- The /VISIBILITY=<vis>[+<vis>*] option limits the disassembly to the items that have the specified visibility and accessibility flags. The <vis> suboptions are three-letter abbreviations of all possible visibility and accessibility flags:

  - *PUB*: Public

  - *PRI*: Private

  - *FAM*: Family

  - *ASM*: Assembly

  - *FAA*: Family and assembly

  - *FOA*: Family or assembly

  - *PSC*: Private scope

For example, /VIS=PUB+FAM+FOA limits the disassembly output to those items that can be accessed from outside the assembly.

- The /NOIL option suppresses the ILAsm source text output. You can use this option when you are interested not in a disassembly but in file statistics, a metadata summary, a headers dump, and so on. This option has no effect if the disassembler is invoked in graphical mode.

- The /RAWEH option forces all structured exception handling clauses to be dumped in canonic (label) form at the end of each method scope.

- The /LINENUM option includes the .language and .line directives in the disassembly text to allow the reassembled code to be bound to the original source files rather than the ILAsm source file. (The section "Compiling in Debug Mode," later in this chapter, discusses the use of these directives in detail.) This option has no effect if the PE file being disassembled is not accompanied by a PDB file that contains all the debug information, including source filenames and sequence points, binding source code lines to offsets in IL.

- The /NOBAR option suppresses the pop-up window showing the disassembly progress. This option is useful if the disassembler is invoked from batch files as part of an automatic process running in the background.

- The /METAINFO[=<met_opt>] option dumps the metadata summary. The <met_opt> suboptions indicate the specifics of this summary:

  - HEX: Add hexadecimal representation of the signatures.

  - CSV: Provide the sizes of string, blob, and GUID heaps and sizes of the metadata tables and their record counts.

  - MDH: Provide the metadata header details.

  - SCH: Provide the metadata header details and schema information.

  - RAW: Provide the metadata header details, schema information, and raw contents of metadata tables.

  - HEA: Provide the raw dump of all heaps.

  - UNR: Provide a list of unresolved method references and method definitions without implementation.

  - VAL: Run metadata validation.

The metadata suboptions can't be concatenated using the plus character, unlike the visibility suboptions. Instead, multiple occurrences of /METAINFO options are permitted in order to set multiple suboptions, such as ildasm /noil /met=hex /met=mdh MyModule.dll /out:MyModule.txt.

All of these options are recognized by their first three letters (/NOBAR means the same as /NOB, for instance) and are case-insensitive (/NOB means the same as /nob). The colon character (:) and the equality character (=) are interchangeable; for example, /vis=pub means the same as /vis:pub. Finally, the option key may be a slash character (/) or a minus character (–), so /nob means the same as –nob. (I am a huge fan of the diversity idea, you see.)

When a PE file is disassembled in full to a file, the managed and unmanaged resources are automatically saved to the respective files so that they can be picked up by the assembler and incorporated into a new PE file during the reassembly. "In full" means that neither /NOIL nor /ITEM nor /VIS options is specified, because these options result in a partial disassembly, whose text is not suitable for reassembling. The unmanaged resources are saved in a file that has the same name as the output file (specified in the /OUT option) and has the extension .res. The managed resources are saved in files named according to the managed resource names specified in the metadata (or aliases if the resource names are not suitable for filenames; see Chapter 6 for details). The resource files are not saved when a PE file is disassembled to a console window using the option /TEXT or /OUT:CON.

Principles of Round-Tripping

The round-tripping of managed PE files includes two steps. The first step is to disassemble the PE file into an ILAsm source file and the managed and unmanaged resource files:

```
ildasm MyModule.dll /out:MyModule.il
```

The second step of round-tripping is to invoke the ILAsm compiler to produce a new PE file from the results of the disassembler's activities:

```
ilasm /dll MyModule.il /out:MyModuleRT.dll /res:MyModule.res
```

The command-line options of the ILAsm compiler are listed in full in Appendix D. The most important of these options are the following:

- The /OUT:<file_name> option specifies the name of the resulting PE file. The default name is the name of the first source file plus the extension .dll or .exe.

- The /DLL option creates a dynamic-link library module. The default is to create an executable (EXE) PE file. The file extension of the output file does not matter; if you specify /OUT:MyModule.dll and neglect to specify /DLL, the result is an executable PE file (EXE) named MyModule.dll. You can try to sell such a PE file to Barnum, but you won't be able to do much more than that.

- The /RES:<unmanaged_resource_file_name> option indicates that the compiler must incorporate the specified unmanaged resource file into the PE file. The managed resources are specified in the ILAsm source code and are picked up by the compiler automatically, whereas an unmanaged resource has no metadata representation and hence must be explicitly specified in a command-line option.

- The /DEBUG option has two effects: a PDB file is created, and the [mscorlib]System. Diagnostics.DebuggableAttribute custom attribute is assigned to the Assembly or Module metadata record. See "Compiling in Debug Mode," later in this chapter, for more details.

- The /KEY:<private_key_file_name> or /KEY:@<private_key_source_name> option makes the IL assembler use the specified private key to strong name sign the output PE file. If you are round-tripping a strong-name-signed prime module and don't have the private key—if, in other words, it's someone else's assembly—you can leave the module unsigned. In this case, you'll be able to use it as a private assembly only. If you decide not to sign the module, you must delete or comment out the `.publickey` directive in the `.assembly` scope. Otherwise, you will produce a delayed-signed assembly—that is, an assembly that must be strong name signed at some moment after the compilation and before it can be used. (Alternatively, you can sign the prime module with your own private key and say that it was your own assembly all along. Do this only if you find true joy in litigation.)

A few items that might be present in a managed PE file don't survive round-tripping. For example, any embedded native code is lost. The exceptions to this rule are the tiny pieces of native code that are automatically generated during the compilation: the common language runtime startup stub and the unmanaged export stubs. Strictly speaking, even these tiny pieces don't really round-trip: they are generated anew rather than reproduced from the disassembly.

Another item that does not survive round-tripping is data on data, which is a data constant containing the address of another data constant. Fortunately, this kind of data is rather rare and not very useful, thanks to the strict limitations the runtime imposes on operations with unmanaged pointers. Among the compilers producing pure-IL modules, only the ILAsm compiler is capable of generating such data.

Local variable names survive round-tripping only if the PDB file accompanying the original PE file is available. The local variable names are part of the debug information rather than the metadata.

Creative Round-Tripping

Simple two-step round-tripping, involving only disassembly and reassembly, is not very interesting, unless you are testing the round-tripping capabilities of the IL assembler and disassembler. A more creative scheme involves three steps: disassembly, *tinkering with the ILAsm source code*, and reassembly.

Generally speaking, you can alter the ILAsm source code during this creative round-tripping in only three ways:

- You can change the code emitted by a high-level compiler or a tool in a way the compiler (the tool) would not allow you to do. From Chapter 18, you might recall mention of the "manual intervention" necessary to correct the interop assemblies produced by the Tlbimp.exe tool. Other scenarios can also call for editing original code. For example, let's suppose you don't believe me when I say that the common language runtime does not permit overriding final virtual methods. You write a test program in Microsoft Visual Basic .NET only to discover that the compiler will not let you explicitly override a final method. Without explicit overriding, the compiler automatically sets the newslot flag of the overriding method, and, alas, there goes your experiment. Then you recall that the ILAsm compiler doesn't have such inhibitions. You disassemble your test application, remove the newslot flag, reassemble the test application, run it, and find out that I was right. As another example, let's suppose you have a nice assembly written in C# that can do a lot of nice things, but your retrograde colleagues insist that in order to be useful your assembly must expose its functionality to the unmanaged legacy components. And those components are so far on the legacy side that they don't even use COM.

Then you recall that ILAsm allows you to export the managed methods as unmanaged entry points, and… I don't think I need to continue.

- You can add the items written in ILAsm to extend your application's functionality beyond the capabilities of a high-level compiler. For example, you can add global fields or methods to applications written in C#.

- Finally, you can disassemble several modules and reassemble them into one module.

Using Class Augmentation

The ILAsm-specific technique of class augmentation can be useful when you want to add new components written in ILAsm to your application written in a high-level language. If you need to add new types, an obvious solution is to declare these classes in a separate ILAsm source file, disassemble your application, and reassemble it with this additional .il file. Class augmentation allows you to apply the same approach if you need to add new members to the types defined in your application. In other words, you don't need to edit the disassembly text of your application, inserting new members in the type definitions, because you can augment the respective type definitions in a separate source file.

For example, suppose that you would like to have a thread local storage (TLS) mapped field in class X defined in your module and a vararg method in class Y (also defined in your module), but the high-level language of your choice does not allow you to specify such items. You can write the following amendment file, Amend.il:

```
.class X
{
    .field public static int32 tlsField at TLSD001
}
.data tls TLSD001 = int32(1234)
.class Y
{
    .method public vararg int64 Sum()
    {
        ...
    }
}
```

Then you can disassemble your original (incomplete) module and reassemble it with an amendment:

```
ildasm MyApp.exe /out:MyApp.il
ilasm MyApp Amend
```

The last line is so laconic because it uses three defaults: the default source file extension (.il), the default output file type and extension (.exe), and the default output filename (the same as the name of the first source file).

Module Linking Through Round-Tripping

Now let's assume that instead of writing the amendment file in ILAsm, you wrote it in another high-level language, compiled it to a module, and then disassembled it. Can you do that? Yes, you can, and it means that round-tripping can be used for linking several modules together to form one. The original language used to write each module does not matter as long as all the modules are pure IL. The modules must be pure IL simply because any mixed-code module will fail to round-trip because of an inability of the IL assembler and disassembler to deal with the embedded native code.

Brad Abrams, a Microsoft colleague I used to work with long ago (I believe in 2001), has written a small tool called Lame Linker, which performed managed module linking through round-tripping. You can have a look at this tool at GotDotNet, http://www.gotdotnet.com/userarea/keywordsrch.aspx?keyword=Lame%20Link. As Brad explained it, he called his linker "lame" because it didn't have many of the features of a good linker. Lame or not, this linker was used rather extensively and has proven to be a useful tool.

Later, I wrote another, less lame module linker called ILLINK and also posted it on GotDotNet as a sample. You can find the ILLINK source code on Apress Web site.

The basic problem with linking multiple modules through round-tripping is that you inevitably run into duplicate declarations. When you write amendment files in ILAsm, you don't need to make sure these files compile per se; they must compile together with the disassembly of the original module. But each module you link *has* been compiled per se, and a significant part of its metadata overlaps with the metadata of other modules being linked.

Let's review the potential effects of multiple declarations of different metadata items.

Multiple Assembly declarations (.assembly) should be avoided. The IL assembler ignores repetitive Assembly declarations as long as the assembly name is the same, but if one of any subsequent declarations specifies a name that differs from that of the first declaration, the compiler diagnoses an error.

Multiple AssemblyRef declarations (.assembly extern) are harmless. The IL assembler ignores them. The same is true for Module declarations (.module), ModuleRef declarations (.module extern), File declarations (.file), and ExportedType declarations (.class extern).

Duplicate ManifestResource declarations (.mresource) should be avoided. The IL assembler will not emit a new ManifestResource record for each declaration encountered, but it will incorporate a copy of the respective managed resource for each .mresource declaration in the output PE file. The resulting PE file will perform as expected, but it will be bloated.

Duplicate member declarations (.field, .method, .event, .property) must be avoided because their presence leads to compilation failure. Duplicate member declarations can happen in two cases only: if you declare a private type in one module and declare an identically named private type in another module so the second type declaration is interpreted by the IL assembler as amendment of the first one and these two types happen to have same-name-and-type members, or if you declare same-name-and-type global fields or methods. Both scenarios are very likely indeed: you usually don't pay much attention to naming private types or global fields and methods because they are an "internal affair" of the module. But when you link several modules to form one, all the private types and global fields and methods from each module wind up together in the resulting module.

Multiple declarations of the module entry point (.entrypoint) must be avoided as well, because they also cause compilation failure.

If several of your original modules use mapped fields, you should watch for duplicate data declarations. ILDASM automatically generates the data labels—D_<data_RVA> for regular data and T_<data_RVA> for TLS data—when it disassembles each original module, so the data labels are almost guaranteed to overlap. Duplicate data labels cause compilation failure.

The list of hazards to watch for in the process of linking through round-tripping looks endless, but in fact all these limitations are reasonable, and their analogs can be found in the traditional linking of object files. Actually, traditional linking is even less tolerant of duplicate definitions. And avoiding (or getting rid of) the dangerous duplications is not rocket science.

The Lame Linker I mentioned earlier eliminated multiple Assembly declarations, but nothing else.

The ILLINK is more sophisticated. It reshuffles the source lines from the disassembled files into "head" and "tail" temporary files, with the manifest declarations and forward class declarations (if any) going to the "head" and class member declarations going to "tail," and in the process of doing that it eliminates duplicate declarations and cross-references between the modules being linked, shifts the v-table entry indexes and export ordinals, and modifies the data labels. You are cordially invited to play with this little tool (524 lines in C including comments) and maybe extend its functionality.

Module linking is necessary whenever you want to create a single-module assembly from a multimodule assembly or a set of assemblies. And it does not matter how you came into possession of the multimodule assembly or a set of assemblies in the first place. Perhaps you developed different modules using different languages. Or perhaps you split your application into subsystems to be developed independently. Or perhaps you split your application for independent development, and the developers of each subsystem chose their own development language. But you don't want to *deploy and service* your product as a set of assemblies and modules, which would be a pain, so here you are.

ASMMETA: Resolving Circular Dependencies

What do you do if you need to do a clean rebuild of a multiassembly project (say, assemblies A, B, and C) in C# or VB .NET (or both), and you have a circular dependency: A references B, B references C, and C references A? The high-level compilers such as C# and VB .NET require all referenced assemblies to be present when you compile an assembly. So which assembly are you going to compile first?

And please don't tell me that it is better to avoid the circular dependencies. I agree whole-heartedly. The question is, what do you do if you have one?

Enter the ASMMETA tool. The ASMMETA is based on the IL disassembler and produces the IL assembly code with some omissions, namely, it does not output the actual IL code of the methods, and it does not output the private members of classes. The drama unfolds as follows (see Figure 19-4):

1. Before starting the rebuild, you run ASMMETA on existing assemblies A, B, and C, producing the IL assembly code files. Or better yet, you take the IL assembly code files you stored in some safe place since the last time you generated the assemblies A, B, and C.

2. You run the IL assembler on the IL assembly code files, producing dummy assemblies A, B, and C. They're "dummies" because those are incomplete assemblies: they don't have the IL code and can't function. But all the metadata pertinent to the assembly identity, the class structure, and the members that might be referenced from other assemblies is present in the dummies. This makes the dummies look, from the point of view of the high-level compilers, exactly like "real" assemblies. The dummies can be

built only because they are built using the IL assembler, which, unlike the high-level compilers, does not care whether the referenced assemblies are present at the compilation time. It does not care for one simple reason: all references in ILAsm are unambiguous and full, so the compiler doesn't need to open and check the referenced assembly to resolve an ambiguity or retrieve missing data.

3. Armed with dummies, which on the outside look exactly like real assemblies, you can rebuild your assemblies A, B, and C in any order. Once you build them, you can run the ASMMETA tool on new assemblies and store the resulting IL assembly code files somewhere for future use. You can also compare old and new IL assembly code files to spot any changes in the "external appearance" of your assemblies.

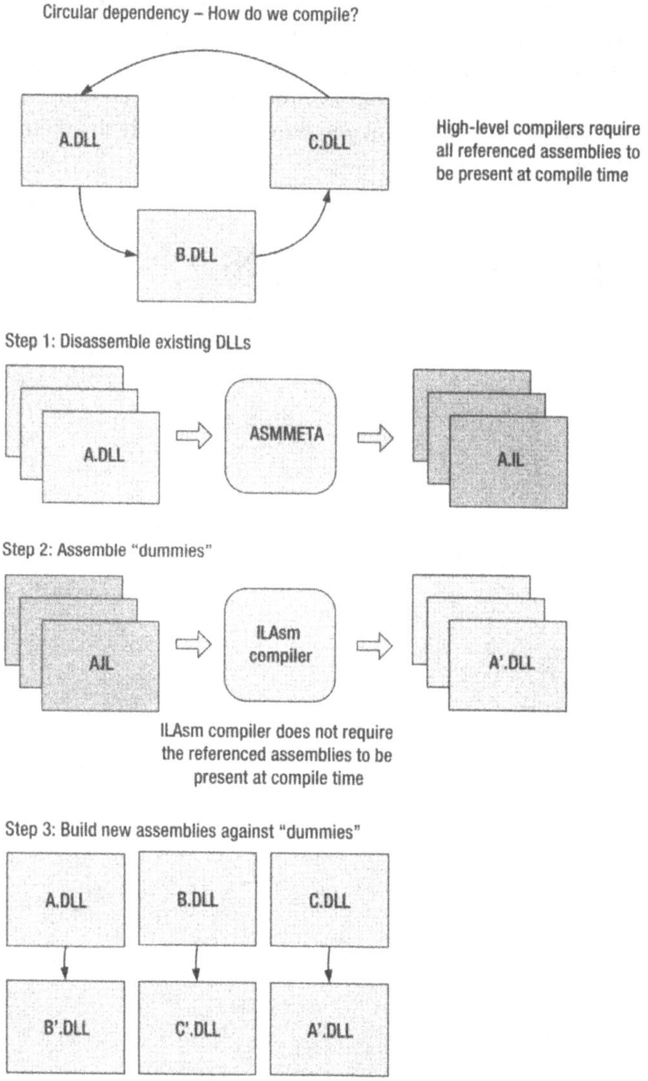

Figure 19-4. *Resolving the circular dependencies with the ASMMETA tool*

The ASMMETA tool and the whole process described previously are used rather extensively at Microsoft when building such large complex systems as .NET Framework and Visual Studio.

The ASMMETA is an internal tool and is not distributed with the .NET Framework SDK, but I am sure you can write a simple tool processing the IL disassembler output that would throw away the method bodies and private members. You can even use "raw" output of the IL disassembler, but throwing away the method bodies has one important advantage: it makes the tool capable of handling the mixed-code assemblies. Another advantage of getting rid of method bodies and private members is that without them you can easily spot the changes in the external appearance of your assembly by comparing the IL assembly code files.

One question (of chicken-and-egg nature) remains unanswered: where do the first IL assembly code files come from? There are two answers: One, as a rule, you don't have a circular dependency from the very beginning of your project. Circular dependencies usually come later (introduced by some enterprising colleague as "great code streamlining"), which means there is a period when you can successfully build your assemblies. Two, in a pinch, you can write the IL assembly code by hand. It is tedious, but you don't need to write the method bodies in ILAsm, so your task is a bit easier.

IL Inlining in High-Level Languages

Mike Stall, my colleague from the common language runtime team, wrote an interesting tool that allows you to insert ILAsm code into the code written in high-level languages such as C# or VB .NET. For example:

```
using System;
class Program
{
    static void Main()
    {
        int x = 3;
        int y = 4;
        int z = 5;
        // Inline IL: "x=x+y+z"
#if IL
        ldloc x
        ldloc y
        add
        ldloc z
        add
        stloc x
#endif
        Console.WriteLine(x);
    }
}
```

The tool, called InlineIL, works as follows (see Figure 19-5):

1. The high-level source is compiled using the respective compiler (C#, VB .NET, and so on) in debug mode (we'll need the PDB file for step 3!). The ILAsm inserts, placed under #if–#endif (or equivalent) pairs, are skipped by the compiler. The resulting module or assembly contains everything except the code defined in the ILAsm inserts.

2. The resulting module or assembly is disassembled, yielding the code in ILAsm.

3. The original source code is analyzed, and the ILAsm inserts are extracted and injected into the disassembly code. The line number information for the injection comes from the PDB file produced in step 1.

4. The modified ILAsm code is assembled. The resulting module or assembly contains everything including the code defined in the ILAsm inserts.

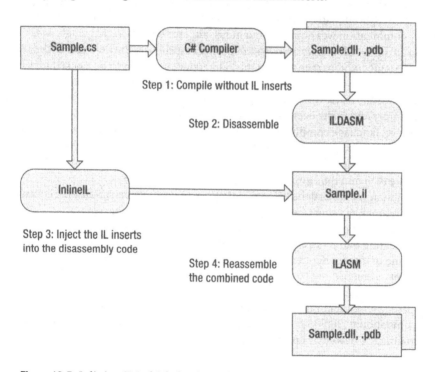

Figure 19-5. *Inlining IL in high-level languages with the InlineIL tool*

Mike has posted this little elegant tool (about 600 lines in C#, including the comments) on his blog (http://blogs.msdn.com/jmstall/archive/2005/02/21/377806.aspx) for everyone to view and play with.

InlineIL is another example of what can be done, and how easily, using the creative round-tripping.

Compiling in Debug Mode

When a managed compiler compiles source code in debug mode, you can expect at least two occurrences. First, the resulting module has the custom attribute [mscorlib]System.Diagnostics.DebuggableAttribute attached to the Module record or, if it is a prime module, to the Assembly record. Second, the compiler produces a PDB file containing data identifying the source files and the compiler itself, the local variable names, and the tables that are binding source lines and columns to the code offsets. Of course, the compiler can perform other tasks as well in debug mode—for example, emitting different IL code.

I need to say several words about the DebuggableAttribute before we proceed. In versions 1.0 and 1.1 of the common language runtime, the constructor of this attribute had two Boolean parameters, the first one indicating whether JIT compiler should track the sequence points defined in the PDB file and the second one indicating whether the JIT compiler optimization is disabled. *Tracking the sequence points* means keeping track of offsets in generated native code corresponding to the IL offsets specified in the sequence points. Obviously, a "false-false" combination was equivalent to not issuing the DebuggableAttribute at all.

Version 2.0 of the CLR offers more sophisticated control over the behavior of the JIT compiler with respect to handling the code points. The sequence points to be tracked may be taken from the PDB file or alternatively may be deduced heuristically "on the fly" by the JIT compiler. The "synthesized" (implicit) sequence points correspond to states when the evaluation stack is empty and to the occurrences of the nop instruction. These heuristics work well for the high-level language compilers, because these compilers usually emit the IL code so that every complete statement in the high-level language begins and ends with the evaluation stack empty. Using the implicit sequence points reduces the overhead of loading the sequence points from the PDB and thus improves the JIT compiler performance.

Accordingly, in version 2.0 the DebuggableAttribute was given an additional constructor, taking as an argument a value of enumeration [mscorlib]System.Diagnostics.DebuggableAttribute/DebuggingModes (an integer value). This value is an OR combination of flag 0x100 indicating that JIT optimizations should be disabled, of flag 0x2 indicating that JIT compiler should ignore the sequence points defined in the PDB and generate the implicit sequence points instead, and of flag 0x1 indicating that the sequence points (wherever they come from) should be tracked.

The old-style constructor of the DebuggableAttribute is preserved in version 2.0 for backward compatibility. Table 19-1 shows correspondence between arguments of the old-style constructor, the new-style constructor, and the ILAsm compiler command-line option.

Table 19-1. *Correspondence of Debuggable Attribute Constructor Arguments and ILAsm Options*

Old-Style Constructor	New-Style Constructor	ILAsm Compiler Option
(true, true)	0x0101	/DEBUG
(true, false)	0x0003	/DEBUG=OPT
(true, true)	0x0103	/DEBUG=IMP

When a module is round-tripped, or when a high-level compiler produces the ILAsm source code as an intermediate step, it is usually desirable to preserve the debug information binding the original source code to the final IL code so the original source code could be displayed correctly (and stepped through) in a debugger and the error messages would indicate correct lines in the original source. ILAsm provides two directives facilitating this:

- The .language <Language_GUID>[,<Vendor_GUID>[,<Document_GUID>]] directive defines the source language and, optionally, the compiler vendor and the source document type. This information is used by the Visual Studio debugger, which displays source code of different languages differently.

- The .line <start_line>[,<end_line>][:<start_col> [,<end_col>]] [<file_name>] directive identifies the line and column in the original source file that are "responsible" for the IL code that follows the .line directive.

For example, the following C# code

```
using System;

public class arr
{
    private static int[,] MakeArray() {
        return (int[,])Array.CreateInstance(typeof(int),
            new int[]{2,3}, new int[]{-1, 0});
    }

    private static void Main() {
        int[,] _aTgt = MakeArray();
        foreach (int i in _aTgt) {
            Console.Write(i + " ");
        }
    }
}
```

compiled in debug mode, is disassembled, using the option *ILINENUM*, into the following ILAsm code:

```
...
.class public auto ansi beforefieldinit arr
       extends [mscorlib]System.Object
{
    .method private hidebysig static int32[0...,0...]
            MakeArray() cil managed
    {
      // Code size      53 (0x35)
      .maxstack  5
```

```
    .locals init ([0] int32[0...,0...] CS$00000003$00000000,
            [1] int32[] CS$00000002$00000001,
            [2] int32[] CS$00000002$00000002)
    .language '{3F5162F8-07C6-11D3-9053- 00C04FA302A1}',
            '{994B45C4-E6E9-11D2-903F- 00C04FA302A1}',
            '{5A869D0B-6611-11D3-BD2A- 0000F80849BD}'
    .line 6,7:7,44 'C:\\MyDirectory\\arr.cs'
    IL_0000:    ldtoken     [mscorlib]System.Int32
    IL_0005:    call class [mscorlib]System.Type
                [mscorlib]System.Type::GetTypeFromHandle(
                    valuetype [mscorlib]System.RuntimeType Handle)
    IL_000a:    ldc.i4.2
    IL_000b:    newarr      [mscorlib]System.Int32
    IL_0010:    stloc.1
    IL_0011:    ldloc.1
    IL_0012:    ldc.i4.0
    IL_0013:    ldc.i4.2
    IL_0014:    stelem.i4
    IL_0015:    ldloc.1
    IL_0016:    ldc.i4.1
    IL_0017:    ldc.i4.3
    IL_0018:    stelem.i4
    IL_0019:    ldloc.1
    IL_001a:    ldc.i4.2
    IL_001b:    newarr      [mscorlib]System.Int32
    IL_0020:    stloc.2
    IL_0021:    ldloc.2
    IL_0022:    ldc.i4.0
    IL_0023:    ldc.i4.m1
    IL_0024:    stelem.i4
    IL_0025:    ldloc.2
    IL_0026:    call class [mscorlib]System.Array
                [mscorlib]System.Array::CreateInstance(
                        class [mscorlib]System.Type,
                        int32[],
                        int32[])
    IL_002b:    castclass   int32[0...,0...]
    IL_0030:    stloc.0
    IL_0031:    br.s        IL_0033

    .line 8,8:4,5
    IL_0033:    ldloc.0
    IL_0034:    ret
} // End of method arr::MakeArray


.method private hidebysig static void  Main() cil managed
{
```

```
.entrypoint
// Code size       103 (0x67)
.maxstack  3
.locals init ([0] int32[0...,0...] _aTgt,
       [1] int32 i,
       [2] int32[0...,0...] CS$00000007$00000000,
       [3] int32 CS$00000264$00000001,
       [4] int32 CS$00000265$00000002,
       [5] int32 CS$00000008$00000003,
       [6] int32 CS$00000009$00000004)
.line 11,11:7,34
IL_0000:  call        int32[0...,0...] arr::MakeArray()
IL_0005:  stloc.0
.line 12,12:25,30
IL_0006:  ldloc.0
IL_0007:  stloc.2
IL_0008:  ldloc.2
IL_0009:  ldc.i4.0
IL_000a:  callvirt instance int32
          [mscorlib]System.Array::GetUpperBound(int32)
IL_000f:  stloc.3
IL_0010:  ldloc.2
IL_0011:  ldc.i4.1
IL_0012:  callvirt    instance int32
          [mscorlib]System.Array::GetUpperBound(int32)
IL_0017:  stloc.s     CS$00000265$00000002
IL_0019:  ldloc.2
IL_001a:  ldc.i4.0
IL_001b:  callvirt    instance int32
          [mscorlib]System.Array::GetLowerBound(int32)
IL_0020:  stloc.s     CS$00000008$00000003
IL_0022:  br.s        IL_0061

IL_0024:  ldloc.2
IL_0025:  ldc.i4.1
IL_0026:  callvirt    instance int32
          [mscorlib]System.Array::GetLowerBound(int32)
IL_002b:  stloc.s     CS$00000009$00000004
IL_002d:  br.s        IL_0055

.line 12,12:16,21
IL_002f:  ldloc.2
IL_0030:  ldloc.s     CS$00000008$00000003
IL_0032:  ldloc.s     CS$00000009$00000004
IL_0034:  call
          instance int32 int32[0...,0...]::Get(int32, int32)
IL_0039:  stloc.1
```

```
    .line 12,12:32,33
    IL_003a:  ldloc.1
    IL_003b:  box         [mscorlib]System.Int32
    IL_0040:  ldstr       " "
    IL_0045:  call        string
              [mscorlib]System.String::Concat(object, object)
    IL_004a:  call void [mscorlib]System.Console::Write (string)
    .line 14,14:7,8
    IL_004f:  ldloc.s     CS$00000009$00000004
    IL_0051:  ldc.i4.1
    IL_0052:  add
    IL_0053:  stloc.s     CS$00000009$00000004
    .line 12,12:22,24
    IL_0055:  ldloc.s     CS$00000009$00000004
    IL_0057:  ldloc.s     CS$00000265$00000002
    IL_0059:  ble.s       IL_002f


    .line 12,12:22,24
    IL_005b:  ldloc.s     CS$00000008$00000003
    IL_005d:  ldc.i4.1
    IL_005e:  add
    IL_005f:  stloc.s     CS$00000008$00000003
    IL_0061:  ldloc.s     CS$00000008$00000003
    IL_0063:  ldloc.3
    IL_0064:  ble.s       IL_0024


    .line 15,15:4,5
    IL_0066:  ret
} // End of method arr::Main

.method public hidebysig specialname rtspecialname
        instance void  .ctor() cil managed
{
    // Code size       7 (0x7)
    .maxstack  1
    IL_0000:  ldarg.0
    IL_0001:  call
              instance void [mscorlib]System.Object::.ctor()
    IL_0006:  ret
} // End of method arr::.ctor


} // End of class arr
```

The .language directive sets the GUIDs for all the following code until it is superseded by another .language directive.

The `.line` directive has five parameters: starting line, ending line, starting column, ending column, and file name:

`.line <start_line>, <end_line> : <start_col>, <end_col> '<file_name>'`

All start/end parameters are 1-based integers. All parameters except the `<start_line>` may be omitted; in this case they are replaced with the following default values:

- `<end_line>` = `<start_line>`

- `<end_col>` = `<start_col>`

- `<start_col>` = `1`

- `<file_name>` = taken from the previous `.line` directive

The `.line` directive had a problem in the first release of the IL assembler and disassembler: the directive specified only the starting line and column of the original source statement that had been compiled into ILAsm code following the `.line` directive. This didn't bode well for the Microsoft Visual Studio debugger, which wanted to see the line/column interval (starting line and column and ending line and column) for each original source statement. This problem was corrected in version 2.0.

In short, if you want the resulting code to be bound to the original source code, you need to do the following:

- If your compiler generates ILAsm source code, it must insert `.language` and `.line` directives at the appropriate points.

- If you are round-tripping a module compiled from a high-level language, use the disassembler option /LINENUM (or /LIN).

- In any case, don't forget to use one of the PDB-generating options of the ILAsm compiler: /DEB, /DEB=OPT, /DEB=IMP, or /PDB (the last option generates the PDB file but doesn't emit the DebuggableAttribute).

In conclusion, let me show you one more trick with round-tripping. It's not a big secret that the Visual Studio debugger (and other popular debuggers such as WinDbg) can show you only two views of your code—the original source code and the JIT-compiled platform (machine) code. But the managed code has in fact three views—the source code, the IL code, and the platform code—and sometimes people want to see all three (from sheer curiosity, I presume). If you are one of those curious individuals, try the following:

1. Compile your application in debug mode so the compiler creates the PDB file.

2. Disassemble your application with option /SOURCE (/SOU); the disassembler will read your PDB file, identify the source files and lines in them corresponding to the IL code in your application, and read the source files and insert the original source lines as comments into the disassembly. The PDB file and the source files, of course, must be available for option /SOURCE to work; the resulting disassembly text will contain ILAsm code plus the original source code (as the comments).

3. Assemble the resulting ILAsm code with option */DEBUG* (*/DEB*); do not use option */DEB=OPT* or */DEB=IMP*, because then the sequence points defined in the PDB will be ignored, or some IL instructions may be optimized out, and as the result the debugger won't be able to walk all IL instructions step by step.

4. Run the reassembled application under the debugger; there will still be only two views (well, we didn't really do anything about the debugger)—the ILAsm and machine code, but the ILAsm code will contain your original source code as comments.

Summary

As you can see, the creative round-tripping offers you a world of possibilities. And these possibilities come cheap: your tools work at the text analysis and editing level, without any concern about emitting correct file headers, metadata structure, and so on.

And if you happen to be a compiler writer implementing a new managed language, ask yourself what is more important for you—implementing your compiler the easiest way (emitting the ILAsm source and letting the assembler take care of the rest) and spending your time fine-tuning it, or showing the world you're a "real macho" and spending your time fiddling with the managed file generation. Many respectable (to say the least) compiler writers already decided they are macho enough and took the first approach, as I mentioned in the introduction.

PART 6

Appendixes

APPENDIX A

■ ■ ■

ILAsm Grammar Reference

Lexical Tokens

ID - C style alphanumeric identifier (e.g. Hello_There2)
DOTTEDNAME - Sequence of dot-separated IDs (e.g. System.Object)
QSTRING - C style quoted string (e.g. "hi\n")
SQSTRING – single-quoted string(e.g. 'hi')
INT32   - C style 32 bit integer (e.g. 235, 03423, 0x34FFF)
INT64   - C style 64 bit integer (e.g. -2353453636235234, 0x34FFFFFFFFFF)
FLOAT64 - C style floating point number (e.g. -0.2323, 354.3423, 3435.34E-5)
INSTR_* - IL instructions of a particular class (see opcode.def).
HEXBYTE - 1- or 2-digit hexadecimal number (e.g., A2, F0).
ILAsm keywords are in bold (e.g., **.class**, **valuetype**, **marshal**).
Comments are enclosed in pairs /* */ (e.g., /* This is a comment */).

Auxiliary Lexical Tokens

TYPEDEF_T - Aliased class (TypeDef or TypeRef).
TYPEDEF_M - Aliased method.
TYPEDEF_F - Aliased field.
TYPEDEF_TS - Aliased type specification (TypeSpec).
TYPEDEF_MR - Aliased field/method reference (MemberRef).
TYPEDEF_CA - Aliased Custom Attribute.

Data Type Nonterminals

compQstring ::= QSTRING | *compQstring* + QSTRING
int32 ::= INT64
int64 ::= INT64
float64 ::= FLOAT64 | **float32**(*int32*) | **float64**(*int64*)
bytes ::= /* EMPTY */ | *hexbytes*
hexbytes ::= HEXBYTE | *hexbytes* HEXBYTE
truefalse ::= **true** | **false**
mdtoken ::= **mdtoken** (*int32*)

Identifier Nonterminals

id ::= ID | SQSTRING
dottedName ::= *id* | DOTTEDNAME | *dottedName.dottedName*
slashedName ::= *dottedName* | *slashedName/dottedName*

Class Referencing

className ::= [*dottedName*] *slashedName*
        | [*mdtoken*] *slashedName*
        | [*] *slashedName*
        | [**.module** *dottedName*] *slashedName*
        | *slashedName*
        | *mdtoken*
        | TYPEDEF_T
        | **.this**
        | **.base**
        | **.nester**

classNameSeq ::= /* EMPTY */ | *className classNameSeq*

Module-Level Declarations

PROGRAM ::= *decls*
decls ::= /* EMPTY */ | *decls decl*

decl ::= *moduleParamDecl*
    | *manifestDecl*
    | *classHead* { *classDecls* }
    | **.namespace** *dottedName* { *decls* } /* obsolete */
    | *methodHead   methodDecls* }
    | *fieldDecl*
    | *dataDecl*
    | *extSourceSpec*
    | *secDecl*
    | *customAttrDecl*
    | *languageDecl*
    | *typedefDecl*
    | *compControl*

Compilation Control Directives

```
compControl ::= #define dottedName
            | #define dottedName QSTRING
            | #undef dottedName
            | #ifdef dottedName
            | #ifndef dottedName
            | #else
            | #endif
            | #include QSTRING
            | ;
```

Module Parameter Declaration

```
moduleParamDecl ::= .subsystem int32
                | .corflags int32
                | .file alignment int32
                | .imagebase int64
                | .stackreserve int64
                | .typelist { classNameSeq }
                | .mscorlib
                | vtableDecl /* deprecated, use .vtfixup instead */
                | vtfixupDecl
```

V-Table Fixup Table Declaration

```
vtfixupDecl ::= .vtfixup [ int32 ] vtfixupAttr at id

vtfixupAttr ::= /* EMPTY */
            | vtfixupAttr int32
            | vtfixupAttr int64
            | vtfixupAttr fromunmanaged
            | vtfixupAttr callmostderived   /* unused */
            | vtfixupAttr retainappdomain   /* unused */

vtableDecl ::= .vtable = ( bytes )    /* deprecated, use .vtfixup instead */
```

Manifest Declarations

```
manifestDecl ::= .module
              | .module dottedName
              | .module extern dottedName
              | assemblyHead { assemblyDecls }
              | assemblyRefHead { assemblyRefDecls }
              | fileDecl
              | exptypeHead { exptypeDecls }
              | manifestResHead { manifestResDecls }
              | moduleHead


assemblyHead ::= .assembly asmAttr dottedName


asmAttr ::= /* EMPTY */
         | asmAttr retargetable
         | asmAttr legacy library /* for backward compatibility only */
         | asmAttr cil
         | asmAttr x86
         | asmAttr ia64
         | asmAttr amd64


assemblyDecls ::= /* EMPTY */
              | assemblyDecls assemblyDecl


assemblyDecl ::= .hash algorithm int32
             | secDecl
             | asmOrRefDecl


intOrWildcard ::= int32 | *


asmOrRefDecl ::= .publickey = ( bytes )
             | .ver intOrWildcard : intOrWildcard : intOrWildcard : intOrWildcard
             | .locale compQstring
             | .locale = ( bytes )
             | customAttrDecl
             | compControl


assemblyRefHead ::= .assembly extern asmAttr dottedName
                | .assembly extern asmAttr dottedName as dottedName


assemblyRefDecls ::= /* EMPTY */
                 | assemblyRefDecls assemblyRefDecl


assemblyRefDecl ::= .hash = ( bytes )
                | asmOrRefDecl
                | .publickeytoken = ( bytes )
                | auto
```

```
fileDecl ::= .file fileAttr dottedName fileEntry .hash = ( bytes ) fileEntry
           | .file fileAttr dottedName fileEntry


fileAttr ::= /* EMPTY */
           | fileAttr nometadata


fileEntry ::= /* EMPTY */
            | .entrypoint


exptypeHead ::= .class extern exptAttr dottedName


exptAttr ::= /* EMPTY */
           | exptAttr private
           | exptAttr public
           | exptAttr forwarder
           | exptAttr nested public
           | exptAttr nested private
           | exptAttr nested family
           | exptAttr nested assembly
           | exptAttr nested famandassem
           | exptAttr nested famorassem


exptypeDecls ::= /* EMPTY */
               | exptypeDecls exptypeDecl


exptypeDecl ::= .file dottedName
              | .class extern slashedName
              | .assembly extern dottedName
              | mdtoken ( int32 )
              | .class int32
              | customAttrDecl
              | compControl


manifestResHead ::= .mresource manresAttr dottedName
                  | .mresource manresAttr dottedName as dottedName


manresAttr ::= /* EMPTY */
             | manresAttr public
             | manresAttr private


manifestResDecls ::= /* EMPTY */
                   | manifestResDecls manifestResDecl


manifestResDecl ::= .file dottedName at int32
                  | .assembly extern dottedName
                  | customAttrDecl
                  | compControl
```

Managed Types in Signatures

```
type ::= class className
     | value class className
     | valuetype className
     | type [ ]
     | type [ bounds ]
     | type &
     | type *
     | type pinned
     | type modreq ( typeSpec )
     | type modopt ( typeSpec )
     | method callConv type * ( sigArgs0 )
     | type < tyArgs >
     | ! ! int32
     | ! int32
     | ! ! dottedName
     | ! dottedName
     | object
     | typedref
     | void
     | native int
     | native unsigned int
     | native uint
     | native float
     | simpleType
     | ... type


simpleType ::= char
          | string
          | bool
          | intType
          | float32
          | float64
          | TYPEDEF_TS


intType ::= int8
        | int16
        | int32
        | int64
        | unsigned int8
        | unsigned int16
        | unsigned int32
        | unsigned int64
        | uint8
        | uint16
        | uint32
        | uint64
```

```
bounds ::= bound | bounds , bound

bound ::= /* EMPTY */
     | ...
     | int32
     | int32 ... int32
     | int32 ...

typeSpec ::= className
        | [ dottedName ]
        | [ .module dottedName ]
        | type
```

Native Types in Marshaling Signatures

```
nativeType ::= /* EMPTY */
        | custom ( compQstring , compQstring , compQstring , compQstring )
        | custom ( compQstring , compQstring )
        | fixed sysstring [ int32 ]
        | fixed array [ int32 ] nativeType
        | variant
        | currency
        | syschar
        | void
        | bool
        | intType
        | float32
        | float64
        | error
        | nativeType *
        | nativeType [ ]
        | nativeType [ int32 ]
        | nativeType [ int32 + int32 ]
        | nativeType [ + int32 ]
        | decimal
        | date
        | bstr
        | lpstr
        | lpwstr
        | lptstr
        | objectref
        | iunknown iidParamIndex
        | idispatch iidParamIndex
        | struct
        | interface iidParamIndex
        | safearray variantType
        | safearray variantType , compQstring
```

```
            | int
            | unsigned int
            | uint
            | nested struct
            | byvalstr
            | ansi bstr
            | tbstr
            | variant bool
            | method
            | as any
            | lpstruct
            | TYPEDEF_TS

iidParamIndex ::= /* EMPTY */ | ( iidparam = int32 )

variantType ::= /* EMPTY */
            | null
            | variant
            | currency
            | void
            | bool
            | intType
            | float32
            | float64
            | *
            | variantType [ ]
            | variantType vector
            | variantType &
            | decimal
            | date
            | bstr
            | lpstr
            | lpwstr
            | iunknown
            | idispatch
            | safearray
            | int
            | unsigned int
            | uint
            | error
            | hresult
            | carray
            | userdefined
            | record
            | filetime
            | blob
            | stream
```

```
                    | storage
                    | streamed_object
                    | stored_object
                    | blob_object
                    | cf
                    | clsid
```

Method and Field Referencing

methodRef ::= *callConv type typeSpec* :: *methodName tyArgs0* (*sigArgs0*)
      | *callConv type methodName tyArgs0* (*sigArgs0*)
      | *mdtoken*
      | TYPEDEF_M
      | TYPEDEF_MR

genMethodRef ::= **method** *callConv type typeSpec* :: *methodName genArity* (*sigArgs0*)

callConv ::= **instance** *callConv*
      | **explicit** *callConv*
      | *callKind*
      | **callconv** (*int32*)

callKind ::= /* EMPTY */
      | **default**
      | **vararg**
      | **unmanaged cdecl**
      | **unmanaged stdcall**
      | **unmanaged thiscall**
      | **unmanaged fastcall**

methodName ::= **.ctor**
      | **.cctor**
      | *dottedName*

genArity ::= /* EMPTY */
      | < [*int32*] >

tyArgs0 ::= /* EMPTY */ | < *tyArgs* >

tyArgs ::= /* EMPTY */ | *tyArgsNotEmpty*

tyArgsNotEmpty := *type* | *tyArgsNotEmpty* , *type*

sigArgs0 ::= /* EMPTY */ | *sigArgsNotEmpty*

sigArgsNotEmpty ::= *sigArg* | *sigArgsNotEmpty* , *sigArg*

```
sigArg ::= ...   /* ellipsis */
        | paramAttr type marshalClause
        | paramAttr type marshalClause id

fieldRef ::= type typeSpec :: dottedName
           | type dottedName
           | TYPEDEF_F
           | TYPEDEF_MR
           | mdtoken

memberRef ::= method methodRef
            | field fieldRef
```

Class Declaration

```
classHead ::= classHeadBegin extendsClause implClause

classHeadBegin ::= .class classAttr dottedName typarsClause

classAttr ::= /* EMPTY */
            | classAttr public
            | classAttr private
            | classAttr value
            | classAttr enum
            | classAttr interface
            | classAttr sealed
            | classAttr abstract
            | classAttr auto
            | classAttr sequential
            | classAttr explicit
            | classAttr ansi
            | classAttr unicode
            | classAttr autochar
            | classAttr import
            | classAttr serializable
            | classAttr nested public
            | classAttr nested private
            | classAttr nested family
            | classAttr nested assembly
            | classAttr nested famandassem
            | classAttr nested famorassem
            | classAttr beforefieldinit
            | classAttr specialname
            | classAttr rtspecialname
            | classAttr flags ( int32 )
```

```
extendsClause ::= /* EMPTY */
              | extends typeSpec

implClause ::= /* EMPTY */
             | implements implList

implList ::= implList , typeSpec
           | typeSpec
```

Generic Type Parameters Declaration

```
typeList ::= /* EMPTY */
           | typeListNotEmpty

typeListNotEmpty ::= typeSpec
                   | typeListNotEmpty , typeSpec

typarsClause ::= /* EMPTY */
               | < typars >

typarAttrib ::= + | - | class | valuetype | .ctor

typarAttribs ::= /* EMPTY */
               | typarAttrib typarAttribs

typars ::= typarAttribs tyBound dottedName typarsRest
         | typarAttribs dottedName typarsRest

typarsRest ::= /* EMPTY */
             | , typars

tyBound ::= ( typeList )
```

Class Body Declarations

```
classDecls ::= /* EMPTY */
             | classDecls classDecl

classDecl ::= methodHead  methodDecls }
            | classHead { classDecls }
            | eventHead { eventDecls }
            | propHead { propDecls }
            | fieldDecl
            | dataDecl
```

```
| secDecl
| extSourceSpec
| customAttrDecl
| .size int32
| .pack int32
| .override typeSpec :: methodName with
    callConv type typeSpec :: methodName ( sigArgs0 )
| .override genMethodRef with genMethodRef
| languageDecl
| compControl
| .param type [ int32 ]
| .param type dottedName
```

Field Declaration

fieldDecl ::= **.field** *repeatOpt fieldAttr marshalClause type dottedName atOpt initOpt*

```
fieldAttr ::= /* EMPTY */
            | fieldAttr static
            | fieldAttr public
            | fieldAttr private
            | fieldAttr family
            | fieldAttr assembly
            | fieldAttr famandassem
            | fieldAttr famorassem
            | fieldAttr privatescope
            | fieldAttr initonly
            | fieldAttr rtspecialname
            | fieldAttr specialname
            | fieldAttr literal
            | fieldAttr notserialized
            | fieldAttr flags ( int32 )
```

```
marshalClause ::= /* EMPTY */
                | marshal ( nativeType )
```

```
atOpt ::= /* EMPTY */
       | at id
```

```
initOpt ::= /* EMPTY */
         | = fieldInit
```

```
repeatOpt ::= /* EMPTY */
           | [ int32 ]
```

Method Declaration

methodHead ::= **.method** *methAttr callConv paramAttr type marshalClause*
                    methodName typarsClause (*sigArgs0*) *implAttr* {

methAttr ::= /* EMPTY */
       | *methAttr* **static**
       | *methAttr* **public**
       | *methAttr* **private**
       | *methAttr* **family**
       | *methAttr* **assembly**
       | *methAttr* **famandassem**
       | *methAttr* **famorassem**
       | *methAttr* **privatescope** /* default */
       | *methAttr* **final**
       | *methAttr* **virtual**
       | *methAttr* **strict**
       | *methAttr* **abstract**
       | *methAttr* **hidebysig**
       | *methAttr* **newslot**
       | *methAttr* **specialname**
       | *methAttr* **rtspecialname**
       | *methAttr* **unmanagedexp** /* unused */
       | *methAttr* **reqsecobj**
       | *methAttr* **flags** (*int32*)
       | *methAttr* **pinvokeimpl** (*compQstring* **as** *compQstring pinvAttr*)
       | *methAttr* **pinvokeimpl** (*compQstring* *pinvAttr*)
       | *methAttr* **pinvokeimpl** (*pinvAttr*)

pinvAttr ::= /* EMPTY */
       | *pinvAttr* **nomangle**
       | *pinvAttr* **ansi**
       | *pinvAttr* **unicode**
       | *pinvAttr* **autochar**
       | *pinvAttr* **lasterr**
       | *pinvAttr* **winapi**
       | *pinvAttr* **cdecl**
       | *pinvAttr* **stdcall**
       | *pinvAttr* **thiscall**
       | *pinvAttr* **fastcall**
       | *pinvAttr* **bestfit** : **on**
       | *pinvAttr* **bestfit** : **off**
       | *pinvAttr* **charmaperror** : **on**
       | *pinvAttr* **charmaperror** : **off**
       | *pinvAttr* **flags** (*int32*)

```
paramAttr ::= /* EMPTY */
          | paramAttr [ in ]
          | paramAttr [ out ]
          | paramAttr [ opt ]
          | paramAttr [ int32 ]


implAttr ::= /* EMPTY */
          | implAttr native
          | implAttr cil        /* default */
          | implAttr optil      /* unused */
          | implAttr managed    /* default */
          | implAttr unmanaged
          | implAttr forwardref
          | implAttr preservesig
          | implAttr runtime
          | implAttr internalcall
          | implAttr synchronized
          | implAttr noinlining
          | implAttr flags ( int32 )
```

Method Body Declarations

```
methodDecls ::= /* EMPTY */
          | methodDecls methodDecl


methodDecl ::= .emitbyte int32
          | mehBlock
          | .maxstack int32
          | .locals ( sigArgs0 )
          | .locals init ( sigArgs0 )
          | .entrypoint
          | .zeroinit    /* deprecated, use .locals init */
          | dataDecl
          | instr
          | id :          /* label */
          | secDecl
          | extSourceSpec
          | languageDecl
          | customAttrDecl
          | compControl
          | .export [ int32 ]
          | .export [ int32 ] as id
          | .vtentry int32 : int32
          | .override typeSpec :: methodName
          | .override genMethodRef
          | scopeBlock
          | .param type [ int32 ]
```

```
        | .param type dottedName
        | .param [ int32 ] initOpt

scopeBlock ::= { methodDecls }
```

External Source Directives

```
languageDecl ::= .language SQSTRING
             | .language SQSTRING , SQSTRING
             | .language SQSTRING , SQSTRING , SQSTRING

extSourceSpec ::= esHead int32 SQSTRING
             | esHead int32
             | esHead int32 : int32 SQSTRING
             | esHead int32 : int32
             | esHead int32 : int32 , int32 SQSTRING
             | esHead int32 : int32 , int32
             | esHead int32 , int32 : int32 SQSTRING
             | esHead int32 , int32 : int32
             | esHead int32 , int32 : int32 , int32 SQSTRING
             | esHead int32 , int32 : int32 , int32
             | esHead int32 QSTRING

esHead ::= .line | #line
```

Managed Exception Handling Directives

```
mehBlock ::= tryBlock mehClauses

mehClauses ::= mehClause mehClauses
           | mehClause

tryBlock ::= .try scopeBlock
         | .try id to id
         | .try int32 to int32

mehClause ::= catch typeSpec handlerBlock
          | filterClause handlerBlock
          | finally handlerBlock
          | fault handlerBlock

filterClause ::= filter scopeBlock
             | filter id
             | filter int32

handlerBlock ::= scopeBlock
             | handler id to id
             | handler int32 to int32
```

IL Instructions

```
instr ::= INSTR_NONE /* nop, add, ldc.i4.1, ldnull, ldarg.0, and so on */
        | INSTR_VAR int32 /* ldarg, ldarga, starg, ldloc, ldloca, stloc */
        | INSTR_VAR id
        | INSTR_I int32   /* ldc.i4 */
        | INSTR_I8 int64 /* ldc.i8 */
        | INSTR_R float64 /* ldc.r4, ldc.r8 */
        | INSTR_R int64
        | INSTR_R ( bytes )
        | INSTR_BRTARGET int32 /* br, beq, ble, brtrue, etc. */
        | INSTR_BRTARGET id
        | INSTR_METHOD methodRef /* call, callvirt, jmp, ldftn, ldvirtftn, newobj */
        | INSTR_FIELD fieldRef  /* ldfld, stfld, ldflda, ldsflda, stfld, stsfld */
        | INSTR_TYPE typeSpec    /* ldobj, stobj, box, unbox, newarr, etc. */
        | INSTR_STRING compQstring  /* ldstr */
        | INSTR_STRING ansi ( compQstring )
        | INSTR_STRING bytearray = ( bytes )
        | INSTR_SIG callConv type ( sigArgs0 ) /* calli */
        | INSTR_TOK ownerType /* ldtoken; ownerType ::= memberRef | typeSpec */
        | INSTR_SWITCH ( labels )

labels ::= /* EMPTY */
         | id , labels
         | int32 , labels
         | id
         | int32
```

Event Declaration

```
eventHead ::= .event eventAttr typeSpec dottedName
            | .event eventAttr dottedName

eventAttr ::= /* EMPTY */
            | eventAttr rtspecialname
            | eventAttr specialname

eventDecls ::= /* EMPTY */
             | eventDecls eventDecl

eventDecl ::= .addon methodRef
            | .removeon methodRef
            | .fire methodRef
            | .other methodRef
            | extSourceSpec
            | customAttrDecl
            | languageDecl
            | compControl
```

Property Declaration

propHead ::= **.property** *propAttr callConv type dottedName* (*sigArgs0*) *initOpt*

propAttr ::= /* EMPTY */
       | *propAttr* **rtspecialname**
       | *propAttr* **specialname**

propDecls ::= /* EMPTY */
       | *propDecls propDecl*

propDecl ::= **.set** *methodRef*
       | **.get** *methodRef*
       | **.other** *methodRef*
       | *extSourceSpec*
       | *customAttrDecl*
       | *languageDecl*
       | *compControl*

Constant Declarations

/* Default values declaration for fields, properties, parameters
    and verbal form of Custom Attribute blob description */

/* Field/property/parameter initialization */
fieldInit ::= *fieldSerInit*
       | *compQstring*
       | **nullref**

fieldSerInit ::= **float32** (*float64*)
         | **float64** (*float64*)
         | **float32** (*int32*)
         | **float64** (*int64*)
         | **int64** (*int64*)
         | **int32** (*int32*)
         | **int16** (*int32*)
         | **int8** (*int32*)
         | **unsigned int64** (*int64*)
         | **unsigned int32** (*int32*)
         | **unsigned int16** (*int32*)
         | **unsigned int8** (*int32*)
         | **uint64** (*int64*)
         | **uint32** (*int32*)
         | **uint16** (*int32*)
         | **uint8** (*int32*)
         | **char** (*int32*)
         | **bool** (*truefalse*)
         | **bytearray** (*bytes*)

```
/* Values for verbal form of CA blob description */
serInit ::= fieldSerInit
        | string ( nullref )
        | string ( SQSTRING )
        | type ( class SQSTRING ) /* class name specified in Reflection notation */
        | type ( className ) /* class name specified in ILAsm notation */
        | type ( nullref )
        | object ( serInit )
        | float32 [ int32 ] ( f32seq )
        | float64 [ int32 ] ( f64seq )
        | int64 [ int32 ] ( i64seq )
        | int32 [ int32 ] ( i32seq )
        | int16 [ int32 ] ( i16seq )
        | int8 [ int32 ] ( i8seq )
        | uint64 [ int32 ] ( i64seq )
        | uint32 [ int32 ] ( i32seq )
        | uint16 [ int32 ] ( i16seq )
        | uint8 [ int32 ] ( i8seq )
        | unsigned int64 [ int32 ] ( i64seq )
        | unsigned int32 [ int32 ] ( i32seq )
        | unsigned int16 [ int32 ] ( i16seq )
        | unsigned int8 [ int32 ] ( i8seq )
        | char [ int32 ] ( i16seq )
        | bool [ int32 ] ( boolSeq )
        | string [ int32 ] ( sqstringSeq )
        | type [ int32 ] ( classSeq )
        | object [ int32 ] ( objSeq )

f32seq ::= /* EMPTY */
        | f32seq float64
        | f32seq int32

f64seq ::= /* EMPTY */
        | f64seq float64
        | f64seq int64

i64seq ::= /* EMPTY */ | i64seq int64

i32seq ::= /* EMPTY */ | i32seq int32

i16seq ::= /* EMPTY */ | i16seq int32

i8seq  ::= /* EMPTY */ | i8seq int32

boolSeq ::= /* EMPTY */ | boolSeq truefalse

sqstringSeq ::= /* EMPTY */
            | sqstringSeq nullref
            | sqstringSeq SQSTRING
```

```
classSeq ::= /* EMPTY */
        | classSeq nullref
        | classSeq class SQSTRING /* class name specified in Reflection notation */
        | classSeq className /* class name specified in ILAsm notation */

objSeq ::= /* EMPTY */ | objSeq serInit
```

Custom Attribute Declarations

```
customAttrDecl ::= customDescr
              | customDescrWithOwner
              | TYPEDEF_CA


customDescr ::= .custom customType
            | .custom customType = compQstring
            | .custom customType = { customBlobDescr }
            | .custom customType = ( bytes )


customDescrWithOwner ::= .custom ( ownerType ) customType
            | .custom ( ownerType ) customType = compQstring
            | .custom ( ownerType ) customType = { customBlobDescr }
            | .custom ( ownerType ) customType = ( bytes )


customType ::= methodRef /* method must be .ctor */


ownerType ::= typeSpec | memberRef
```

Verbal Description of Custom Attribute Initialization Blob

```
customBlobDescr ::= customBlobArgs customBlobNVPairs


customBlobArgs ::= /* EMPTY */
              | customBlobArgs serInit
              | customBlobArgs compControl


customBlobNVPairs ::= /* EMPTY */
              | customBlobNVPairs fieldOrProp serializType dottedName = serInit
              | customBlobNVPairs compControl


fieldOrProp ::= field | property


serializType ::= simpleType
            | type
            | object
            | enum class SQSTRING /* class specified in Reflection notation */
            | enum className /* class name specified in ILAsm notation */
            | serializType [ ]
```

Security Declarations

```
secDecl ::= .permission secAction typeSpec ( nameValPairs )
       | .permission secAction typeSpec = { customBlobDescr }
       | .permission secAction typeSpec
       | .permissionset secAction = ( bytes )
       | .permissionset secAction bytearray ( bytes )
       | .permissionset secAction compQstring
       | .permissionset secAction = { secAttrSetBlob }


secAttrSetBlob ::= /* EMPTY */
             | secAttrBlob
             | secAttrBlob , secAttrSetBlob


secAttrBlob ::= typeSpec = { customBlobNVPairs }
          | class SQSTRING = { customBlobNVPairs }


nameValPairs ::= nameValPair
           | nameValPair , nameValPairs


nameValPair ::= compQstring = caValue


caValue ::= truefalse
       | int32
       | int32 ( int32 )
       | compQstring
       | className ( int8 : int32 )
       | className ( int16 : int32 )
       | className ( int32 : int32 )
       | className ( int32 )


secAction ::= request
         | demand
         | assert
         | deny
         | permitonly
         | linkcheck
         | inheritcheck
         | reqmin
         | reqopt
         | reqrefuse
         | prejitgrant
         | prejitdeny
         | noncasdemand
         | noncaslinkdemand
         | noncasinheritance
```

Aliasing of Types, Methods, Fields, and Custom Attributes

```
typedefDecl ::= .typedef type as dottedName                  /* TYPEDEF_TS */
              | .typedef className as dottedName              /* TYPEDEF_T  */
              | .typedef memberRef as dottedName              /* TYPEDEF_M, _F, _MR */
              | .typedef customDescr as dottedName            /* TYPEDEF_CA */
              | .typedef customDescrWithOwner as dottedName   /* TYPEDEF_CA */
```

Data Declaration

```
dataDecl ::= ddHead ddBody


ddHead ::= .data section id =
         | .data section


section ::= /* EMPTY */  /* defaults to .sdata section */
          | tls  /* .tls section */
          | cil  /* .text section */


ddBody ::= { ddItemList }
         | ddItem


ddItemList ::= ddItem , ddItemList
             | ddItem


ddItemCount ::= /* EMPTY */ /* defaults to 1 */
              | [ int32 ]


ddItem ::= char * ( compQstring )
         | & ( id )  /* data is pointer to another data */
         | bytearray ( bytes )
         | float32 ( float64 ) ddItemCount
         | float64 ( float64 ) ddItemCount
         | int64 ( int64 ) ddItemCount
         | int32 ( int32 ) ddItemCount
         | int16 ( int32 ) ddItemCount
         | int8 ( int32 ) ddItemCount
         | float32 ddItemCount
         | float64 ddItemCount
         | int64 ddItemCount
         | int32 ddItemCount
         | int16 ddItemCount
         | int8 ddItemCount
```

APPENDIX B

■■■

Metadata Tables Reference

Table Entry Types

Type	Description
BYTE	Unsigned 1-byte integer
SHORT	Signed 2-byte integer
USHORT	Unsigned 2-byte integer
ULONG	Unsigned 4-byte integer
RID: <table>	Record index to <table>
STRING	Offset in the #Strings stream
GUID	Offset in the #GUID stream
BLOB	Offset in the #Blob stream
<coded_token_type>	Coded token (see the "Coded Token Types" table at the end of the appendix)

Module; RID Type: 00; Token Type: 0x00000000; Metadata (MD) Streams: #~, #-

Entry Name	Entry Type	Comments
Generation	USHORT	For edit-and-continue
Name	STRING	No longer than 512 bytes
Mvid	GUID	Generated automatically
EncId	GUID	For edit-and-continue
EncBaseId	GUID	For edit-and-continue

TypeRef; RID Type: 01; Token Type: 0x01000000; MD Streams: #~, #-

Entry Name	Entry Type	Comments
ResolutionScope	ResolutionScope	
Name	STRING	
Namespace	STRING	

TypeDef; RID Type: 02; Token Type: 0x02000000; MD Streams: #~, #-

Entry Name	Entry Type	Comments
Flags	ULONG	Validity mask: 0x001173DBF
Name	STRING	
Namespace	STRING	
Extends	TypeDefOrRef	Base type
FieldList	RID: Field	
MethodList	RID: Method	

FieldPtr; RID Type: 03; Token Type: None; MD Stream: #-

Entry Name	Entry Type	Comments
Field	RID: Field	

Field; RID Type: 04; Token Type: 0x04000000; MD Streams: #~, #-

Entry Name	Entry Type	Comments
Flags	USHORT	Validity mask: 0xB7F7
Name	STRING	No longer than 1023 bytes
Signature	BLOB	Cannot be 0

MethodPtr; RID Type: 05; Token Type: None; MD Stream: #-

Entry Name	Entry Type	Comments
Method	RID: Method	

Method; RID Type: 06; Token Type: 0x06000000; MD Streams: #~, #-

Entry Name	Entry Type	Comments
RVA	ULONG	Must be 0 or point at read-only section
ImplFlags	USHORT	Validity mask: 0x10BF
Flags	USHORT	Validity mask: 0xFDF7
Name	STRING	No longer than 1,023 bytes
Signature	BLOB	Cannot be 0
ParamList	RID: Param	

ParamPtr; RID Type: 07; Token Type: None; MD Stream: #-

Entry Name	Entry Type	Comments
Param	RID: Param	

Param; RID Type: 08; Token Type: 0x08000000; MD Streams: #~, #-

Entry Name	Entry Type	Comments
Flags	USHORT	Validity mask: 0x3013
Sequence	USHORT	0 means return value
Name	STRING	

InterfaceImpl; RID Type: 09; Token Type: 0x09000000; MD Streams: #~, #-

Entry Name	Entry Type	Comments
Class	RID: TypeDef	Class implementing the interface
Interface	TypeDefOrRef	Implemented interface

MemberRef; RID Type: 10; Token Type: 0x0A000000; MD Streams: #~, #-

Entry Name	Entry Type	Comments
Class	MemberRefParent	Cannot be TypeDef
Name	STRING	No longer than 1,023 bytes
Signature	BLOB	Cannot be 0

Constant; RID Type: 11; Token Type: None; MD Streams: #~, #-

Entry Name	Entry Type	Comments
Type	BYTE	
Parent	HasConstant	
Value	BLOB	

CustomAttribute; RID Type: 12; Token Type: 0x0C000000; MD Streams: #~, #-

Entry Name	Entry Type	Comments
Parent	HasCustomAttribute	
Type	CustomAttributeType	
Value	BLOB	Can be 0

FieldMarshal; RID Type: 13; Token Type: None; MD Streams: #~, #-

Entry Name	Entry Type	Comments
Parent	FieldMarshal	
NativeType	BLOB	Cannot be 0

DeclSecurity; RID Type: 14; Token Type: 0x0E000000; MD Streams: #~, #-

Entry Name	Entry Type	Comments
Action	SHORT	
Parent	HasDeclSecurity	
PermissionSet	BLOB	Cannot be 0

ClassLayout; RID Type: 15; Token Type: None; MD Streams: #~, #-

Entry Name	Entry Type	Comments
PackingSize	USHORT	*Power of 2, from 1 through 128*
ClassSize	ULONG	
Parent	RID: TypeDef	

FieldLayout; RID Type: 16; Token Type: None; MD Streams: #~, #-

Entry Name	Entry Type	Comments
OffSet	ULONG	Offset in bytes or ordinal
Field	RID: Field	

StandAloneSig; RID Type: 17; Token Type: 0x11000000; MD Streams: #~, #-

Entry Name	Entry Type	Comments
Signature	BLOB	Cannot be 0

EventMap; RID Type: 18; Token Type: None; MD Streams: #~, #-

Entry Name	Entry Type	Comments
Parent	RID: TypeDef	
EventList	RID: Event	

EventPtr; RID Type: 19; Token Type: None; MD Stream: #-

Entry Name	Entry Type	Comments
Event	RID: Event	

Event; RID Type: 20; Token Type: 0x14000000; MD Streams: #~, #-

Entry Name	Entry Type	Comments
EventFlags	USHORT	0x0000, 0x0200 or 0x0600
Name	STRING	
EventType	TypeDefOrRef	

PropertyMap; RID Type: 21; Token Type: None; MD Streams: #~, #-

Entry Name	Entry Type	Comments
Parent	RID: TypeDef	
PropertyList	RID: Property	

PropertyPtr; RID Type: 22; Token Type: None; MD Stream: #-

Entry Name	Entry Type	Comments
Property	RID: Property	

Property; RID Type: 23; Token Type: 0x17000000; MD Streams: #~, #-

Entry Name	Entry Type	Comments
PropFlags	USHORT	Validity mask: 0x1600
Name	STRING	
Type	BLOB	Property signature

MethodSemantics; RID Type: 24; Token Type: None; MD Streams: #~, #-

Entry Name	Entry Type	Comments
Semantic	USHORT	
Method	RID: Method	
Association	HasSemantic	

MethodImpl; RID Type: 25; Token Type: None; MD Streams: #~, #-

Entry Name	Entry Type	Comments
Class	RID: TypeDef	
MethodBody	MethodDefOrRef	Overriding method
MethodDeclaration	MethodDefOrRef	Overridden method

ModuleRef; RID Type: 26; Token Type: 0x1A000000; MD Streams: #~, #-

Entry Name	Entry Type	Comments
Name	STRING	No longer than 512 bytes

TypeSpec; RID Type: 27; Token Type: 0x1B000000; MD Streams: #~, #-

Entry Name	Entry Type	Comments
Signature	BLOB	Cannot be 0

ENCLog; RID Type: 28; Token Type: None; MD Stream: #-

Entry Name	Entry Type	Comments
Token	ULONG	
FuncCode	ULONG	

ImplMap; RID Type: 29; Token Type: None; MD Streams: #~, #-

Entry Name	Entry Type	Comments
MappingFlags	USHORT	Validity mask: 0x0747
MemberForwarded	MemberForwarded	Method only
ImportName	STRING	Entry point name
ImportScope	RID: ModuleRef	ModuleRef to unmanaged DLL

ENCMap; RID Type: 30; Token Type: None; MD Stream: #-

Entry Name	Entry Type	Comments
Token	ULONG	

FieldRVA; RID Type: 31; Token Type: None; MD Streams: #~, #-

Entry Name	Entry Type	Comments
RVA	ULONG	
Field	RID: Field	

Assembly; RID Type: 32; Token Type: 0x20000000; MD Streams: #~, #-

Entry Name	Entry Type	Comments
HashAlgId	ULONG	
MajorVersion	USHORT	
MinorVersion	USHORT	
BuildNumber	USHORT	
RevisionNumber	USHORT	
Flags	ULONG	Validity mask: 0x0000C031
PublicKey	BLOB	
Name	STRING	No path, no extension
Locale	STRING	

AssemblyProcessor; RID Type: 33; Token Type: None; Unused

Entry Name	Entry Type	Comments
Processor	ULONG	

AssemblyOS; RID Type: 34; Token Type: None; Unused

Entry Name	Entry Type	Comments
OSPlatformID	ULONG	
OSMajorVersion	ULONG	
OSMinorVersion	ULONG	

AssemblyRef; RID Type: 35; Token Type: 0x23000000; MD Streams: #~, #-

Entry Name	Entry Type	Comments
MajorVersion	USHORT	
MinorVersion	USHORT	
BuildNumber	USHORT	
RevisionNumber	USHORT	
Flags	ULONG	0x00000000 or 0x00000001
PublicKeyOrToken	BLOB	
Name	STRING	No path, no extension
Locale	STRING	
HashValue	BLOB	

AssemblyRefProcessor; RID Type: 36; Token Type: None; Unused

Entry Name	Entry Type	Comments
Processor	ULONG	
AssemblyRef	RID: AssemblyRef	

AssemblyRefOS; RID Type: 37; Token Type: None; Unused

Entry Name	Entry Type	Comments
OSPlatformId	ULONG	
OSMajorVersion	ULONG	
OSMinorVersion	ULONG	
AssemblyRef	RID: AssemblyRef	

File; RID Type: 38; Token Type: 0x26000000; MD Streams: #~, #-

Entry Name	Entry Type	Comments
Flags	ULONG	0x00000000 or 0x00000001
Name	STRING	No path; only filename
HashValue	BLOB	

ExportedType; RID Type: 39; Token Type: 0x27000000; MD Streams: #~, #-

Entry Name	Entry Type	Comments
Flags	ULONG	Validity mask: 0x00200007
TypeDefId	ULONG	TypeDef token in another module
TypeName	STRING	
TypeNamespace	STRING	
Implementation	Implementation	File, ExportedType, AssemblyRef

ManifestResource; RID Type: 40; Token Type: 0x28000000; MD Streams: #~, #-

Entry Name	Entry Type	Comments
Offset	ULONG	
Flags	ULONG	0x000001 or 0x000002
Name	STRING	
Implementation	Implementation	0, File, AssemblyRef

NestedClass; RID Type: 41; Token Type: None; MD Streams: #~, #-

Entry Name	Entry Type	Comments
NestedClass	RID: TypeDef	
EnclosingClass	RID: TypeDef	

GenericParam; RID Type: 42; Token Type: 0x2A000000; MD Streams: #~, #-

Entry Name	Entry Type	Comments
Number	USHORT	Ordinal
Flags	USHORT	Constraint flags
Owner	TypeOrMethodDef	Generic type or method
Name	STRING	Can be 0

MethodSpec; RID Type: 43; Token Type: 0x2B000000; MD Streams: #~, #-

Entry Name	Entry Type	Comments
Method	MethodDefOrRef	Instantiated method
Instantiation	BLOB	Instantiation signature

GenericParamConstraint; RID Type: 44; Token Type: 0x2C000000; MD Streams: #~, #-

Entry Name	Entry Type	Comments
Owner	RID: GenericParam	Constrained parameter
Constraint	TypeDefOrRef	Type the parameter must extend or implement

Coded Token Types

Type	Tag
TypeDefOrRef (64): 3 referenced tables, tag size 2	
TypeDef	0
TypeRef	1
TypeSpec	2
HasConstant (65): 3 referenced tables, tag size 2	
Field	0
Param	1
Property	2

(continued)

Coded Token Types (continued)

Type	Tag
HasCustomAttribute (66): 22 referenced tables, tag size 5	
Method	0
Field	1
TypeRef	2
TypeDef	3
Param	4
InterfaceImpl	5
MemberRef	6
Module	7
Permission	8
Property	9
Event	10
Signature	11
ModuleRef	12
TypeSpec	13
Assembly	14
AssemblyRef	15
File	16
ExportedType	17
ManifestResource	18
GenericParam	19
GenericParamConstraint	20
MethodSpec	21
HasFieldMarshal (67): 2 referenced tables, tag size 1	
Field	0
Param	1
HasDeclSecurity (68): 3 referenced tables, tag size 2	
TypeDef	0
Method	1
Assembly	2
MemberRefParent (69): 5 referenced tables, tag size 3	
TypeDef	0
TypeRef	1
ModuleRef	2
Method	3
TypeSpec	4

Type	Tag
HasSemantics (70): 2 referenced tables, tag size 1	
Event	0
Property	1
MethodDefOrRef (71): 2 referenced tables, tag size 1	
Method	0
MemberRef	1
MemberForwarded (72): 2 referenced tables, tag size 1	
Field	0
Method	1
Implementation (73): 3 referenced tables, tag size 2	
File	0
AssemblyRef	1
ExportedType	2
CustomAttributeType (74): 2 referenced tables, tag size 3	
none	0
none	1
Method	2
MemberRef	3
none	4
ResolutionScope (75): 4 referenced tables, tag size 2	
Module	0
ModuleRef	1
AssemblyRef	2
TypeRef	3
TypeOrMethodDef (76): 2 referenced tables, tag size 1	
TypeDef	0
Method	1

■ ■ ■

IL Instruction Set Reference

Instruction Parameter Types

Type	Description
int8	Signed 1-byte integer
uint8	Unsigned 1-byte integer
int32	Signed 4-byte integer
uint32	Unsigned 4-byte integer
int64	Signed 8-byte integer
float32	4-byte floating-point number (IEEE-754)
float64	8-byte floating-point number (IEEE-754)
<Method>	MethodDef or MemberRef token
<Field>	FieldDef or MemberRef token
<Type>	TypeDef, TypeRef, or TypeSpec token
<Signature>	StandAloneSig token
<String>	User-defined string token

Evaluation Stack Types

Type	Description
int32	Signed 4-byte integer
int64	Signed 8-byte integer
Float	80-bit floating-point number
&	Managed or unmanaged pointer
o	Object reference
*	Unspecified type

IL Instructions, Their Parameters, and Stack Operations

Opcode	Name	Parameter(s)	Pop	Push
00	nop			
01	break			
02	ldarg.0			*
03	ldarg.1			*
04	ldarg.2			*
05	ldarg.3			*
06	ldloc.0			*
07	ldloc.1			*
08	ldloc.2			*
09	ldloc.3			*
0A	stloc.0		*	
0B	stloc.1		*	
0C	stloc.2		*	
0D	stloc.3		*	
0E	ldarg.s	uint8		*
0F	ldarga.s	uint8		&
10	starg.s	uint8	*	
11	ldloc.s	uint8		*
12	ldloca.s	uint8		&
13	stloc.s	uint8	*	
14	ldnull			&=0
15	ldc.i4.m1, ldc.i4.M1			int32=-1
16	ldc.i4.0			int32=0
17	ldc.i4.1			int32=1
18	ldc.i4.2			int32=2
19	ldc.i4.3			int32=3
1A	ldc.i4.4			int32=4
1B	ldc.i4.5			int32=5
1C	ldc.i4.6			int32=6
1D	ldc.i4.7			int32=7
1E	ldc.i4.8			int32=8
1F	ldc.i4.s	int8		int32
20	ldc.i4	int32		int32
21	ldc.i8	int64		int64
22	ldc.r4	float32		Float
23	ldc.r8	float64		Float
25	dup		*	*,*

Opcode	Name	Parameter(s)	Pop	Push
26	pop		*	
27	jmp	*<Method>*		
28	call	*<Method>*	N arguments	Ret.value
29	calli	*<Signature>*	N arguments	Ret.value
2A	ret		*	
2B	br.s	int8		
2C	brfalse.s, brnull.s, brzero.s	int8	int32	
2D	brtrue.s, brinst.s	int8	int32	
2E	beq.s	int8	*,*	
2F	bge.s	int8	*,*	
30	bgt.s	int8	*,*	
31	ble.s	int8	*,*	
32	blt.s	int8	*,*	
33	bne.un.s	int8	*,*	
34	bge.un.s	int8	*,*	
35	bgt.un.s	int8	*,*	
36	ble.un.s	int8	*,*	
37	blt.un.s	int8	*,*	
38	br	int32		
39	brfalse, brnull, brzero	int32	int32	
3A	brtrue, brinst	int32	int32	
3B	beq	int32	*,*	
3C	bge	int32	*,*	
3D	bgt	int32	*,*	
3E	ble	int32	*,*	
3F	blt	int32	*,*	
40	bne.un	int32	*,*	
41	bge.un	int32	*,*	
42	bgt.un	int32	*,*	
43	ble.un	int32	*,*	
44	blt.un	int32	*,*	
45	switch	(uint32=N) + N(int32)	int32	
46	ldind.i1		&	int32
47	ldind.u1		&	int32
48	ldind.i2		&	int32
49	ldind.u2		&	int32
4A	ldind.i4		&	int32

Continued

IL Instructions, Their Parameters, and Stack Operations (Continued)

Opcode	Name	Parameter(s)	Pop	Push
4B	ldind.u4		&	int32
4C	ldind.i8, ldind.u8		&	int64
4D	ldind.i		&	int32
4E	ldind.r4		&	Float
4F	ldind.r8		&	Float
50	ldind.ref		&	&
51	stind.ref		&,&	
52	stind.i1		int32,&	
53	stind.i2		int32,&	
54	stind.i4		int32,&	
55	stind.i8		int32,&	
56	stind.r4		Float,&	
57	stind.r8		Float,&	
58	add		*,*	*
59	sub		*,*	*
5A	mul		*,*	*
5B	div		*,*	*
5C	div.un		*,*	*
5D	rem		*,*	*
5E	rem.un		*,*	*
5F	and		*,*	*
60	or		*,*	*
61	xor		*,*	*
62	shl		*,*	*
63	shr		*,*	*
64	shr.un		*,*	*
65	neg		*	*
66	not		*	*
67	conv.i1		*	int32
68	conv.i2		*	int32
69	conv.i4		*	int32
6A	conv.i8		*	int64
6B	conv.r4		*	Float
6C	conv.r8		*	Float
6D	conv.u4		*	int32
6E	conv.u8		*	int64
6F	callvirt	*<Method>*	N arguments	Ret.value

Opcode	Name	Parameter(s)	Pop	Push
70	cpobj	*<Type>*	&,&	
71	ldobj	*<Type>*	&	*
72	ldstr	*<String>*		o
73	newobj	*<Method>*	N arguments	o
74	castclass	*<Type>*	o	o
75	isinst	*<Type>*	o	int32
76	conv.r.un		*	Float
79	unbox	*<Type>*	o	&
7A	throw		o	
7B	ldfld	*<Field>*	o/&/*	*
7C	ldflda	*<Field>*	o/&	&
7D	stfld	*<Field>*	o/&,*	
7E	ldsfld	*<Field>*		*
7F	ldsflda	*<Field>*		&
80	stsfld	*<Field>*	*	
81	stobj	*<Type>*	&,*	
82	conv.ovf.i1.u n		*	int32
83	conv.ovf.i2.u n		*	int32
84	conv.ovf.i4.u n		*	int32
85	conv.ovf.i8.u n		*	int64
86	conv.ovf.u1. un		*	int32
87	conv.ovf.u2. un		*	int32
88	conv.ovf.u4. un		*	int32
89	conv.ovf.u8. un		*	int64
8A	conv.ovf.i.un		*	int32
8B	conv.ovf.u.u n		*	int64
8C	box	*<Type>*	*	o
8D	newarr	*<Type>*	int32	o
8E	ldlen		o	int32
8F	ldelema	*<Type>*	int32,o	&
90	ldelem.i1		int32,o	int32
91	ldelem.u1		int32,o	int32
92	ldelem.i2		int32,o	int32
93	ldelem.u2		int32,o	int32
94	ldelem.i4		int32,o	int32
95	ldelem.u4		int32,o	int32
96	ldelem.i8, ldelem.u8		int32,o	int64

Continued

IL Instructions, Their Parameters, and Stack Operations (Continued)

Opcode	Name	Parameter(s)	Pop	Push
97	ldelem.i		int32,o	int32
98	ldelem.r4		int32,o	Float
99	ldelem.r8		int32,o	Float
9A	ldelem.ref		int32,o	o/&
9B	stelem.i		int32,int32,o	
9C	stelem.i1		int32,int32,o	
9D	stelem.i2		int32,int32,o	
9E	stelem.i4		int32,int32,o	
9F	stelem.i8		int64,int32,o	
A0	stelem.r4		Float,int32,o	
A1	stelem.r8		Float,int32,o	
A2	stelem.ref		o/&,int32,o	
A3	ldelem, ldelem.any	*<Type>*	int32,o	*
A4	stelem, stelem.any	*<Type>*	o/&,int32,o	
A5	unbox.any	*<Type>*	o	*
B3	conv.ovf.i1		*	int32
B4	conv.ovf.u1		*	int32
B5	conv.ovf.i2		*	int32
B6	conv.ovf.u2		*	int32
B7	conv.ovf.i4		*	int32
B8	conv.ovf.u4		*	int32
B9	conv.ovf.i8		*	int64
BA	conv.ovf.u8		*	int64
C2	refanyval	*<Type>*	*	&
C3	ckfinite		*	Float
C6	mkrefany	*<Type>*	&	&
D0	ldtoken	*<Type>/<Field>/<Method>*		&
D1	conv.u2		*	int32
D2	conv.u1		*	int32
D3	conv.i		*	int32
D4	conv.ovf.i		*	int32
D5	conv.ovf.u		*	int32
D6	add.ovf		*,*	*
D7	add.ovf.un		*,*	*
D8	mul.ovf		*,*	*
D9	mul.ovf.un		*,*	*
DA	sub.ovf		*,*	*

Opcode	Name	Parameter(s)	Pop	Push
DB	sub.ovf.un		*,*	*
DC	endfinally, endfault			
DD	leave	int32		
DE	leave.s	int8		
DF	stind.i		int32,&	
E0	conv.u		*	int32
FE 00	arglist		*	&
FE 01	ceq		*,*	int32
FE 02	cgt		*,*	int32
FE 03	cgt.un		*,*	int32
FE 04	clt		*,*	int32
FE 05	clt.un		*,*	int32
FE 06	ldftn	*<Method>*		&
FE 07	ldvirtftn	*<Method>*	o	&
FE 09	ldarg	uint32		*
FE 0A	ldarga	uint32		&
FE 0B	starg	uint32	*	
FE 0C	ldloc	uint32		*
FE 0D	ldloca	uint32		&
FE 0E	stloc	uint32	*	
FE 0F	localloc		int32	&
FE 11	endfilter		int32	
FE 12	unaligned.	uint8		
FE 13	volatile.			
FE 14	tail.			
FE 15	initobj	*<Type>*	&	
FE 16	constrained.	*<Type>*		
FE 17	cpblk		int32,&,&	
FE 18	initblk		int32,int32,&	
FE 1A	rethrow			
FE 1C	sizeof	*<Type>*		int32
FE 1D	refanytype		*	&
FE 1E	readonly.			

■ ■ ■

IL Assembler and Disassembler Command-Line Options

This appendix describes the command-line options of the IL assembler (ilasm.exe) and the IL disassembler (ildasm.exe).

IL Assembler

The command-line structure of the IL assembler is as follows:

```
ilasm [<options>] <sourcefile> [<options>][<sourcefile>*]
```

The default source file extension is .il. Multiple source files are parsed in the order of their appearance on the command line. Options do not need to appear in a prescribed order, so options and names of source files can be intermixed. All options specified on the command line are pertinent to the entire set of source files.

All options are recognized by the first three characters following the option key, and all are case insensitive. The option key can be a forward slash (/) or a hyphen (-). In options that specify parameters, the equality character (=) is interchangeable with the colon character (:). So, for example, the following option notations are equivalent:

- /OUTPUT=MyModule.dll

- -OUTPUT:MyModule.dll

- /out:MyModule.dll

- -Outp:MyModule.dll

The following command-line options are defined for the IL assembler:

- */NOLOGO*. Suppress typing the logo and copyright statement.

- */QUIET*. Suppress reporting the compilation progress.

- */NOAUTOINHERIT*. Suppress the default inheritance of classes (from System.Object, System.ValueType, or System.Enum). This option is used for testing purposes.

- */DLL*. Compile to a dynamic-link library.

- */EXE*. Compile to a runnable executable (the default).

- */PDB*. Create a PDB file, but don't enable the debug information tracking.

- */DEBUG*. Disable JIT optimization, and create a PDB file; when running under the debugger, use sequence points from PDB.

- */DEBUG=IMPL*. Disable JIT optimization, and create a PDB file; when running under the debugger, use implicit (heuristically calculated) sequence points.

- */DEBUG=OPT*. Enable JIT optimization, and create a PDB file; when running under the debugger, use implicit sequence points.

- */OPTIMIZE*. Optimize long instructions to short when possible.

- */FOLD*. Fold identical method bodies into one. If two or more methods have identical bodies (method headers, IL code, and exception handling clauses), emit only one body and set the RVA of the respective method records to point at this body. This option reduces the size of managed executable but slows the assembler down.

- */CLOCK*. Measure and report the compilation times.

- */RESOURCE=<res_file>*. Link the specified unmanaged resource file (*.res) into the resulting PE file. *<res_file>* must be a full filename, including the extension. Only one .res file can be linked into a managed executable.

- */OUTPUT=<targetfile>*. Compile to the file whose name is specified. The file extension must be specified explicitly; there is no default. If this option is omitted, the IL assembler sets the name of the output file to that of the first source file and sets the extension of the output file to DLL if the */DLL* option is specified and to EXE otherwise.

- */KEY=<keyfile>*. Compile with a strong name signature. *<keyfile>* specifies the file containing the private encryption key.

- */KEY=@<keysource>*. Compile with a strong name signature. *<keysource>* specifies the name of the source of the private encryption key.

- */INCLUDE=<path>*. Set the search path for files specified in #include directives. If a file specification in the #include directive contains the path, the include search path is ignored. The include search path can be set alternatively via the environment variable ILASM_INCLUDE. The command-line option */INCLUDE* has precedence over the environment variable.

- */SUBSYSTEM=<int>*. Set the Subsystem value in the PE header. The most frequently used *<int>* values are 3 (Microsoft Windows console application) and 2 (Microsoft Windows GUI application).

- */FLAGS=<int>*. Set the Flags value in the common language runtime header. The most frequently used *<int>* values are 1 (pure-IL code) and 2 (mixed code). The third bit of the *<int>* value, indicating that the PE file is strong name signed, is ignored.

- */ALIGNMENT=<int>*. Set the FileAlignment value in the NT Optional header. The *<int>* value must be a power of 2, in the range 512 to 65536.

- */BASE=<int>*. Set the ImageBase value in the NT Optional header (maximum 2GB for 32-bit executables).

- */STACK=<int>*. Set the SizeOfStackReserve value in the NT Optional header.

- */MDV=<version_string>*. Set the metadata version string. Use */MDV=1.0.3705* to generate metadata in version 1.0 format and */MDV=1.1.4322* to generate metadata in version 1.1 format.

- */MSV=<int>.<int>*. Set the metadata stream version number. Use */MSV=1.0* to generate metadata in version 1.0 or 1.1 format.

- */PE64*. Create a 64-bit image (PE32+ file). Default target processor: Intel Itanium.

- */ITANIUM*. Target processor: Intel Itanium. Target file format: PE32+.

- */X64*. Target processor: AMD/Intel X64 architecture. Target file format: PE32+.

- */NOCORSTUB*. Suppress emission of COERExeMain stub (CLR start-up stub).

- */STRIPRELOC*. Indicate that no base relocations are needed. Set the flag IMAGE_FILE_RELOC_STRIPPED in the COFF header.

- */ENC=<file>*. Create Edit-and-Continue delta files from the specified source file. This option is intended for internal CLR testing purposes. Do not use this option; you won't be able to make anything useful out of it.

- */ERROR*. Attempt to create the PE file even if compilation errors have been reported. Using the */ERROR* option does not guarantee that the PE file will be created: some errors are abortive, and others lead specifically to a failure to create the PE file. This option also disables the following IL assembler automatic correction features:

  - An unsealed value type is automatically marked *sealed*.

  - A method declared as both *static* and *instance* is automatically marked *static*.

  - A nonabstract, nonvirtual instance method of an interface is automatically marked *abstract* and *virtual*.

  - A global abstract method is automatically marked *nonabstract*.

  - Nonstatic global fields and methods are automatically marked *static*.

⬛**Caution** Don't use the */ERROR* command-line option unless you're positive you know what you're doing. It is dangerous! You can create a monster that will crash your application.

IL Disassembler

The command-line structure of the IL disassembler is as follows:

```
ildasm [<options>] [<in_filename>] [<options>]
```

If no filename is specified, the disassembler starts in graphical mode. You can then open a specific file by using the File ➤ Open menu command or by dragging the file to the disassembler's tree view window.

All options are recognized by the first three characters following the option key, and all are case insensitive. The option key can be a forward slash (/) or a hyphen (-). In options that specify parameters, the equality character (=) is interchangeable with the colon character (:).

Output Redirection Options

These are the options:

- */OUT=<out_filename>*. Direct the output to a file rather than to a GUI.

- */OUT=CON*. Direct the output to the console window from which ildasm.exe was started rather than to a GUI.

- */TEXT*. A shortcut for */OUT=CON*.

- */HTML*. Output in HTML format. This option is valid for file-directed output only.

- */RTF*. Output in RTF. This option is invalid for console-directed output (option */OUT=CON* or */TEXT*).

If the */OUT* option or the */TEXT* option is specified, <in_filename> must be specified as well.

ILAsm Code-Formatting Options (PE Files Only)

The code-formatting options specify what information, and in what form, will be included in the disassembly text:

- */BYTES*. Show the actual IL stream bytes (in hexadecimal notation) as instruction comments.

- */RAWEH*. Show structured exception handling clauses in canonical (label) form.

- */TOKENS*. Show metadata token values as comments.

- */SOURCE*. Show original source lines as comments. This requires the presence of the PDB file accompanying the PE file being disassembled and the original source files. If the original source files cannot be found at the location specified in the PDB file, the disassembler tries to find them in the current directory.

- */LINENUM*. Include references to original source lines (.line directives). This requires the presence of the PDB file accompanying the PE file being disassembled.

- */VISIBILITY=<vis>[+<vis>...]*. Disassemble only the items with specified visibility. Visibility suboptions (<vis>) include the following:

- • PUB: Public

- • PRI: Private

- • FAM: Family

- • ASM: Assembly

- • FAA: Family and assembly

- • FOA: Family or assembly

- • PSC: Private scope

- */PUBONLY*. A shortcut for */VIS=PUB*.

- */QUOTEALLNAMES*. Enclose all names in single quotation marks. By default, only names that don't match the ILAsm definition of a simple name are quoted.

- */NOCA*. Suppress output of the custom attributes.

- */CAVERBAL*. Output the custom attribute initialization blobs in verbal form. The default is hexadecimal form.

- */NOBAR*. Suppress the pop-up window showing the disassembly progress bar.

File Output Options (PE Files Only)

These options specify the encoding of the disassembly text file. The options are ignored if the output is directed to GUI or to the console.

- */UTF8*. Use UTF-8 encoding for output. The default is ANSI.

- */UNICODE*. Use Unicode (UTF-16) encoding for output.

File or Console Output Options (PE Files Only)

These options are used for output directed to a file or to the console and are ignored if the output is directed to GUI:

- */NOIL*. Suppress ILAsm code output.

- */FORWARD*. Use forward class declaration, similar to ILDASM versions 1.0 and 1.1.

- */TYPELIST*. Output full list of types defined in the module to preserve the type declaration order in round tripping.

- */HEADERS*. Include PE header information, runtime header information, and metadata headers information in the output (as comments).

- */ITEM=<class>[::<method>[(<sig>)]]*. Disassemble the specified item only. If *<sig>* is not specified, all methods named *<method>* of *<class>* are disassembled. If *<method>* is not specified, all members of *<class>* are disassembled. For example, */ITEM="Foo"* produces the full disassembly of the Foo class and all its members; */ITEM="Foo::Bar"* produces the disassembly of all methods named Bar in the Foo class.

If the method name and signature are specified, the last closing parenthesis of the signature should be omitted (a known bug in the IL disassembler 2.0). For example, */ITEM="Foo::Bar(void(int32,string)"* produces the disassembly of a single method, `void Foo::Bar(int32,string)`.

- */STATS.* Include statistics of the image file (as comments).

- */CLASSLIST.* Include the list of classes defined in the module (as comments).

- */ALL.* Combine the */HEADER, /BYTES, /TOKENS, /CLASSLIST,* and */STATS* options.

Metadata Summary Option

The metadata summary option is suitable for file or console output, and it is the only option that works for both PE and COFF managed files. If an object file or an object library file is specified as an input file, the IL disassembler automatically invokes the metadata summary, ignoring all other options. The metadata summary is output as comments.

- */METAINFO[=<specifier>].* Show the metadata summary. The optional *<specifier>* is one of the following:

  - `MDH`: Show the metadata header information and sizes.

  - `HEX`: Show the hexadecimal representation of the signatures.

  - `CSV`: Show the sizes of the #Strings, #Blob, #US, and #GUID streams and the sizes of the metadata tables and their records.

  - `UNR`: Show the list of unresolved method references and unimplemented method definitions.

  - `SCH`: Show the metadata header and schema information.

  - `RAW`: Show the metadata tables in raw form.

  - `HEA`: Show the metadata heaps in raw form.

  - `VAL`: Invoke the metadata validator and show its output.

- */OBJECTFILE=<obj_file_name>.* Show the metadata summary of a single object file in the object library. This option is valid for managed LIB files only.

APPENDIX E

■■■

Offline Verification Tool Reference

An offline verification tool for managed PE files, PEVerify.exe, is distributed with the Microsoft .NET Framework SDK. The tool includes two components: the metadata validator (MDValidator) and the IL verifier (ILVerifier).

MDValidator works on the module level, running validity checks of the metadata of a specified managed module (PE file). It does not matter whether the specified module is a prime module or an auxiliary. If the specified module is a prime module of an assembly, MDValidator does not automatically check other modules of the same assembly.

ILVerifier works on the assembly level, loading the assembly in full in memory, resolving internal references, and verifying the IL code of the methods contained in the assembly. Consequently, ILVerifier fails if the specified PE file is not the prime module of the assembly.

The result of this discrepancy in the approaches taken by MDValidator and ILVerifier is that only single-module assemblies can be fully validated and verified in one pass of the verification tool.

The PEVerify tool sets the exit code to 1 if errors are found during the PE file verification and sets the code to 0 otherwise.

The command-line format is as follows:

```
peverify <PE_file> <option>*
```

Unlike the IL assembler and the IL disassembler, the PEVerify tool does not allow arbitrary positioning of the filename and options on the command line; rather, the name of the PE file being verified must be the first command-line parameter. Also, unlike the assembler and disassembler options, which are recognized by their first three characters only, PEVerify options must be fully spelled out.

PEVerify options are case insensitive, and the option key can be a forward slash (/) or a hyphen (-). The equality character (=) cannot be replaced with the colon character (:).

The command-line options include the following:

- */IL*: Check the PE structure and verify the IL code.

- */MD*: Check the PE structure and validate the metadata. If neither */MD* nor */IL* is specified, the metadata validation is performed first; then, if no metadata errors were found, the IL verification is performed. If either the */MD* or */IL* option is specified, only the metadata validation or the IL verification, respectively, is performed. If both the */MD* and /IL options are specified, the metadata validation is performed, followed by the IL verification, regardless of whether errors were found during the metadata validation phase.

- /UNIQUE: Disregard repeating error codes; report only the first occurrence of each error type.

- /HRESULT: Display error codes in hexadecimal format.

- /CLOCK: Measure and report validation and verification times.

- /IGNORE=<err_code>[,<err_code>...]: Ignore the specified error codes. Error codes must be specified in hexadecimal format.

- /IGNORE=@<err_code_file>: Ignore the error codes specified in <err_code_file>, which is a text file containing comma-separated and/or line-separated hexadecimal error codes.

- /BREAK=<maxErrorCount>: Abort verification after <maxErrorCount> errors. The value of <maxErrorCount> is a decimal number; if it is negative or unspecified, <maxErrorCount> is set to 1.

- /VERBOSE. Display additional information in IL verification error messages.

- /NOLOGO: Don't display the product version and copyright information.

- /QUIET: Suppress reporting the errors; report only the file being verified and the end result of the verification.

The following example shows verification of an exceptionally buggy PE file, created using the IL assembler with the /ERROR option:

```
D:\MTRY>peverify mtry.exe /md /il /hresult /unique

Microsoft (R) .NET Framework PE Verifier  Version 2.0.50727.42
Copyright (C) Microsoft Corporation. All rights reserved.

[MD](0x8013121D): Error: TypeDef is marked ValueType but not marked
    Sealed. [token:0x02000002]
[MD](0x80131256): Error: TypeDef is not marked Nested but has an encloser
    type. [token:0x02000006]
[MD](0x8013126D): Error: Global item (field,method) must be Public, Private, or
    PrivateScope. [token:0x04000002]
[MD](0x8013126E): Error: Global item (field,method) must be Static.
    [token:0x04000002]
[MD](0x8013126A): Error: Field name value__ is reserved for Enums only.
    [token:0x04000008]
[MD](0x80131B24): Error: Illegal use of type 'void' in signature.
    [token:0x06000001]
[MD](0x801312DB): Error: Constructor, initializer must return void.
    [token:0x06000005]
[MD](0x801312DF): Error: ELEMENT_TYPE_SENTINEL is only allowed in MemberRef
    signatures. [token:0x06000009]
```

[MD](0x801312E2): Error: Trailing ELEMENT_TYPE_SENTINEL in signature.
    [token:0x06000009]
[MD](0x80131239): Error: Signature has invalid calling convention=0x00000023.
    [token:0x0600000D]
[MD](0x801312E0): Error: Signature containing ELEMENT_TYPE_SENTINEL must be VARARG.
    [token:0x0A000006]
[MD](0x801312E1): Error: Multiple ELEMENT_TYPE_SENTINEL in signature.
    [token:0x0A000006]
[MD](0x80131230): Error: FieldLayout2 record has Field token=0x04000003 marked
    Static. [token:0x00000001]
13 Errors Verifying mtry.exe

Error Codes and Messages

In Tables E-1 and E-2, 0xff, 0xffff, and 0xffffffff denote hexadecimal numbers, and 99 denotes a decimal number.

Table E-1. *Metadata Validation Error Codes and Messages*

HRESULT	Error Message
0x80131203	Error (Structural): Table=0xffffffff, Col=0xffffffff, Row=0xffffffff, has rid out of range.
0x80131204	Error (Structural): Table=0xffffffff, Col=0xffffffff, Row=0xffffffff, has coded token type out of range.
0x80131205	Error (Structural): Table=0xffffffff, Col=0xffffffff, Row=0xffffffff, has coded rid out of range.
0x80131206	Error (Structural): Table=0xffffffff, Col=0xffffffff, Row=0xffffffff, has an invalid String offset.
0x80131207	Error (Structural): Table=0xffffffff, Col=0xffffffff, Row=0xffffffff, has an invalid GUID offset.
0x80131208	Error (Structural): Table=0xffffffff, Col=0xffffffff, Row=0xffffffff, has an invalid BLOB offset.
0x80131209	Error: Multiple module records found.
0x8013120A	Error: Module has no MVID.
0x8013120B	Error: TypeRef has no name.
0x8013120C	Error: TypeRef has a duplicate, token=0xffffffff.
0x8013120D	Error: TypeDef has no name.
0x8013120E	Error: TypeDef has a duplicate based on name+namespace, token=0xffffffff.
0x8013120F	Warning: TypeDef has a duplicate based on GUID, token=0xffffffff.
0x80131210	Error: TypeDef that is not an Interface and not the Object class extends Nil token.
0x80131211	Error: TypeDef for Object class extends token=0xffffffff which is not nil.
0x80131212	Error: TypeDef extends token=0xffffffff which is marked Sealed.
0x80131213	Error: TypeDef is a Deleted record but not marked RTSpecialName.
0x80131214	Error: TypeDef is marked RTSpecialName but is not a Deleted record.

Table E-1. *Continued*

HRESULT	Error Message
0x80131215	Error: MethodImpl overrides private method (token=0xffffffff).
0x80131216	Error: Assembly name contains path and/or extension.
0x80131217	Error: File has a reserved system name.
0x80131218	Error: MethodImpl has static overriding method (token=0xffffffff).
0x80131219	Error: TypeDef is marked Interface but not Abstract.
0x8013121A	Error: TypeDef is marked Interface but extends non-Nil token=0xffffffff.
0x8013121B	Warning: TypeDef is marked Interface but has no GUID.
0x8013121C	Error: MethodImpl overrides final method (token=0xffffffff).
0x8013121D	Error: TypeDef is marked ValueType but not marked Sealed.
0x8013121E	Error: Parameter has invalid flags set 0xffffffff.
0x8013121F	Error: InterfaceImpl has a duplicate, token=0xffffffff.
0x80131220	Error: MemberRef has no name.
0x80131221	Error: MemberRef name starts with _VtblGap.
0x80131222	Error: MemberRef name starts with _Deleted.
0x80131223	Error: MemberRef parent is Nil but the module is a PE file.
0x80131224	Error: MemberRef signature has invalid calling convention=0xffffffff.
0x80131225	Error: MemberRef has MethodDef parent, but calling convention is not VARARG (parent:0xffffffff; callconv: 0xffffffff).
0x80131226	Error: MemberRef has different name than parent MethodDef, token=0xffffffff.
0x80131227	Error: MemberRef has fixed part of signature different from parent MethodDef, token=0xffffffff.
0x80131228	Warning: MemberRef has a duplicate, token=0xffffffff.
0x80131229	Error: ClassLayout has parent TypeDef token=0xffffffff marked AutoLayout.
0x8013122A	Error: ClassLayout has invalid PackingSize; valid set of values is {1,2,4,...,128} (parent: 0xffffffff; PackingSize: 99).
0x8013122B	Error: ClassLayout has a duplicate (parent: 0xffffffff; duplicate rid: 0xffffffff).
0x8013122C	Error: FieldLayout2 record has invalid offset (field: 0xffffffff; offset: 0xffffffff).
0x8013122D	Error: FieldLayout2 record for Field token=0xffffffff has TypeDefNil for parent.
0x8013122E	Error: FieldLayout2 record for field of type that has no ClassLayout record (field: 0xffffffff; type: 0xffffffff).
0x8013122F	Error: Explicit offset specified for field of type marked AutoLayout (field: 0xffffffff; type: 0xffffffff).
0x80131230	Error: FieldLayout2 record has Field token=0xffffffff marked Static.
0x80131231	Error: FieldLayout2 record has a duplicate, rid=0xffffffff.
0x80131232	Error: ModuleRef has no name.
0x80131233	Warning: ModuleRef has a duplicate, token=0xffffffff.
0x80131234	Error: TypeRef has invalid resolution scope.
0x80131235	Error: TypeDef is marked Nested but has no encloser type.

HRESULT	Error Message
0x80131236	Warning: Type extends TypeRef which resolves to TypeDef in the same module (TypeRef: 0xffffffff; TypeDef: 0xffffffff).
0x80131237	Error: Signature has zero size.
0x80131238	Error: Signature does not have enough bytes left at byte=0xffffffff as indicated by the compression scheme.
0x80131239	Error: Signature has invalid calling convention=0xffffffff.
0x8013123A	Error: Method is marked Static but calling convention=0xffffffff is marked HASTHIS.
0x8013123B	Error: Method is not marked Static, but calling convention=0xffffffff is not marked HASTHIS.
0x8013123C	Error: Signature has no argument count at byte=0xffffffff.
0x8013123D	Error: Signature missing element type after modifier (modifier: 0xff; offset: 0xffffffff).
0x8013123E	Error: Signature missing token after element 0xffff.
0x8013123F	Error: Signature has an invalid token (token: 0xffffffff; offset: 0xffffffff).
0x80131240	Error: Signature missing function pointer at byte=0xffffffff.
0x80131241	Error: Signature has function pointer missing argument count at byte=0xffffffff.
0x80131242	Error: Signature missing rank at byte=0xffffffff.
0x80131243	Error: Signature missing count of sized dimensions of array at byte=0xffffffff.
0x80131244	Error: Signature missing size of dimension of array at byte=0xffffffff.
0x80131245	Error: Signature missing count of lower bounds of array at byte=0xffffffff.
0x80131246	Error: Signature missing lower bound of array at byte=0xffffffff.
0x80131247	Error: Signature has invalid ELEMENT_TYPE_* (element type: 0xffffffff; offset: 0xffffffff).
0x80131248	Error: Signature missing size for VALUEARRAY at byte=0xffffffff.
0x80131249	Error: Field signature has invalid calling convention=0xffffffff.
0x8013124A	Error: Method has no name.
0x8013124B	Error: Method parent is Nil.
0x8013124C	Error: Method has a duplicate, token=0xffffffff.
0x8013124D	Error: Field has no name.
0x8013124E	Error: Field parent is Nil.
0x8013124F	Error: Field has a duplicate, token=0xffffffff.
0x80131250	Error: Multiple assembly records found.
0x80131251	Error: Assembly has no name.
0x80131252	Error: Token 0xffffffff following ELEMENT_TYPE_CLASS (_VALUETYPE) in signature is a ValueType (Class, respectively).
0x80131253	Error: ClassLayout has parent TypeDef token=0xffffffff marked Interface.
0x80131255	Error: AssemblyRef has no name.
0x80131256	Error: TypeDef is not marked Nested but has an encloser type.
0x80131258	Error: File has no name.

Continued

Table E-1. *Continued*

HRESULT	Error Message
0x80131259	Error: ExportedType has no name.
0x8013125A	Error: TypeDef extends its own child.
0x8013125B	Error: ManifestResource has no name.
0x8013125C	Error: File has a duplicate, token=0xffffffff.
0x8013125D	Error: File name is fully-qualified, but should not be.
0x8013125E	Error: ExportedType has a duplicate, token=0xffffffff.
0x8013125F	Error: ManifestResource has a duplicate by name, token=0xffffffff.
0x80131260	Error: ManifestResource is not marked Public or Private.
0x80131262	Error: Field value__ (token=0xffffffff) in Enum is marked static.
0x80131263	Error: Field value__ (token=0xffffffff) in Enum is not marked RTSpecialName.
0x80131264	Error: Field (token=0xffffffff) in Enum is not marked static.
0x80131265	Error: Field (token=0xffffffff) in Enum is not marked literal.
0x80131267	Error: Signature of field (token=0xffffffff) in Enum does not match enum type.
0x80131268	Error: Field value__ (token=0xffffffff) in Enum is not the first one.
0x80131269	Error: Field (token=0xffffffff) is marked RTSpecialName but not named value__.
0x8013126A	Error: Field name value__ is reserved for Enums only.
0x8013126B	Error: Instance field in Interface.
0x8013126C	Error: Non-public field in Interface.
0x8013126D	Error: Global item (field,method) must be Public, Private, or PrivateScope.
0x8013126E	Error: Global item (field,method) must be Static.
0x80131270	Error: Type/instance constructor has zero RVA.
0x80131271	Error: Field is marked marshaled but has no marshaling information.
0x80131272	Error: Field has marshaling information but is not marked marshaled.
0x80131273	Error: Field is marked HasDefault but has no const value.
0x80131274	Error: Field has const value but is not marked HasDefault.
0x80131275	Error: Item (field,method) is marked HasSecurity but has no security information.
0x80131276	Error: Item (field,method) has security information but is not marked HasSecurity.
0x80131277	Error: PInvoke item (field,method) must be Static.
0x80131278	Error: PInvoke item (field,method) has no Implementation Map.
0x80131279	Error: Item (field,method) has Implementation Map but is not marked PInvoke.
0x8013127A	Warning: Item (field,method) has invalid Implementation Map.
0x8013127B	Error: Implementation Map has invalid Module Ref, token 0xffffffff.
0x8013127C	Error: Implementation Map has invalid Member Forwarded, token 0xffffffff.
0x8013127D	Error: Implementation Map has no import name.
0x8013127E	Error: Implementation Map has invalid calling convention 0xff.
0x8013127F	Error: Item (field,method) has invalid access flag.
0x80131280	Error: Field marked both InitOnly and Literal.

HRESULT	Error Message
0x80131281	Error: Literal field must be Static.
0x80131282	Error: Item (field,method) is marked RTSpecialName but not SpecialName.
0x80131283	Error: Abstract method in non-abstract type (token=0xffffffff).
0x80131284	Error: Neither static nor abstract method in interface (token=0xffffffff).
0x80131285	Error: Non-public method in interface (token=0xffffffff).
0x80131286	Error: Instance constructor in interface (token=0xffffffff).
0x80131287	Error: Global constructor.
0x80131288	Error: Static instance constructor in type (token=0xffffffff).
0x80131289	Error: Constructor/initializer in type (token=0xffffffff) is not marked SpecialName,RTSpecialName.
0x8013128A	Error: Virtual constructor/initializer in type (token=0xffffffff).
0x8013128B	Error: Abstract constructor/initializer in type (token=0xffffffff).
0x8013128C	Error: Non-static type initializer in type (token=0xffffffff).
0x8013128D	Error: Method marked Abstract/Runtime/InternalCall/Imported must have zero RVA, and vice versa.
0x8013128E	Error: Method marked Final/NewSlot but not Virtual.
0x8013128F	Error: Static method can not be Final or Virtual.
0x80131290	Error: Method can not be both Abstract and Final.
0x80131291	Error: Abstract method marked ForwardRef.
0x80131292	Error: Abstract method marked PInvokeImpl.
0x80131293	Error: Abstract method not marked Virtual.
0x80131294	Error: Nonabstract method not marked ForwardRef.
0x80131295	Error: Nonabstract method must have RVA or be PInvokeImpl or Runtime.
0x80131296	Error: PrivateScope method has zero RVA.
0x80131297	Error: Global method marked Abstract,Virtual.
0x80131298	Error: Signature contains long form (such as ELEMENT_TYPE_CLASS<token of System.String>).
0x80131299	Warning: Method has multiple semantics.
0x8013129A	Error: Method has invalid semantic association (token=0xffffffff).
0x8013129B	Error: Method has semantic association (token=0xffffffff) that does not exist.
0x8013129C	Error: MethodImpl overrides non-virtual method (token=0xffffffff).
0x8013129E	Error: Method has multiple semantic flags set for association (token=0xffffffff).
0x8013129F	Error: Method has no semantic flags set for association (token=0xffffffff).
0x801312A1	Warning: Unrecognized Hash Algorithm ID (0xffffffff).
0x801312A4	Error: Constant parent token (0xffffffff) is out of range.
0x801312A5	Error: Invalid Assembly flags (0xffff).
0x801312A6	Warning: TypeDef (token=0xffffffff) has same name as TypeRef.
0x801312A7	Error: InterfaceImpl has invalid implementing type (0xffffffff).
0x801312A8	Error: InterfaceImpl has invalid implemented type (0xffffffff).

Continued

Table E-1. *Continued*

HRESULT	Error Message
0x801312A9	Error: TypeDef has security information but is not marked HasSecurity.
0x801312AA	Error: TypeDef is marked HasSecurity but has no security information.
0x801312AB	Error: Type constructor must have no arguments.
0x801312AC	Error: ExportedType has invalid Implementation (token=0xffffffff).
0x801312AD	Error: MethodImpl has body from another TypeDef (token=0xffffffff).
0x801312AE	Error: Type constructor has invalid calling convention.
0x801312AF	Error: MethodImpl has invalid Type token=0xffffffff.
0x801312B0	Error: MethodImpl declared in Interface (token=0xffffffff).
0x801312B1	Error: MethodImpl has invalid MethodDeclaration token=0xffffffff.
0x801312B2	Error: MethodImpl has invalid MethodBody token=0xffffffff.
0x801312B3	Error: MethodImpl has a duplicate (rid=0xffffffff).
0x801312B4	Error: Field has invalid parent (token=0xffffffff).
0x801312B5	Warning: Parameter out of sequence (parameter: 99; seq.num: 99).
0x801312B6	Error: Parameter has sequence number exceeding number of arguments (parameter: 99; seq.num: 99; num.args: 99).
0x801312B7	Error: Parameter #99 is marked HasFieldMarshal but has no marshaling information.
0x801312B8	Error: Parameter #99 has marshaling information but is not marked HasFieldMarshal.
0x801312BA	Error: Parameter #99 is marked HasDefault but has no const value.
0x801312BB	Error: Parameter #99 has const value but is not marked HasDefault.
0x801312BC	Error: Property has invalid scope (token=0xffffffff).
0x801312BD	Error: Property has no name.
0x801312BE	Error: Property has no signature.
0x801312BF	Error: Property has a duplicate (token=0xffffffff).
0x801312C0	Error: Property has invalid calling convention (0xff).
0x801312C1	Error: Property is marked HasDefault but has no const value.
0x801312C2	Error: Property has const value but is not marked HasDefault.
0x801312C3	Error: Property has related method with invalid semantics (method: 0xffffffff; semantics: 0xffffffff).
0x801312C4	Error: Property has related method with invalid token (0xffffffff).
0x801312C5	Error: Property has related method belonging to another type (method: 0xffffffff; type: 0xffffffff).
0x801312C6	Error: Constant of type (0xff) must have null value.
0x801312C7	Error: Constant of type (0xff) must have non-null value.
0x801312C8	Error: Event has invalid scope (token=0xffffffff).
0x801312CA	Error: Event has no name.
0x801312CB	Error: Event has a duplicate (token=0xffffffff).
0x801312CC	Error: Event has invalid EventType (token=0xffffffff).

HRESULT	Error Message
0x801312CD	Error: Event's EventType (token=0xffffffff) is not a class (flags=0xffffffff).
0x801312CE	Error: Event has related method with invalid semantics (method: 0xffffffff; semantics: 0xffffffff).
0x801312CF	Error: Event has related method with invalid token (0xffffffff).
0x801312D0	Error: Event has related method belonging to another type (method: 0xffffffff; type: 0xffffffff).
0x801312D1	Error: Event has no AddOn related method.
0x801312D2	Error: Event has no RemoveOn related method.
0x801312D3	Error: ExportedType has same namespace+name as TypeDef, token 0xffffffff.
0x801312D4	Error: ManifestResource refers to non-PE file but offset is not 0.
0x801312D5	Error: Decl.Security is assigned to invalid item (token=0xffffffff).
0x801312D6	Error: Decl.Security has invalid action flag (0xffffffff).
0x801312D7	Error: Decl.Security has no associated permission BLOB.
0x801312D8	Error: ManifestResource has invalid Implementation (token=0xffffffff).
0x801312DB	Error: Constructor, initializer must return void.
0x801312DC	Error: Event's Fire method (0xffffffff) must return void.
0x801312DD	Warning: Invalid locale string.
0x801312DE	Error: Constant has parent of invalid type (token=0xffffffff).
0x801312DF	Error: ELEMENT_TYPE_SENTINEL is only allowed in MemberRef signatures.
0x801312E0	Error: Signature containing ELEMENT_TYPE_SENTINEL must be VARARG.
0x801312E1	Error: Multiple ELEMENT_TYPE_SENTINEL in signature.
0x801312E2	Error: Trailing ELEMENT_TYPE_SENTINEL in signature.
0x801312E3	Error: Signature is missing argument # 99.
0x801312E4	Error: Field of byref type.
0x801312E5	Error: Synchronized method in ValueType (token=0xffffffff).
0x801312E6	Error: Full name length exceeds maximum allowed (length: 99; max: 99).
0x801312E9	Error: ManifestResource has invalid flags (0xffffffff).
0x801312EA	Warning: ExportedType has no TypeDefId.
0x801312EB	Error: File has invalid flags (0xffffffff).
0x801312EC	Error: File has no hash BLOB.
0x801312ED	Error: Module has no name.
0x801312EE	Error: Module name is fully-qualified.
0x801312EF	Error: TypeDef marked as RTSpecialName but not SpecialName.
0x801312F0	Error: TypeDef extends an Interface (token=0xffffffff).
0x801312F1	Error: Type/instance constructor marked PInvokeImpl.
0x801312F2	Error: System.Enum is not marked Class.
0x801312F3	Error: System.Enum must extend System.ValueType.
0x801312F4	Error: MethodImpl's Decl and Body method signatures do not match.
0x801312F5	Error: Enum has method(s).

Continued

Table E-1. *Continued*

HRESULT	Error Message
0x801312F6	Error: Enum implements interface(s).
0x801312F7	Error: Enum has properties.
0x801312F8	Error: Enum has one or more events.
0x801312F9	Error: TypeDef has invalid Method List (> Nmethods+1).
0x801312FA	Error: TypeDef has invalid Field List (> Nfields+1).
0x801312FB	Error: Constant has illegal type (0xff).
0x801312FC	Error: Enum has no instance field.
0x801312FD	Error: Enum has multiple instance fields.
0x80131B00	Error: InterfaceImpl's implemented type (0xffffffff) not marked tdInterface.
0x80131B01	Error: Field is marked HasRVA but has no RVA record.
0x80131B02	Error: Field is assigned zero RVA.
0x80131B03	Error: Method has both RVA!=0 and Implementation Map.
0x80131B04	Error: Extraneous bits in Flags (0xffffffff).
0x80131B05	Error: TypeDef extends itself.
0x80131B06	Error: System.ValueType must extend System.Object.
0x80131B07	Warning: TypeDef extends TypeSpec (0xffffffff), not supported in Version 1.
0x80131B09	Error: Value class has neither fields nor size parameter.
0x80131B0A	Error: Interface is marked Sealed.
0x80131B0B	Error: NestedClass token (0xffffffff) in NestedClass record is not a valid TypeDef.
0x80131B0C	Error: EnclosingClass token (0xffffffff) in NestedClass record is not a valid TypeDef.
0x80131B0D	Error: Duplicate NestedClass record (0xffffffff).
0x80131B0E	Error: Nested type token has multiple EnclosingClass tokens (nested: 0xffffffff; enclosers: 0xffffffff, 0xffffffff).
0x80131B0F	Error: Zero RVA of field 0xffffffff in FieldRVA record.
0x80131B10	Error: Invalid field token in FieldRVA record (field: 0xffffffff; RVA: 0xffffffff).
0x80131B11	Error: Same RVA in another FieldRVA record (RVA: 0xffffffff; field: 0xffffffff).
0x80131B12	Error: Same field in another FieldRVA record(field: 0xffffffff; record: 0xffffffff).
0x80131B13	Error: Invalid token specified as EntryPoint in CLR header.
0x80131B14	Error: Instance method token specified as EntryPoint in CLR header.
0x80131B15	Error: Invalid type of instance field (0xffffffff) of an Enum.
0x80131B16	Error: Method has invalid RVA (0xffffffff).
0x80131B17	Error: Literal field has no const value.
0x80131B18	Error: Class implements interface but not method (class:0xffffffff; interface:0xffffffff; method:0xffffffff).
0x80131B19	Error: CustomAttribute has invalid Parent token (0xffffffff).
0x80131B1A	Error: CustomAttribute has invalid Type token (0xffffffff).

HRESULT	Error Message
0x80131B1B	Error: CustomAttribute has non-constructor Type (0xffffffff).
0x80131B1C	Error: CustomAttribute's Type (0xffffffff) has invalid signature.
0x80131B1D	Error: CustomAttribute's Type (0xffffffff) has no signature.
0x80131B1E	Error: CustomAttribute's blob has invalid prolog (0xffff).
0x80131B1F	Error: Method has invalid local signature token (0xffffffff).
0x80131B20	Error: Method has invalid header.
0x80131B21	Error: EntryPoint method has more than one argument.
0x80131B22	Error: EntryPoint method must return void, int or unsigned int.
0x80131B23	Error: EntryPoint method must have vector of strings as argument, or no arguments.
0x80131B24	Error: Illegal use of type 'void' in signature.
0x80131B25	Error: Multiple implementation of interface method (class: 0xffffffff; interface: 0xffffffff; method: 0xffffffff).
0x80131B26	Error: GenericParam has no name.
0x80131B27	Warning: GenericParam has nil owner.
0x80131B28	Error: GenericParam has a duplicate based on owner and name, token=0xffffffff.
0x80131B29	Error: GenericParam has a duplicate based on owner and number, token=0xffffffff.
0x80131B2A	Error: GenericParam is out of sequence by owner.
0x80131B2B	Error: GenericParam is out of sequence by number.
0x80131B2C	Error: GenericParam is co-or-contra variant but its owner, token (0xffffffff), is not an interface or delegate.
0x80131B2D	Error: GenericParam is a method type parameter and must be non-variant, not co-or-contra variant.
0x80131B2E	Error: GenericParam has invalid variance value in flags (0xffffffff).
0x80131B2F	Error: GenericParam has inconsistent special constraints ReferenceTypeConstraint and ValueTypeConstraint in flags (0xffffffff).
0x80131B30	Error: GenericParamConstraint has nil owner.
0x80131B31	Error: GenericParamConstraint has a duplicate based on owner and constraint, token=0xffffffff.
0x80131B32	Error: GenericParamConstraint is non-contiguous with preceding constraints for same owner, token=0xffffffff.
0x80131B33	Error: MethodSpec has nil method.
0x80131B34	Error: MethodSpec has a duplicate based on method and instantiation, token=0xffffffff.
0x80131B35	Error: MethodSpec signature has invalid calling convention=0xffffffff.
0x80131B36	Error: MethodSpec signature is missing arity at byte=0xffffffff.
0x80131B37	Error: MethodSpec signature is missing type argument # 99.
0x80131B38	Error: MethodSpec has generic method of arity 99 but instantiation of different arity 99.

Continued

Table E-1. *Continued*

HRESULT	Error Message
0x80131B39	Error: MethodSpec method is not generic.
0x80131B3A	Error: Signature missing arity of instantiated generic type at byte=0xffffffff.
0x80131B3B	Error: Signature has generic type of arity 99 instantiated at different arity 99 at byte=0xffffffff.
0x80131B3C	Error: Method cannot be both generic and a class constructor.
0x80131B3E	Error: Method cannot be both generic and defined on an imported type.
0x80131B3F	Error: Method cannot be both generic and have non-default calling convention.
0x80131B40	Error: Entry point in CLR header is the token for a generic method.
0x80131B41	Error: Method signature is generic but is missing its arity at byte=0xffffffff.
0x80131B42	Error: Method signature is generic but its arity is zero at byte=0xffffffff.
0x80131B43	Error: MethodSpec signature has arity 0 at byte=0xffffffff.
0x80131B44	Error: Signature has generic type instantiated at arity 0 at byte=0xffffffff.
0x80131B45	Error: MethodDef signature has arity 99 but the token owns 99 GenericParams.
0x80131B46	Error: Entry point in CLR header is the token for a method in a generic type.
0x80131B47	Error: MethodImpl overrides non-generic method (token=0xffffffff) with generic method.
0x80131B48	Error: MethodImpl overrides generic method (token=0xffffffff) with non-generic method.
0x80131B49	Error: MethodImpl overrides generic method (token=0xffffffff) of arity 99 with generic method of arity 99.
0x80131B4A	Error: TypeDef extends a TypeSpec (0xffffffff) that is not an instantiated type.
0x80131B4B	Error: Signature has type instantiated at ByRef at offset 0xffffffff.
0x80131B4C	Error: MethodSpec has type instantiated at ByRef at offset 0xffffffff.
0x80131B4D	Error: TypeSpec has empty signature.
0x80131B4E	Error: TypeSpec has signature containing one or more sentinels.
0x80131B4F	Error: TypeDef is generic but has explicit layout.
0x80131B50	Error: Signature has token following ELEMENT_TYPE_CLASS (_VALUETYPE) that is not a TypeDef or TypeRef (token: 0xffffffff; offset: 0xffffffff).
0x80131B51	Warning: Class does not implement interface method in this module (class: 0xffffffff; interface: 0xffffffff; method: 0xffffffff).

Table E-2. IL *Verification Error Codes and Messages*

HRESULT	Error Message
0x80131810	Unknown opcode [0xffffffff].
0x80131811	Unknown calling convention [0xffffffff].
0x80131812	Unknown ELEMENT_TYPE [0xffffffff].
0x80131818	Internal error.
0x80131819	Stack is too large.

HRESULT	Error Message
0x8013181A	Array name is too long.
0x80131820	fall thru end of the method
0x80131821	try start >= try end
0x80131822	try end > code size
0x80131823	handler >= handler end
0x80131824	handler end > code size
0x80131825	filter >= code size
0x80131826	Try starts in the middle of an instruction.
0x80131827	Handler starts in the middle of an instruction.
0x80131828	Filter starts in the middle of an instruction.
0x80131829	Try block overlaps with another block.
0x8013182A	Try and filter/handler blocks are equivalent.
0x8013182B	Try shared between finally and fault.
0x8013182C	Handler block overlaps with another block.
0x8013182D	Handler block is the same as another block.
0x8013182E	Filter block overlaps with another block.
0x8013182F	Filter block is the same as another block.
0x80131830	Filter contains try.
0x80131831	Filter contains handler.
0x80131832	Nested filters.
0x80131833	filter >= code size
0x80131834	Filter starts in the middle of an instruction.
0x80131835	fallthru the end of an exception block
0x80131836	fallthru into an exception handler
0x80131837	fallthru into an exception filter
0x80131838	Leave from outside a try or catch block.
0x80131839	Rethrow from outside a catch handler.
0x8013183A	Endfinally from outside a finally handler
0x8013183B	Endfilter from outside an exception filter block
0x8013183C	Missing Endfilter.
0x8013183D	Branch into try block.
0x8013183E	Branch into exception handler block.
0x8013183F	Branch into exception filter block.
0x80131840	Branch out of try block.
0x80131841	Branch out of exception handler block.
0x80131842	Branch out of exception filter block.
0x80131843	Branch out of finally block.
0x80131844	Return out of try block.

Continued

Table E-2. IL *Continued*

HRESULT	Error Message
0x80131845	Return out of exception handler block.
0x80131846	Return out of exception filter block.
0x80131847	jmp / exception into the middle of an instruction
0x80131848	Non-compatible types depending on path.
0x80131849	Init state for this differs depending on path.
0x8013184A	Non-compatible types on stack depending on path.
0x8013184B	Stack depth differs depending on path.
0x8013184C	Instance variable (this) missing.
0x8013184D	Uninitialized this on entering a try block.
0x8013184E	Store into this when it is uninitialized.
0x8013184F	Return from ctor when this is uninitialized.
0x80131850	Return from ctor before all fields are initialized.
0x80131851	Branch back when this is uninitialized.
0x80131852	Expected byref of value type for this parameter.
0x80131853	Non-compatible types on the stack.
0x80131854	Unexpected type on the stack.
0x80131855	Missing stack slot for exception.
0x80131856	Stack overflow.
0x80131857	Stack underflow.
0x80131858	Stack empty.
0x80131859	Uninitialized item on stack.
0x8013185A	Expected I, I4, or I8 on the stack.
0x8013185B	Expected R, R4, or R8 on the stack.
0x8013185C	Unexpected R, R4, R8, or I8 on the stack.
0x8013185D	Expected numeric type on the stack.
0x8013185E	Expected an Objref on the stack.
0x8013185F	Expected address of an Objref on the stack.
0x80131860	Expected Byref on the stack.
0x80131861	Expected pointer to function on the stack.
0x80131862	Expected single dimension array on the stack.
0x80131863	Expected value type instance on the stack.
0x80131864	Expected address of value type on the stack.
0x80131865	Unexpected value type instance on the stack.
0x80131866	Local variable is unusable at this point.
0x80131867	Unrecognized local variable number.
0x80131868	Unrecognized argument number.
0x80131869	Unable to resolve token.

HRESULT	Error Message
0x8013186A	Unable to resolve type of the token.
0x8013186B	Expected memberRef/memberDef token.
0x8013186C	Expected memberRef/fieldDef token.
0x8013186D	Expected signature token.
0x8013186E	Instruction can not be verified.
0x8013186F	Operand does not point to a valid string ref.
0x80131870	Return type is BYREF, TypedReference, ArgHandle, or ArgIterator.
0x80131871	Stack must be empty on return from a void function.
0x80131872	Return value missing on the stack.
0x80131873	Stack must contain only the return value.
0x80131874	Return uninitialized data.
0x80131875	Illegal array access.
0x80131876	Store non Object type into Object array.
0x80131877	Expected single dimension array.
0x80131878	Expected single dimension array of pointer types.
0x80131879	Array field access is denied.
0x8013187A	Allowed only in vararg methods.
0x8013187B	Value type expected.
0x8013187C	Method is not visible.
0x8013187D	Field is not visible.
0x8013187E	Item is unusable at this point.
0x8013187F	Expected static field.
0x80131880	Expected non-static field.
0x80131881	Address-of not allowed for this item.
0x80131882	Address-of not allowed for byref.
0x80131883	Address-of not allowed for literal field.
0x80131884	Cannot change initonly field outside its ctor.
0x80131885	Cannot throw this object.
0x80131886	Callvirt on a value type method.
0x80131887	Call signature mismatch.
0x80131888	Static function expected.
0x80131889	Ctor expected.
0x8013188A	Can not use callvirt on ctor.
0x8013188B	Only super::ctor or typeof(this)::ctor allowed here.
0x8013188C	Possible call to ctor more than once.
0x8013188D	Unrecognized signature.
0x8013188E	Can not resolve Array type.
0x8013188F	Array of ELEMENT_TYPE_PTR.

Continued

Table E-2. IL *Continued*

HRESULT	Error Message
0x80131890	Array of ELEMENT_TYPE_BYREF or ELEMENT_TYPE_TYPEDBYREF.
0x80131891	ELEMENT_TYPE_PTR can not be verified.
0x80131892	Unexpected vararg.
0x80131893	Unexpected Void.
0x80131894	BYREF of BYREF
0x80131896	Code size is zero.
0x80131897	Unrecognized use of vararg.
0x80131898	Missing call/callvirt/calli.
0x80131899	Cannot pass byref to a tail call.
0x8013189A	Missing ret.
0x8013189B	Void ret type expected for tail call.
0x8013189C	Tail call return type not compatible.
0x8013189D	Stack not empty after tail call.
0x8013189E	Method ends in the middle of an instruction.
0x8013189F	Branch out of the method.
0x801318A0	Finally handler blocks overlap.
0x801318A1	Lexical nesting.
0x801318A2	Missing ldsfld/stsfld/ldind/stind/ldfld/stfld/ldobj/stobj/initblk/cpblk.
0x801318A3	Missing ldind/stind/ldfld/stfld/ldobj/stobj/initblk/cpblk.
0x801318A4	Innermost exception blocks should be declared first.
0x801318A5	Calli not allowed on virtual methods.
0x801318A6	Call not allowed on abstract methods.
0x801318A7	Unexpected array type on the stack.
0x801318A9	Attempt to enter a try block with nonempty stack.
0x801318AA	Unrecognized arguments for delegate ctor.
0x801318AB	Delegate ctor not allowed at the start of a basic block when the function pointer argument is a virtual method.
0x801318AC	Dup, ldvirtftn, newobj delegate::.ctor() pattern expected (in the same basic block).
0x801318AD	Ldftn/ldvirtftn instruction required before call to a delegate ctor.
0x801318AE	Attempt to load address of an abstract method.
0x801318AF	ELEMENT_TYPE_CLASS ValueClass in signature.
0x801318B0	ELEMENT_TYPE_VALUETYPE non-ValueClass in signature.
0x801318B1	Box operation on TypedReference, ArgHandle, or ArgIterator.
0x801318B2	Byref of TypedReference, ArgHandle, or ArgIterator.
0x801318B3	Array of TypedReference, ArgHandle, or ArgIterator.
0x801318B4	Stack not empty when leaving an exception filter.
0x801318B5	Unrecognized delegate ctor signature; expected I.

HRESULT	Error Message
0x801318B6	Unrecognized delegate ctor signature; expected Object.
0x801318B7	Mkrefany on TypedReference, ArgHandle, or ArgIterator.
0x801318B8	Value type not allowed as catch type.
0x801318B9	ByRef not allowed as catch type.
0x801318BA	Filter block should immediately precede handler block
0x801318BB	ldvirtftn on static
0x801318BC	callvirt on static
0x801318BD	initlocals must be set for verifiable methods with one or more local variables.
0x801318BE	branch/leave to the beginning of a catch/filter handler
0x801318BF	call to .ctor only allowed to initialize this pointer from within a .ctor. Try newobj.
0x801318C0	Value type, ObjRef type or variable type expected.
0x801318C1	Expected address of value type, ObjRef type or variable type on the stack.
0x801318C2	Unrecognized type parameter of enclosing class.
0x801318C3	Unrecognized type parameter of enclosing method.
0x801318C4	Unrecognized type argument of referenced class instantiation.
0x801318C5	Unrecognized type argument of referenced method instantiation.
0x801318C6	Cannot resolve generic type.
0x801318C7	Method instantiation contains non boxable type arguments.
0x801318C8	Method parent instantiation contains non boxable type arguments.
0x801318C9	Field parent instantiation contains non boxable type arguments.
0x801318CA	Unrecognized calling convention for an instantiated generic method.
0x801318CB	Unrecognized generic method in method instantiation.
0x801318CC	Missing ldelema or call following readonly prefix.
0x801318CD	Missing callvirt following constrained prefix.
0x801318CE	Method parent has circular class type parameter constraints.
0x801318CF	Method has circular method type parameter constraints.
0x801318D0	Method instantiation has unsatisfied method type parameter constraints.
0x801318D1	Method parent instantiation has unsatisfied class type parameter constraints.
0x801318D2	Field parent instantiation has unsatisfied class type parameter constraints.
0x801318D3	Type operand of box instruction has unsatisfied class type parameter constraints.
0x801318D4	The 'this' argument to a constrained call must have ByRef type.
0x801318D5	The operand to a constrained prefix instruction must be a type parameter.
0x801318D6	The readonly prefix may only be applied to calls to array methods returning ByRefs.
0x801318D7	Illegal write to readonly ByRef.
0x801318D8	A readonly ByRef cannot be used with mkrefany.
0x801318D9	Alignment specified for 'unaligned' prefix must be 1, 2, or 4.
0x801318DA	The tail.call (or calli or callvirt) instruction cannot be used to transfer control out of a try, filter, catch, or finally block.

Continued

Table E-2. IL *Continued*

HRESULT	Error Message
0x801318DB	Stack height at all points must be determinable in a single forward scan of IL.
0x801318DC	Call to base type of valuetype.
0x801318DD	Cannot construct an instance of abstract class.
0x801318DE	Unmanaged pointers are not a verifiable type.
0x801318DF	Cannot LDFTN a non-final virtual method.
0x801318E0	Accessing type with overlapping fields.
0x801318E1	The 'this' parameter to the call must be the calling method's 'this' parameter.
0x801318E2	Expected I4 on the stack.
0x801318F0	Unverifiable PE Header/native stub.
0x801318F1	Unrecognized metadata, unable to verify IL.
0x801318F2	Unrecognized appdomain pointer.
0x801318F3	Type load failed.
0x801318F4	Module load failed.

Index

Find it faster at http://superindex.apress.com/

You Need the Companion eBook

Your purchase of this book entitles you to buy the companion PDF-version eBook for only $10. Take the weightless companion with you anywhere.

We believe this Apress title will prove so indispensable that you'll want to carry it with you everywhere, which is why we are offering the companion eBook (in PDF format) for $10 to customers who purchase this book now. Convenient and fully searchable, the PDF version of any content-rich, page-heavy Apress book makes a valuable addition to your programming library. You can easily find and copy code—or perform examples by quickly toggling between instructions and the application. Even simultaneously tackling a donut, diet soda, and complex code becomes simplified with hands-free eBooks!

Once you purchase your book, getting the $10 companion eBook is simple:

❶ Visit **www.apress.com/promo/tendollars/**.

❷ Complete a basic registration form to receive a randomly generated question about this title.

❸ Answer the question correctly in 60 seconds, and you will receive a promotional code to redeem for the $10.00 eBook.

2560 Ninth Street • Suite 219 • Berkeley, CA 94710

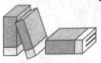

eBookshop

THE EXPERT'S VOICE™

Offer valid through 2/07.